1. Church Through the Ages

THE CATHOLIC CHURCH
THROUGH THE AGES

THE
CATHOLIC
CHURCH
THROUGH THE
AGES

MARTIN P. HARNEY, S.J.

St. Paul Editions

In conformity with the decrees of Pope Urban VIII, all expressions regarding the sanctity of persons not yet canonized or beatified by the Holy Apostolic See, as well as all discussion of miraculous cures, are made without any anticipation of the judgment of the Church.

Imprimi potest:
William G. Guindon, S.J.
PROVINCIAL, NEW ENGLAND PROVINCE

Nihil Obstat:
Rev. Shawn G. Sheehan

Imprimatur:
✠ Humberto Cardinal Medeiros
ARCHBISHOP OF BOSTON

February 4, 1974

Library of Congress Catalog Card Number 73-76312

Copyright, © 1974, by the Daughters of St. Paul

Printed in U.S.A. by the Daughters of St. Paul
50 St. Paul's Ave., Boston, Ma. 02130

The Daughters of St. Paul are an international religious congregation serving the Church with the communications media.

Daughters of St. Paul

IN MASSACHUSETTS
    50 St. Paul's Avenue, Boston, Ma. 02130
    172 Tremont Street, Boston, Ma. 02111
IN NEW YORK
    78 Fort Place, Staten Island, N.Y. 10301
    625 East 187th Street, Bronx, N.Y. 10458
    525 Main Street, Buffalo, N.Y. 14203
IN NEW JERSEY
    84 Washington Street, Bloomfield, N.J. 07003
IN CONNECTICUT
    202 Fairfield Avenue, Bridgeport, Ct. 06603
IN OHIO
    2105 Ontario St. (at Prospect Ave.), Cleveland, Oh. 44115
    25 E. Eighth Street, Cincinnati, Oh. 45202
IN PENNSYLVANIA
    1719 Chestnut St., Philadelphia, Pa. 19103
IN FLORIDA
    2700 Biscayne Blvd., Miami, Fl. 33137
IN LOUISIANA
    4403 Veterans Memorial Blvd.,
      Metairie, La. 70002
    86 Bolton Avenue, Alexandria, La. 71301

IN MISSOURI
    1001 Pine St. (at North 10th), St. Louis, Mo. 63101
IN TEXAS
    114 East Main Plaza, San Antonio, Tx. 78205
IN CALIFORNIA
    1570 Fifth Avenue, San Diego, Ca. 92101
    278 17th Street, Oakland, Ca. 94612
    46 Geary Street, San Francisco, Ca. 94108
IN HAWAII
    1184 Bishop St., Honolulu, Hi. 96813
IN ALASKA
    511 H. St.
    Anchorage, Ak. 99501
IN CANADA
    3022 Dufferin Street, Toronto 395, Ontario, Canada
IN ENGLAND
    57, Kensington Church Street, London W. 8, England
IN AUSTRALIA
    58, Abbotsford Rd., Homebush, N.S.W., Sydney 2140, Australia

Acknowledgements

I wish to thank His Eminence John Cardinal Wright for the splendid preface which he has written for this book. I wish to express my gratitude to the Daughters of St. Paul, who through nine years printed the chapters of this work in their magazine, *The Family,* and now are bringing it out in book form. Sister Paula, Sister Concetta and Sister Mary Catherine have been constant assistants; indeed the sisters of the Boston Motherhouse made the publication a special community project. I must express my gratitude to several Jesuit colleagues, especially to Father Maurice V. Dullea, S.J.; from no other person have I received more personal help. Also I must give my thanks to Father Carl J. Thayer, S.J.; Father William J. Burke, S.J.; Father Francis X. Weiser, S.J.; Father Joseph D. Gauthier, S.J.; and to Father Heinrich Huthmacher, S.J. With reverence I must mention the late Father Edward L. Murphy, S.J., who always shared with me, even in his last painful illness, his wisdom, loyalty to the Church and to the papacy, and his own spiritual strength. Finally, I must thank Mrs. Helen Fitzgerald for her generous typing of the texts of the magazine articles and of the book.

Sincerely,

Father Martin P. Harney, S.J.

Feast of St. Ignatius Loyola, S.J.

To
His Holiness

POPE PAUL VI

Vicar of Christ
Bishop of Rome
Captain of Peter's Barque

October 11, 1973

Rev. Martin P. Harney, S.J.
Jesuit Community
Boston College
Chestnut Hill, Ma. 02167

Dear Martin: P.C.

It is a real pleasure to give my enthusiastic approval
(imprimi potest) for the publication of your new book, *The
Catholic Church Through the Ages*. It is most edifying to see
this real evidence of your continuing literary activities, and
I know how much the book will be appreciated, not only
by your faithful readers, but also by your brother Jesuits.

Please do send me two copies, one for our library here
and the other to be sent to Father General.

Congratulations on your fine work, and be assured
of a remembrance in my Masses and prayers that our Lord
will continue to bless you with every grace and good health
in His service.

Sincerely yours in Christ,
William G. Guindon, S.J.
PROVINCIAL

Contents

Prefatory Note

Father Martin Harney was teaching history at
Boston College to types like the undersigned before
most of those who hopefully will read his book were
born. Some of these latter, noting the absence of foot-
notes, critical apparatus and carefully selective bibli-
ography, will decide the work is highly readable but not
as "scientific" as they might wish; others, seeking out
denunciations of some action or inadequacy of the Church
or the discrediting of a personality, preferably a prelate
or even a saint, will find Father Harney's book a
profession of faith, hope and love so fervent as to seem
"triumphalistic." These will have missed the point of
the book and the purpose of the author. Alas, they know
not the author nor, in fact, *the Church.*

Many, please God very many, surfeited with mere
negativism, will welcome the chance to hear "the other
side" again or, at least, for a change. Not a few, sharing
the widespread conviction that Catholics as a community
are suffering at the moment from a severe case of
collective amnesia, with all the symptomatic *malaise* and
confusion of such an identity crisis in the case of
individual persons, will be grateful to Father Harney
for reminding us with passionate enthusiasm of whence
we came and what were our great adventures along the
way of that coming. For these readers, the book will be
therapeutic, a welcome and providential tonic.

It is perhaps this consideration that prompts the
special warmth of the words with which the Very
Reverend William G. Guindon, S.J., Father Harney's
Provincial, gave his unqualified approval for the publication of this book: "It is most edifying to see this real
evidence of your continuing literary activities, and I

15

know how much the book will be appreciated, not only by your faithful readers, but also by your brother Jesuits." The word edifying is clearly used here in its positive, Scriptural sense of something that builds up the strength of God's people and furthers His purposes.

For any readers dejected because of the absence of elaborate breast-beating or because of touches of exaltation in Father Harney's text, there will be more persons moved by holy pride to be reminded that, sinners though they be, they have experienced joyful and glorious mysteries intermingled with the sorrowful or even scandalous mysteries encountered along the way from Peter (as, indeed, from Abraham, our Father in Faith!) to Vatican Council II, Pope Paul and today.

Such readers will be prayerfully grateful for the loving memories, the poetic insights, the unashamed joy with which a resilient Jesuit, at home with learning and in love with the Church of his Fathers, recalls the high road of history we have walked, despite its pitfalls, to arrive at our present state, with all its exciting frontiers yet to reach—and also its own particular pitfalls.

Perhaps the most impatient, perhaps well-founded complaint of the critical will be that our author, despite so many pages packed with history from Christian beginnings to modern times, has not given sufficient space to the Second Vatican Council, to the contemporary problems and promise of the "post-conciliar" Church. This may well be. But on the other hand Father Harney is painting with a broad brush, as the very title of his book *The Catholic Church Through the Ages* proclaims. Vatican II is, indeed, a major page in that history, but history has not yet come to a full stop and it no more began in 1962 than in 1492. Many of the implications and hopes of Vatican II form the content of current events, more than of soberly reviewed history, and some of Vatican II is still the premise of prophecy.

Moreover, one repeats, Father Harney is attempting to describe the road along which we reached the present point in history; he does not undertake to evaluate the present (save in passing details and occasionally in parallels with the past) nor anticipate the future, this being the domain of the seer rather than that of the historian. He writes with unconcealed attachment to his view of history. Who does not?

Nor can one exaggerate the presumed therapeutic purpose of the labor of love summed up in this book, a work designed to recall, in a crisis of frequent bewildered amnesia, the historically impressive reasons, running across the centuries, why we should never forget the mandate of Pope St. Leo the Great to the children of the Church: *Recognize your dignity!*

Not long ago one of America's most sensitive and intelligent religious columnists, Monsignor Norbert Gaughan of Greensburg, weary of the "sick" downgrading of Catholicism so often characteristic of the moment, cried out in these, among other, words:

"Shouldn't somebody defend the Catholic Church? When the barbarians attacked Rome and threatened to overrun civilization, who was there to protect art, literature, letters? A Catholic Pope. When the Emperor at Constantinople massacred thousands for refusing his version of Christianity, only Ambrose, the Catholic bishop of Milan, challenged him. In the "dark ages" when savages overran Europe, who was there to save civilization, guard learning, help literacy, except Catholic missionaries, Boniface, Cyril and Methodius, Patrick?

"Today's universities began with small cathedral schools and became the universities at Paris, Padua, Bologna and Oxford. As kings grew mighty and demanded complete domination over the lives of their serfs, who resisted them but Popes, bishops and monks? Our hospitals today began with loving care given in the name of Christ by medieval monks, by Friars and Sisters, by the lay volunteers of St. Vincent de Paul.

"Some claim that Catholics worship the statues of saints. But they exult over carved madonnas, sculptured saints, exquisitely wrought angels, painted masterpieces of the lives of the saints. They rejoice in the glowing imagery of stained glass, the exquisitely balanced cathedrals reaching up to the sky, all of which were done because Catholics believed in God, His angels and His saints.

"They say Catholics ignore the Bible, but who saved the Bible for them but Jerome and Pope Damasus, Cyril and Methodius, and the Fathers of the Church?

"Hang in there, Catholics. America needs you!"

Father Harney has developed this plea at greater length and with more detail, broadening the final appeal, in effect, to read: *"Civilization,* not to mention *salvation,* needs the Church! Stand fast!"

John Cardinal Wright
VATICAN CITY

Introduction

EVERY ONE OF US should know how our holy religion, God's kingdom on earth, has fulfilled in the past her divine commission of imparting to the human race the fruits of the Redemption. And since the gates of hell have striven unceasingly to destroy her, everyone should also know how our faith has endured and overcome every onslaught. Nothing can be more absorbing than the study of the achievements, the trials and tribulations, and the ultimate victories of the Mystical Body of Christ.

The origins of the Catholic Church are familiar to all of us. We have read in the Gospels how our Lord chose the twelve apostles, bestowing on them the office of teaching the doctrine and of administering the sacraments, and endowing them with the power to rule and to create their successors. And we know how Jesus chose one from among them, Saint Peter, to be their head. He purposely changed this supreme ruler's name, which had been Simon Bar-Jona, to Peter. The significant words of our Lord were: "Blessed are you, Simon Bar-Jona.... And I say to you: you are Peter, and upon this rock I will build my church, and the gates of hell shall not prevail against it." Now the name "Peter" means "rock." Actually what our Lord said was: "You are Rock and upon this Rock I will build my church."

It was to St. Peter that our Lord gave the power of the keys: "And I will give to you the keys of the kingdom of heaven. And whatsoever you shall bind upon earth shall be bound also in heaven; and whatsoever you shall loose on earth shall be loosed also in heaven." All these promises of the primacy the risen Jesus fulfilled on the shores of the Lake of Genesareth when He bade St. Peter: "Feed my lambs," and, "Feed my sheep."

Let us recall that Jesus, the Second Person of the Blessed Trinity, guaranteed that His Church would never fail nor disappear. His words are so definite: "All power is given to me in heaven and on earth. Going therefore teach all nations, baptizing them in the name of the Father, and of the Son, and of the Holy Spirit, teaching them to observe all things whatsoever I have commanded you; and behold I am with you all days, even to the consummation of the world."

And further Christ guaranteed that His Church would always teach the truth, would never be deceived and would never fall into doctrinal error. There are His words: "And I will ask the Father, and he will send you another Paraclete, that will abide with you forever.... But the Paraclete, the Holy Spirit, whom the Father will send in my name, he will teach you all things, and will bring all things to your mind, whatsoever I shall have said to you."

Some important phases of the history of very early Christianity, especially the works of the apostles after the descent of the Holy Spirit, the labors of St. Peter, and the apostolic journeys of St. Paul are narrated in the *Acts of the Apostles,* the last historical book in the New Testament. Unfortunately many Catholics have never read the *Acts.* It is a pity. They have missed a truly absorbing history.

Primitive Christianity is an especially important topic today. For the last century and a half the main historical attack against the Church has been made in that area. Modern scepticism, stemming from the infidelity of the eighteenth century, has been assailing the existence and nature of primitive Christianity. It has affected countless non-Catholic intellectuals; vast numbers have lost their faith, or at least have been greatly weakened in their acceptance of traditional Christianity. Few of them today retain an interest in the old controversies between Protestantism and Catholicism. Questions far more fundamental confront them: Did Jesus claim to be God? Did He act as one claiming to be divine? Did He establish a visible Church at all? Some, admitting a primitive religious organization, are confused about the nature of it: Did bishops rule it? Did the bishops of Rome exercise a perpetual primacy? What was the character of its worship? What was the content, if any, of its doctrinal teaching? Did it have sacraments (rites for obtaining the fruits of the Redemption)?

If Catholics in reply cited texts from the Gospels and the Epistles, they were met with denials that the sacred books were authentic history. Questions such as the following were raised: Were the Gospels written in the first century? Were the Evangelists really their authors? Or were the sacred books composed by Greek enthusiasts in the second or third century? Were not these later writers responsible for the dogma and the organizational functions found in the accepted versions?

If these denials were true then most of the ideas long accepted as the essentials of Christianity would have to be abandoned. Such would be the divinity of Jesus Christ, the visible Church, the primacy of the Popes, the office of bishops, the sacraments, and all the doctrines implied in these concepts.

The leaders of the attacks were for the most part able and sincere scholars, but having been raised in backgrounds of scepticism and rationalism they could not help but reach such disintegrating conclusions. There is no question that they presented their objections with a wealth of apparent scholarship. And that explains why their attacks destroyed the religious faith of large numbers of Protestant intellectuals, or at least weakened it decisively. Many educated non-Catholics, including a considerable number of ministers, if asked whether they believe that Jesus Christ is God, or that He established a visible Church, will reply with a decided "no," or at the least with a confused and inconclusive answer.

Now the Church had her scholars, experts in biblical and historical studies, and these she rallied to her defense. By learned research and wise interpretation the Catholic scholars forced back step by step the sceptical rationalists until today the outstanding among them acknowledge that the Gospels were written some time in the last quarter of the first century (when men were still living who knew Christ and the apostles). Some will even admit that the Catholic Church in all its fundamentals was in existence before the close of the first century. These fundamentals are: belief in the divinity and humanity of Jesus Christ, and in the Holy Trinity, a visible Church, a hierarchy of bishops, the primacy of the Pope, and the seven sacraments. These are the fundamentals of the Catholic Church, and they have been back through all the ages.

Some of the rationalists who concede so much, however, assert that these fundamentals were not established by Jesus, nor were they held by the first Christians until the last decades of the first century. There would be consequently neither faith nor organization until forty or so years after the death of Christ. Then suddenly there came into existence a full-blown church with dogmas and a united body. For such a tremendous change there is not a shred of historical evidence. On the contrary, as the Gospels and the Epistles reveal, during the thirty or forty years following the death of Christ the apostles taught the essential doctrines of the Trinity and of the divinity and humanity of Jesus Christ. These sacred documents also show them working in a visible Church which they governed under the primacy of St. Peter. Finally history recounts that the apostles and large numbers of the Christians, especially in the persecution of Nero, suffered cruel martyrdoms for those truths and that organization.

Always remember this: no matter how formidable may appear objections raised against our Catholic Faith, we have the scholars who will solve them—and always there is the presence and the guidance of the Holy Spirit.

The Beginnings

THE FIRST HOUR of the Catholic Church is described thus in the *Acts of the Apostles* (2:2-4): "And when the days of the Pentecost were completed, the disciples were all gathered together in one place. And suddenly there came a sound from heaven as of a rushing mighty wind, and it filled the whole house where they were sitting. And there appeared to them parted tongues as of fire, and it sat upon every one of them. And they were all filled with the Holy Spirit, and began to speak with other tongues, as the Holy Spirit gave them to speak."

From this assembly the apostles went forth to the nations and preached to them Christ and His Redemption. Infused with wisdom by the Holy Spirit they taught without shadow of error. Strong in His gift of fortitude they braved every peril until finally they sealed their testimony with the blood of their martyrdoms.

It was in the Roman Empire that the apostles propagated the Christian Church. This mighty state ruled all the lands and all the peoples of the then-known civilized world. Its regime held sway from the headwaters of the Tigris and the Euphrates in the east, all around the shores of the Mediterranean Sea, to the long stretching seaboard of the Atlantic Ocean in the west. Its strongly organized government and its large, disciplined army maintained peace and prosperity everywhere. An immense network of excellent roads bound all its provinces together and kept even the most remote in constant contact with its capital on the Tiber. Three centuries of foreign conquest had amassed for it untold wealth and luxury, so strikingly evidenced in its several thousand cities, all busily engrossed in commerce and industry and all resplendent with temples and public buildings. The superb Greco-Roman culture, matchless in literature, art and philosophy, permeated all phases of its life and produced "the glory that was Greece and the grandeur that was Rome."

At first St. Peter preached only to the children of Israel. But soon he was instructed by a vision that the Gentiles were to be admitted into the Church. At Caesarea in Palestine there was stationed a Roman centurion, Cornelius, who with his household worshiped God and served Him. This Gentile requested St. Peter to teach him and his family the religion of Christ. While the Apostle was in the act of explaining the doctrine to them the Holy Spirit manifestly descended upon his listeners. Peter recognizing the fulfillment of his vision baptized Cornelius and his friends. They were the first Gentile Christians.

As the Church was spreading rapidly through the Near East, St. Peter moved the seat of his authority to Antioch, its most important city. Here it was that the followers of Jesus were first called Christians. At length when Christianity was organized in the capital city of the Empire, the Prince of the Apostles established permanently his primatial see in Rome. St. Peter governed the Church from Rome for about twenty years, until his crucifixion in 69 A.D.

No one did more for the propagation of the early Church than St. Paul. Indeed he is the greatest of all Christian missionaries. Our Lord Himself spoke of St. Paul as "a vessel of election to carry my name before Gentiles and kings and the children of Israel." In four missionary journeys he preached Christ through Palestine, Syria, Cyprus, several provinces in Asia Minor, Macedonia, Greece, Crete, Rome, and possibly Spain. The bitterest oppositions failed to quench the living flame of this apostle's zeal: neither stoning, scourging, prison-chains, shipwrecks, hunger nor thirst. Learned in Hebrew Law, conversant with Greek thought, taught by the Holy Spirit, St. Paul was uniquely able to interpret Christianity to Jew and Gentile. Especially did he achieve this in his fourteen Epistles which are among the most important

HEAD OF CHRIST. One of the earliest representations of the Lord, dating from the fourth century. *Cemetery of Commodilla, Rome.*

The Eucharistic Fish

From the Catacomb of St. Callistus. Early second century.

The symbolism of the fish to represent Christ as God, as man, and as Redeemer was widely used in the primitive church, especially in the catacombs. It was based on the initial letters of five Greek words: Jesous Christos, Theou Uios, Soter. Arranged in a line these initial letters made the word *Ichthus*, the Greek word for *fish*. In English it would read: "Jesus Christ, of God the Son, Savior"; and it would stand for: "Jesus the Man, Jesus the second Person of the Divine Trinity, and Jesus the Redeemer."

To the early Christians the fish also symbolized their beliefs in the Oneness of God, the Holy Trinity, the divine and human natures of Christ, and His Redemption of mankind by His sacrifice on the cross. When the fish bore a basket filled with loaves of bread and containing in a small compartment a glass of wine, then the fish became the symbol of the Eucharistic Christ. The bread and wine changed into the Body and Blood of Jesus Christ, is now *"Jesus Christ, of God the Son, Savior."* The Eucharistic Fish testified that the primitive Christians believed in the total change of the bread and wine into the Body and Blood of Christ at the Sacrifice of the Mass.

foundations of Catholic theology. Since he held that the Gospel was for all nations, he devoted the major part of his labors to the Gentiles. St. Paul *is* the Apostle of the Gentiles. He was beheaded at Rome during the persecution of Nero in 69 A.D.

Christianity was scarcely a decade old when its character, even its existence was threatened by internal controversy. A group among the Jewish Christians in Jerusalem, the Judaizers, insisted that the prescriptions of the Mosaic Law regarding circumcision and prohibited foods were necessary for salvation and hence binding on all Christians. The quarrel grew in bitterness as the rapid increase of Gentile converts made it evident that soon they would outnumber the Jewish Christians. St. Paul, constituting himself the champion of the Gentiles, maintained energetically that the non-Jewish converts were free from such prescriptions of the Mosaic Law. His stand was supported by St. Peter, St. James, St. John and many of the Jewish Christians. The Council of Jerusalem, presided over by St. Peter, definitely proclaimed the freedom of the Gentile Christians. Henceforth belief and Baptism only were obligatory for the Gentiles. It was a momentous decision, for the defeat of the Judaizers meant that Christianity was to be the Church for all nations, as her Founder intended. In the Providence of God the Jewish religion and culture had played a gigantic part in preserving the worship of the true God and in maintaining His moral law. Now and until the end of time that part was to be carried on by Jesus and the Church founded by Him.

Of the labors of the other apostles very little is known for certain. Numerous legends portray them as spreading the Gospel in many eastern lands, even as far as India. It is commonly accepted that all died martyrs' deaths, save St. John; and he too because of his sufferings is reckoned a martyr. We may safely hold that all the apostles spent themselves preaching and establishing Christ's religion. When St. John died at Ephesus about the year 100, the time of revelation came to an end. There can be no new doctrines, although there can be better understanding and clearer definition of the revealed Faith.

How far had Christianity extended at the end of the Apostolic Age? It would be impossible to give an exact answer. Besides the *Acts of the Apostles* and the *Epistles*, practically no authentic documents of the period exist. The ravages of time, of wars and disasters, and the policy—pursued by the later persecuting emperors—of burning all the books of the Christians, destroyed whatever was written. True, there is a mass of piously cherished traditions about the introduction of Christianity into this region or that; but the substrata of truth they contain, if they contain any, have never been established.

Christianity was spoken about and preached in numerous and diverse parts of the Greco-Roman world and beyond by 100. But organized Christian Churches were few. Here are the principal cities in which Christian communities had been established and the regions (in parentheses) which they were evangelizing: Jerusalem (Palestine), Antioch (Syria), Alexandria (Egypt), Ephesus and Smyrna (Asia Minor), Thessalonica (Macedonia), Corinth (Greece), Naples (Southern Italy), Rome (Central Italy). Possibly Dalmatia, Southern Gaul, Spain and North Africa each had Christian communities. It might be well to note here that Christianity was largely urban until the fourth century, when St. Martin of Tours undertook a large scale evangelization of rural areas in Gaul.

Yet the knowledge of Christianity may well have spread over far wider areas of the Empire. On the great network of Roman roads there was constant movement, much going and coming from city to city. At a time when all Christians were filled with the missionary spirit, it is reasonable to assume that the story of Christ and His teachings was told in cities and provinces far distant from Rome. Travelers, merchants, artisans, soldiers and slaves brought the good news to individual acquaintances, or shared it with fellow travelers. It is quite probable that they explained its meaning to sympathetic groups. Women too, of high or low estate, imparted the holy message to their sisters. Later on, priests would arrive to teach, to baptize and to organize a Christian community.

No Array of Human Reason Can Explain...

CHRISTIANITY WAS NOT long in existence when it found itself in total conflict with the Greco-Roman world. The conflict was inevitable, for this brilliant civilization as far as spiritual and moral values went was a complete failure. The mighty empire despite its strong government, far-reaching power, wise laws, tremendous wealth, superb culture and magnificent art was materialistic to the core. Its people were possessed with insatiable, cold-blooded avarice, unbounded pride and voluptuousness that brooked no restriction either of right or decency.

The root evil was idolatry. St. Paul so states it in the beginning of his powerful indictment of the Greco-Roman world (Rom. 1:20-33): "For professing themselves to be wise, they became fools. And they changed the glory of the incorruptible God into the likeness of the image of corruptible man, and of birds, and of four-footed beasts, and of creeping things.... Who changed the truth of God into a lie, and worshiped and served the creature rather than the Creator." The Greeks and the Romans adored all kinds of pagan deities, no matter how unreal or imaginary, no matter how sinister or diabolical. Many of their gods were nought but the materializations of their ambitions or their vices. The lowest depths were reached when they offered divine honors to the living emperors, even to those who were human monsters. Religious ignorance prevailed everywhere, and superstition held all classes, learned as well as illiterate, in an iron vise.

Closely bound up with its idolatry was the moral depravity of society, whose sins St. Paul denounced in such strong terms. At the best its paganism was indifferent to morals, at the worst it offered positive incitement to vice. Throughout the empire impurity was deeply rooted and shamelessly open. It pervaded every aspect of life, of literature and of art. Countless millions were corrupted in mind and heart to an appalling degree. Unnatural vice was common, and leniently dealt with. Adultery had become almost a fashion, and divorce dreadfully frequent. Wholesale and unspeakable degradation—that was the moral condition of Greco-Roman society.

Idolatry and moral depravity begot fearful cruelty in the populace. Unwanted or crippled children they cast out pitilessly, abandoning them to die from exposure, to be devoured by wolves, or to become the prey of slave-hunters. The highest classes of Roman society, as well as its dregs, thronged the arenas to amuse themselves with the deathfights of the gladiators and to shout mercilessly for the victors to slaughter the vanquished. Their vaunted empire was largely the result of brutal wars waged with savage aggression and ruthless conquest. Caesar's cold enumerations of the massacrings by his legions of Gaulish tribes makes frightful reading.

Almost half the population were slaves. And although there were some kind masters, generally the lot of the slave was a terrible one. Until the second century there were no laws to protect them from the cruelties of their masters. The abyss of vice which pagan slavery was, needs no description. In life the slave was the sport of the master's, or the mistress', passion or caprice. In death he perished undeplored and unvalued, of overlabor, on the rack, or in the underground workhouse.

Such was the world that confronted Christ's disciples when they set out to conquer it for His name. Idolatrous, superstitious, ignorant, lascivious, cruel, totally blind in

Anderson

Detail of a reconstruction of the original, based on the works of C. DeRossi.

MADONNA AND CHILD ANNOUNCED BY A PROPHET. Second-century fresco; the earliest extant representation of the Blessed Virgin with the Infant Christ. *Cemetery of Commodilla, Rome.*

SAINTS PAUL AND PETER. Medallion of the two martyred
apostles, discovered in the catacombs. Dating from the second
century, it provides the basis for the traditional features
of Peter and Paul used throughout the history of religious art.

its intellectual pride, and cynical of any values save the crass materialism in which it was absorbed, this Greco-Roman world constituted not one mountain-high barrier to the zeal of the apostles, but an entire mountain range of opposition.

Who were these apostles, advancing undauntedly against the might and the cruelty of ancient paganism? To start off with, they were Jews. From the beginning they had to face hateful prejudices — widespread through the empire — against their race. What were they? Humble fishermen mostly; and fishermen, not of the Mediterranean or the Atlantic, but of a small lake hidden in the mountains bordering the remote eastern frontier. Surely Roman government officials would resent such insignificant fellows telling them how to manage their own destinies. How much erudition could they claim? Scarcely more than a modicum of reading and writing. St. Matthew, a small tax collector, possibly had a little more. From their familiarity with the Hebrew Scriptures they were wise in the knowledge of God and of His law. But that knowledge counted for nothing with the pagans of the empire. Not one of them, save St. Paul, knew anything of the classical literatures and philosophies. Certainly Greek rationalizers would waste no time on such uncultured ignoramuses.

Yet they were from the east, whence had been coming for two hundred years the mystery cults that had captivated the upper-class Greeks and Romans. As strange prophets with promises of salvation by secret knowledge reserved exclusively to their initiates they might gain a following. Perhaps they might offer to satiated dilettantes bizarre rites, intriguing to the curious or, in some cases, frankly inducive to the depraved. Possibly they might win adherents by teachings that flattered their pride, stimulated their greed for power and riches, or pandered to their vicious propensities.

Far, far otherwise did the apostles act. They preached against almost every opinion of the Greeks and Romans. They proclaimed the one true God, announcing emphatically His command: "I am the Lord, your God. You shall not have strange gods before me." They demanded faith in the unseen, for God is a pure spirit, simple and unseen. They insisted on the acceptance of mysteries, the Holy Trinity, the divinity and the humanity of Christ; and they required the acceptance of miracles, especially the resurrection of Jesus from the dead. They scorned every single deity of the pagans as a mere fancy of human imagination or, in some instances, a disgusting symbolism of human vice.

The apostles preached a stern, all-comprehensive moral code, which they announced as binding upon every last man. To a world dominated by hate, a world that did not have even the word "charity," they counseled love of all men, bond or free. To a people that made revenge, and at times murder, a duty, they enjoined the forgiveness of injuries. From a populace steeped in avarice and scrupling at nothing in the accumulation of wealth, they demanded honesty and detachment from worldly riches. To a lecherous society that condoned the vilest iniquities, they glorified chastity as a primary virtue.

Neither in doctrine nor in morality did the apostles minimize or compromise. Indeed at the climactic moment of their preaching they commanded the power-grasping Romans, the intellectually proud Greeks and the fanatically emotional Easterners to get down on their knees and adore Jesus Christ dying on His cross, for He was not only man but God, eternal and almighty.

The pagan world, infuriated by such challenges, determined on the complete obliteration of this Christianity that spurned its power, rejected its gods, questioned its wisdom, wounded its pride, and rebuked its sinful life. Its warfare lasted for two hundred and fifty years. But the apostles and their successors held their lines firm against each murderous onslaught of the world, the flesh and the devil. With them always was the invincible power of their divine Founder, as He had promised. Moreover, even during the most furious assaults, Christ's religion continued to spread rapidly and deeply. No array of human reasons can explain such wonderful expansion—only the miraculous power of God.

The
Early
Persecutions

FOR TWO HUNDRED and fifty years the pagan world waged against the Christians a war of extermination. Every method of obliteration was employed: not only uncountable executions, frightful tortures and wholesale massacres, but also widespread slander, bitter literary attacks and the destruction of all Christian books and documents. Occasionally there were letups in the persecutions; one such lasted for almost forty years. But the anti-Christian edicts were seldom repealed; most of the time they hung ominously over the heads of the faithful. Bigoted governors could enforce them in their own provinces, and often did. Two of the bloodiest persecutions were local onslaughts that occurred in the second century, one at Lyons and one in Proconsular Africa. How many great persecutions there were would be difficult to determine. It is generally said that there were ten, but this is not to be taken as an exact figure.

The history of the persecutions divides into three periods. In the first, 64 A.D. to 112 A.D., the attacks were largely mob movements blindly striking at the fanatically hated, though little understood, Christians. The Emperor Nero, a half-mad monster of cruelty, inaugurated the first persecution to divert suspicion from himself, for the infuriated Roman populace believed that he had enkindled the great fire of 64 A.D. which had destroyed almost two-thirds of their city with a terrible holocaust of lives. This first persecution was one of the cruelest. Nero's officials filled the jails with Christians, and then executed them in the Circus Maximus with brutalities calculated to satisfy the frenzy of the mobs. Some were beheaded or crucified in public spectacles. Some were wrapped in the skins of animals to be hunted and worried to death by ferocious mastiffs. Some were drowned in the Tiber. Some were covered with pitch and resin, elevated on posts and set on fire, to be human torches illuminating the night in the imperial gardens. Nero's persecution reached a pitch of horror never surpassed although often equalled in the later persecutions.

Before the first century was out, during the years 92 to 96, the Christians were again subjected to a violent persecution. The instigator was the Emperor Domitian, in cruelty another Nero. The inhumanities of the executions probably rivaled Nero's horrors. Among the victims were members of the imperial family, an indication of the deep extension of Christianity even at this early date.

As the followers of Christ increased, the hatred of them increased. Popular hostility was nourished by false accusations and vile calumnies, which were spread, broadcast and believed in all circles. The necessary secrecy of the Christian worship, whose rites were not properly understood and were often scurrilously interpreted, lent credence to odious tales of gross crimes and orgies. Yet the chaste conduct of Christians was resented by the pagans as intentional rebuking of their own immoral lives. Most relentless foes were those whose material interests were bound up with the pagan worship, the priests, temple officials, makers and sellers of heathen ornaments, soothsayers and charlatans. In every public calamity the superstitious, and that included almost everyone in the empire, placed the blame upon "the revilers of the national gods." Tertullian, the Christian apologist, could write, "If the Tiber arises above its banks, if the Nile does not overflow, if the skies are not clear, if the earth quakes, if famine or pestilence come, up goes the cry, 'The Christians to the lions.'" The mobs hastened to the arenas to satisfy their blood lust.

The second period of the persecutions extended from 112 to 186 A.D., the years when the best and the most humane

THE CATACOMBS. The crypt of one of the Roman catacombs

ST. CECILIA. The Maderno statue (sixteenth century) shows the virgin-martyr professing her faith in the unity and trinity of God. *Basilica of St. Cecilia, Rome.*

emperors ruled. The persecutions remained mob movements; but the emperors entered into them by establishing the legal principle that the profession of Christianity, with its refusal to adore the gods of the empire, was a capital crime. The principle was first set forth in Trajan's reply to his agent in Asia Minor, the younger Pliny. This official had requested instructions for dealing with the Christians, apparently virtuous citizens despite their superstitions. The emperor's reply was: (1) Christianity is in itself a crime; (2) those legally accused of it must be tried and, if convicted, punished by death; (3) those who renounce their beliefs are to be freed; (4) magistrates need not search out Christians nor notice anonymous denunciations. Apparently a mild decision, actually it placed the Christians at the mercy of provincial governors, informers and fanatics. Bloody persecutions occurred sporadically under Trajan, Hadrian and Antonius Pius. Marcus Aurelius, despite his stoic philosophy, proved himself a genuine persecutor. Not only did he allow full rein to outbursts of popular violence in Asia Minor and at Lyons and Vienne in Gaul, but he ordered the Christians to be arraigned under charges of atheism and unnatural vices. His laws called for the severest tortures to break the constancy of the Christians.

The third period of the persecution lay between 189 and 313 A.D. During these years the Empire itself became the chief persecutor. Certain emperors formulated campaigns of total proscription, which were to be carried out by all administrative, judicial and military forces. Then imperial edicts put into effect and extended to the whole Greco-Roman world these plans for the wholesale liquidation of Christians and Christianity. Not all the emperors acted so, indeed there were several long intervals of peace. But whenever the edicts were carried out, there were bloody executions and horrible massacres everywhere. The persecuting emperors and their edicts were: Septimius Severus (201), forbidding conversion to Christianity; Maximian (235), against the bishops; Decius (250-251), against all persons suspected of being Christians, in what may have been the bloodiest of the persecutions; Valerian (257), against the bishops and against all Christian assemblies, confiscating all Church and private property;

Diocletian (295 to 305), the last and the greatest persecution, a campaign of total extermination which lasted for ten years.

What capital punishments were visited on the Christians? Imprisonment, because it proved fatal to countless victims, must be considered of capital nature. Confinement in the dark, horrible jails, or exile to prison camps in the centers of malarial swamps, or forced labor in the metal and salt mines, from which only one in ten survived — all were looked upon by the Romans as capital punishments. An enormous toll of human lives was taken by beheading, crucifixion, burning at the stake, exposure to famished and maddened lions, tigers and leopards in the public spectacles. Such is but a pale enumeration of the deaths meted out to the Christian martyrs. The excruciating tortures designed by sadistic officials, especially those inflicted on Christian women, cannot be described.

Who were the martyrs? The men and women who freely and unresistingly endured death rather than sacrifice to pagan gods. How many martyrs were there? It would be impossible to give any definite number; scarcely any documents have survived the ravages and disasters of two thousand years. It must be remembered that one of the chief points aimed at in the last persecutions was the total destruction of all Christian books and writings. A reasonable estimate has placed the number at over a million martyrs. Rationalists of the eighteenth and nineteenth centuries dismissed the early Christian martyrs as an insignificant number of ignorant fanatics drawn from the dregs of the Roman slums. Some modern Catholic apologists have been willing to concede as the lowest possible minimum one hundred and fifty thousand, though holding personally the number of over a million.

Even one hundred and fifty thousand persons freely and unresistingly accepting most horrible tortures and death for the sake of Christ constitute a most stupendous testimony to the divinity of Christ and to His perpetual and omnipotent protection of His Church. They came from every time of life, from old age to childhood. They were drawn from every rank of society: senators, women of nobility, scholars, merchants, artisans, freemen and free women, male and female slaves. They represented every racial group in the vast empire: Romans, Greeks, Syrians, Egyptians, Africans, Spaniards, Germans from the Rhine and the Danube, Celts from Gaul and Britain. They were not wiped out in one or two vast obliterations; but they died in persecution after persecution extending over two hundred and fifty years. No collection of human reasons can explain their sacrifices, so variant in time, place and character. The divine grace of the God-man for whom they willingly died is the only answer. One of the greatest miracles of the early Church is the heroic constancy of her martyrs.

The
Victory

AT THE MILVIAN Bridge that spans the Tiber not far from Rome a battle was fought on the 28th of October, 312, for the rule of the western half of the Roman Empire. The contending leaders were Constantine, at the head of an army of Gauls, Germans and Britons, and Maxentius, supported by an army of Italians and North Africans. Constantine's seasoned veterans routed the larger but inexperienced forces of Maxentius, who was drowned in the flight across the Tiber. The battle at the Milvian Bridge was not, as it has often been represented, a struggle between a Christian army and a pagan army; the vast majority of Constantine's soldiers were pagans. At the moment it was nothing more than a contest for imperial power. It was only in the aftermath that the importance of the struggle at the Milvian Bridge developed: the victor, and now the sole ruler of the western half of the empire, was a powerful soldier who at least in mind was a Christian. He might be classed as a catechumen, although he did not receive Baptism until he was on his deathbed some twenty-five years later.

Yet even before Milvian Bridge Constantine had turned to Christianity. Towards the end of his life he stated under oath to his biographer, Eusebius, that one day, while invoking the God of the Christians, he and his whole army beheld in the sky a cross with the Greek inscription over it, "In this conquer." He also affirmed that later Christ appeared to him and ordered him to place the monogram of Christ, ☧ , (the Greek letters ✗–Chi, and ᚹ–Rho) on the shields of his soldiers, and to display the cross on his banner. On the triumphal arch which he erected in Rome, and which is still standing, Constantine had engraved the statement that he conquered "by an inspiration of the Deity." He also had inscribed on his coins and medals the monogram of Christ. Certainly from that time Constantine was the staunch friend and protector of the Christians.

The importance of the victory of the Milvian Bridge became evident in a little less than five months when Constantine, as emperor of the West, and Licinius, as emperor of the East conjointly issued at Milan the famous edict of toleration. It was not a single document, but a series of regulations. These regulations guaranteed the Christians liberty of worship; they permitted Roman citizens the freedom to embrace Christianity, and restored all the confiscated properties of the Christians. Henceforward the religion of Christ possessed legal status in Roman Law. The era of persecutions was terminated.

It was a most glorious victory for Christianity. Yet it did not come as the triumph of a successful military revolt. Never once in all the two hundred and fifty years had the Christians risen in arms against their persecutors. Nor was it a yielding to the weight of great numbers. At the time of the Edict of Milan the Christians were far from being even a large minority in the population of the empire. They counted only one-ninth of the imperial populace. There were many regions, particularly in the west, where a Christian was scarcely to be found. The victory of the followers of Christ was achieved solely by the sword of the spirit.

Many factors contributed to Christianity's triumph. First there was the force of truth in the teachings of Christ. Reasonably and completely these doctrines explained everything about God, about man and about the relations between God and man. Further they were taught in so simple a form that they were as easily comprehensible by the unlearned as by the learned. And they satisfied every craving of the human soul: knowledge and possession of God, hope and confidence of eternal salvation, salutary fear and penitent sorrow, limitless love of God and ardent affection for mankind. Shallow paganism had nothing at all like this to offer to puzzled and troubled hearts.

The miracles wrought by the apostles and their successors immensely strengthened their preaching. The apostles spoke with the gift of tongues on the day of Pentecost itself; at the gates of the Temple Peter cured a man lame from birth; Paul cured a similar cripple at Lystra; and Paul brought a dead youth back to life at Troas. The times demanded miracles, for it was only by striking manifestations of God's power that the hearts of the heathen could be softened. But the Christians put forth no claims to personal magic. St. Peter said: "In the name of Jesus Christ of Nazareth, arise and walk." Christ had foretold that his disciples would perform miracles: "And these signs shall attend those who believe; in my name they shall cast out devils; they shall speak in new tongues; they shall take up serpents; and if they drink any deadly thing, it shall not hurt them; they shall lay hands upon the sick and they shall get well" (Mk. 17:17-18).

The words of the apostles had tremendous effects when they spoke as witnesses of Christ's resurrection. They could declare: "After the Master had risen from the dead we spoke with Him; we saw Him eat the broiled fish and the honeycomb which we gave Him; we were fed by fish which He broiled on the shores of the Lake of Genesareth." How often, and with what vehemence, Thomas must have repeated: "These fingers, at His command, I placed in the wounds in His hands and in His side, in His actually glorified body."

The early disciples and all their successors continually appealed to the fulfillment of the Jewish prophecies in the person of Jesus Christ. They were but following His own example when He discoursed with the two disciples on the road to Emmaus: "'O foolish ones and slow of heart to believe in all that the prophets have spoken! Did not Christ have to suffer these things before entering into his glory?' And beginning with Moses and with all the prophets, he interpreted to them in all the Scriptures the things referring to himself" (Lk. 24:25-27). The Christian preachers appealed also to Jesus' own prophecies, especially after the destruction of Jerusalem which with great sorrow He had so clearly foretold.

ST. PETER IN CATHEDRA. Third-century sculpture. *Vatican
Basilica, Rome.*

Alinari

ST. PAUL THE APOSTLE. From a woodcut of the middle ages.

The early Christians all participated in the propagation of the Faith. Often the first to introduce the doctrines of Christ to his fellows was the artisan at the work-bench, the soldier on a route-march, or the merchant at his stall. Many times it was the matron, or the housewife, who unfolded before her sisters the high and revered position of the Christian woman. And frequently it was the slave, male or female, who strengthened companions in bondage with the fortitude of the crucified Redeemer, or inspired them with the joyful Christian hope of God's eternal mansions. The Christians preached no stronger sermon than that of their own virtuous lives. It was plain to see that they were reverent, humble and honest. Their warmhearted, all-embracing charity won from the admiring pagans the exclamation: "Behold, how these Christians love one another." The chastity of their conduct convinced the better type of their neighbors that purity in personal and in family life was not only a possible theory but a realizable achievement.

Of all the arguments for Christianity the most convincing was the glorious constancy of the Christian martyrs. Most of the pagans could not hear the proponents of the Christian Gospels. Many would not even listen. But none could close their eyes forever to the heroism of the million men and women of all conditions and all ranks who during two hundred and fifty years endured the most terrible tortures and gladly made the supreme sacrifice of their lives in testimony of the truth of the religion of Jesus Christ.

The supreme reason, and it was the basis of all others, was the infinite power of God Almighty. Never did He make it more evident that the gates of hell would not prevail against the Rock of Peter than in the first three centuries of the Church. Never did His promise that He would abide with His Church forever shine out more clearly.

First
Internal
Storms

THE MARTYRS WITH their numbers and their heroism constitute the most inspiring tradition of the Catholic Church. Were they truly representative of their brethren in the early Church? Yes, at least to the extent that heroes manifest the ideals of their peoples. Yet it would be incorrect to imagine that all the early Christians measured up to the courage and sanctity of the martyrs. Unhappily there were apostates. In the persecutions of the first two centuries they were few, but in the conflicts of the third century they were fairly common. In the terrible days of Decius perhaps there were as many apostates as martyrs. These apostates can be separated into three classes: the *sacrificati,* who actually offered sacrifices to the heathen deities; the *thurificati,* who burned incense before the statues of the gods, especially the divine emperors; and *libellatici,* who obtained by bribery or through influential connections false certificates of sacrificing. One might add a fourth class: those who purchased immunity by delivering to the authorities the Christian books for destruction.

How explain these sad failures? Fear, overwhelming fear, caused most of them. Living in an atmosphere charged with terror, witnessing, perhaps many times, the excruciating agonies of the martyrs, when the unfortunate's hour of personal trial came, his courage collapsed before the terrible prospect. The moral fiber of many Christians had weakened during the long periods of relative peace. This was especially true of defaulters from among the well-to-do. Worldliness contributed heavily to their apostasy. For them life held too many good things to lose: luxurious living, high social connections, great financial possessions. Persuasions of relatives and friends, often non-Christians, or, at the best, half-hearted Christians, weakened the resolution of many of them. Some sought to rationalize their apostasies by the false argument that their treason was only superficial and that it would save them for great good when peace returned. The apostasies of the highly-placed and the wealthy set an oft-repeated example for the weak-of-faith in the lower classes. Finally there were the excitable hotheads who rushed headlong into dangers for which they were not prepared. The Church has never encouraged rash seeking of martyrdom; she has always counseled her children to await its trial prayerfully and with humble trust in God.

Pagan persecutions were not the only evils against which Christianity had to struggle during the first three centuries. Within her own ranks arose quarrels and controversies so bitter as to threaten more than once the breaking up of her essential unity into factions permanently irreconcilable. Differences of opinions were to be expected in developing the knowledge of the Faith, in probing its mysteries, and in presenting its truths to non-Christians, especially of the learned class. The work was good and it was necessary. But the work was also extremely difficult. Many of the Christian truths were new concepts, and hence terms to express them had to be invented. Further the organization of the Church, particularly in matters of authority and discipline, had hardly progressed very far beyond the primitive, essential stages. All would have been well if the Christians had worked humbly and with loyal deference to the divinely appointed teachers, the Pope, first of all, and the bishops. But the early Christians were human, with decided differences of personalities and with sharply clashing racial characteristics. They had too their share of the ambitious and the jealous, who abetted the controversies for their own advantages. Small wonder that the quarrels were often whipped up into fierce, intransigent fanaticism.

The controversies sometimes ended in heresy, a far worse evil since it denied essential truths of Christianity. Heresies cropped up very early in the Church's history. Some started within the Christian body itself, others seeped in from the outside world. All such teachings would have radically changed Christianity; indeed some of them aimed at nothing less than absorbing or obliterating Christ's religion. Heresies often arose from exaggerations, either of a special truth or of the role of knowledge in the Faith. Some heretics stumbled into error, others in an endeavor to save one truth sacrificed another, others still clung stubbornly to false interpretations of the Scriptures or of the Christian doctrines. Some, not satisfied with the Church's moral teachings and practices, pushed on into extreme rigorism; some, on the other hand, scorning the Church's reasonable strictness, fell into laxist morality. Whatever their theories or intellectual pretensions — and many lapsed through intellectual pride — all were one in rejecting the teaching office of the Church confided to her by Christ and safeguarded perpetually by the Holy Spirit.

It would be a useless, tedious task to list all these strange sects and their odd systems. Three, since they constituted extremely grave threats to Christianity, must be noticed. Gnosticism was the worst; its attack was more sinister and its tentacles penetrated into every area. It sought to absorb all religions, appropriating doctrines and rites from each for its own peculiar cult, and then stripping each religion of its special characteristics. There was a pagan Gnosticism, a Jewish Gnosticism and a Christian Gnosticism. It was a collection of systems rather than a single organized religion. All the Gnostic systems claimed to confer salvation, but only through a special knowledge, which was imparted solely to the initiates. No false religion ever flattered so the intellectually proud. As for Christianity, Gnosticism would have smothered it to death. Marcionism, a rigoristic sect, claimed to return to the Gospel's primitive Christianity. Guided by its founder Marcion, an organizing genius, it set up strong communities in many provinces to become a formidable rival of Christianity. Montanism preached an early second coming of Christ. The Montanists claimed special inspirations of the Holy Spirit, and hence rejected the guidance of the Church. It too was an extremely rigoristic sect. One of the greatest tragedies of the early Church was the lapse into Montanism of Tertullian, the eloquent Christian apologist.

But enough of faults and failures. For the far, far greater part, her first three centuries were glorious for Christianity. The heroism of her martyrs and the wisdom of her teachers already have been noticed. But there was much more. Even in the first century Christianity was beginning to transform society.

The Church introduced a clear and pure concept of the Deity: God, all good, all wise, all powerful, eternal; God, the Father of mankind, who gave His only-begotten Son to save the human race; God, the loved of all, who desired to be loved by all. By her teaching on the resurrection and immortality of the soul and body she gave unlimited hope and courage to the lowliest. She gave a new meaning to humility, which in the pagan writers signified only that which was base. With Christians, humility now means lowliness and mild-ness and submission to God and His creatures. No wonder it came to be considered essential to all the virtues. Christianity brought her followers to such heights of sanctity that the pagans were amazed that such holiness could be a reality. This was especially true of the chastity manifested in the lives of countless Christian men and women. Also, the Christian teaching of the fatherhood of God had as a necessary corollary the teaching of the brotherhood of man. This fraternal love of the Christians brought into society for the first time institutions for the orphans, the aged, the sick and the indigent.

The early Christians introduced social ideals that have ever since been characteristic of western civilization. One was the priceless value of the human soul, an idea which is the basis of all true liberty. Another was the sanctity of the family. Christianity not only restored the family to its ancient stability but also made it a blessed institution, elevated by Christ to the dignity of a holy sacrament. There followed of necessity Christianity's elevation of women in reverence and in honor, as was witnessed by the numerous Christian women saints, especially the Christian women martyrs. The sanctifying of the family also brought new ideas about the holiness and sacredness of childhood. Significantly there is scarcely a statue of a child in Greek sculpture. But the images of children appear everywhere in medieval and modern art. The Baby-God of Nazareth made all childhood holy. Another concept fostered by the early Church was the dignity of labor. Only the Jewish people, among the ancients, reverenced the worker. Christianity spread this veneration throughout the Greco-Roman world. The toilers in Nazareth's carpenter shop blessed forever the hands of the laborer. Finally the early Church raised man from pre-occupation with temporary material gains to the vision and pursuit of the eternal happiness of heaven. Grief, pain and poverty, all were endured in the hope of the boundless celestial blessedness which God had prepared for those who had loved Him well.

A New Force in a Worn-Out World

IN THE EARLY YEARS of the fourth century Christianity emerged from the darkness of persecution. As the decades moved along it grew in numbers and in depth, although at the same time it had to overcome several serious threats to its essential character. When the century came to a close Christianity was the legally established religion of the Roman Empire.

The religion of Christ began at once to spread widely. Christians increased rapidly in the areas where they were fairly numerous: Asia Minor, Syria, Egypt, North Africa, Southern and Central Italy. More strikingly they multiplied in regions where the followers of the Gospel were sparsely numbered: Gaul, Spain, Britain and Northern Italy. The growth was astonishing. At the Edict of Milan the Christians amounted to only about one-ninth of the imperial population, by the middle of the century they had reached the one-third mark, and at the end they numbered far more than one half. They had even established churches in Armenia, Persia, Ethiopia and possibly in other lands to the east.

Christianity was also increasing in depth. Hitherto it drew its membership largely, though not exclusively, from the urban middle class and the slaves. Now it began to enroll considerable numbers from the imperial and local nobilities. Not all were converted; the final defenders of the dying paganism were Roman aristocrats. Of much greater import, the Church was gathering into her fold the peasantry, the coloni and the serfs of Gaul, Britain and northern Italy. There were many zealous apostles of the rural people. Outstanding was St. Martin of Tours, who devoted years and years of his life, as a monk and a bishop, travelling the roads of the northern half of Gaul to lead the Gallic country-people into the true fold. But the rural peoples were not all converted. For a century or two some lingered in heathenism. It was hard for them to forsake the superstitions and rites that so impregnated their sowing and harvesting. The word "pagan" indicates how slowly idolatry died in the remote regions; it originally meant one who dwelt in the "pagus," the countryside.

Development of organization kept pace with increasing numbers. The single Christian community of each town now had to be divided into sections, each with its own church and its own priests. The parish system was beginning. The bishop's jurisdiction was also growing; now it reached out to the independent villages and to the surrounding countryside. The diocesan system too was starting. As the Faith spread through the western provinces, or into the lands beyond the eastern frontiers, many new dioceses appeared, always located in the leading cities.

The numerous bishops were organized into groups, each group under the superiority of the most important local see. The bishop of such a see was given the title, "Metropolitan." In later times he would also be called, "Archbishop." The jurisdiction of the metropolitan see corresponded roughly to that of the local Roman province; its geographical limits were practically the same. There were 120 provinces and there were almost 120 metropolitan sees. It may be noticed that the organization of the Church followed that of the Roman Empire. This was but to be expected from ecclesiastics who were all Roman citizens and inheritors of the Roman traditions of government. It was a fortunate development, for the Roman Empire was the most efficiently organized government in history.

Later the metropolitans were gathered into groups, which in the following century would serve as the bases of the patriarchates. These groupings were a marked feature of

Eastern Catholicism: Antioch in Syria and the neighboring regions; Ephesus in Asia Minor; Alexandria in Egypt; Caesaria in Persia; Heraclea, or Constantinople, in Greece. Similarly the metropolitans of North Africa were united under the see of Carthage. The system, however, scarcely penetrated into Spain and Gaul. It did not appear at all in Italy, owing to the pre-eminence of the bishopric of Rome.

During this time of organization the primacy of the Pope of Rome was conclusively acknowledged. "Conclusively" is the word to note. There was no innovation of doctrine. From the beginning the venerable tradition of the superiority of the see of Peter was accepted as a fact. But in the fourth century it was more distinctly expressed and more strikingly asserted by Christians everywhere, even in those ancient sees, Jerusalem, Antioch and Alexandria, which claimed St. Peter as their founder. It was held to be a true authority, not a mere primacy of honor. Fathers of the Church, flourishing in the fourth century, referred to the superiority of the Bishop of Rome as a traditional fact. Thus spoke St. Athanasius, St. Hilary, St. John Chrysostom and St. Ambrose. St. John Chrysostom asserted that attachment to Peter's succession was the only principle of cohesion in the Faith. St. Ambrose declared that where Peter is, there is the Church.

The Popes exercised their universal authority in the areas of faith and discipline. In matters of faith they took the supreme leadership of the orthodox all through the long conflict with the Arian heresy. In matters of discipline they were the recipients of final appeals of many Christian leaders from local superiors or ecclesiastical councils. Among such appellants were St. Athanasius, Paul of Constantinople, Marcellus of Ancyra and (in the early fifth century) St. John Chrysostom. The Council of Sardica, 343, declared: "It seems right and proper that the bishops should refer from their own provinces to the head of the Church, that is to say, to the see of the Apostle Peter."

The fourth century was by no means a golden age. Christianity had to struggle continuously against sinister enemies. Troubles arose from diverse sources: unworthy members, widely supported heretics, domineering emperors and pagan resurgents.

Unworthy members, a perennial weakness for the Catholic Church, were never more unworthy than in the fourth century. Then a deluge of converts produced vast numbers of poorly prepared and untried Christians. Some were hardly more than sham converts, entering the Church for social or political advancement. Even among the more genuine, many persisted in their superstitions, and many remained slaves of sensuality. These last received little virtuous example from the nominal Christians of the imperial court and the higher circles. The invading barbarians merely compounded their own coarseness and brutality with the vices of the conquered. The great Christian thinkers, who were beginning to appear, found the pagan philosophers strongly posted in the higher schools as in so many citadels. And though the new glorious Christian literature was attracting many, pagan thought still dominated classical studies.

And yet a balance must be struck in favor of the innumerable Christians who were as staunch in their faith and its practice as were the martyrs. They produced countless holy persons, they distributed charity on an even vaster scale and they remained loyal to the Faith in all the heretical controversies. From their ranks came forth many apostles of the rural peoples, and many evangelists who went to the peoples beyond the imperial frontiers. And it was the fourth-century Christians who developed and spread monasticism through the East and the West.

For sixty years, 321 to 381, the Church had to struggle with the heresy of Arianism. Daniel-Rops has called Arianism the most formidable heresy that has ever confronted the Church. Certainly it denied the most fundamental doctrine, the divinity of Christ. Arianism and other fourth century heresies will be treated more extensively in the subsequent chapter. Let it here be thought of as a very widespread doctrinal revolt that was backed by powerful personages of state and church.

During the fourth century the Church suffered repeatedly from domineering emperors. Some of the emperors, it is true, replaced pagan laws and practices by Christian principles. But others interfered in the Church's government and even sought to dictate its teachings. One, Valens, an

Arian, fanatically persecuted the orthodox believers. At times Constantine proved difficult. As far as building churches he was truly a munificent benefactor. To the great Council of Nicaea he furnished the strongest support. And as the years passed on he grew in devoted loyalty to Christianity. His moving of the capital to Byzantium, later Constantinople, turned out an unmixed blessing for the Popes in the freedom that it afforded them in old Rome — a development the great emperor doubtlessly never envisioned. As a matter of fact in the new capital Constantine laid the groundwork for the later Caesaro-Papism. In his last years, mingling in dogmatic controversies for which he had not the slightest competence, he was deceived by Arian intriguers into supporting their program. It need scarcely be said that in this matter Constantine acted in good faith.

Several efforts were made to revive paganism. Only one was important, that of the Emperor Julian in 361. On becoming sole ruler, he publicly repudiated the religion of the Galilean, as he was wont to refer contemptuously to Christ. Although baptized and brought up a Christian, Julian in his youth had secretly embraced paganism, especially after his studies in the school of Athens, the refuge of Neo-Platonism. History has ever called him "Julian the Apostate." Assuming the office of pontiff of the pagan cult, he ostentatiously performed the sacrifices. He strove to rejuvenate paganism by urging its priests to learned pursuits and virtuous lives. As for the Christians, he banished them from the court and closed to them forever careers in the government, the law, the higher positions in the army, the teaching profession and the opportunities for study in the higher schools. He did not himself inflict death on the followers of the Galilean, but he allowed his officials to torture and murder them. Many martyrs are listed in the persecution of Julian the Apostate. Sadly enough there were also large numbers of defectors, chiefly from among the worldly-minded and the sham Christians. Julian's effort collapsed within two years, when he met his death fighting the Persians. The oft-told story of the emperor's dying words, "Galilean, You have conquered," may possibly be legendary; but it truly summarizes his failure.

Confusion
Runs
Rampant

THE FOURTH AND fifth centuries have been called "The Age of the Great Heresies." At no time before or afterwards, at least until the sixteenth century, were heresies more numerous, more widespread and more violent. There were even differences between the heresies that arose in the East and those which appeared in the West. The western heretics, in keeping with the practicality of the Latin mind, were more likely to discuss how men saved their souls, or how the Church was governed. The eastern heretics were apt to busy themselves with the nature and person of Jesus, the God-man. Greeks, Syrians and Egyptians, rationalistic and speculative, loved to probe the mysteries of the Infinite's relations with humanity. The disputants, intense by nature, struggled fiercely as they debated most vital truths. All ranks of the populace participated, even the street-gangs of the imperial cities. The controversialists, as partisans of Alexandria, Antioch or Constantinople, were further inflamed by the rivalries of these great intellectual centers. By their intrigues, ambitious ecclesiastics often complicated and prolonged the conflicts, as did interfering emperors. In extenuation it might be said that this was a period in which the debaters were trying to explain more clearly and to define more accurately the mysteries of the faith, and they were right in fearing inexact terms and incorrect statements.

The greatest of the eastern heresies was Arianism, named after its founder, Arius, a priest of Alexandria, who had been trained at Antioch. In regard to the Holy Trinity he taught that the Son is not of one nature with the Father, not His equal in dignity, and not co-eternal with Him. Arius' doctrine rejected immediately the Holy Trinity and ultimately the redemption of mankind. Though condemned by the Council of Nicaea in 325, and vigorously opposed by St. Athanasius, Bishop of Alexandria, Arius found strong and widespread support from confused or intriguing ecclesiastics through the East and, to a lesser extent, in the West. The Emperor Constantius militantly supported Arianism, as did the Emperor Valens. Persecutions deprived many Catholic bishops of their sees and sent some of them to their deaths. St. Athanasius, the heroic champion of orthodoxy, was five times banished and more than once placed in danger of death. St. Hilary of Poitiers, second only to St. Athanasius in the defense of truth, was exiled from his see for years. The bishopric of Constantinople was held by an Arian for forty years.

After the death of Constantius in 361, Arianism declined. It was done away with by the Emperor Theodosius in 380. It survived for a century and a half outside the empire as the national religion of several Germanic nations. In the subsequent invasions Arianism was to prove a formidable obstacle to Germanic amalgamation with the Romans. Very early in the course of the heresy the Semi-Arians appeared. They taught that the Son had a nature similar to the Father's, but not the same divine nature. What did "similar" mean? Two equally divine natures? But this idea was repugnant to the essential oneness of God, the single Supreme Being. This meaning would have brought back the many gods of polytheism. "Similar," a nature like, but inferior to the Father? This meaning was but the Arian doctrine that the Son was not God. Semi-Arianism was condemned by the Council of Constantinople in 381. There are no modern descendants of Arianism, although many, such as the Unitarians, hold similar views.

The next great eastern heresy, Nestorianism, dealt with the person of Jesus. The Church teaches that Jesus possesses two natures: one, divine, as God the Son; and one human, as a true man. The Church also teaches that these two natures are united in one Person, but are not fused nor absorbed in each other. But how could the same individual at the same time be God and man, eternal and temporal, infinite and finite? Some asserted that Christ was two independent persons, a God and a man. Their teaching contradicted the doctrine of the Redemption. Since mortal sins were human acts, the expiation of Christ had to be a human act; but since mortal sins were infinite offenses against God, Christ's expiation had to have infinite (divine) value.

Nestorius, a priest of Antioch, who in 428 had been made Patriarch of Constantinople, declared that the Blessed Virgin was the mother only of Christ the man. Further Nestorius excommunicated certain monks for giving to Mary the title, "Mother of God." The writings of the patriarch gave grounds for the notion of two separate Christs, although Nestorius would not have admitted that they did. The outstanding opponent of Nestorianism was the learned, though bellicose, St. Cyril of Alexandria. The rivalries of Alexandria, Antioch and Constantinople inflamed the dogmatic dispute. Finally the General Council of Ephesus in 431 condemned Nestorianism. The citizens of Ephesus, convinced that the decision vindicated Mary's title of "Mother of God," held jubilant torch-light processions to celebrate her victory.

The Nestorians disappeared in the empire after their banishment by the Emperor Zeno in 489. They persisted in Persia where those who were Christians were mostly Nestorians, and they founded missions in India and China. Most of these Nestorians were submerged later on by Mohammedanism or heathenism. Here and there small communities managed to exist. In the sixteenth century many in Mesopotamia united themselves with Catholicism and today constitute the Chaldaean Rite. So also did some in India, who now form the Malabar Rite. There still exist in Iraq small groups of Nestorians, who call themselves Assyrian Christians.

Upholders of the truth in acute religious controversies always run the danger of pushing their own ideas too far and themselves falling into error. Such was the fate of the Monophysites. As opponents of Nestorianism rightly they upheld the oneness of the person of Jesus, the God-man. But some of them, when they endeavored to explain how one person could be God and man at the same time, fell into the error of submerging the human nature. They taught that the divine nature of Christ absorbed His human nature, so that in Him there was practically but one nature. So their doctrine was named "Monophysitism," or the doctrine of one nature.

A conflict of intense partisanship raged through the eastern patriarchates. Monophysitism was condemned by the Council of Chalcedon's acceptance of the definitions of Pope St. Leo I in 451. But the struggle was far from ended. Several times the imperial court interfered; with some important exceptions the emperors supported the orthodox side. The Monophysites entrenched themselves in Syria, Egypt and Armenia. Resentment against the superiority of the patriarchate of Constantinople and also against the imperial government led to the final break which produced three independent Monophysite Churches, the Jacobite in Syria, the Coptic in Egypt and the Gregorian in Armenia. Despite some reunions with Rome, the three Churches still exist.

The one great heresy of the West was Pelagianism, which dealt with man's eternal salvation. The Church holds two essentials for salvation: God's grace and man's cooperation with that grace. God's grace is absolutely required for man to begin, to continue and to persevere unto salvation. But God endowed man with a free will; hence He has conditioned the efficacy of His grace on man's acceptance or rejection of it. About the year 400, Pelagius, a British monk, began to teach a contrary doctrine at Rome. Rejecting original sin and exaggerating man's natural powers, he asserted that man without the help of grace could lead a stainless life and obtain eternal salvation. Pelagius achieved a considerable following by his proclaiming that man through intellectual culture and will-training could attain to spiritual greatness.

The scholar who more than anyone else defeated Pelagius was St. Augustine. He based his refutation on St. Paul's doctrine and in so masterful a manner that he has been ever afterwards hailed as the "Doctor of Grace." The heresy disappeared after its condemnation by the Council of Ephesus in 431.

A group of monks in southern Gaul mistakingly suspected St. Augustine of excluding human liberty. They were called Semi-Pelagians because they wrongly affirmed that grace was merited by man and was made efficacious by his human will. St. Augustine opposed them as did several Gallic saints. They were condemned by the Council of Arles in 475. Problems about grace did not seriously bother the Church for the next one thousand years, not until the advent of Luther and Calvin.

The Church in Northern Africa suffered grievously during this period in the schism of the Donatists, which arose from an extreme rigorism that held apostasy during the persecutions to be an unforgivable sin. Donatism had one dogmatic error, namely that the efficacy of the sacraments depended on the spiritual condition of the minister. The Donatists' stubborn refusal to accept the Pope's decision was long enduring and wide-extending; at one time almost half the African hierarchy refused submission. St. Augustine was its great opponent. Fourteen centuries later his writings on the unity of the Church against the Donatists made clear to John Henry Newman the ancient unchangeable rule of faith.

The Age
of the
Fathers

IF THE FOURTH AND fifth centuries were the disastrous "Age of the Great Heresies," they were also the glorious "Age of the Fathers." In no other period of her history was the Church served by so many outstanding literary champions. The productivity and originality of these writers and orators in explaining, interpreting and defending the truths of the faith have never been equalled. They originated Christian education and they began Christian literature. Succeeding generations have accorded them the title, "Fathers of the Church." Their collected works would fill more than a thousand volumes. Cardinal Newman has said that no one, even in a lifetime, could read all the works of the Fathers. One branch of modern ecclesiastical learning is devoted to the study of these early writers; it is the vast and scholarly science of Patrology.

There are four requisites for the title, "Father." The first is antiquity: the writer must have lived before 800; so the last Father in the East is St. John Damascene (676-700), and the last Father in the West is St. Bede the Venerable (672-735). The second is orthodoxy of doctrine: the writer must be free from formal heresy, though his works may contain occasional mistakes; accordingly, despite the great value of their works in general, Tertullian (a formal heretic), Origen (an objective, but probably not a formal heretic), and Eusebius (a Semi-Arian), are not considered Fathers. The third is sanctity of life: all the great Fathers and most, at least, of the minor Fathers were saints. The fourth is the approbation of the Church: this need not be a formal approbation; a general acceptance suffices.

It might be well here to distinguish between the titles, "Father of the Church" and "Doctor of the Church." The differences are in the requisites of formal approbation and of antiquity. The Church by formal document bestows the title "Doctor" on one of her learned teachers and orders a Mass and office for his feast day. So far the Church has designated only thirty-one doctors. No note of antiquity is required: 17 were Fathers, 8 flourished in the Middle Ages, 5 were prominent in the Counter-Reformation, and one lived in the eighteenth century — St. Alphonsus Liguori, who died in 1787. Recently the title, "Doctor," was bestowed on St. Catherine of Siena and St. Teresa of Avila.

The golden age of the Fathers was from 320 to 461, the very years of the great heresies. Indeed they composed most of their works in maintaining the Christian teaching against the attacks of the heresiarchs, or in elaborating the meaning of the doctrinal or moral truths debated in the controversies. These great Christian writers are commonly divided into the Greek and the Latin Fathers according to the language in which they wrote.

The first of the Greek Fathers was St. Athanasius, 296-373, the mightiest opponent of Arianism, and the intrepid defender of the Church against imperial domination. In the face of the bitterest persecution — five times he was banished from Alexandria, and once his death was plotted — he produced an immense literary effort: controversial and dogmatic treatises, scriptural commentaries, moral dissertations and biographies. His life of St. Anthony the hermit (written while in exile in Rome) started Western monasticism.

Next were the Three Cappadocians, called so from their native province: St. Gregory Nazianzen, 325-389; Saint Gregory of Nyssa, 331-386; and St. Basil, 329-379. St. Gregory Nazianzen, close friend of St. Basil, wrote poems and orations of high literary value. He was a staunch opponent of Arianism. St. Gregory of Nyssa, brother of St. Basil, was a gentle mystic, yet a champion against heresy; his principal extant

ST. AUGUSTINE OF HIPPO. *Botticelli, Church of
All Saints, Florence.*

Alinari

ST. BASIL. Twelfth-century mosaic.
Palatine Chapel, Palermo.

work is a defense of Catholic doctrine. One of the supreme personages of Greek Catholicism was, and is, St. Basil. A great thinker, a man of action, a master of spirituality, an outstanding administrator, he remained always a completely human personality. He was the Father of Greek Monasticism; to this day his is the only rule in Greek monasteries. St. Basil's considerable writings were directed largely against Arianism and Manichaeism.

St. John Chrysostom, 347-407, the most eloquent of Christian preachers, was called "Chrysostom" (the Golden Mouth) by his hearers. He preached as a simple priest for twelve years in his native Antioch, and for ten years as the Patriarch in Constantinople. His impassioned sermons were more than emphasized by his piety and heroic courage. That courage brought him to his death on the road to a barren exile. In hundreds of sermons he treated every topic: dogma, morality, Scripture and social justice. To this day St. John Chrysostom is the model for Christian orators.

The last of the Greek Fathers was St. John Damascene (of Damascus), 676-770, a saint profoundly wise and advanced in spirituality. His foremost achievement was his defense of the veneration of holy statues and paintings against the heresy of the Iconoclasts who called them idols. One of his large theological works anticipated the *Summa* and was cited by St. Thomas Aquinas. He composed manuals of asceticism and countless sermons. His hymns are still sung in the churches of the Greek Rite.

St. Hilary of Poitiers, 309-368, earliest of the Latin Fathers, was the leading opponent of Arianism. He was one of the chief supporters of St. Athanasius, and like him was exiled from his see for many years. He produced several dogmatic treatises, biblical commentaries and hymns.

St. Ambrose, 304-397, was the first of the "Four Latin Doctors." Archbishop of Milan for twenty-four years, his excellent administration made him the model of Christian bishops. To all his people he was a father, but especially was he the lover and the provider of the poor. He did not hesitate to rebuke the highest; even the Emperor Theodosius he brought to public penance. His hymns and popularization of antiphonal chanting has given him the name, "Father of

Church Music." His eloquent sermons drew immense crowds; one of his converts was Augustine. He wrote many religious works, and his treatise on virginity is a priceless classic. He opposed Arianism unrelentingly and successfully.

St. Jerome, 340-420, the second of the "Latin Doctors," was the Church's outstanding biblical authority. A native of Dalmatia he served for a time as a civil official. Then he retired to the East for a life of penitence and scriptural studies: four years in the Syrian desert, then the priesthood, then thirty-five years in a monastery in Bethlehem. He mastered Hebrew and other Semitic languages, collected and collated texts, consulted rabbinical sources, and finally produced the Vulgate, the Latin translation of the entire Bible. For almost sixteen hundred years the Vulgate has been the official Latin text used by the Church. St. Jerome's numerous writings included scriptural commentaries, histories, sermons, letters and controversial works.

St. Augustine, 354-430, the third of the "Latin Doctors," is supreme among all the Fathers. He is mighty in every facet of his career: penitent, shepherd of souls, monastic pioneer, preacher of truth, controversialist against Manichaeans, Donatists, Arians and Pelagians. A partial list of his extant writings include 93 major works, 263 sermons and 260 letters. Possibly there are many more letters which have been lost. Because of his works on salvation he has been called the "Doctor of Grace." Two of his writings are eternal classics for all peoples and all places: *The Confessions,* the account of his struggles for conversion; and *The City of God,* a theology framed in history and explaining the actions of God in the world. Peter the Venerable ranked Augustine among the apostles; Bossuet hailed him the Doctor of Doctors.

St. Gregory the Great, 540-604, was the fourth "Latin Doctor." He is universally considered one of the greatest Popes because of his sanctity, spirituality, missionary zeal, administrative achievements and his vast correspondence. Coming a century after the theological controversies he wrote principally on morals and devotions: *Moralia,* a treatise on moral conduct; *Regula Pastoralis,* on priestly life; *Dialogues,* including some biographies. His summaries of the Fathers served as texts for centuries. His spiritual writings nurtured medieval Catholic life.

The last of the Latin Fathers was St. Bede, the Venerable, 672-735. He was an Englishman who was born, lived and died in Northumbria. He was an excellent educator and the foremost scholar of his day. His *Ecclesiastical History of the Anglo-Saxons* was a work of fine scholarship, one of the best books produced in the Middle Ages. The last work of his life was a translation of St. John's Gospel.

The Teutonic Invasions

WHEN THE EMPEROR Theodosius in 394 made Christianity the official religion of the Roman Empire, almost everyone concluded that the future of Christianity was linked in perpetuity with the destinies of eternal Rome. A decade passed and the dream was rudely shattered. The invasions of the Teutons — or, if you will, the migrations of the Germanic nations — were bringing down the Roman Empire, at least the western Latin half, into total destruction.

In 407, the Rhine barrier fell, and Burgundians, Suevians, Vandals, Alans and Franks swarmed over the length and breadth of Gaul. Even earlier the Visigoths had ravaged the Balkans; later they invaded Italy, and in 410 they captured and sacked the "immortal" city of Rome. After a brief tarrying in the Italian peninsula they invaded Gaul and occupied the southwest quarter, Aquitaine; then they continued into Spain, drove out the Vandals, occupied most of the land and set up the Visigothic Kingdom of Spain. The Vandals moved into northern Africa, which they seized and turned into their Vandal Kingdom. About the fourth decade of the century,

Jutes, Angles and Saxons launched their conquest of Britain. In 451, Attila at the head of his Mongolian Huns and his Teutonic satellites swept in frightful devastation through Northern Gaul, leaving everywhere a desert of smoking cities and ravaged countrysides.

The Italian peninsula all during these terrible years suffered one invasion after another; Rome was sacked for a second and a third time. In 475, the last Roman emperor ruling in the West, a puppet and a child, was deposed, but actually long before that date the western half of the empire had disappeared. The Ostrogoths took over the peninsula to give Italy a respite of three decades of peace. The Franks during the last half of the century extended their dominion over all Gaul from the Rhine to the Atlantic and the Pyrenees. In the middle of the next century the Lombards, the last of the Teutons, established themselves in the wasted and depopulated areas of Northern Italy.

The Teutons came out of the primeval forests east of the Rhine and north of the Danube and from the plains and marshes stretching farther to the East. Most were crude barbarians, and some were fierce savages. Those near the Roman frontier had attained some civilization; a few of their leaders, those who as hostages had been brought up at Constantinople, had achieved considerable culture.

It was in the last century of the Republic that the Germanic peoples had begun their efforts to invade the Roman dominion. The Romans on their part had planned to conquer the Germans in the same manner as they had conquered the Celts of Gaul. But after an overwhelming defeat early in the first century A.D. the Romans relinquished the idea of conquest and settled for a policy of keeping the Teutons out of the Empire. To implement the project they constructed the famous Rhine-Danube fortified frontier. The plan worked successfully, and, except for some rare instances, for four hundred years the Teutonic tribes pounded in vain against the long stretching defense. However, because the Romans had a policy of employing Germans as military auxiliaries, chiefly in cavalry units, a considerable number of Germans did get into the empire. Later many more entered when the Teutons were enlisted in the legions to fill up the ranks depleted by pestilences and a low birth rate. By the end of the second century the legions had become largely Teutonic in personnel and minor officers; by the fourth century most of the general officers were Teutonic. These northern soldiers proved themselves loyal; they adopted Roman names and they accepted Roman ideas. In the dark days to come they were Rome's staunch defenders against the newer Germanic invaders.

The new invasions were more than pillaging, destroying and murdering raids. They were all these, but they were also large-scale migrations. An entire nation bringing along all its goods fought its way and wandered along until it seized some part of the western empire for its permanent possession. Though there were several Teutonic groups migrating, it would be a mistake to consider the migrations as a vast movement of German nationalism. That would be interpreting the fifth century in terms of the nineteenth century. The different groups nourished no consciousness of a common nationality. Each worked out its own destiny alone. At the most they spoke similar languages and they used similar structures of government. They often fought each other, even as agents in the pay of the Romans. All this contributed immensely to the universal chaos.

The invading groups were not numerous. Some were hardly more than tribes, and the largest were only small nations. Their strength lay in the fact that almost every man was a soldier, whereas the Latins had become unwarlike. None of the invaders were as numerous as the Latins in the particular sector which they conquered. The new Teutonic kingdoms of the fifth and sixth centuries were really military minorities. In the beginning most of the leaders, including such powerful rulers as Clovis of the Franks and Theodoric of the Ostrogoths, sought from the Emperors at Constantinople the title of "Patricius" (Viceroy) so that they might have a legal claim to rule the far larger Latin populations under them. For their own people alone were they "kings." Only towards the end of the sixth century, when Teuton and Roman had become fused in several national groups, were the Teutonic leaders "kings" of all their subjects and no longer "patricii" of Constantinople.

In the whirlwind the Catholic Church alone survived. It did more. It eventually converted the Teutons to the true Faith and endowed them with the Greco-Roman culture. A chaos of devastation, slaughter, rapine and anarchy inundated western Europe for a century and a half. Heaps of corpses and smoking ruins marked the courses of the invaders. Of the great cities Rome was sacked three times, Trier, five times, and Speyer, Mainz, Strasburg, Rheims, Soissons and London were left smouldering ruins. Very many smaller cities disappeared forever. Ravaged countrysides stood totally deserted. In Burgundy six large districts lapsed back into virginal forests, Northern Italy was practically depopulated, and a tidal wave of destruction cut Britain off from the continent for one hundred and fifty years. To survive in such total chaos was truly miraculous. Yet that is what the Church did. It lifted up the crushed spirits of the Latin provincials; it started rebuilding its ruined edifices as soon as the worst was over; and it negotiated through its bishops with barbarian kings for the alleviation of its afflicted flocks.

These negotiations were often broken up by religious hatreds. The majority of the Teutons were Arians; such were the Visigoths, the Ostrogoths, the Burgundians, the Suevians, the Vandals and the Lombards. Their theology was meager, their comprehension of doctrines hazy, and their practice of rites more military than pious. But their propagation of the Arian creed was often fanatical. The Vandals persisted ferociously anti-Catholic to the end, adding many martyrs to the Church's rolls. The Visigoths persecuted the Spanish Catholics, at times to blood. Some Teutonic nations were heathen; so were the Franks, the Angles and the Saxons. The last two long endeavored to liquidate the Catholicism of the Britons. Yet in the long run the Teutons who survived and participated in the amalgamation with the Latins were the ones who were converted to Catholicism. The others who were not converted, such as the Vandals and the Ostrogoths, faded from history.

The civilizing of the barbarians, a necessary concomitant of their conversion, proved extremely difficult. It took numerous generations to bring the bloodthirsty nomad to the pursuits of peace, to imbue the ignorant plunderer with an appreciation of learning, to instill into the licentious savage submission to the holy yoke of Christ. At the same time the Latin provincials too had to be elevated. Even before the invasions their culture had fallen considerably. Now, cowed and bewildered amid the ashes of their cities and their seats of learning, they sadly needed revival. Many of them, weakened still by the former pagan corruption, had to be reformed. Actually, upon the amalgamated society that was emerging there fell a long night of wholesale barbarism. The elevation of the Teuto-Roman world eventually was achieved by the faith, patience, and zeal of the bishops and the monks.

The Bishops and the Teutonic Invaders

THE CHURCH WAS SAVED and the barbarians were converted and civilized by the bishops and the monks. The role of the bishops will be considered first. They directed the Church's activities, protecting the Latin peoples, negotiating with the invaders, leading heretic and heathen into the true fold, and fostering the fusion of the Latins and the Teutons. The monks played their important part in carrying out the details of Christianizing and civilizing.

In the beginning of the fifth century the Church was blessed with a very large number of bishops who were leaders of the first order. They were, above all, saints, strongly self-disciplined, humble of heart, just in deed and wise in judgment, and devoted completely to God. They were energetic administrators carrying out a plenitude of duties. They were the principal preachers of faith and morals in their dioceses; the leaders in the celebration of the liturgies; the managers of the properties of their bishoprics, widespread and ever increasing; the builders of many new churches in their jurisdictions; the fathers of the faithful, caring for the poor, the sick and the abandoned; the propagators of the Faith among the still numerous heathens; and the founders of monasteries — many of them had been monks before their elevation to the episcopacy. In religion alone these mighty bishops stood out as the leaders of the Latin provincials, the peoples of the Roman provinces of Italy, Gaul, Britain, Spain and North Africa.

In the whirlwinds of invasion the Roman civil officials rapidly declined in influence; the tasks before them were too great. When the imperial government disappeared, bureaucrats and soldiers ceased to be the people's representatives. Only the bishops were left; they became the sole champions of the people.

In consequence of their position as the sole leaders, there devolved upon the bishops a political role, something they neither desired nor sought for. On numerous occasions as the barbarian hordes were approaching, the bishops actually became the "defenders of the city." Sometimes they were ordered by the fading imperialists to provide for the defense; so were the Popes of Rome, to cite but one example. But more often the bishops had to take over on their own initiative. The unaccustomed tasks they performed courageously, displaying a capable political, and even military, leadership. More than once, bishops, casting aside all regard for their own safety, penetrated the besieging lines to confront personally barbarian kings, seeking the best terms possible, striving to dissuade invaders from sacking their cities, always pressing for merciful treatment for the beleaguered people.

From among the many bishops who stood guardians of the people only a few can be mentioned here. St. Germanus of Auxerre, at the age of 70, journeyed to northwestern Gaul to save the provincials of Amorica from the Alans. When the barbarians' leader strove to ignore him, the heroic old bishop stopped the invader's horse by seizing its bridle and forced the Alan chief to hear his pleas. St. Exsuperius of Toulouse stirred up so strong a resistance to the Vandals that he was condemned to deportation. The aged St. Augustine, sick unto death in his episcopal city of Hippo as it lay under siege by Vandals, by his burning words inspired his flock in their desperate defense. St. Quodvultdeus was so much the soul of resistance of his people of Carthage, beleaguered by the ruthless Vandals, that after the city's fall he was banished to Italy, in which devastated land he had to live out his life in the direst poverty.

POPE ST. LEO THE GREAT MEETING ATTILA. *Raphael, the Vatican.*

When Attila the Hun drove his fierce Mongolian raiders and his savage Teutonic satellites through northern Gaul in 461, in the bloodiest and most devastating campaign of all, the bishops alone stood up to the ferocious "Scourge of God." St. Nicasius of Rheims, as he stood in the doorway of his cathedral encouraging the people of his captured city, was slain in the holy precincts. St. Lupus of Troyes dauntlessly confronted the terrible Hun and somehow persuaded him to bypass his city. At the strategic town of Orleans, its bishop, St. Anianus, worked at strengthening the walls, organized the defense and nerved the citizens to meet the attack of the ruthless hordes. Repeatedly he sent appeals to Aetius, the Roman commander-in-chief to hurry his troops and his Visigothic allies to the relief of Orleans. It was shortly afterwards that the Roman-Visigothic forces defeated the Hunnish army in one of the most decisive battles of history, fought on the Catalaunian Plains.

The most significant "Defense of the City" took place in the next year. Attila, still heading a powerful and terrible army, swept down into Italy aiming at Rome. Everywhere people fled from his ravaging horsemen; even the Imperial Court abandoned Ravenna. The Mongolian savage paused at Mantua on the River Mincio. He could take his time; not a single army stood between him and Rome. But one day a strange procession approached the Mincio. It numbered less than a hundred persons, mostly priests and monks, chanting psalms and hymns, and bearing aloft crosses and banners. In their midst rode a venerable, white-bearded ecclesiastic. He was Pope St. Leo I, commissioned by Emperor Valentinian III to halt the invasion. A conference between the Hunnish leader and the old Pope took place; at its end Attila agreed to abandon the conquest of Rome. Shortly afterwards he turned and led his fierce marauders out of Italy. No one has ever learned what exactly took place at that conference. All that Pope St. Leo would say to Emperor Valentinian was: "Let us give thanks to God, for He has delivered us from great danger." St. Leo was truly the "Defender of the City," and of Christianity and civilization.

In the kingdoms quickly arising from the invasions, the Latin provincials constituted the great bulk of the population; the Teutons were but a ruling, military minority. Differences of race, speech, social customs, political practices and, above all, religion led to constant clashes. More than ever the bishops stood out as the representatives of the people. The Teutonic kings came to realize this. When they sought to govern the Latin majorities, they found only the bishops with whom to deal; they saw no civil leaders at all. In the presence of these great churchmen the barbarian kings were awed into reverence, for they were meeting with Roman fortitude, deep intelligence and evident holiness. Even while still Arian or pagan the Teutonic kings began to employ the Catholic bishops as peacemakers, ambassadors and personal advisers.

But until the fusion of the Germanic barbarians and the Latin provincials occurred there could be no ending of the confusion ruling the western world. None realized this better than the bishops. With greater certainty they knew that the fusion would never take place until the barbarians had become Catholics. The Vandals' effort in Africa to obliterate Catholicism had failed; and so too had the more civilized Ostrogoths' plan in Italy of establishing a double society. Paganism, where it existed, would have to disappear. So the bishops now made their first objective the conversion of Arians and pagans to the true faith. So labored St. Avitus of Vienne among the Burgundians, St. Remigius and his fellow bishops among the Franks, St. Leander of Seville among the Visigoths, St. Martin of Braga among the Suevians, St. Augustine of Canterbury among the Jutes and Saxons, and St. Aidan of Lindisfarne among the Angles. The prime mover in the work of conversion was Pope St. Gregory the Great; he sent missionaries to the Lombards, as he had done to the Angles and the Saxons, and he supported St. Leander in his apostolate to the Visigoths of Spain.

The civilizing of the barbarians, the imparting to them of the Greco-Roman culture, was the second great task of the bishops of the sixth, seventh and eighth centuries. Softening savage natures, inculcating habits of industry, introducing learning, and creating a love of knowledge were achieved only by long and slow processes, filled with wide-scaled reverses and hopeless disappointments. The bulk of the Latin provincials afforded little help; their culture had fallen to low standards. Fusion too had its sinister aspects. The coarseness of the barbarians, the ignorance of the provincials, and often the mingled vices of both, brought on a veritable centuries-enduring night of barbarism. But the bishops persevered in their gigantic task of Christianizing and civilizing. After generations they did succeed. For the realization of almost super-human projects they welcomed the assistance of the monks.

Work
and
Prayer

THE MONKS performed most of the actual work in the Christianizing and civilizing of the barbarians. Their achievements were but developments of their own monastic lives, the goal of which was the complete service of God obtained by the conquest of self. To realize this objective they practiced perpetual poverty, chastity and obedience. Early in monastic history these three virtues became the subjects of distinct vows. The monks always located their habitations in remote places for the opportunities these solitary sites offered for uninterrupted prayer and penitential practices. All activities were done under the prescription of written approved rules interpreted and directed by the superiors of monasteries, who were called abbots.

Christian monasticism began in the last decades of the third century. Egypt was the place, in a sandy, rocky, desert region, known as the Thebaid, to the west of the Nile. St. Anthony was the first monk; he instituted the solitary life of the hermit. St. Pachomius, about the same time and in the same locale, organized the communal life, in which the monks prayed, worked and lived together. This last type of monasticism spread rapidly through Egypt, Palestine, Syria and Greece. It was among the Greeks that monastic life was first solidly organized. St. Basil did this by his great rule. He is rightly called the Father of Eastern Monasticism; even to the present day St. Basil's rule is the only religious rule observed in the East.

St. Athanasius, not himself a monk, is said to have introduced monasticism to the Latin West by the life of St. Anthony, which he wrote while in exile at Rome. The writing of the first rule in the West is attributed to St. Augustine. Many monasteries were soon established in Africa, Spain and Italy; in the last country St. Eusebius of Vercelli and St. Paulinus of Nola were outstanding abbots. To the Celtic peoples monasticism had an especially strong appeal; indeed for a long time Irish, Welsh and Breton Catholicism possessed a marked monastic character. The great abbots among the Gauls were St. Martin of Tours, St. Vincent of Lerins, John Cassian of Lerins and St. Caesarius of Arles. The great abbots among the Welsh were St. David and St. Kentigern. The great abbots among the Irish were St. Columcille of Derry, Swords and Iona, St. Comghall of Bangor, St. Finian of Clonard, St. Carthaach of Lismore and St. Kevin of Glendalough.

The supreme figure among all Latin monks, however, was St. Benedict (480-550). He lived two centuries after the pioneers, and yet he is considered the Father of Western Monasticism. St. Benedict established his great monastery at Monte Cassino and it became the motherhouse of all Benedictines. It was there that the patriarch of western monasticism composed his marvelous constitution, known ever since as *The Rule of St. Benedict.* Its practicality and its adaptability have suited monastic life to all circumstances of time and place. Its spirit of love and peace, so characteristic of St. Benedict, breathes life into every page and raises it far above a dry set of formularies. Eventually St. Benedict's rule was accepted by all monasteries in the Latin West; from the early Middle Ages all monks, with rare exceptions, have been Benedictines.

The daily activities of the monks were divided into prayer and physical work. *"Ora et Labora"* (Pray and Work) was the motto to be found painted or carved on the walls of every monastery. The prayer was specified; it consisted of the chanting of the psalms and the recitation of designated prayers. The Sacred Office which all priests read today is

Anderson

ST. BENEDICT. *Memling, Uffizi Gallery, Rome.*

derived from this prayer of the monks. In the monastery it was chanted at fixed hours during the day: Matins and Lauds (after midnight), Prime (at dawn), Terce (at nine), Sext (at noon), Nones (at three), Vespers (in the evening), Compline (before retiring). Immediately after Prime the Communal Mass was celebrated. In the beginning most monks were not priests, although in every monastery there were a few ordained for the offering of the Holy Sacrifice, the supreme religious act of the monastery. Early in the middle ages the present practice of ordaining most of the monks was introduced.

Such was the prayer. The monks esteemed it their most important employment; they called it the "Opus Dei" (the Work of God). They also called it the "Laus Dei" (the Praise of God), for they felt that by it they were inaugurating in this life their own praise of God which they would continue eternally in heaven. It was to give this formal praise to God that monasteries were established. Some writers, Catholic included, tremendously impressed by the vast achievements of the monks for the civilizing and the Christianizing of the barbarians have missed this point of the primacy of prayer in the endeavors of the monks. The medieval monks were not primarily civilizers. They were not primarily even evangelists. Only the Irish and the Anglo-Saxon missionary monks, such as St. Columban and St. Boniface for example, seemed to have made the apostolate of the heathen one of the primary goals.

After the prayer came the labor of the monks. They ranked labor just short of prayer. In fact they looked upon labor as a form of prayer, for they did their work for the praise and glory of God. They drew the motivation for their hard tasks from the official prayer. They valued painful, wearisome toilings as true penitential practices. Finally they knew that physical exertions and the tiredness that accompanied them balanced well the emotionalism and exaltation that can come in prayer.

The labors of the monks embraced manual works, intellectual activities and religious propagation. As has been noted, when the monks planned a monastery they sought remote solitude and hard physical surroundings. The first would aid their prayer and contemplation. The second would afford them plentiful penitential labors. So they built in the depths of the forests, on the edge of swamps, or in rugged mountain valleys. Such localities were numerous in all parts of Europe. In the course of the invasions whole areas of arable lands reverted to woods and brambles, while east of the Rhine primeval forests covered the land for hundreds and hundreds of miles. Uncountable swamps, fens and morasses were to be found through the length and breadth of Europe. The arable sides of mountain valleys lay practically untouched.

The monks cleared the forests, drained the marshes and terraced the mountain fields. They brought back countless square miles of farm lands and they also opened up countless new areas. Historians unanimously have hailed the monks as "the restorers of European agriculture." But they made an even greater contribution: the monks made the barbarians farmers. They persuaded the wanderers to abandon nomadic life and settle around the monasteries as helpers of the monks. They showed them the valuable returns of agriculture: a permanent food supply, so immeasurably superior to their hitherto feast-or-famine existence. They taught them how to plow, to sow and cultivate the crop and to reap the harvest. In a sense the monasteries were the first agricultural schools; of course there were no classes, but there was much practical instruction illustrated by example.

The monks were their own carpenters, stone-masons and iron-workers in the construction of their monastic buildings, which were few and simple in the beginning but eventually numerous and imposing. In these crafts also the monks trained the barbarians; they taught them to wield the saw and hammer, to mix the cement and lay the true line of the stone walls, to turn and shape the iron at the forge. As time went on the monks turned to the finer crafts, fashioning gold and silver chalices, crosiers, processional crosses and various other ecclesiastical ornaments. These skills they too imparted to their neophytes. In a sense the monasteries were the first technical schools.

Most importantly the monks convinced the barbarians of the dignity of manual labor. Hitherto the barbarians had disdained labor as the lot of the slave. But now they beheld monks, whom they knew to have been great nobles or learned scholars, toiling in the fields or at the craftsman's bench. Eventually they learned that all this was being done in imitation of the Savior of men, Jesus. He was God; but as a man He had been the Carpenter of Nazareth, earning by the toil of His hands sustenance for His Mother and for Himself. Nothing that Jesus had done could be low or disgraceful. The monks did not aim at being philanthropists, teaching skills only to elevate human beings materially. They were apostles all the time; and they were teaching the barbarians to labor in imitation of Christ, out of love for Him. Further they impressed upon the barbarians that to do so was a great act of adoration and praise of Jesus the God-man.

The
Monastic
Apostles and
Civilizers

THE MONKS ACHIEVED a tremendous advance in the civilizing of the barbarians when they elevated them intellectually. This they accomplished by their monastic schools. Not all monasteries maintained schools, but most did. The monks began by teaching the young barbarians, mostly their own novices, to read, write and speak the Latin language, the common language of the West. They endowed their pupils with a working knowledge of Latin from grammar to rhetoric. Once the students had obtained a command of the language, the monks introduced them to the study of Sacred Scripture and to the writings of the Fathers, especially St. Augustine, St. Gregory the Great and St. Isidore of Seville. They added training in geometry and music (for the chanting of the Office). And thus the monks imparted to the barbarians the fundamentals, at least, of Greco-Roman culture. Of course intellectual ideals were seldom reached in the beginning; indeed they were often obscured by recurring tides of war and barbarism. But if the monastic teacher had not persevered steadfastly in his classroom, the barbarian might never have been civilized and the Greco-Roman culture might have passed into the limbo of forgotten civilizations.

The books that formed the bases of learning in the monastic schools—the Bible, the Latin classical writings and the works of the Fathers—from whence did they come? Not, of course, from the printing presses; seven or eight hundred years would have to pass before the invention of the printing presses. All the books were produced by the pens of the monastic copyists, who prepared also the parchments (there was no paper), the pens and the inks. The task of the copyist was one of the most difficult, yes, and one of the most penitential, of all the monastic labors. Infinite care had to be exercised at all times. The text had to be reproduced with exact faithfulness; there could be no mistakes or omissions. Each letter had to be formed with careful legibility, with all the sharp definiteness of a modern poster. The copyist was producing his manuscript not for the pleasure of a single person but for the profit of generations to come. The labor was as long drawn out as it was tedious; to make a complete copy of the Bible took a whole year. What the world, and the barbarian in particular, owes to the monastic copyist can never be fully evaluated. Without books, or with very few, how could the Bible, the Latin classics, the works of the Fathers and the historical chronicles of eleven centuries have remained in existence—to be the literary treasures of western civilization? Justly has there been placed in the Library of Congress a mural painting depicting monks working in the scriptorium (the copying room of the monasteries).

More than civilizers, the monks were apostles. The ultimate object of all monastic labors for the barbarians was their conversion to the Catholic religion and, once converted, the intensification of their Catholicism. As has been previously noted some—the Irish monks especially—seemed to have made the conversion of the heathen to Christ an essential goal of their monastic lives. So did St. Columcille among the Scots and the Picts, St. Aidan among the Angles, St. Columban among the Franks and the Lombards, St. Fridolin and St. Gall among the Alamanni, St. Kilian among the Franconians, and St. Virgilius among the Bavarians. The Anglo-Saxon monks—the early fruits of the Italian missionary

CELTIC CROSS. East face
of the cross of the
Scriptures. *Clonmacnois,
Ireland.*

ST. PATRICK. Contemporary sculpture by Cascieri.
St. Ignatius Church, Boston College.

monks, St. Augustine and his companions—journeyed to the Continent in quest of souls; notable among them were St. Boniface, the patron saint of Germany; his cousin, the holy nun, St. Lioba; St. Willibald, St. Wunibald, and their sister, St. Walburga. These Irish and Anglo-Saxon missionary monks were significant of the large numbers of their countrymen who labored with them, or were their contemporaries in the conversion of the Teutonic pagans. Nor should there be passed over the numerous Frankish monks and nuns who sought directly the salvation of the heathen. Typical of the Frankish religious were St. Ansgar and St. Norbert.

Everywhere the monks made their particular monasteries active centers for the propagation of the Catholic Faith. They evangelized the barbarians who had settled around their abbeys and they made missionary circuits through the nearby areas preaching Christ and His redemption. If their efforts seem at first glance not to be so striking as those of the more definitely missionary monks, the end results were as great. The first generations of monks and nuns, almost all natives, converts or the first descendants of converts, produced a glorious flowering of monastic saints. The names of these holy religious show them to be of various races: Celts, Angles, Saxons, Franks, Burgundians, Goths, Alamanni, Bavarians and Lombards. Let it be remembered that this flowering of holiness came during one of the darkest periods of Christian history.

Most effective in the conversion of the barbarians were the holy lives of the monks and the nuns. In the beginning, no doubt, the wanderers were attracted by the sounds of the chanted Office; certainly they were fascinated by the colorful vestments and the solemn, devout ceremonies of the Mass. After a time deeper thoughts came with the frequent sight of the monks or nuns laboring in the fields and in the shops. It was plain to see: here were dedicated people devoted to doing good to all, especially the sick and the needy. Here were disciplined people, humble, poor, obedient and chaste. How could they have become so, especially those who had held high positions, were of noble birth, or had long mingled in the decadent society of the times? A partial answer dawned on the barbarians as they began to recognize the monks and nuns as people of prayer and holy lives. The full answer was obtained when the barbarians finally grasped the motivation of these dedicated and saintly persons, their acceptance of God, their love for Jesus, and their complete confidence in the truth of Jesus' doctrines. The Catholic teaching was now understandable and acceptable to the barbarians for it was living before their eyes in the holy lives of the monks and nuns.

The Mohammedan Flood

AROUND THE YEAR 600, while western Christians were immersed in barbarism and laboring for the conversion of the Teutons, while eastern Christians were weakened by theological conflicts and struggling under the checkered fortunes of Byzantine emperors, there appeared a hostile force that seemed about to wipe out the Greco-Roman world. This alien force was Mohammedanism. It swept up from the mysterious depths of Arabia, a belligerent religion of Bedouin warriors and caravan guards bent on world conquest.

Fanatical fighters, they spurned any assimilation with Christianity and western civilization. In an amazingly short time they broke the unity of the Mediterranean world. Their founder had not been dead a hundred years when they had conquered Syria and Palestine, almost the whole eastern shore of the great sea, Egypt, Northern Africa and Morocco, the entire southern shore, and Spain, the whole western shore. They made Arabic-Moslem culture dominant in the eastern and western conquests, and the sole culture in the entire south from Egypt to Morocco.

The Church suffered overwhelming disasters. Henceforth Christians under Moslem rule lived in isolated groups. The chances of reunion of the Syrian, Palestinian and Egyptian Monophysites with Catholicism were for the future practically nil. Many, induced by material prospects under Islam, abandoned Christianity. True, Christian communities in Spain and Sicily, and to a lesser extent in Syria and Palestine, remained steadfast to Christ and His religion. But in Egypt,

North Africa and (later) Asia Minor the losses were almost complete and permanent. Further the Mohammedan control of the Mediterranean Sea impeded contacts between Rome and Constantinople, thus contributing immeasurably to the growing cleavage.

No one could ever have predicted this mighty assault upon the Christian world, much less its origin in Arabia. This vast peninsula, with its sandy wastes and its bare granite hills, was for Europeans a totally unknown land. The region was sparsely populated by Bedouin tribes wandering in the deserts and by isolated dwellers of the few commercial towns on the caravan routes. Nomads or merchants, they were all fierce and warlike, brave and passionate, predatory and ambitious. They were at war continually, tribe with tribe among the Bedouins, clan with clan in the town vendettas. The Arabians lacked any sense of nationality, for them the state was only a congeries of families.

The religion of the Arabians was a low type of heathenism. They adored objects of nature; their chief idol was the Kaaba, a black stone venerated in Mecca by great pilgrimages. Even in their native paganism they held no unity. Further on the northeastern fringes dwelt followers of Persian Zoroastrianism. Some Jews were to be found, and a few Christians, the last mostly on the northwestern border. There seemed no possibility that the various religious trends could be welded into a unity, no more than the bellicoseness of the desert nomads could be whipped into a national thrust outwards.

At Mecca in 571, or shortly afterwards, was born the genius who would give a new religion and its unity to the Arabians and who would turn the bloodfeuds into national conquest. He was named Mohammed. The impoverishment of his youth drove him to the caravans and he soon became the leading camel-driver for a rich widow, Khadija. His travels brought him familiarity with the ways of desert life, and also some fragmentary knowledge of Judaism and Christianity. Mohammed developed into something of a mystic. In the beginning his highly sensitive soul, wracked with religious questions and doubts, alternated between profound despair and violent exaltation. Later he became subject to dreams and trances. His marriage to his employer afforded him a retirement in which, ministered to by his faithful wife, he gave himself to introspective contemplation of his experiences. At length he came forth proclaiming a national religion: the worship of the true God, and the acceptance of Mohammed as His supreme and last prophet.

The Meccans, except for his family and a few friends, refused to accept him. Some actually plotted his assassination. He had to flee in 622 to Yatreb where he was accepted completely. The flight is called the Hegira; from it the Mohammedans date their calendar. Yatreb's name was changed to Medina (the City of the Prophet); and there Mohammed developed his teachings, organized his supporters and made war upon Mecca and its caravans. After eight years the Prophet captured Mecca, made it the capital of his well-knit state, that now controlled a considerable part of Arabia, and extended his influence from it over the whole peninsula. He also designated Mecca the sanctuary of his new religion. Mohammed died in 632. He had unified the Arabians in a political-religious system to which he gave the name "Islam."

His new religion was simple enough for the most unlettered nomads. It had but one cardinal principle: "There is no God but Allah, and Mohammed is His prophet." Allah is the name of the true God worshipped by the Jews and the Christians. Islam called for surrender to God and acceptance of Mohammed as His prophet. It had no mysteries in its belief, nor did it have a sacrifice or a priesthood. It taught the immortality of the soul, total fatalism, and the reward of a sensual paradise.

Islam made much of its moral code. In some parts it was not exacting: polygamy was sanctioned by the permission for four wives; divorce was easily obtainable and slavery was condoned. In other parts the morality was severe and rigoristic: strictly forbidden were not only idolatry, apostasy and adultery, but also gambling and the use of wine and pork. Islam also prescribed a ritualism: prayers (five times a day) preceded by ablutions and prostrations, strict fasting during the month of the Ramadan, and pilgrimages to Mecca. The faithful believed that by such external practices they were justified and maintained in holiness. All Mohammedans constituted a single fellowship regardless of race, trade or rank. The teachings of the Prophet were assembled in the Koran, the sacred book of the Mohammedans, venerated by them as the Bible is venerated by Jews and Christians.

Mohammedanism was a convert-making religion. That it propagated itself by the sword has been widely, if inaccurately asserted. Certainly on all believers lay the obligation of propagating Islam and waging holy war to destroy unbelievers. Idolators were offered the choice of the Koran or death; Jews and Christians were offered the choice of the Koran, tribute or death. Some writers claim that Mohammed planned such a course only for Arabia and that its extension to the outside was the work of his successors. After the first flush of conquest, with its mixed motivation of religion, booty, and power, the Arabs showed themselves rather tolerant. If the Christians accepted the inferior status, they could live comfortably and even hold important offices in the state. The Arabs wanted more their tribute than their conversion. The later Christians' apostasies came from the worldly-minded who sought the greater material prospects hitherto denied them. The multiplying conquests, however, were frequently marked by fanatical persecutions. The hopeless lot of the Christians in the east and more so in the south has already been noted.

The extent and the rapidity of the Mohammedan conquests were fantastic. In less than eighty years Moslem territory stretched from the Indus River to the Spanish coasts of the Atlantic Ocean. Only the Christian lands must here be considered. From 633-661 Syria, Palestine, Cyprus, Rhodes, Egypt and Lybia were subjected; from 661-718 the rest of Northern Africa, Morocco and Spain were completely subdued. How can such phenomenal conquests be explained? First, there were the militant faith, fanaticism, warlike propensities and exaltation in victory of the Arabians. Second, there was the exhaustion of the Byzantines after their long wars with the Persians. Third, there were the disaffection of Syrian and Egyptian Monophysites and the popular enmity in those regions for the Byzantine "tyrants." North Africans nursed similar estrangements, plus separatists' tendencies of their own. Spain was paralyzed by decadence and political anarchy.

The Mohammedan surge was finally turned back. In the east the Byzantines by two tremendous defenses of besieged Constantinople stopped the Moslems. The first defense, 673-678, was against five attacks from land and sea in five successive years. The second defense, 717-718, was Leo the Isaurian's defeat of the year-long siege by the Mohammedans when they were at the very peak of their conquering successes elsewhere. In the west the Arabians were stopped by the victory of Charles Martel and his Franks over Abd-er-Rahman at the battle of Tours, 732. After seven days of watching each other the two armies clashed at Tours. Time after time the white clad horsemen of the desert flung themselves in whirlwind charges on the solid ranks of the mail-clad, iron-helmeted warriors of the forests. The iron wall held. Abd-er-Rahman's death in a charge decided the outcome. Tours is universally considered one of the decisive battles of the world. Christianity was saved there, and also at Constantinople. But how much was lost forever elsewhere?

The Temporal Sovereignty of the Popes

THE YEAR 756 witnessed an extremely important event in the Church's history, the establishment of the Papal States. The locale of this new government was the central portion of the Italian peninsula. Geographically it consisted of two areas, one in the west along the Mediterranean coast and the other in the east along the Adriatic coast. The western area extended for 150 miles, about 75 miles south and 75 miles north of Rome; it went inland for some 50 miles. A long and narrow corridor, stretching northeasterly through the Apennines, connected the western with the eastern part. This eastern part also extended for 150 miles, from south of Ancona to north of Ravenna; and it too went inland for some 50 miles. The figures are approximate, and intended only to give an idea of the original extent of the Papal States. The new sovereignty lasted for 1,114 years, until it was ended by the Italian unification movement in 1870. It was revived, in a modern form, by the Lateran Treaty of 1929 between Italy and the Papacy, which established the Vatican City State.

The temporal sovereignty of the Popes was not an overnight creation. Rather it was the culmination of a process which was four centuries in development. Circumstances compelled the Popes to be what the emperors could not or would not be, the protectors of the Italian people in times of extraordinary disasters. One of the earliest of the causes was the Patrimony of St. Peter. For three centuries after the end of the persecutions great Roman families had donated to the Bishop of Rome for religious and charitable purposes estates with farms, pasture lands, villages and even small towns. In time there grew up the vast accumulation of such gifts, which came to be known as the Patrimony of St. Peter. Although found in all parts of the western empire, the great majority of the papal estates were located in central Italy. The Popes employed the revenues for the building of churches and monasteries, the maintenance of hospices and hospitals, the freeing of slaves, the providing of legal advocates for the poor and oppressed, the relieving of the sufferings of the peoples of Italy and elsewhere in the ravages of the barbarian invasions. Because of the Patrimony of St. Peter, the Popes were by far the largest landowners in all Europe, and hence the lords of the innumerable coloni and serfs who cultivated the Patrimony's estates.

The emperors through the centuries entrusted the Popes with many executive functions; as a consequence the Popes became important officials in civil, legal, business and governmental affairs. In times of invasion they were frequently commanded by the emperors to organize the military defense of Rome and the episcopal cities of Italy. And since the emperors or the exarchs, their viceroys, often neglected their duties of protecting the people, the Popes were obliged to negotiate with the leaders of hostile armies and to conclude treaties of peace with invading kings. Sometimes the Popes had to defray, out of the properties of the Church, all the costs of the defense of Rome and the Byzantine possessions in Italy. Twice Rome was saved only by St. Leo the Great.

For some time the peoples of Italy had become estranged from their loyalty to the emperors at Constantinople. With mounting indignation they followed the treacherous dealings of heretical and Caesaro-papist rulers of Byzantium with the Popes. They were horrified at the banishment in chains of Pope St. Martin and his subsequent death in prison in Constantinople. In sorrowful impotency they witnessed the imperial soldiers plundering the Roman churches. On one occasion they rose in arms to prevent the arrest of Pope Sergius, and on another they fought to protect the life of Pope St. Gregory II. Their feelings were completely outraged when they beheld the emperors Leo the Isaurian and Constantine Copronymous enforcing with fire and sword the Iconoclastic heresy.

This heresy held that the honoring of sacred icons or holy statues or pictures was pure idolatry, and taught that all such objects must be totally destroyed. The iconoclastic emperors ruthlessly enforced such doctrines. Everywhere they smashed and burned the most sacred shrines. In the East they added many names to the roll of the martyrs. In Italy, besides the universal demolishing of statues and paintings, the imperial troops confiscated the patrimonies of St. Peter in Sicily and devastated them on the mainland. Yet the Popes strove to restrain the people. Against the heresies of the emperors they spoke out with apostolic freedom; but not one of them failed in his civil obedience, even to the worst of rulers.

What precipitated the establishment of the Papal States, however, was the ambition of the Lombard kings to conquer the entire Italian peninsula. They held in a strong grip almost the whole of the north as their own kingdom. Below them, and as far south as Naples, there was a confusion of small governments. Some were semi-independent Lombard duchies; while others were Latin duchies, restless under the Byzantine exarchs at Ravenna. The rest of the peninsula, from Naples south to Sicily, lay under the undisputed but weak rule of the Byzantine emperors.

Conquest of the peninsula by the Lombards was not a welcome prospect. The last of the invaders were among the fiercest of the barbarians. Even after conversion, though their treatment of the conquered greatly improved, they still kept their Italian subjects in an inferior status. The two races never coalesced. Rule by the Lombards on the whole was feared and even hated.

The southward invasions of the Lombards were begun by Luitprand, the ablest of their kings. His life was a constant conflict between the deep reverence of a pious Catholic for the Popes and the ambitions of a successful conqueror for the whole Italian peninsula. Luitprand's first attack, 727, ended outside the walls of Rome when he yielded to the pleas of Pope St. Gregory II and abandoned the siege of the city. His second campaign, 738, brought him again to the gates of Rome. This time he was determined not to be turned from his purpose. Pope Gregory III in desperation appealed to Charles Martel. But the Frankish leader refused to make war upon his Lombard friends and allies. He did, however, by friendly mediation induce the Lombard king to raise the siege. Luitprand generously restored to the new Pope, St. Zachary, a number of towns and patrimonies within and without the Duchy of Rome.

About ten years later the then reigning Lombard king, Aistulf, began the last invasion. He captured Ravenna and all the imperial territories in Central Italy. Then he turned against the Duchy of Rome, treating with contempt the papal embassies. Pope Stephan II sent letter after letter to the Emperor begging for an army to defend Rome. Constantine V, the Iconoclast, did not deign even to reply. His refusal to protect his subjects in their grave peril was equivalent to the abdication of his claims. Stephan had been rebuffed by Lombard and Byzantine. Only one course was left open to him: an appeal to the Frankish king, Pepin the Short.

Pepin first sent a peaceful mission to Aistulf. When it was rejected, the Frankish king and his nobles marched through the passes of the Alps and besieged Aistulf in Pavia, his capital. The Lombard sued for peace; and by the terms of the treaty he had to surrender the Exarchate, the Pentapolis and other captured places to the Roman Church and Republic. But the Franks had hardly left Italy when Aistulf broke the treaty. Again he laid siege to Rome, this time burning and devastating the countryside, and brutally attacking the unarmed peoples.

Pepin once more led his armies into Italy and captured Aistulf at Pavia. The Lombard king was forced to carry out his previous engagements and to pay a heavy indemnity. Then Pepin dispatched the Abbot of St. Denis, Fulrad, on a significant mission. First he went from city to city of the Exarchate, Emelia and the Adriatic Pentapolis and received the keys of each city in the name of the conquerors (the Franks). Then he proceeded to Rome and upon the tomb of St. Peter he placed the keys together with a document, a written donation by Pepin granting these towns and territories to the Holy See as a free and independent possession. Thus were established the Papal States. Their long history has had many glorious chapters, and some unfortunate ones. But through it all most of the time they preserved the independence of the Popes. Today in their modern abbreviated form, the Vatican City State, they are succeeding in their task of emphasizing the Pope's independence better than at any time in the past.

Charlemagne

CHARLEMAGNE IS THE only hero in whose name men have incorporated the word "Great." In medieval Latin he was always designated "Carolus Magnus" (Charles the Great) —he is still called in German "Karl der Grosse." But in the developing French and English of the middle ages a fusion of the two words was made into "Charlemagne." Few men have deserved the term "great" more than this vigorous Frankish monarch who completed the amalgamation of the Germanic world with the Greco-Roman civilization and who laid the basis of Christendom, the family of Christian nations, which was to be the very foundation of Europe for the next thousand years.

Through the forty-five years of his reign, 769-814, Charlemagne was to move without ceasing in vast undertakings: numerous military campaigns, superintendence of large government agencies, maintenance of strong educational programs, and unremitting support for religion in all its activities. He was not a saint. There still lingered in him something of the barbarian in his ambitions, his ruthlessness and the moral delinquencies of his earlier years. Yet the Church permits the ancient veneration of him as a Blessed in Aachen and Poitou; his heart was usually right and his death was truly pious. In every role in which he appears

Charlemagne stands pre-eminently great: statesman, ruler, warrior, organizer, administrator, law-giver, promoter of education, reformer of morals (clerical and lay), or protector and propagator of Christianity. This chapter must concern itself primarily with the Frankish monarch as the protector and propagator of Christianity, a role, however, which affected all his other achievements.

One first thinks of Charlemagne as the champion of Christianity. The early half of his reign amounted to one long war in defense of the Church. It was a war filled with an astounding series of rapid marches from end to end of a continent intersected with mountains, morasses and forests, and scantily provided with roads; it was a struggle replete with fiercely contested, sanguinary battles. Of fifty-three distinct campaigns, forty were undertaken principally, if not entirely, by Charlemagne in his mission as soldier and protector of the Church. His destruction of the Lombard Kingdom, 773 and 776, freed the Papacy from the two-hundred-year-old threat to its independence. His invasion of Moorish dominated Spain, 778, and his subsequent establishment of the Spanish March, south of the Pyrenees, was the beginning of the Christian reconquest. His destruction of the pagan Avars, 796, removed the Mongolian terror from Eastern Europe and restored Christianity to the lands of the Danube.

The bitterest and the most difficult strife was waged with the pagan Saxons on the northeastern frontier. It was a protracted conflict, starting in 772 and ending only in 803. From the beginning the wars were a life and death struggle between Christianity and the last of Teutonic heathenism. The terrain, mostly primeval forest, was extremely difficult. The Saxons were numerous and fought unrelentingly and stubbornly; one cannot but admire their heroic tenacity to their ancient liberties, customs and religion. Time and again the Franks invaded the region, overcame the opposition, built fortresses, set up a judicial system, erected monasteries and set about conversions not only by the word but by the sword. But as soon as Charlemagne was afar off engrossed in some great project in a distant province, the Saxons would erupt into revolt, destroy the fortresses, burn the monasteries, slaughter the Christians wholesale and move devastatingly into the

Frankland. Charlemagne would have to hasten back and begin the conquest all over again. Only after nine expeditions were the Saxons finally beaten. Most regrettably the suppressions were marked with fierce cruelties, which gained only feigned submissions, simulated baptisms and new revolts. Peace finally came when the Saxon leader, Widukind, disillusioned with the Teutonic heathen deities, freely sought baptism. Modern Christians must be shocked at the bloody ruthlessness of Charlemagne and the Franks. Not in defense, but in explanation, it must be remembered that the time was the barbaric eighth century and that there were horrible cruelties on the other side.

Charlemagne was patron of the Church quite as much as her champion. His founding of seven bishoprics among the Saxons is but an indication of his unfailing support of countless missionaries and monks. He was continually issuing laws for the support of religion: the Holy See and the clergy must be honored throughout his domains; tithes must be regularly maintained for the expenses of worship, the building of churches, the support of the clergy, and the assistance of widows and orphans. He even made laws guaranteeing Sunday observance and regulating the sacred chant. Largely through his backing, the Benedictine rule became universal in the monasteries. Some of Charlemagne's most earnest efforts were directed to the reform of the clergy. Perhaps the chief reason for his tremendous educational work, for which he is as much renowned as for military victories, was his desire for the intellectual and moral training of the priests.

But in all his devotion to the Church's welfare there lay grave dangers. Charlemagne was actually maintaining a theocratic state in which he exercised the major control. He chose the bishops and the administrators, he regulated worship and he directed the course of religion. One of his contemporaries, a monk of St. Gall, hailed him as "The Pious Overseer of the Bishops," a well-intentioned but dubious compliment. Even in regard to the Pope, Charlemagne considered himself his guardian; and sometimes he was a masterful guardian. The great monarch, confusing the spiritual and the temporal, was apt to identify his own glory with the exaltation of religion. Sometimes he interfered in the very life of the Church, in her discipline and, on a few occasions, even in her dogmatic prerogative. The description of him as the "Christian Caliph" holds a measure of truth. His motives were the highest, but he entered into fields that were not his. Later rulers would copy his intrusions with great disaster to religion.

After the third Mass on Christmas Day, 800, in St. Peter's in Rome came the supreme moment of Charlemagne's career. As he knelt before St. Peter's altar Pope Leo III proclaimed him Emperor and placed upon his head the imperial crown. Historians have made the date, 800, the dividing line between ancient history and medieval history; at least it marks the consolidation of Christendom, that binding basis of Europe which lasted for a thousand years.

What was the meaning of this empire? Legal historians have disputed about it for centuries, especially during the conflicts of the medieval Popes and civil rulers. One thing it was not — a revival of the old Roman Empire, despite certain terms and ceremonies. Nor was it a tranference of the imperial office from the Byzantines to the Franks. The emperors of Constantinople, who deeply resented the whole affair, continued to be the lineal descendents of Augustus, Constantine and Justinian. Further, the Pope's act bestowed no new territories upon Charlemagne; he possessed practically everything in the Christian West except a few small countries.

It is the significances of the act of 800 which really count. For one thing it meant the final incorporation of the Teutons in the eternal Roman civilization. What resulted from Pope Leo's action might well be called the Christian Empire of the West, presided over in temporal affairs by the Frankish ruler and his successors and governed in spiritual concerns by the Popes of Rome. In pursuance of this idea Charlemagne was made officially the protector of the Church and the guardian of public order. On him was bestowed a primacy of honor and dignity over the other kings of the family of Christian nations, the union called Christendom. It is well to note these rulers were not subjects of the new emperor.

The relations of Pope and emperor were those of mutual dependence and loyalty; at least such was the theory.

Vigorous almost to his very last year Charlemagne died in 814. He was buried in the cathedral of Aachen; he loved the town and he had built the cathedral. The actual political structure of Charlemagne's domain did not long remain after him; but the reality of Christendom survived until the Religious Revolution of the 16th century. In the contemplation of the tremendous majesty of Charlemagne's plans and achievements, his personal faults fade out. Truly he was Charles the Great.

The Darkest Age

THE EXPRESSION, "The Dark Ages," is rightfully resented by Catholics. It is a propaganda slander of the Religious Revolution of the 16th century; possibly it originated with that faction of the Renaissance which cultivated a pagan outlook. The term was continually repeated by the sceptics of the 17th century, emphatically proclaimed by the Voltairian infidels of the 18th century, and unquestioningly believed in by the secularists and materialists of the 19th century. "The Dark Ages" summarizes this charge: the thousand years from Constantine's Catholicism to Luther's revolt was one long period of intellectual stagnation, in which civilization and liberty were kept imprisoned in the darkness of ignorance and superstition by the tyrannical, obscurant and corrupt Catholic priesthood — Popes, bishops, clerics and monks. No sensible Catholic denies the periods of intellectual retrogression in the course of those thousand years; such disasters are common in every civilization. Nor does he deny that there were many human failings in the Church's representatives during those centuries. What he does strongly resent is the blanket indictment of the whole Catholic priesthood with its thousands and thousands of saints, martyrs, missionaries, scholars, worthy Popes and holy clerics.

Those who accepted the term tended to close their eyes, ears and intellects to the writings of the Fathers, the apostolates of the missionaries, the civilizing labors of the monks, the codification of the Roman Law by Justinian and his lawyers, the achievements of emperors and kings, the heroic deeds of the Crusaders, the glories of Byzantine, Romanesque and Gothic architecture, the educational accomplishments of some eighty universities, the depth and value of Scholasticism, the system of theology and philosophy developed by the medieval thinkers, the beauties of literature in the national epics, the *Divina Commedia* and the Latin hymns, the charm of the Italian, Netherlandish and German paintings of the 14th and 15th centuries. Today a real scholar would hesitate to use the term, "The Dark Ages," without qualifying his words.

However, we can properly speak of "The Dark Ages" if we use the term to designate the terrible century and a half that followed the death of Charlemagne. In that period the vast Carolingian Empire disintegrated in chaos and anarchy. The internal causes of the catastrophe were the chronic wars of Charlemagne's descendants. In the place of the one strong government they eventually produced fifty small sovereignties, the semi-independent duchies, incessantly quarrelling and making war on each other. The external causes of the catastrophe were the continual invasions of savage heathens from the east, north and west, and the ceaseless raidings of fanatical Moslems from the south. Fiery destruction and merciless slaughter yearly descended upon the frontiers, and often swept far inland. This century and a half amounted to one long agony of fighting, pillage, animal lust, elemental blood-thirstiness and ruthless devastation. In such political chaos, social anarchy and economic ruin, a grave moral collapse was inevitable. It was wholesale and it affected all classes of Christians. The worst scandals in the history of the Church, some reaching even to the very throne of Peter, occurred in these fearful times. Truly this era can be called "The Dark Age," even "The Darkest Age."

The invasions will be considered first; they began forty years before the start of the internal disintegration. Hostile forces, hating Catholicism bitterly, encircled all Christendom, not only the Frankish Empire, but the Anglo-Saxon Heptarchy, Ireland, the remnant of Catholic Spain, and the Byzantine provinces of southern Italy. Occupying the whole of the south from the Nile to the Atlantic and up the Spanish peninsula to the Ebro River were the Mohammedans, zealous for Islam and eager for booty and slaves. Their great fleets captured Corsica, Sardinia, and brought powerful, fanatical armies into Calabria. Their piratical corsairs continually ravaged with fire and sword the coasts and the hinterlands of the southern Frankland and central Italy. In no time they made the Mediterranian a Mohammedan sea. A Saracen fleet in 846 sailed up the Tiber, attacked Rome and sacked the basilicas of St. Peter and St. Paul. Pope St. Leo IV fortified the Vatican Hill and built the Leonine City against the Moslem marauders, and in 849 his fleet completely defeated theirs off Ostia. Pope John X in 916 drove the Saracens from their strong base on the Garigliano, whence, from 852, they had constantly raided central Italy. The Saracens held their grip on Sicily, overrunning Calabria again in 976 and for several years afterwards. The Moslems were finally ousted from Sicily only at the end of the 11th century.

The enemies on the eastern frontier were heathens and, racially, Slavs or Magyars. The Slavs (Moravians, Slovaks and Czechs) launched no invasions; they were too occupied battling German conquest. About 863, Sts. Cyril and Methodius brought Christianity to the Slavs. But its complete acceptance was complicated by disputes over the Slavonic Liturgy and was long delayed by the bitter conflicts of the Christian and heathen parties. The Poles, who appeared later, were converted in 966.

The Magyars were the terrifying scourge of the eastern regions. They were of Mongolian origin and were often called Hungarians. A vigorous nation of disciplined warriors, they were passionate for war and plunder and were pitiless to either age or sex. After destroying ruthlessly the kingdom of Moravia in 906, for the next half century the "Magyars" were a byword in Europe for terror. Mounted on fleet horses, they roamed in hordes, slaying and burning, over Germany, northern Italy and even France.

Only in 955 were they stopped, when Otto I overwhelmingly defeated them in the battle of Lechfeld. The Magyars settled down in Hungary, where Christianity was introduced among them in 979. Their complete conversion was accomplished by their great king, St. Stephen, 997-1039.

The most terrible of all the invaders were the Norse, whose raids for two centuries surpassed all others in ferocity and who devastated the entire northwest of Europe. They were known variously as Norsemen, Danes or Vikings. The last term has no royal significance; it merely meant a dweller along a creek or fjord. By whatever name, they were pirates, fearless and cruel, ever on the lookout for plunder. Prowess in combat and physical courage were the only qualities they esteemed; mercy was unknown to them. In their long ships, narrow of beam and low of keel, they skirted the coasts, entered the most shallow inlets and bore down upon any defenseless places, pillaged and burned them, and were off before any resistance could be offered.

There were three phases in the Norse invasions. The first lasted a hundred and fifty years and consisted of piratical raids whose principal objects were churches and monasteries. The second period witnessed the construction of permanent settlements at river mouths, bases for controlling the surrounding areas and for invading further inland. The third phase was occupied with the founding of states, like the Norse Kingdom of Dublin or the Duchy of Normandy in France.

Ireland was the first to be overwhelmed by the whirlwind. In 795, the Norse began raiding. Annually for the next century, and intermittently after that, the murderous savages scoured the entire country. Their fiercest and bloodiest blows they delivered against the monasteries. It is doubtful if a single monastery was spared; some like Clomacnoise were repeatedly destroyed. The Vikings seemed to delight especially in desecrating shrines and in "drowning" books. The Golden Age of Irish monasticism was brought to an end in the Norse invasions.

Norse pirates harried every mile of the coastline of the East Frankland and of the West Frankland. They pushed up every river fighting, devastating and carrying off captives. Forty-seven great invasions are listed by the Frankish chroniclers. Not an important city from Cologne to Bordeaux escaped Viking assaults; Paris in forty years was four times besieged, three times pillaged and twice burned. Little wonder that the northern and western regions of the Frankland were demoralized. The tide was turned by the defeats of the Norsemen at Saucourt, 881, and Louvain, 891, and above all by the successful defense of Paris during an eleven month siege, 885-886. The Norse peril was ended by the creation of the Duchy of Normandy in 911.

England, directly in the path of the Vikings, suffered as much as, if not more than Ireland or the Frankland. Under pressure of the Norse attacks the Anglo-Saxons were forced to unite into one nation, which came to be known as England. The invasions, starting with the destruction of the great monastery of Lindisfarne in 787, brought along the same terrible devastations as elsewhere, with the same intense hatred of Christianity. The same debasement of culture and morals resulted in England. In 876, the Norsemen conquered the whole of England. The danger was great that they might stamp out Christianity. But England was rescued and Christianity was saved by the resolute courage of King Alfred the Great. Still so powerful were the Norse that Alfred himself was able to gain back only half of England. He did however prepare the way for his sons and grandsons to reconquer the other half.

Anarchy, Feudalism and the Papacy

THE CENTURY AND A HALF following Charlemagne's death has been called "The Dark Age" because of the frightful devastations of the frontiers of Christendom by the Moslems, Magyars and Northmen. The period must also be called so because of the chaotic disintegration of the Carolingian Empire and because of the terrible moral collapses in clerical ranks, high and low.

The disintegration began during the reign of Louis the Pious, Charlemagne's heir, in the quarrels of Louis and his four sons over the division of power. Chronic wars, raging in all parts of the empire for the next hundred years, produced first three kingdoms, then further divisions into seven, finally a coalescing into two, the East Frankland (including Italy and Provence) and the West Frankland. Each kingdom though headed by a descendant of Charlemagne, actually was but a loose collection of powerful duchies, paying but nominal allegiance to a weak monarch. These practically independent sovereignties, totalling about fifty, were strong only against their kings; among themselves they were constantly waging civil wars. In 911, the Carolingian line disappeared in the East Frankland; in 961, the Saxon ruler, Otto I, transformed the realm into the Holy Roman Empire. In 987, the last Carolingian in the West Frankland died, and his successor, Hugh Capet, Count of Paris, turned the region into the Kingdom of France. Both new states continued for a long time to be collections of feudal duchies.

The social anarchy in this chaotic century of disinte-gration beggars description. The royal power was almost extinguished; there was no national government, army, system of justice, or economy. Tyrannical dukes and counts destroyed the freedom of the lower nobles and the common people. Their armies in the never-ending baronial wars mercilessly ravaged the fields and homes of the defenseless tillers of the soil. The excesses of some of these "Christians" rivaled the outrages of the Moslems and heathen.

Yet the mailed horsemen and the strong-walled castles of feudalism foiled the Moslems, Magyars and Norsemen, and eventually brought some order into the chaos of the decaying empire. A knowledge of feudalism is important, especially because of its connections with the Church. Feudalism was the system that organized the politics, the social life and the economy of medieval Europe. It was based upon a graduated land tenure involving military, judicial and financial services. Feudalism came into full existence in the 9th and 10th centuries to answer the need for pro-tection against the terrors of savage invasion and domestic anarchy. Smaller landowners gave over their holdings to more powerful ones, who took upon themselves the duty of defending the smaller proprietors and their possessions. The defender was known as the lord, the defended as the vassal, the holdings as the fief. The lord gave back the land to the vassal but with the latter's obligation of furnishing troops, keeping peace in the possession and contributing financial dues. A sort of double ownership arose: the lord's, who gave protection, and the vassal's, who gave services. In conse-quence a relationship of mutual rights and duties came into existence. The vassal did not pay rent for the use of the property; he and his heirs held it in permanent title, but with the added obligation of services. It should be noted that the vassals were not poor men; the lowest among them were owners of large estates, the highest were powerful dukes.

Feudalism was maintained in a graduated system of land tenure. A feudal kingdom was a vast pyramid of fiefs, each with its particular set of rights and duties, great or small depending on its position. At the apex was the king. Directly under him were his immediate vassals, the great dukes, who in turn were the lords of the next line of vassals, important nobles, who in turn were lords of the next in line of vassals, lesser nobles. The succession spread down through one or two more ranks to the lowest vassals, the rural gentry who held the manors. It is important to note that the particular rights and duties of each feudal fief adhered to that fief. If by purchase, or forfeiture, or donation the fief changed hands, the new owner inherited all its duties and rights. Since wealth was largely in lands, substantial gifts to the Church would have to be feudal lands; in consequence bishops and abbots would obtain not only landed estates, but the adherent feudal rights and duties. It could not have been otherwise in a society whose whole structure was feudal. In time bishops and abbots became great feudal landholders, with vassals and lords and all sorts of secular obligations.

A great amount of good was accomplished for the Church by the feudal system. In practice it was the main and, in many cases, the only support of religion, education and charity. But there were ominous possibilities of abuse. Unfortunately they were only too terribly realized when, in the anarchic chaos, evil men seized control of religion in many places all over Christendom. These wicked tyrants would prove how seriously bad Catholics can cripple, even though they cannot destroy, Christ's Church.

In the turmoil of civil wars unscrupulous barons began seizing and despoiling bishoprics and abbeys. From these devastations and, of course, from the ravaging invasions, churchmen had to seek the protection of the great feudal lords. Under feudalism this involved some concessions in the nominations to ecclesiastical office. Aggressive and avaricious kings and nobles pushed such concessions to an almost unlimited control over bishops, abbots and parish priests. The results were appalling. Offices with grave spiritual responsibility were bestowed upon kinsmen or favorites, with no regard for their virtues or intellectual qualifications. Sometimes these holy offices were sold, thus adding to outrage the sin of simony. Such simoniacal prelates sought to reimburse themselves by financial oppression of their unfortunate subjects, or by simoniacal selling of the benefices under them. The Church has never known, before or since, such evil bishops. They lived like the bellicose, brutal and licentious nobles who were their kin; often as vassals they led their men-at-arms in the battles of their overlords. They brazenly violated celibacy, claiming the right to marry, and strove to transmit their sees to their illegitimate offspring. They gave the minor benefices, which they often attempted to sell, to ignorant and untrained priests, who knew scarcely more than the bare essentials of doctrine and the minimum of sacramental rites. In consequence the people were uninstructed and neglected. These poor clerics also failed grievously in the practice of celibacy, and, like their unworthy shepherds, essayed to marry openly. But let it not be thought that the clerical body was totally corrupt. There were holy bishops and saintly priests during these dark times, as will be shown.

The worst stages of anarchy were reached in northern and central Italy, the most remote regions of the Carolingian Empire. After the death of Charlemagne orderly government disappeared rapidly. The high barriers of the Alps effectively blocked any intervention by the weak Frankish rulers. So in these isolated parts chaotic forces struggled with each other unchecked for more than a century. The northern area, when it was not being overrun by Magyar horsemen, was fought over time and again by rival Carolingian princelings claiming the petty Kingdom of Italy. The central area was overwhelmed by violent and sanguinary contentions of factions of the Roman nobility aiming to dominate the Papacy. The Moslem raids in the same region were far less evil.

When the Carolingian regime disappeared in central Italy, its protectorate of the Pope and the papal state were taken over by the military aristocrats of Rome. For the next century and a half, violent and licentious factions among them battled in sanguinary rivalry for complete lay domination of the Papacy. First the Theophylacti, then the Crescentii and finally the Tusculans laid their hands on the Holy See and dictated the nominations of Popes. Shameful scandals disgraced the first of all sees. These Roman nobles did more harm to the Church than had ever been done by Byzantines or Lombards. At least two unworthy Popes were seated upon the throne of Peter. The majority of the Popes were not evil; many were zealous reformers. But too many of the good Popes met violent death at the hands of their opponents. The depths were reached when the wicked Princess Marozia, the leader of the Theophylactic faction, determined who were to be Popes. It is true that contemporary records are obscure and that there have been many gross exaggerations and lurid myths; nevertheless this period remains the darkest hour in the history of the Church.

Why did God permit such evils? It is to show that His Church cannot be destroyed from within, that the dry-rot of the sins of wicked Catholics cannot bring down in ruins the structure of His timeless Church. Never was Christ's prophecy about the perpetual failure of the gates of hell more evident than in the dark night of the 9th and 10th centuries. What of the unworthy Popes? God guarantees His vicars on earth only infallibility in their official teaching of faith and morals; He does not endow them with sinlessness. They retain their free will and, being sons of Adam, they may fail. It is remarkable that of all the 262 Popes, the unworthy ones were three, at the most five. Many of the Popes were capable and exemplary, a large number of them were martyrs and canonized saints. They are among the glories of the Church.

Not
All
Was
Dark

THE BARQUE OF PETER is a staunch ship—it outrides every storm. Christ sails in it always; and He, the Second Person of the Blessed Trinity, has guaranteed its indestructibility. And so in the darkest night its light shines, dimmed sometimes by the fury of the tempests, but never extinguished. In the tumultuous violence of the "Darkest Age," the light of Peter's barque gleamed steadily.

There was the Christianization of many pagan people. In the 9th century the conversion of the Scandinavians began when in 831, St. Ansgar started his thirty-four years of evangelizing the Danes, Norwegians and Swedes. Peril from heathen vikings and discouragement from wholesale relapses failed to deter him from laying the foundations of Christianity in the Northland. Rightly is St. Ansgar revered as the Apostle of the Scandinavians. In 863, St. Cyril and St. Methodius, the Apostles of the Slavs, came from Greece to introduce Christianity among the Moravians and Bohemians. They won numerous converts for, not only did they preach in Slavonic, but they translated the Gospels and the liturgy into Slavonic. However, they encountered powerful opposition from the German princes and bishops. The brothers personally brought their case to Rome. Pope Adrian II approved of their methods and made St. Methodius archbishop of Moravia. The opposition did not relent and sometime later imprisoned St. Methodius. He was liberated on the insistence of Pope

John VIII, who renewed the approval of the Slavonic liturgy. Unfortunately the locale of the mission was in an area beset by the conflicting interests of the Frankish and the Byzantine empires. Finally the intrigues of the East Franks deceived Pope Stephen IV who forbade the Slavonic liturgy. Pope John X and later Popes renewed the prohibition. The action was disastrous for it turned most of the Slavic peoples from Rome to Constantinople. The Moravian-Bohemian mission disappeared in the Magyars' destruction of Moravia.

The last half of the 10th century witnessed the total conversion of the Scandinavians. The Norse settlers in Ireland, the Frankland and England first accepted Christianity. Then Benedictines from Bremen, but more especially from England, brought the Gospel to the homelands, overcoming strong heathen opposition. What won the Danes, Norwegians and Swedes were the austere lives and fervent faith of the monks and the prestige of Christian civilization. The Scandinavian kings strongly supported the missionary monks. The Wends, Pomeranians and Prussians along the Baltic in spite of furious pagan resistance were brought into the Faith by monks under the leadership of St. Adalbert of Magdeburg. The final Christianization of Bohemia came after the bitter conflicts between pro-German Christians and nationalist pagans. St. Wenceslaus, the king, and St. Adalbert of Prague, both martyrs (the latter by Prussian heathens) had leading parts in the conversion of the Bohemians. The greatest triumph came with the acceptance of Christianity by the Polish people. It was the result of the missionary labors of German and Bohemian monks, supported by the kings, Miesko and Boleslaus. Next in significance was the conversion of the Hungarians, or Magyars, by missionaries sent by St. Adalbert of Prague. The greatest of all persons connected with the conversion of the Hungarians was their own holy king, St. Stephen. The Bohemians, Moravians, Slovenes, Croats and the Poles received their Christianity from Rome; the Serbs, Bulgarians, Ruthenians, Ukranians and Russians received theirs from Constantinople. The period of the conversions of all was in these difficult times.

The dark shadows hovering over the See of Peter were dissipated from time to time by the lives of zealous pontiffs.

Several Popes were energetic reformers. Their reforms failed because of the circumstances of the times; but their efforts kept alive the memory of holy ideals. Of the forty-nine Popes reigning during these terrible centuries four are canonized saints. St. Nicholas I, the Great, 858-867, is one of the three Popes in the history of the Church who bear this title. St. Nicholas resisted imperial encroachments on the papacy, denounced evil princes and prelates, upheld the sanctity of Christian marriage against the bigamous King Lothair, maintained the papal authority over local bishops, nullified the election of Photius to the Patriarchate of Constantinople and restored there the deposed St. Ignatius.

During these turbulent times when war was the normal condition of society, one promise of a better day was the "Peace of God." It was a device of the Church to lessen violence during the constant feuds and private wars. In the complete decentralization of feudal governments there existed no effective machinery for punishing offenders or settling disputes. Great lords fought each other with impunity, lesser barons battled their rivals unrestrainedly. Ruined shrines and violated sanctuaries were the Church's lot; brutal outrages and ravaged farms with consequent famine and disease were the peasants' fate.

In 989, the Synod of Charroux in Aquitaine directed by Archbishop Gumbald of Bordeaux inaugurated the first "Peace of God" by excommunicating those who broke into churches, or struck clerics, or robbed the poor. In the next year the bishop of Puy, Guy of Anjou, published another "Peace of God." This document, retaining the sanctions of the first, further decreed excommunication against those who seized ecclesiastical lands, those who made peasants captives and held them for ransom, those who injured monks and their unarmed companions, those who robbed merchants on a journey, and those who killed or carried off cattle — unless required for a lawful expedition.

The "Peace of God" spread to all parts of France. Various church synods and assemblies of nobles passed laws in its support. Some nobles bound themselves by oath to observe it. But given the decentralized and military structure of feudal society, anything like a complete acceptance of the

"Peace of God" was hardly to be expected. What is significant is that in anarchic times some advance towards peace was made and the way prepared for the "Truce of God," which was started fifty years later in 1041. The "Truce of God," also devised by the Church, proposed a truce to all warfare during certain parts of each week and certain periods of each year. It gained a much wider acceptance.

Monastic reform produced the most successful counter-action to the evils of the times. During the invasions and the civil wars religious communities deteriorated sadly. There always remained some good monasteries. But many communities, when dominated by feudal lords and prelates, fell victims of most pernicious secular influences, lost their ideals of sanctity and became infested with the contemporary evils of incontinence and simony. The very institution that should have been an inspiration to priests and laymen became a scandal. The root evil lay in the choosing of the abbots. Greedy barons and vicious prelates, all sprung from the same ruthless warrior caste, thrust lax monks upon the abbatial throne or sold the office to evil religious.

A salutary change began in 910, when William the Pious, Duke of Aquitaine, endowed a monastery for St. Berno at Cluny, near Macon. Monastic observance flourished in the new foundation from the beginning and its monks earned a high reputation for holiness. Poverty and chastity were practiced with rigorous faithfulness; strict silence assured a spirit of prayer, and meager diets disciplined the body. A careful regulation of time properly provided for the offices of prayer and labor. Great emphasis was placed on the full carrying out of the liturgy. Charity abounded so that every day crowds of poor people were fed and cared for.

But much more than a holy monastery had been founded; a great movement had been inaugurated, the Cluniac Reform. First the Abbey of Cluny was placed directly under the Pope. The foundation provided complete immunity from lay inter-ference and from local episcopal control. This guaranteed that the monks alone chose the abbot and that he and his community alone regulated the affairs of the community. Secondly the abbot of Cluny was made the head of a large collection of monasteries. He was empowered by the Popes to establish new houses dependent on Cluny, or to incorporate other monasteries into the Cluniac system. He named the superiors of the dependent houses, he sanctioned the professions, he made annual visitation of all the dependent houses. By the 12th century Cluny was at the head of some 314 monasteries, all enjoying the exemptions of the mother-house from outside control and all living the holy life of Cluny. The Cluniac Reform in consequence gave immense strength to the great Hildebrandine reform of Pope Saint Gregory VII.

Under papal direction Cluniac monasteries were established in Italy, Spain, France, Normandy, England, Germany and Poland. The first six superiors were exceptional personalities: St. Berno, St. Odo, Abbot Aymard, St. Maieul, St. Odilo and St. Hugh. They were also long-lived rulers; in 250 years Cluny had only six abbots; they had time for their great reform program. Several cardinals and bishops, and three Popes started as Cluniac monks. Cluny's influence went far beyond its confines. Many Benedictine abbeys, while maintaining their independence, adopted the ideals and practices of Cluny. Some formed similar amalgamations on a smaller scale in local areas, as at Metz, Brogne, Fleury, Hirschau and Farfa. Within a hundred years from the foundation the abbot of Cluny was, after the Pope, the most influential personage in the Church, the trusted advisor of Popes and kings. Cluny was to remain a vital force in the Church for the next three hundred years.

Lay
Investiture

THE LIGHTS OF FAITH and virtue gleaming in the 10th century's darkness presaged the Church's heroism in her 11th century battles with kings for her freedom in the titanic struggles over lay investiture. The roots of this conflict were the secular rulers' intrusions into the nominations of bishops and abbots, and even of Popes. Bishoprics and abbeys because of their feudal possessions, the main sources of their support, had become royal fiefs with vast *regalia*, that is, large castles, wide countrysides and even towns. As holders of these fiefs the ecclesiastical lords exercised the same temporal rule over them as the lay lords did over their fiefs. Like them too the bishops and abbots were vassals of the king.

The trouble arose in the ceremony of investiture which marked the transferral of the fief. After the new vassal had sworn homage the king placed in his hands a banner, symbolizing his military duty. Since a martial ensign was considered inappropriate for an ecclesiastic, the king presented the bishop, or abbot, with a crosier and a ring. Because these were tokens of spiritual jurisdiction the symbolism was not felicitous. However, if the ceremony followed the canonical election, the freedom of the election was not destroyed. But gradually the king began to hand the crosier and the ring to a churchman of his own choosing *before* the clergy of the cathedral or the abbey had a chance to elect and present their candidate. An archbishop was then ordered by the king to consecrate the royal appointee. Lay investiture thus destroyed the freedom of the Church in the election of the shepherds of the flock.

In consequence pernicious evils spread over all Christendom. A most sinister meaning was now attached to lay investiture. Formerly it expressed merely the transference of fiefs and their regalia; now it signified the handing over of a church, or its properties (feudal and non-feudal), of its pastoral care and jurisdiction, of everything but consecration. Under bad monarchs the door was opened to unholy ambition, bribery and the terrible sin of simony. Unprincipled clergymen unblushingly offered enormous sums to obtain a bishopric or an abbey. To reimburse themselves they sold minor benefices to clergy of lower rank. The evil traffic filled many higher and lower offices with unworthy clerics who, lost to the sense of their vocation, attempted marriage or brazenly lived in concubinage. A large number of the clergy thus defied a law binding in the Latin Church since the 6th century. Many speciously defended their transgression as lawful custom.

There developed a more basic evil. Lay investiture tended to break up the unity and catholicity of the Church by nationalizing it in the various countries. Had this divisiveness eventuated, the ecclesiastical order would have been completely merged in the feudal system, and the priesthood would have become a caste holding benefices on a secular tenure and, owing to the influence of clerical marriage, on an hereditary tenure.

But once again the gates of hell crashed in vain against the Rock of Peter. About the middle of the century a vigorous reform movement swung into action. It was called the Hildebrandine Reform, from its chief activator, Cardinal Hildebrand (later Pope Gregory VII). Through the next three decades its successes mounted yearly until it culminated in the pontificate of St. Gregory VII, one of the greatest of the Popes.

Who participated in the reform? First, there were the five Popes who directed it—especially St. Leo IX, who devised its methods, and Nicholas II under whose inspiration the election of Popes was restricted to the cardinals alone—thus abolishing the emperor's nomination. These Popes held synods in almost every country of Western Europe and presided over them personally or by their legates. At these

synods, by preaching a moral revival and by deposing simoniacal prelates, the Popes labored for an ecclesiastical
reform based on a celibate clergy, elected without the use
of money or violence, and inducted into office by the Church
alone.

Then must be noted the supporters of the Popes. First
were able collaborators, such as St. Peter Damian, Cardinal
Hildebrand and Cardinal Humbert. Second was the congregation of Cluny, established in all parts of Europe, with more
than ten thousand monks and some three hundred houses,
all under the Pope's authority alone. Third was the Pataria,
a society of priests and simple laymen organized to oppose
the married clergy; founded in Milan it had spread to the
principal cities of Italy. Fourth were the Normans of Sicily,
since 1059 vassals of the Holy See. Though turbulent and
difficult to control, these indomitable warriors could satis-
factorily defend the Popes against any imperial armies that
might march against the sovereign Pontiffs. Fifth were the
rulers of Tuscany, the Countess Beatrice and her daughter, the
Countess Matilda. Enthusiasts for the reform, they devoted
their wealth, their castles and their troops to the cause. The
Countess Matilda, as heroic as she was saintly, commanded
her own vassals in defense of Rome. Finally there was the
loyalty of all true Christians of the age.

The reform had to overcome most virulent opponents:
the bishops deposed for simony or incontinence, or those
about to be deposed; the Roman baronage, excluded from
papal affairs for thirty years; and the imperial court, deprived
of its appointing of the Popes. The opponents struggled in
vain; by 1073, when Pope Alexander II died, the reform was
ascendant. But victory was not yet certain; the root evil,
lay investiture, remained.

The uprooting of lay investiture was to be done by the
next Pope, St. Gregory VII (Cardinal Hildebrand). His first
acts were to renew the decrees against simony and clerical
incontinence, and to continue the depositions. Undismayed
by new storms of opposition and obloquy he appealed
directly to the people to avoid the ministrations of unworthy
shepherds and to refuse obedience to bishops who tolerated
immoral priests. In 1075, Gregory VII promulgated the vital

POPE GREGORY VII AND HENRY IV AT CANOSSA. Visible behind
the kneeling figure of the Emperor is Countess Matilda of
Tuscany. *Frederico Zuccari, the Vatican.*

decree against lay investiture: excommunication for any cleric who received from a lay person a bishopric or an abbey; and excommunication for any emperor or king who gave such investiture. The infuriated opponents attempted to depose St. Gregory.

Heading the opposition was the profligate emperor, Henry IV. By his open simony he had made his court a market for bishoprics and abbeys. When he contemptuously disobeyed the decree against lay investiture, Gregory VII excommunicated him and absolved his subjects from their allegiance. Henry's situation became desperate. Disaffection was widespread in Germany owing to his cruel suppression of the Saxon revolt and to his status as an excommunicate. A strong movement to depose him developed. One way out was left to him, reconciliation with the Pope within a year: the time of grace allowed an excommunicated monarch.

In the middle of the winter, with a few attendants Henry crossed the Alps. The Pope, fearing treachery, sought the protection of Countess Matilda's castle at Canossa in the northern Apennines. Henry made his way to Canossa. Then occurred one of history's most dramatic incidents. For three days the emperor stood constantly before the castle's gate, garbed as a penitent and beseeching with many tears the Pope's forgiveness. Gregory VII had his doubts about Henry; but he yielded to his evident sincerity, and to the entreaties of St. Hugh of Cluny and Countess Matilda, and absolved the emperor.

The Pope's misgivings were only too justified. Within a short time the fickle monarch had returned to investing bishops and abbots. Victory in Germany freed him for war against Gregory VII. Setting up an anti-pope, the Archbishop of Ravenna, long a leader of the Italian opposition, Henry led an army against Rome. On his fourth attempt he captured the city and installed his creature on the papal throne. Gregory VII, holding out in the Castel Sant'Angelo, summoned his Norman vassals. Before these powerful fighting men reached the city, Henry fled. They easily occupied Rome. Unfortunately, owing to a street brawl, the unruly Normans, heedless of Gregory's remonstrances, pillaged and burned a considerable part of the city. When they returned to Salerno the Pope had to go with them.

There on May 25, 1085, Pope Gregory VII died. These were his last words: "I have loved justice and hated iniquity, therefore I die in exile." Apparently defeated, actually he was victorious. He had established the principle of the Church's freedom in the election of her shepherds, and he had obtained for it the acceptance of the people. Never again would secular princes exercise unchallenged control over the papacy. Acceptance by the imperial court would take longer; it came only after thirty-seven years of struggling by Gregory's successors, especially Urban II and Calixtus II. Imperial acceptance was achieved by the Concordat of Worms, 1122.

The Hildebrandine Reform was more or less effective in most European countries. In England, however, William the Conqueror would not relinquish lay investiture. As his choices, under the guidance of the worthy Archbishop Lanfranc, were good, Gregory VII, hard pressed by Henry IV, had to let the situation stand. The next king, the thoroughly bad William Rufus, exceeded the worst evils on the continent, and his successor, Henry I, aimed at complete control of the bishoprics. The defender of the Church's liberties was St. Anselm, unmoved by bitter persecutions and two exiles.

The last encyclical of St. Gregory VII epitomizes the Hildebrandine Reform and the war against lay investiture: "That the Holy Church, the Spouse of God, our Mistress and Mother, returning to her innate splendor, may continue to be *free, chaste* and *Catholic*."

Schism
in the
East

THE 11th CENTURY Church, preoccupied with the investiture struggle in the West, encountered a much graver evil in the East, the schism of Constantinople. The patriarch, Michael Cerularius, rejected the primacy of the Pope and cut off all relations with the Latin Christians. Later his separatism spread through most of Eastern Christendom. It has remained to the present day.

The break did not originate with Cerularius, nor did it derive solely from the great schism of Photius in the 9th century. It was rooted in divergencies between Rome and Constantinople that had been developing from the day when Constantine transferred the imperial capital from old Rome on the Tiber to New Rome on the Bosporus. That was far back in the 4th century.

Difference in church government led to the first divergencies. Christians were grouped around different centers, the patriarchates; after the Council of Chalcedon (451) these were: Rome, Antioch, Alexandria, Constantinople and Jerusalem. The bishop of Rome held two jurisdictions: as patriarch he was the sole leader of the entire Latin West; as Pope he was the supreme Pontiff of all Christianity. The Easterners acknowledged his universal headship. Because of his remoteness, however, they referred to him only the rare cases that were locally unsolvable. Ordinarily they gave their immediate obedience to their own patriarchs. Therein lay dangers of divided allegiance. In a quarrel between Pope and patriarch, the local bishops, priests and laity might be apt to follow their patriarch. In the beginning there were only contrasts, but these could and did develop into serious rivalries.

Differences of rites multiplied divergencies. With the Roman rite completely supreme in the West and the Byzantine rite almost as universal in the East two unities began to appear, one Latin, the other Greek. Diversities of rites were easily comprehensible. The simplest layman, who could hardly understand the canon law of patriarchates, could easily recognize the different and, to him, strange ceremonies of another liturgy. Each division knew that the other's rites were equally legitimate; and up to the 11th century both sides manifested great mutual charity. But differences of rites made it increasingly hard to pray together. When the great conflicts came, Photius and Cerularius made the most telling arguments in attacks on the "false" and "evil" religious practices of the Latins.

Language differences raised the barriers higher. Religious disputes were complicated by the fact that neither the Westerners nor the Easterners could understand one another. St. Gregory I, though a papal agent at Constantinople, seems not to have learned Greek; Pope Virgilius, despite his eight unhappy years at the eastern capital, did not acquire the language; Photius, one of the most learned scholars of the Middle Ages, knew no Latin; St. Peter III, Patriarch of Antioch, had to seek an interpreter for Pope St. Leo IX's Latin letter. Facility in foreign languages had to wait for the Renaissance, six centuries later, to produce convenient grammars and dictionaries. Language difficulties shackled the most vital negotiations. At the Councils, held at or near Constantinople and made up exclusively of Greek speakers, the fathers could make nothing out of addresses of the Latin-speaking papal legates, nor could the legates follow the fathers debating in Greek. Interpreters had to be used, but their versions might not always be trusted by the Latins. The legates were asked to sign documents which they did not understand, on the assurance that nothing really compromising was contained in them. The legates hesitated in matters where a brief expression might have made a world of difference.

Yet all these divergencies of government, rite and language were not sufficient to account for a permanent schism. In the four centuries after Constantine not all the Popes were Latin; some were Greeks or Syrians. What turned the contrasts into persisting rivalries was the advance of the See of Constantinople towards supremacy in the East and leadership of the other three patriarchates.

The ultimate promoters of the advance were the emperors of Constantinople, who despite the heroic opposition of many a holy patriarch dominated the choice and policies of the patriarchs. It was owing to these caesaro-papist rulers that Byzantium, only a suffragan see of Heraclea, was raised to an archbishopric when it became Constantinople, then later elevated to patriarchal rank (over Asia Minor and Thrace), and finally declared an ecumenical patriarchate second only to Rome. The basic reason was always: it was the bishopric of the capital city of the empire; as Caesar could locate political pre-eminence where he wished, so he could locate ecclesiastical pre-eminence where he wished. The final move would come when an emperor transferred the supreme pontificate to the bishopric of his imperial city. The Popes vigorously opposed every step of the advance, incurring thereby the enmity of caesaro-papist emperors and of such ambitious ecclesiastics as supported them.

Constantinople, backed by the emperors, gradually assumed leadership over the other eastern patriarchates. These could offer little opposition; they had lost the bulk of their populations in the Monophysite heresy, and the Moslems had reduced the remnants to abject isolation. They yielded to the leadership of Constantinople. When Cerularius' schism came, even though it was not a quarrel between the East and the West but a revolt of one see, such was the influence of Constantinople that eventually it drew the other three patriarchates along with it.

Doctrinal controversies were fertile sources of divergence between the speculative Greek and the practical Latin. Let it be remembered that large numbers of Greek theologians, learned and holy, always upheld the true faith. The Church Universal honors seven with the title, "Doctor," three of whom were bishops of Constantinople: Sts. Basil, Gregory Nazianzen and John Chrysostom. Behind the heresies that arose often would be found a meddlesome emperor. The list of conflicts involving schisms is formidable: between the founding of Constantinople and the patriarchate of Photius there were five periods of schism, totalling 203 out of 537 years. Each schism was healed in time; but all tended to weaken the conviction of essential unity. Other strains on unity there were: the disputes between Rome and Constantinople over jurisdiction in the Balkans and over the evangelizing of the Bulgars and the Slavs. One event that caused great resentment in the East was Pope St. Leo III's crowning of Charlemagne, a barbarian Frank, as Roman Emperor. Though the title had only western significance, Constantinople was incensed: there was but one Roman Empire and one Roman Emperor.

Divergencies finally climaxed in the Photian Schism (857-867). The proximate cause was the resignation of the Patriarch of Constantinople, St. Ignatius, forced by the regent, Bardas. The saint had publicly refused Communion to Bardas, a notoriously evil living person. To fill the vacancy the council of bishops chose Photius, a layman, who was quickly ordained, consecrated, and named patriarch. Photius was a great scholar, one of the most learned of the Middle Ages, or of any other time; he was also a man of irreproachable life and character. But his elevation was not accepted entirely in the East; and when appeal was made to the Pope, St. Nicholas I, he sided with St. Ignatius and condemned Photius. Then followed a dozen years of the most involved conflict: mutual condemnations and excommunications, schism, real and pseudo councils, depositions and restorations. On the death of St. Ignatius, Photius was accepted as patriarch at Constantinople and recognized as such at Rome.

The unfortunate consequence of the schism of Photius was the rise of an anti-Roman party. It never disappeared, but nourishing the old resentments and charges against the West, it waited for the opportunity of permanently breaking the union. Its main reliance was the anti-Roman writings of Photius. His fundamental charge was heresy: that the Latins were heretics in regard to the Holy Trinity because they introduced into the Creed the *Filioque* clause (that the Holy Spirit proceeds from the Father *and the Son*). The addition was not heretical; in no way did it deny the equality of each of the Three Divine Persons. But accusation of heresy, backed by the great prestige of Photius, colored and immensely strengthened his popular accusations against the Latins' "evil" ritual and ecclesiastical disciplinary practices, practices that had no connection at all with heresy. These petty differences eventually came to be treated like fundamental dogmas.

The opportunity appeared when Michael Cerularius, one of the most extreme anti-Romans, became patriarch in 1043. By letters to the East and the West (the last intended for the Pope's eyes), he attacked Latin practices, especially the Saturday Fast, the use of unleavened bread in the Eucharist, and the celibacy of the clergy. Then he closed all churches of the Latin rite in Constantinople. Before their doors were locked the blessed Hosts were cast outside and trampled underfoot because they had been consecrated from unleavened bread. Pope St. Leo IX in protest solemnly reminded Cerularius of the divinely founded primacy and of the heinousness of schism. The patriarch did not submit, but sought rather an equality. To the papal legates sent for the crisis Cerularius refused the customary precedence; he even strove to place them below his own metropolitans. When the legates refused to accept his rankings, he terminated all negotiations and erased the Pope's name from the liturgy. The legates in reply, July 16, 1054, placed an excommunication of Cerularius on the high altar of Sancta Sophia and departed from Constantinople. The schism was a fact. Most people of the time never dreamed that it was to extend through most of the East and to last to the present day.

"Taking the Cross"

DANIEL-ROPS SUMMARIZES the High Middle Ages in two words, "Cathedral" and "Crusade." This chapter will discuss the second of those two words. The crusades came in the twelfth and thirteenth centuries. They were mighty military expeditions against the Mohammedan powers of the Near East, undertaken by western Christians. Their purpose was the protection of the Christians in that area and in the adjacent Byzantine lands. The western forces epitomized their efforts by declarations that they sought to rescue the Holy Places of Palestine, especially the Holy Sepulcher, from the hands of the Moslems. The term "crusade" arose from the custom of the Christian warriors of sewing a small cross upon the shoulder of their garments — later the cross was enlarged and sewn on the breast of the tunics. Such warriors were said to have "taken the cross"; they were known as "crusaders" and their expeditions were called "crusades."

The protection of the native Christians of the East, or the western Christians who had gone there on pilgrimage, was the fundamental motive of the crusading movement. During the entire eleventh century, after the fall of the tolerant Arab caliphs, the lot of the Christians in the Near East became extremely perilous. In the first decades they were in danger of complete destruction by the new masters of Palestine, the Fatimites of Egypt. These Moslems, ferociously fanatical, by the bloodiest atrocities and total oppression aimed at liquidating the Christians. In the second half of the century a far more powerful force persecuted the Christians, the Seljuk Turks, who had made themselves masters of Baghdad and taken over the headship of the Mohammedan world. In

Palestine and Syria their bloody outrages and ruthless extortions reduced the Christians, native or pilgrim, to a bare, miserable existence. The Turks, by their victory at Manzikert, 1071, annihilated the main Byzantine army and marched as conquerors through the whole of Asia Minor. Before long they were occupying fortified cities within the very neighborhood of Constantinople. The Greek Empire seemed doomed.

The fearful plight of their eastern brethren deeply affected Christians of the West. Reports of their terrible trials enkindled the religious fervor of the westerners, and in the military spirit of the age they vowed to march to the rescue of their Greek and Syrian co-religionists. The Popes from the very start headed the movement. As early as 1000, Pope Sylvester II projected armed assistance, but his death and that of the Emperor Otto III nullified the plans. For some time nothing further could be attempted; the bitterly contested reform monopolized all papal efforts. St. Gregory VII, when he became Pope, planned on raising an army and leading it personally to Palestine. He wrote to Henry IV that 50,000 men were ready beyond the Alps to follow him. He also was in frequent epistolary contact with the Greek Emperor, Michael Dukas. The lay-investiture struggle with Henry IV prevented the realization of St. Gregory's hopes for aid to the East. However, the delay was not of long duration, for a few years after his death, his ideas were activated by his chosen disciple, Pope Blessed Urban II in a manner greater than he had originally planned.

In 1095, Pope Urban inaugurated the Crusades. The souls of men had been prepared by the Hildebrandine Reform; and their hearts had been aroused by eloquent preachers, notably Peter the Hermit, a returned pilgrim from the ravaged Holy Land. An embassy from the eastern Emperor, Alexius Comnenus, was also in the West appealing to the princes for their help against the Moslem conquerors. The Pope made his first appeal to a large gathering at Piacenza in Italy. Then he delivered his supreme effort to an immense throng of nobles, warriors and common people at Clermont in France. Urban's glowing oratory was interrupted time and again by shouts, "God wills it! God wills it!" The response far exceeded his most sanguine expectations. He wrote to Alexius Comnenus that 300,000 men had taken the vow of an armed pilgrimage to Jerusalem to deliver the Holy Sepulcher.

In his appeal for defenders of the persecuted eastern brethren Pope Urban begged his hearers to stop their endless wars. The western European states were actually only loose confederations of semi-independent, powerful feudal duchies, each with a large feudal army. They were constantly at war with their kings, their fellow dukes, or their subordinate barons. Their armies in the aggregate counted up to an enormous force of men-at-arms, mostly minor nobles whose sole occupation was fighting. The Pope urged the leaders to establish mutual peace that they might channel their vast military potential to the relief of the suffering Syrian and Greek Christians.

The enthusiastic response to Pope Urban can only be explained in that he touched the hearts of men who considered Jesus Christ, the Redeemer, as claiming their highest allegiance. The Holy Places, and above all the Holy Sepulcher, they revered as the visible embodiment of the mysteries of redemption. Contemporary writers called the crusades the *Opus Dei* (The Work of God) and the exploits of the crusaders the *Gesta Dei* (The Deeds of God). Daniel-Rops calls the crusades a mystical fact. The crusaders battled so bravely because they believed that they were fighting for the cause of Christ. They placed the cross on their shoulders that they might offer Christ cross for cross, suffering for suffering, that they might by mortifying their desires share with Christ in the resurrection. So motivated, the soldier of the cross looked upon failure and death as no less blessed than success and victory.

Such idealism made the crusades one of the most inspiring enterprises in all history. However it would be absurd to fancy all the crusaders as saintly heroes. The crusade was a human movement and not a romance of the Round Table. One cannot arouse large human groups without stirring up the bad with the good. The religious enthusiasm of many crusaders was mixed with less worthy motives: the thirst for adventure, worldly ambition, avidity for gain, weakness in luxury and vice. With some few, base motives were the mainsprings of their activities. There were merchant traders over-occupied with the accumulation of gold and the precious materials of the East. More than one baron schemed for large feudal possessions, and impoverished younger sons of great families sought for rich estates in the Orient.

It would be most unfair to pronounce such selfishness as the primary and determining motives of the general body of the crusaders. Always there was abundant evidence of Christian piety, holy resignation, and religious heroism in the crusading ranks. But the baser causes explain those sinister episodes of the campaigns wherein were revealed egotism, unbridled lust, ferocious cruelty and heartless rapacity. They explain too those leaders who were unscrupulous adventurers and scheming politicians. One, however, must never forget the surprising number of noble, generous leaders, and the many examples of sublime unselfishness they displayed. The human defects put the crusades in proper perspective; they were splendid, but also human enterprises. In considering the crusaders as a whole one must emphasize the nameless mass, the rank and file, who prayed and worshiped, thirsted and starved, fought against overwhelming odds and died for Christ, for His Holy Sepulcher and for His afflicted people.

The greatest single power in the crusades was the Church. She originated the idea, and inspired men to rally to it. She received the vows of the crusaders. She financed a large part of the expenses from her own revenues. The Cluniac reform afforded the ascetical spirit that taught the warriors of the cross to consider the hardships and the sacrifices as fit penances for past sins. The Church granted indulgences to all who took the cross with the spirit of true contrition, and she thus opened up new means of expiation and conversion. The Popes exercised the leadership of this common undertaking of Christendom. The Popes kept alive in all the subsequent crusades the religious motives that inspired the First Crusade. The Popes placed the families, the properties and the countries of the crusades under the special protection of St. Peter, and defended them with the entire power and authority of the Holy See. As Urban II set the First Crusade in motion, so it was that the Popes who followed him organized all the later crusades.

Death
of a
Dream

THE ERA OF THE CRUSADES lasted for about two hundred years (1095-1291). There were about seven great expeditions and some minor campaigns. The Latin Kingdom of Jerusalem, the creation of the First Crusade, was in perpetual need of European help. In area it was small, a narrow strip of petty feudal states stretching along the coasts of Palestine and Syria. Its defensive forces were totally inadequate to withstand the certain return of the Moslem hordes from Egypt, Arabia, Mesopotamia and Turkey. The military orders (warrior monks vowed to defend the Holy Places) and the Christian peoples, the Knights Hospitallers, the Knights Templars and, later, the Teutonic Knights, despite their prodigies of valor and their mighty fortresses, could but temporarily hold back disaster.

When reconquest became imminent Pope Eugenius III in 1146 commissioned St. Bernard to preach a crusade. Wherever the great ascetic spoke, in France or Germany, vast crowds moved by his inspired eloquence took the cross. The Emperor Conrad III set forth at the head of a mighty army of Germans; King Louis VII led a tremendous host of Frenchmen. But the best hopes of both expeditions were obliterated by overwhelming defeats in their attempts to battle their way across the hot, semi-arid mountain defiles of central Asia Minor. Many causes contributed to the disasters: lack of unity in leadership and plans, excessive numbers of foot-soldiers unable to cope with the swarms of Turkish horsemen, the secret undertakings of the Emperor Manuel Comnenus with the Turks and the terrible hardships of climate, lack of provisions and disease. When the two monarchs arrived at Jerusalem with small detachments of their armies in 1149, they were forced to abandon the entire project.

The prospects of the Latin Kingdom worsened from year to year: weak rulers, a divisive and totally unsuited feudal system, interminably quarreling inhabitants, and scarcely any possibility of western military help. Moslem reconquest seemed as certain as tomorrow's sun. It was a certainty after Saladin, the Turkish Sultan, forged the unification of all Mohammedans from Egypt to the Caspian Sea. Saladin, ablest of all Moslem leaders, now led his disciplined hosts against Palestine. Storming town after town, finally, on October 3, 1187, he captured Jerusalem.

The news of the disaster moved Christendom profoundly. In a short time Pope Clement III was multiplying appeals to kings and peoples to rally for a new crusade. His legate for the crusade, William, Archbishop of Tyre, preached and organized tirelessly. A *Saladin* tax was levied in England and elsewhere. King William II of Sicily dispatched to Syria a fleet and an army which saved Antioch and strengthened other Christian garrisoned cities. A mighty force of 100,000 warriors in 1189 started from Germany under the leadership of the greatest of the medieval emperors, Frederick I, Barbarossa.

Despite his advanced years Frederick exercised the full command. He provided for ample supplies and safe passages, and he maintained excellent order and strict discipline; in consequence Barbarossa's expedition was the best in the whole history of the Crusades. Owing to the hostility of the eastern emperor, Isaac Angelus, who was in alliance with Saladin, Frederick at times had to fight his way through the Byzantine empire. In 1190, he gained two great victories over the Seljuk Turks in Asia Minor. But shortly afterwards the aged emperor met his death by drowning while attempting to swim the rapid River Calycadmus, near Seleucia. It was a supreme disaster, and as one of its results the great army broke up. Frederick of Suabia, however, succeeded in bringing a large part to Antioch. Barbarossa's death was the greatest loss of the Third Crusade; his experience and his imperial prestige were sadly needed when numerous quarrels were wrecking the other expedition.

The combined forces of the king of France, Philip Augustus, and of the king of England, Richard I, had sailed eastward to join the besiegers of the important port of Acre. The Christian besiegers were themselves besieged by a powerful army of Saladin's fighting men. After much bloodshed and loss of life on both sides Acre surrendered in 1191. But future action was gravely weakened by the quarreling of the two monarchs and the return of Philip to France. For a year Richard carried the war all over Syria and Palestine, capturing several cities, but not Jerusalem. His fantastically heroic exploits earned for him the immortal name of "the Lion-Hearted." Saladin matched Richard and no decision seemed possible. Finally both sides wearied of the resultless conflict and agreed to a three-year truce. Acre and a long strip of the coastline was allowed to the Crusaders; but permission for free pilgrimages to Jerusalem was all that could be obtained in regard to the Holy Sepulcher. Thus the Third Crusade, the best organized of all, ended in a stalemate.

The next crusade, the Fourth, though inaugurated by Innocent III, the ablest of the medieval Popes, ended in gravest disorder. Flemish and French counts organized the expedition, while the republic of Venice agreed to transport men and supplies, though for an extremely high price. A minor part of the crusaders decided to leave from Brindisi; so when the bulk of the expedition arrived at Venice they found themselves unable to pay the original charges. The Venetians refused to transport them except for the original price. Finally a solution was offered by the Doge, Dandolo, a blind man but sharply astute: the Venetians would carry out the contract if the crusaders would assist them in their war with a rival Christian port, Zara. Simon de Montfort and a few other leaders refused, but the majority joined the Venetians. When Innocent III learned of the news, he was incensed, and he excommunicated all who took part in the campaign. But Zara was captured before the papal condemnation arrived. Innocent, anxious to get the crusaders fighting in defense of the Holy Land, lifted the excommunication conditionally if the crusaders promised to depart for Syria.

But his hopes were defeated by a much more serious diversion. An imperial refugee from Constantinople,

Alexius IV, son of the imprisoned and blinded emperor, Isaac Angelus, obtained from Dandolo and the crusaders at Zara an engagement to restore him and his father to the throne at Constantinople. Alexius IV on his part agreed to a union of the Churches, a gift of money and a Greek army for the crusade. Again Simon de Montfort protested and left the crusading camp for Syria. Innocent III on being informed of the engagement condemned it most vigorously.

The crusaders occupied Constantinople but only by the force of arms. They found no enthusiasm for their protégé. Their presence in winter-quarters nearby only aggravated the evil situation. Finally popular riotings, hatred of the Latins and numerous street-conflicts erupted into a full-scale struggle. The crusaders stormed the city, burned the eastern part and pillaged the rest for three days. Then they set up a Latin empire and crowned Baldwin of Flanders in the Sancta Sophia as the first ruler. The Latin Empire was short-lived, 1204-1261. But the capture of Constantinople lives on as a vivid memory to the present day, standing as a mighty block in the way of reunion.

Several expeditions from 1217 to 1229, have been grouped under the term, "Fifth Crusade." Some were in Syria, one was in Egypt. Many heroic deeds were done and the leaders acted in the best traditions of the crusades. The last expedition, that of the evil emperor Frederick II, was the most disgraceful and the costliest campaign in the whole history of the Crusades. Under excommunication when he departed, avoided by the resident Christians, Frederick II fought no battles but negotiated with the Saracens. The truce which he obtained did irreparable injury to the entire position of the Christians, whom the sinister monarch did not deign to consult but whom he forced to accept a disastrous ten-year truce. Further, he deprived the Christians of their defenders by ordering all crusaders to depart with him for Europe.

The last crusades, the Sixth and Seventh, were organized and led by the holiest of the soldiers of the cross, St. Louis IX of France. In the first, 1248-1254, St. Louis attacked Egypt. He was successful until the rashness of his brother brought about total defeat at the battle of Mansurah; the king and the whole army were captured by the Moslems. The noble bearing of St. Louis in captivity so won the admiration of the Saracens that they offered him their royal crown if he would embrace Mohammedanism. In the second expedition, 1270, St. Louis moved his forces into Tunis with the design of using it as a base for another attack on Egypt. But in the plague that attacked the camp at Tunis, St. Louis met his death.

There were a few other expeditions to the East towards the close of the century; but all were in vain, and one by one every Christian stronghold was lost, except on the island of Cyprus. The Crusading Era had come to an end. One must note, however, a happier turn of events in the Spanish peninsula. There the supreme threat of the Moslem Almohades from Morocco to the Christian recovery was obliterated in the decisive battle of Las Navas de Tolosa, 1212. The victory was gained by an army recruited by Innocent III not only from Castilians, Portuguese, Navarrese and Aragonese, but from warriors of every Christian country of Western Europe. Shortly after the victory, and as a result of it, the whole peninsula, save the small kingdom of Granada, was permanently in Christian hands.

Age
of
St. Bernard

DURING THE ELEVENTH and twelfth centuries there occurred some remarkable developments in monasticism. The wonderful work of the Cluniac movement of the previous century has been noted: by centralizing hundreds of monasteries under the rule of the Abbot of Cluny and by strong emphasis on the liturgy the Cluniac monks freed great areas of monastic life from secular control and brought about a glorious and most saving reform. By their own reform they laid the basis for the far greater reform of the whole Church, the Hildebrandine Reform.

First one must note the revival among the canons regular, in which the Premonstratensian Canons, founded by St. Norbert at Prémontré, near Laon, were outstanding. The institution of canons regular goes back to Carolingian times. Their life was a combination of the monk's activities with those of the parish priest. They lived in monasteries but they also operated parishes. St. Norbert founded his order in 1120, and received papal confirmation for it in 1136. His sons were to do much for the conversion of the Slavic peoples. Similar orders founded about this time were the Canons of St. Victor, the Canons of St. John Lateran and the Crosier canons.

The life of the ancient hermits was restored in mitigated form by St. Bruno when he founded the Carthusians in 1084, at Chartreuse, near Grenoble. The Carthusian hermits led

ST. BERNARD OF CLAIRVAUX. *Sebastian del Piombo,*
Vatican Gallery.

their lives of isolation with their severe mortifications and their perpetual silence in little huts with gardens attached, all adjacent to one another and all connected with the central monastic church. Over all was a hermit-abbot, who governed his community of hermits according to a fixed rule. The first Carthusian rule came in 1142. It might be well to note that long periods of trial and experimenting often intervened between the founding of religious orders and their confirmation by the Popes. Like the Carthusians were the Camaldolese hermits and the Vallombrosian monks.

In 1098, at Citeaux in Burgundy, Robert of Molesme, a Cluniac monk, founded the outstanding monastic order of the Middle Ages, the Cistercians, whose most well known branch today is the order of the Trappists. The rule was the Benedictine, but special emphasis was placed upon the practice of austerities. In the beginning numbers remained small, even though one of the first abbots was the learned and holy St. Stephen Harding, an English monk. Growth began when Bernard of Fontaine, a Burgundian nobleman, and several of his relatives including his brothers and eventually his father, entered Citeaux in 1113. Two years later Bernard was sent to Clairvaux to establish a Cistercian abbey and to be its first abbot. The virtues and the spiritual accomplishment of Clairvaux under its now celebrated abbot, St. Bernard, prompted the foundation of Cistercian monasteries throughout Christendom. St. Malachy O'More induced his friend, St. Bernard, to make the first non-Celtic monastic foundations in Ireland. Later St. Malachy died at Clairvaux in the arms of St. Bernard who immortalized his memory by writing his biography.

Pope Calixtus II, in 1119, approved the Cistercian constitutions, the celebrated *Charter of Charity*. In this great document the self-renunciation, the obligation of agricultural labor and the strictness of daily life brought the austerity of the Cistercians much beyond the original Benedictine rule. The document also provided a unique form of government for the Cistercian order, one midway between the separatism of the Benedictine monasteries and the centralization of the Cluniac system. It placed the supreme power in a general chapter made up of a council of all the abbots. A general chapter of such a nature was later placed upon all religious orders by the Fourth Lateran Council in 1215. The Cistercians by their hundreds of abbeys brought an intense and solid revival of Christian life in every European country. Together with the Premonstratensians, the Cistercians Christianized and civilized the Slavic tribes of Poland, Bohemia and eastern Germany. Their piety, self-denial and indefatigable work in clearing the wild forest lands made them the benefactors of eastern Europe.

St. Bernard was the greatest of the Cistercians. It is extraordinary how this monk, always the most austere of ascetics and ever a contemplative gifted with the highest mystical prayer, was yet the most active man of affairs of his time. He so dominates the mid-twelfth century that the period is known as "The Age of St. Bernard." A brief listing of some of his activities shows that the term is not a rhetorical exaggeration. He preached the Second Crusade, both in France and along the Rhine. He aided the Pope against his enemies; and for Pope Eugenius III, the first Cistercian Pope, he composed a notable treatise on the papal office and its responsibilities. He helped the French monarch in settling ecclesiastical problems. He engaged in controversy with the great Abelard. He wrote great essays on spirituality and mysticism; he composed strong sermons and he wrote beautiful poems. One of his poems is considered among the loveliest of the medieval Latin hymns, "Jesu, dulcis memoriae" (Jesus, the Very Thought of You); even today Catholics of every European language love to sing a vernacular version. One has only to recite slowly and devoutly St. Bernard's prayer, the "Memorare" to appreciate the intensity and confidence of his spirit of piety.

One writer thus describes St. Bernard of Clairvaux: "His activity took in the whole of Christendom. His correspondence was enormous, his works numerous and varied, and his authority hardly questioned. The rulers of Church and State flocked to the rude huts of Clairvaux as to an oracle. It shows that the days of brute force were over, when a simple monk, whose singleness of purpose and zeal for righteousness were never so much as questioned, could rule with such astounding power over the minds of men."

The Friars

GOD WONDERFULLY AIDS His Church at every turn of the changing ages. His providence is especially evident in the founding of religious orders. Continually He inspires saintly men and women to establish institutes which by newer developments successfully answer the challenges of newer problems. Yet these changes do not entail the abandonment of older institutes. There was and always will be need for the hermit and for the monk. The significant words are "newer developments." Such were produced when St. Francis of Assisi, St. Dominic and other holy persons founded the "Friar" orders.

These saints were answering the challenges that were confronting the Church in the twelfth and thirteenth centuries. The High Middle Ages with all their glorious achievements had yet their full measure of evil problems. The large increases of wealth consequent on the great commercial expansion brought in their train much materialism, worldliness and luxury. The laity was most affected, but the contamination spread also in clerical ranks. The teeming populations of the new towns, that had sprung up all over Europe, heavily overtaxed the Church's facilities for the care of souls; the urban clergy were not numerous enough to cope with the situation. The monasteries, rural institutions by nature, and usually remote from the populace-centers, could offer little effective help. Problems were further complicated by the poor education and inadequate training of the parish clergy, urban and rural. Small wonder that heresies, as evil as ever assailed the Church, spread widely and deeply. Finally, among the

ST. FRANCIS OF ASSISI. *Cimabue, Basilica
of St. Francis, Assisi.*

ST. DOMINIC DE GUZMAN. *Titian, Borghese Gallery, Rome.*

heathen beyond the frontiers, new missionary opportunities were beginning to open up. But these prospects were in areas so remote and so vast that they could be cultivated only by disciplined itinerant missionaries.

The most distinctive development of the new religious institutions was complete poverty—of the order as well as of the individual friars. The members obtained their material support only in the alms they solicited; hence they were officially designated as "mendicant friars" or "begging friars." Their ideal was total detachment from earthly possessions and complete dependence on God's providence. They dedicated themselves to this ideal; but they also offered it to the world for consideration and application. Their proposal of strict poverty for the order as an organization was aimed at offsetting the effects of wealth that might develop from great co-operative possessions. The friars did not condemn the monks for their imposing monastic buildings nor for their wide-extending estates; they agreed that such possessions were needed to support these rural institutions in the vast good works they accomplished. But the friars' convents belonged in the towns, to be centers of preaching and teaching in urban apostolates; vast landed estates would have been useless encumbrances for such labors. The friars felt also that a large convent subsisting solely on alms preached poverty of spirit very tangibly to materialistic town-dwellers.

The urban apostolate brought on a second new development in the friar's life: a specific dedication to preaching, teaching and promoting devotional spirituality. With the monk such labors were incidental; his primary occupations were the celebration of the Liturgy and the chanting of the Sacred Office in choir. The friar retained the choir as a vital part of his spiritual life; but along with it he made the active apostolate a major function of his vocation.

The disciplined efficiency needed for journeying across the length and breadth of Europe preaching, teaching and disputing for the faith, in villages and in the fields as well as in the towns, produced the third development—highly centralized organization. In this the friars went far beyond the Cluniac monks. The convents were united into local groupings, called provinces, under a superior, called a provincial. All provinces were united into one great international body, called the order, under the government of a general superior, assisted by a permanent council or chapter. The superiors general were known by such names as: Master General, Guardian General, or Superior General. Neither convents nor provinces were autonomous. The order worked its apostolate as one great body. Unlike the monks there was constant change of all superiors — general, provincial and local. These changes were effected by elections in local convents or provinces. The election of the general superior was made by the representatives of the whole order meeting in a general chapter.

The fourth development in the friars' life was dedication to the teaching of theology, philosophy and general learning. Their goal was two-fold: first, their own personal mastery of these subjects for their labors in the apostolate, and secondly, the elevation of the standards of ecclesiastical knowledge among all the clergy. They entered into the new universities, where despite strong initial opposition, they became the outstanding thinkers and teachers of the sacred studies. Most of the leading medieval masters of Scholasticism were friars. One need but recall the Dominicans, St. Albertus Magnus and St. Thomas Aquinas; and the Franciscans, St. Bonaventure and John Duns Scotus. The pioneers in the field of natural sciences were Roger Bacon, the Franciscan, and St. Albertus Magnus, the Dominican.

The principal friar orders were the Franciscans, the Dominicans, the Carmelites and the Augustinians. There were a number of lesser orders, among whom the Servites were outstanding. The members of all these bodies bore the title of friar, which means brother. The title was retained by the priests, even when they constituted the majority of the membership, as was the case with some orders from the beginning and with all eventually. St. Francis of Assisi, in 1207, founded the Franciscans, designating them, for humility's sake, the Order of Friars Minor (O.F.M.). Because their original habit was grey they were popularly known as the Grey Friars. St. Dominic de Guzman, a Spanish canon, in 1215, founded the Dominicans, designating them as the

ST. CLARE OF ASSISI.
*Giotto, Basilica of
Santa Croce,
Florence.*

Alinari

ST. ELIZABETH OF HUNGA-
RY. The saint giving alms.
Popular art of the eight-
eenth century. *Val
Gardena, Ortisei.*

Order of Preachers (O.P.), since this ministry was their distinctive vocation. Because of the black cloak which they wore over their white habit they came to be called the Black Friars. Blessed Albert of Jerusalem, in 1219, united the hermits on Mt. Carmel into the Friar Hermits of Mt. Carmel. Later one group was called the Order of Carmelites Discalced (O.C.D.) because they went barefoot, and the other group, the Order of Calced Carmelites (O.C.C.) because they used footwear. Since the Carmelites wore a white cloak over their brown habit they were known as White Friars. The Augustinians came from an amalgamation, in 1255, of several communities of Hermits of St. Augustine. Sometimes they are known by this name, but more often by the title, the Order of St. Augustine (O.S.A.). Their habit was always black. Influenced by the friar movement they spread all over Europe. In England they were called the Austin Friars.

All the friar institutes maintained three-fold groupings of first orders, second orders and third orders. The First Order, embracing the priests and brothers, has already been treated. The Second Order consisted of nuns following an adaptation of a particular friar rule. They dwelt in strictly enclosed cloisters, chanted the office, practiced severe reparational penances and prayed for the Church, the clergy and the Christian people. Like the members of first orders they were bound by solemn vows. The Poor Clares were the second order of the Friars Minor; the Second Order Dominicans, of the Friars Preacher; the Carmelite Nuns, of the Carmelites; and the Canonesses of St. Augustine, of the Augustinians. Several other orders of nuns followed the Augustinian rule. In the late middle ages the second orders produced an extraordinary number of holy women. A few names only can be cited: St. Clare, co-foundress with St. Francis of the Poor Clares; Bl. Marguerite of Hungary, a Dominican; St. Clara of Montefalco and St. Catherine of Sweden for the Augustinians. The second order of the Carmelites became prominent only around the fifteenth century.

The third orders brought the laity into the friars' ranks. Laymen and laywomen, married or single, still in the world and not bound by vows, obtained membership in the friars' orders, occasionally wore the particular habit and continually participated in the good works. The tertiaries dressed simply, led pious lives, practiced penances and assembled at definite times in church for common prayers and the recitation of the office. They carried on apostolic works under direction of the friars, who extended to these zealous lay people their orders' ideals of love of God, detachment from earthly riches, devotion to the Blessed Mother, the practice of the Community of Saints, charitable and spiritual help of fellow men, and the intensification of their own personal holiness. Later two branches of the third orders appeared: one, the Third Order Secular, which continued in the original manner; the other, the Third Order Regular, which lived in community and took simple vows.

The greatest of the tertiaries was the Dominican, Saint Catherine of Siena. Foremost among the Franciscan tertiaries were St. Elizabeth of Hungary and St. Louis of France. But from all ranks of society there were produced holy tertiaries. The third orders were among the chief means by which the friars accomplished so much for God, His Church and the salvation of souls.

Royal
Dominance
and
Ecclesial
Freedom

THE MIDDLE AGES witnessed a continuing struggle for the liberty of the Catholic Church. Sometimes it erupted into violent, even sanguinary conflicts; always it was raising up questions to plague men's thoughts. Its conflicts and controversies were but phases of the old and never-ending problem of the relations of Church and state. In theory nothing was more easy of solution: both were perfect societies; both had their proper spheres; both should refrain from interfering in the other's area of activity. In practice nothing was more difficult of solution. People cannot divide their living between hermetically sealed compartments. This was especially true in the Middle Ages. Then everyone confessed the same Faith and everyone was influenced in every phase of his life by its religious motivation. At the same time these people owed a common allegiance to the same state (be it the Empire or one of the great monarchies). Hence both Church and State had vital interests in many common areas: economic, social and political. At the best it was hard to draw the line delimiting the Church's power and the state's power. It was extremely difficult when the spheres of influence shifted as they were bound to shift in the changes of time and circumstances.

Practical adjustments begot numerous and bitter disputes. Far mightier controversies arose when the question was raised as the possessor of the final supremacy. Was it the spiritual power or the temporal power; or, more specifically, was it the Pope or the monarch? Debates raged interminably between canon lawyers, developing papal claims in the emerging Church Law, and civil jurists, reviving the Roman Law with its exaltation of the Imperial office. Under all the conflicts and all the contentions lay the fundamental issue, the liberty of the Church. In bringing men to God, her divinely appointed task, the Church had to teach religious truth uncompromisingly and she had to proclaim and fearlessly maintain Christian morality. The Church could do this only when she was free to govern her own affairs, to appoint her chief officers, the bishops, and to discipline equally all her members.

Otherwise the Church would become a mere governmental department, a pious auxiliary of the police as it were. The principal functions assigned to the Church then would be: to keep the populace docile and subservient; to enhance the prestige of emperors and kings by solemn, colorful liturgical ceremonies; to carry out the religious programs of the monarchs — even to defend and to teach the doctrinal compromises dictated by the supreme civil ruler. Emperors and kings would completely dominate the Church's organization for they would nominate all of the bishops. Such dominance would have frightful consequences. Rulers, using bishoprics to reward sycophant clerics or to pay off old retainers, would have little concern about the holiness or the capabilities of their nominees. Evil monarchs would not scruple to sell holy offices to simoniacal, immoral clerics. The Church would strive in vain to reform incompetents or to discipline the hireling shepherds; she would find herself blocked at every step. What an ignominious slavery for the Bride of Christ!

Royal dominance of the Church would be immensely strengthened if there were royal dominance of the revenues and resources of the Church. The everyday expression that the control of the purse strings guarantees the control of the organization is as true in ecclesiastical affairs as in mundane affairs. A monarch who held the revenues of a see during its vacancy not only would have its financial returns but could keep it vacant until his choice of bishop was accepted. The monarch who could impose great taxes arbitrarily on the bishoprics of his realm held a practical power over them greater than that of any primate or Pope. Finally an emperor or a king, appealing either by himself or by the bishops of his realm to local prejudices, could seriously threaten the universality of the Church and foster wholesale disobedience or heresies.

If the Church were subordinate to the State, then the Pope would become a decorative chaplain of the emperor; and the local bishops, inferior functionaries of the kings. There was always the danger of the emperor making himself a lay Pope. Constantine told the Fathers of the Council of Nicea that as they were the internal bishops of the Church, he was the external bishop. The "Theologian Emperors" of Constantinople earned that term by their attempts to make their definitions in the Christological heresies the official doctrines of the Church. Not without reason was Charlemagne called the Christian Caliph. Otto I solved the scandals of the Roman See during the Dark Age by deposing an unworthy Pope and intruding his own candidate. Several of the succeeding Popes, all worthy Pontiffs, were nevertheless the appointees of the Holy Roman Emperors. Truly then the fundamental issue of the long struggle between Church and State in the Middle Ages was the liberty of the Church. If some Popes, such as St. Gregory VII, Innocent III and Boniface VIII, and their supporters advanced propositions which today may seem extreme, their ideas must be considered in the circumstances of their times—circumstances which have not obtained in later ages. Their propositions must also be placed in comparison with the extreme claims advanced by the regalist lawyers during the controversies.

The struggle for the liberty of the Church became a mighty pageant of Medieval history. There were four episodes, and each episode contained two acts. The first act in each episode was a major conflict between the Popes and the powerful continental rulers. The second act was a contemporary conflict in England, almost as important as the first.

Episode the First was the contest over lay investiture. The first act covered the long struggle between the Popes St. Gregory VII, Urban II, Paschal II and Callixtus II and the Emperors Henry IV and Henry V, 1075-1122. It had two significant incidents: the Penance of Canossa and the Concordat of Worms. The second act dealt with conflict over lay investiture in England between St. Anselm, Archbishop of Canterbury and Primate, with King William Rufus and Henry I, 1095-1107. Its significant events were the persecutions of St. Anselm and his two exiles.

Episode the Second was the warfare of the Emperor Frederick I, "Barbarossa" against the Popes. The first act was Barbarossa's campaigns against Popes Adrian IV (the only English Pope) and Alexander III and their allies, the League of the Lombard Cities, 1154-1186. The significant events were: the six Italian expeditions of Barbarossa, the Caesaro-Papism of the decrees of the Diet of Roncaglia, the anti-popes, the Peace of Venice and the Peace of Constance. The second act was the dispute between St. Thomas à Becket, Archbishop of Canterbury, with Henry II of England over the Royal Customs, 1164-1170. The significant events were the murder of St. Thomas à Becket and the Penance of Henry II.

Episode the Third was the long protracted conflict of the Emperor Frederick II, aiming at mastery of the papacy. The first act covered the warfare of the Emperor against Popes Honorius III, Gregory IX and Innocent IV, 1215-1250. The significant events were the atrocities and crimes of Frederick II, his excommunication and his dilatory tactics on the Fifth Crusade. The second act presented the dispute over the Archbishopric of Canterbury between Cardinal Stephen Langton, backed by Pope Innocent III, and King John of England, 1205-1213. Its significant events were the cruelties of John, the Interdict, the excommunication of the king and the Magna Carta.

Episode the Fourth was the dispute over royal taxation of ecclesiastics and their properties in France and in England. The king of France now was the chief enemy of the papacy; the Holy Roman Empire was in a state of chaos. The French monarch was the powerful Philip IV, "The Fair." The first act was the quarrel between Philip IV and Pope Boniface VIII, 1300-1303. The significant events were the Bull, "Unam Sanctum"; the beginnings of Gallicanism (the semi-independence from the Pope of the Church in France, though under royal control); the origins of secularism and the Sacrilege of Anagni, when Boniface was assaulted and thrown into prison by French and Italian partisans of Philip IV. The second act was a similar dispute over taxation of clerics between King Edward I and Archbishop Winchelsey of Canterbury, backed by Boniface VIII, 1297. Its significant event was the success of Edward I, but also the first enunciation of the principle, "No taxation without representation."

During the two centuries of strife the Popes did maintain the liberty of the Church, but not with complete success. The opposition was too strong, and other problems were intermingled in the conflicts. Episode the First has already been described in the chapter on lay investiture. Episodes the Second, the Third and the Fourth will be treated in the following chapters.

Barbarossa
and
Henry II

THE SECOND EPISODE in the struggle for the liberty of the Church embraced in its Act One the contention of the Emperor Frederick I, Barbarossa, with Pope Adrian IV and Pope Alexander III, and in its Act Two the strife between King Henry II of England and St. Thomas à Becket, Archbishop of Canterbury.

The imperial conflict lasted from 1154 to 1183. Frederick I, called Barbarossa due to his red beard, was the ablest and the most powerful ruler of the Holy Roman Empire. He had many excellent qualities: high-mindedness as a sovereign, brilliancy as a soldier, affability as a monarch. But he balanced these by pride and ambition. He was impatient of all opposition and on occasions he could ruthlessly suppress his adversaries. It was special misfortune that he had for his closest advisors legalists, products of the revival of the Roman Law at the University of Bologna, who instilled into his mind the absolutism and the caesaropapism of the Byzantine emperors. Frederick's supreme ideal was the Holy Roman Empire. He envisioned it as a universal monarchy over which absolute power was given to him immediately from God alone. He would protect the Church, provided the Popes, the prelates and the clergy acknowledged his lordship over the Church and modeled their administrations according to the dictates of his supreme will.

The Popes who stood up to Frederick I were Adrian IV and Alexander III. It is worth noting, for those days of the high medieval prestige of the papacy, that Adrian IV was born the son of a humble English serf. Adrian IV was the only English Pope. The longest period of the struggle fell to Alexander III, who bore the brunt of Barbarossa's attacks for eighteen years. At his side, however, were brave allies, the Lombard city-states who themselves were battling the Emperor for their municipal liberties. The Lombard League fought persistently and courageously for the Pope and the freedom of the Church; Alexander III faithfully supported them in the defense of their civic freedom.

While Frederick I was achieving a complete mastery over the Holy Roman Empire, such as no other emperor had ever possessed, he was also aiming at similar control over the Church. He interfered in the management of strictly ecclesiastical affairs; he appointed bishops in violation of the Concordat of Worms; he connived at the imprisonment in his Burgundian territory of the papal legate, Eskyll, Archbishop of Lund and metropolitan of Denmark; and he restricted journeys and appeals to Rome. Frederick claimed as his own the city of Rome and the sovereign right of the Holy See, the lands left by Matilda of Tuscany to the Popes, and also all episcopal palaces of central and northern Italy. Further he planned to take over the Kingdom of Sicily (the whole of southern Italy) and unite it to the German crown; such an acquisition would have put the Pope between two millstones of imperial power. As for the Lombard cities, Frederick abolished their communal immunities and set over them imperial officers with dictatorial powers.

Frederick Barbarossa acted with swiftness and power in carrying out his vast plans. Of his six moves into Italy, all but one were military expeditions. And these campaigns were marked by destruction and ravaging of Italian towns. In one expedition he seized Rome and drove Pope Alexander into exile; previously he had refused to recognize Alexander's election as Pope. Three times he tried to set up antipopes. But his grand plans and mighty moves all came to nought. They were brought down into ultimate defeat by the heroism of the Lombard League in several fiercely-contested battles, by the refusal of many German princes and bishops to support Barbarossa, and by the steadfastness of Alexander III.

The alarming extremes of the absolutism of Frederick I were revealed in the proceedings of the Diet of Roncaglia, where in 1158, during his second expedition into Italy, he had summoned his Italian vassals. The decrees of this diet proclaimed the policy of Justinian absolutism as it was taught by the jurists of Bologna. The Emperor was declared to be the Lord of the World, the sole fountain of legislation, "the living law on earth," the embodiment of right and justice. The Archbishop of Milan, an imperial partisan, addressed Frederick with these words: "Do and ordain whatever thou wilt; thy word is the law." How far Barbarossa embraced this absolutism may be learned from the negotiations of himself and his evil genius, Raynald of Dassal, with the representatives of the foreign kings who had remained loyal to Alexander III. Their rejection of Frederick's anti-pope was termed an infringement of imperial rights. It was asserted that Rome being *the first city of the Empire* it concerned the emperor alone to appoint or confirm the *bishop of his Capital.* It was further asserted that it would be as unwarranted a presumption on the part of the *provinces of the empire* (France and England—really they were independent nations) to claim the right of declaring who should be considered the *bishop of Rome,* as it would be for the emperor to interfere in some episcopal dispute in France or England. To battle against such absolutistic policies surely made Alexander III and the cities of the Lombard League the champions of all liberty, civil or ecclesiastical.

The strife between Henry II and St. Thomas à Becket brought into conflict two strong characters. Henry, the most powerful of the medieval English monarchs, was able, sagacious and strong-willed. But he was also of such an ungovernable temper that at times in paroxysms of anger he lost all control of himself. Thomas à Becket, brilliant as a courtier and skillful as a diplomat, was the closest friend and chief helper of Henry, and by him was made Chancellor of the realm. When the primatial see of Canterbury was open, Henry nominated his trusted helper for the prelacy. Thomas à Becket tried to dissuade the king, declaring to him that the duties of archbishop might very probably change their friendship into enmity. Henry ignored the warnings for he expected that the new primate would maintain the "Royal Customs," if not extend them. This was just where à Becket feared the rupture would come. So, reluctantly he accepted the nomination; he was then raised from the diaconate to the priesthood and consecrated a bishop. Straightway Archbishop à Becket resigned the chancellorship; and he changed his life of magnificence to one of austerity, penitential practices and prayer.

The struggle was not long delayed, and it was precisely over the "Royal Customs." These were practices which Henry's royal predecessors had carried on in contradiction to the laws of the Church. Henry assembled a great council of barons, spiritual and temporal, at his castle in Clarendon in 1164, for the purpose of defining these practices and committing them to written law.

The Articles of Clarendon, as they were called, gave the king vast control over the revenues of bishoprics and abbeys during their vacancies and total domination over their subsequent elections. They ordered that criminal clerics must be tried by the king's courts, even though they had been already tried in the Church's courts. They forbade the excommunication of tenants-in-chief of the king, except after his consent. They required the king's permission for beneficed clergymen, from the primate down, to leave the country (i.e., to go to Rome). They prohibited all appeals to the Holy See without the consent of the king's council, and they made the king's court the last resort for all ecclesiastical appeals. If such usurpations, which had never been acknowledged by the Church, had ever received the sanction of written law, they would have cut off England from the rest of Christendom and would have intruded the king into the Pope's place.

From the beginning St. Thomas stood almost alone in opposition; the majority of the bishops had gone over to the king's side. All sorts of pressures, intrigues, false reports and personal enmities were brought to break his constancy.

Finally, doubtful, fearful and reluctant he yielded, signed the articles, and sent them to the Pope. But Alexander III refused to ratify the Clarendon code. As soon as the archbishop learned this, he withdrew his signature and imposed upon himself the severest penances. Fierce persecution broke upon the head of St. Thomas. He was summoned to the royal court to answer charges of malfeasance in office. When he refused to appear he was accused of treason. He had to flee to France. But he was not secure from Henry's power. His relatives and friends were punished and reduced to beggary, and the Cistercians who gave him refuge were threatened with the seizure of all their English possessions. The persecuted prelate, however, did find protection with King Louis VII. The French monarch labored to effect a reconciliation between Henry and St. Thomas. The English king, fearing excommunication by Alexander III, yielded and made a simulated reconciliation.

The archbishop, on his return to England, found his enemies as strongly and actively opposed as before. He stood up to them, to the great anger of Henry who was living in his duchy of Normandy. Beside himself with rage the king cried out: "Of the cowards who eat my bread, is there no one to free me from this turbulent priest?" Four knights left shortly for England.... On the afternoon of December 29, 1170, they entered the cathedral of Canterbury, shouting out for "the traitor," and getting no answer, shouting out for "the archbishop." Then from his place of prayer Saint Thomas walked towards them saying, "Here I am, no traitor, but the Archbishop." Three of the knights cut him down with their swords, and one of them scattered his brains upon the cathedral's floor. St. Thomas' last words, faintly murmured, were, "For the name of Jesus and the defense of the Church I am ready to die." Like his Savior's, his death was the triumph of his cause. The advocates of the "Royal Customs" were silenced in the face of the revulsion at the horrible deed, that swept over all Europe. Their projects were completely lost in the universal joy of England and Europe, when three years later the martyr, St. Thomas à Becket was canonized.

King John
and
Frederick II

THE CLIMAX IN THE CONFLICT between medieval Popes and rulers came in the Third Episode. Act One occurred in England. It was a struggle for control of the primatial see of Canterbury, and, in consequence, for the Church in England. The protagonists were King John and Cardinal-Archbishop Stephen Langton, supported by Pope Innocent III. John, arrogant, cynical and cruel, was one of the most evil of kings. Act Two included the wars of Frederick II, Emperor of the Holy Roman Empire and King of Sicily, against the papacy. The wars were constant and protracted, lasting through thirty years; and they were horrible because of the frightful cruelties of this tyrant's soldiery. These wars were supremely dangerous, since they held the threat of the complete enslavement of the Church by this most powerful and most capable of medieval kings.

The English conflict started in 1205, in a disputed election for the archbishopric of Canterbury. The monks of the monastery attached to the cathedral actually formed the chapter.

Such a practice existed among some of the cathedrals of England, but nowhere else. Theoretically the monks were free, but actually they had to elect the nominee of the king.

The younger monks, to forestall royal interference, hurriedly elected Reginald, their sub-prior. John was furious and ordered the election of his treasurer, John de Gray, bishop of Norwich. For the sake of peace the older monks complied. On an appeal to Rome Innocent III rejected both candidates. Fifteen delegates of the monastery elected at Rome, on the Pope's suggestion, Cardinal Stephen Langton, an Englishman, a renowned scholar and a man of piety and strength of character. King John angrily refused to accept Cardinal Langton. When he persisted in his refusal Innocent placed the kingdom under interdict. All religious services were stopped, except the essential sacraments of Baptism, Penance and Matrimony; and these were administered outside the churches. No bell could be tolled. The silence of death fell upon England. It was a desperate measure, perhaps hard for moderns to comprehend, but easy for medievalists to understand. It was a powerful, in many cases a necessary, in most instances an effective weapon for bringing a ruthless tyrant to his knees. In opposition John inaugurated a period of oppression and persecution. Church lands were seized, bishops were driven into exile, priests were executed, even crucified. The laity who obeyed the interdict had their lands burdened with most oppressive taxes. John lived in fear of treason everywhere. He forced his chief vassals to give him their sons as hostages. Some of the hostages were hanged, and others starved to death. John became so hated that he could not rely on a single Englishman to defend him, when the French King Philip was preparing an army to carry out the sentence of excommunication.

Finally the evil monarch was forced to make his peace with Innocent III. He received Cardinal Langton, freed all prisoners and offered restitution for his confiscations. On his own accord John went a step further and made England a feudal fief of the Holy See. This meant little besides the payment of an annual sum; there was no mention of fealty or homage in his document. The great barons united with him in the document. Several motives have been suggested for the wily monarch's move. One perhaps was to prevent Philip's coming into England. Another was an attempt to safeguard himself in the case of a rebellion of the great barons, who under the leadership of Cardinal Langton made such an attempt two years later when they forced the Magna Carta out of John. Whatever were his motives in making England a fief of the Holy See, King John, the worst king that England ever had, was defeated by Innocent III in his effort to enslave the Church in England.

The continental struggle, as has been already inferred, was longer and very much more dangerous because of the strength and ability of the emperor. Frederick II was the grandson of Frederick I, Barbarossa, and the ward of Innocent III. This double prestige obtained for him election as Emperor of the Holy Roman Empire. Born in Italy he was an Italian quite as much as he was a German. From his mother Constance, the heiress of Sicily, he had obtained the kingship of that region. The Kingdom of Sicily, a feudal fief of the Holy See, embraced not only the island but the whole southern mainland of the Italian peninsula, from Naples south. Frederick II was one of the most contradictory figures in history. He was so capable a ruler, so cultured a personality, such a promoter of arts and letters that he was hailed by his contemporaries as the "Stupor Mundi" (the Marvel of the World). Yet because of his cruelties, cynicism, sensualities and scepticism many people of his day wondered if he were not Antichrist. Certainly he was one of the most sinister and evil enemies the Church has ever encountered. Three goals the young emperor-king set for himself: first, the uniting of all of Italy and Germany; second, the destruction of the freedoms of the Italian municipalities; third, his own rule as absolute monarch over Church and state.

Three strong Popes combated his designs upon the liberty of the Church: Honorius III (1216-1227); Gregory IX (1227-1241), who was well over eighty when elected Pope and who struggled unflinchingly for fourteen years until his death; and Innocent IV (1243-1254), who was elected after the papal throne had been kept vacant for twenty months by the interferences of Frederick II. These Popes were supported by the city-states of Northern Italy, and by some

German bishops and princes. But it must be noted that the Ghibellines, the Italian imperialists, were powerful in all parts of the peninsula, while in Germany the prelates and dukes who supported Frederick were often more numerous than those who were loyal to the Popes. The troubles began in the studied delays by Frederick of the fulfillment of his vows to go on the Fifth Crusade—ten broken oaths in ten years of procrastination. The loyal crusaders who had gone to Palestine waited in vain for his important forces, as they wasted away, plagued by the great heat, the lack of water and the ravages of disease. Eventually they were overwhelmed by the Moslem hordes. Gregory IX at length had to excommunicate the faithless leader. In answer, Frederick's Roman supporters rose as a mob and drove the Pope from Rome. Frederick finally, though under excommunication, lead his own expedition to the Holy Land. It was more like a buccaneering campaign. The emperor ruined almost the whole crusading effort with his highhanded negotiations with Saracen leaders who conceded to him lands that belonged to other Moslem leaders. His immoralities scandalized all his fellow Christians.

Before embarking for Palestine, Frederick had busied himself with another project—the union of Italy and the Holy Roman Empire. To further his designs he established a military colony of Saracens at Lucera near the frontiers of the papal territories. These Mohammedan soldiers became a curse to the countryside of that part of Italy. Frederick issued despotic laws to oppress the clergy of the south, and to overcome the resistance of the city-states of the north. Pope Gregory IX could not ignore the menace to the freedom of the papacy and of religion certain to follow the union of the two crowns. Fight he must lest he, and all he stood for, be crushed between the upper and the nether millstones. Recognizing that the same fate threatened their municipal liberties, the Lombard cities hastened to ally themselves with Gregory IX.

But the fundamental issues ran far deeper: Frederick's theories of royal autocracy clashed essentially with the old medieval ideas of limited monarchy. His despotism would establish a conception of the monarch as the sole source of rights and powers, supreme in both spiritual and temporal affairs, and responsible to no other authority. With Frederick II the state became an end in itself—a theory that has much acceptance today. His idea of the Church was completely anticlerical: to him it was but a part of the state. Accordingly it was the mission of the emperor, not of the Popes and the priests, to keep the Church true to itself, to reform the Church when necessary, and to restore the Church to the original simplicity of the Gospels. Small wonder all the anticlerical spirit of previous heresies rallied to support Frederick in this most subversive of heresies: the destruction of the *sacerdotium* (the papal and priestly rule of the Church).

The conflict between Frederick II and the Popes, Honorius III, Gregory IX and Innocent IV, endured for three decades. Its most striking features were the violence and the cruelties of the emperor. His callous failures to come to the aid of the suffering crusaders has been noted. When finally, though an excommunicate, he did go, an army of his vassals and Saracens invaded and wasted the papal territories in Italy.

Each of the emperor's three major conflicts with the Popes was noted for cynicism and cruelty. The campaign of his captain, Ezzolino de Romano, is remembered for its horrible atrocities. Frederick attempted the capture of Gregory IX, stirred up the Roman mobs to revolt, forcibly retained ambassadors from and to the Holy See and imprisoned a papal legate. In Sicily he kept twenty bishoprics vacant, his agents proscribed and executed clergymen, and his Saracen mercenaries desecrated and destroyed churches. He shocked Christian Europe by maintaining a Moslem harem. The depth of his evil deeds was reached when Frederick essayed to capture every prelate going to the General Council of Rome. After the destruction of the Genoese fleet, which was conveying a large number of delegates, the emperor cast into his loathsome Apulian dungeons 100 bishops or episcopal vicars, the deputies of Lombardy and 4,000 Genoese sailors. The stern demands of St. Louis IX forced him to release the French bishops and delegates. Of the rest, many died of ill-treatment in that terrible captivity. His siege of Parma was marked with hideous cruelties. At a later time, in Italy, he extended his cruelties to the wives and children of his opponents.

Death stopped him from further evil deeds. The terrible monarch died on December 19, 1250. It must be noted that before his end Frederick II was reconciled to the Faith, humbly and with contrite heart acknowledging the Holy Roman Church as his Mother, making full reparation and receiving absolution from the Archbishop of Palermo. It has been said that he died clothed in the habit of the Cistercians, whom despite all his aberrations, he sincerely revered.

Earthly
Failure and
Eternal Triumph

THE FOURTH AND LAST episode should bear the title, "Tragic Failure," because it terminated in defeat. Yet that defeat was but another instance of the paradox — earthly failure and eternal triumph — ever recurring in Christian history; the first instance was the paradox of Calvary. Act One deals with the struggle between Pope Boniface VIII and King Philip IV of France. Act Two describes the conflict between Archbishop Winchelsey of Canterbury and Edward I of England. In both kingdoms the Church was opposing the royal policies of arbitrary and extortionate taxation of ecclesiastical revenues and properties. Such policies could only end in the royal domination of religion. It should be noted that the Empire, leaderless and enmeshed in internal rivalries, was no longer the first state of Europe. France, with strong kings and powerful armies, had succeeded to that position. And England, which also had strong kings and powerful armies, pressed France in bitter rivalry.

The outstanding personage in the contentions was Pope Boniface VIII (1294-1303). To a fine mind, cultivated by profound learning and matured by wide experience in ecclesiastical affairs, he added the energies of a strong will. As Pope he dedicated his great abilities to enforcing the laws of the Church and to pacifying the Christian nations. Yet his pontificate was a troubled one, and he failed in most of his dealings with secular princes. Boniface had his faults —

sternness of manner and severity in measure. Much, however, must be said for this unfortunate Pontiff. He governed the Church during a period of uncertainty in public affairs, when emerging nationalities were fragmenting the unity of Christendom. Of the changes involved he possessed little or no understanding. He was forced to struggle with faithless and ruthless adversaries, who did not hesitate at the vilest calumnies and the cruelest violence. Further, these opponents rivaled in ability any of the previous antagonists of the medieval papacy.

The most malign of Boniface's enemies were Philip IV and his coterie of evil advisers. The trouble began in the king's forcing money from ecclesiastical revenues for his secular wars. His royal officials were so extortionate in their demands that the entire French clergy petitioned the Pope for his protection. Pope Boniface in 1296 published the Bull *Clericis laicos* in which he forbade under pain of excommunication any ruler to take, and the clergy to pay, taxes on ecclesiastical revenues without the consent of the Holy See. He was thus only enforcing a well-known ecclesiastical law. But Philip IV declared that the Bull was an infringement of the plenitude of his royal power. He inhibited the exportation of money and valuables so as to deprive the Holy See of the subsidies of the French Church. When the Pope later explained that the bull had been misinterpreted and that it did not affect voluntary grants for national defense, nor contributions from royal fiefs, the king suspended his hostile measures.

There could be no permanent peace between the Pope and the king. Boniface strove to maintain the rights of the Church and the Holy See as he had received them from his predecessors. Philip was determined to rule with absolute independence of any spiritual control. He proceeded to annex Christian domains to the crown, to confiscate pious foundations for his treasury, to depose bishops devoted to the Pope and to intrude royal favorites in their sees, and to appropriate the revenues of bishoprics and abbeys. Finally he imprisoned the papal legate, who was then robbed of his papers and declared guilty of treason by Philip's council of state. The Pope determined on more severe measures to defend so many violated rights.

First Boniface demanded the liberation of his legate. Then he summoned the bishops and doctors of the French Church to Rome, where he might deliberate with them and, from their knowledge of circumstances and from their love of the king, he might devise the best means for preserving the Church's freedom and for obtaining the reformation of the king. Finally he addressed a bull to Philip reminding him in a grave and fatherly way of the evils he had caused the Church and the French citizens, advising him of the synod to be held, and inviting the king to send his representatives. The document on its delivery, early in 1301, was seized and burned by the Count of Artois. A fictitious bull was substituted. In this fabrication, written in insulting language, the Pope is made to claim superiority over the king in temporal affairs. This imposture, together with an insulting answer of the king, was spread broadcast among the people to rouse their national anger and hatred. The States General (the French parliament) was summoned to Paris; before them was laid a garbled account of the conflict, with a demand for a stand by them for the king against papal pretensions. The barons and the bourgeoise so acted; the barons and probably the bourgeoise, dispatched an arrogant letter to the Cardinals at Rome. The clergy hesitated, but under the threat of high treason they promised to uphold the king in his person and rights. The clergy wrote to the Pope asking him to withdraw his summons.

Boniface refuted the charges raised in the States General. In spite of Philip's closing of the frontiers forty-five bishops went to the Roman synod. The principal results of the synod's deliberations were laid down in the Bull *Unam Sanctam,* which the Pope then published. In this famous document Pope Boniface upheld the Catholic doctrine of the indirect powers of the papacy over temporal affairs, as far as they touch upon sin or the spiritual welfare of souls. He maintained also two other propositions: the distinction of the two highest powers and the superiority of the spiritual over the temporal. These propositions date back to the most remote Christian antiquity, and were asserted by the Fathers and by the Popes of the first six centuries as well as by the Popes of the medieval period. It is not true that after the publication of the Bull *Unam Sanctam* Boniface VIII deposed Philip IV and absolved his subjects from their allegiance.

In 1303, while Pope Boniface was working for a reconciliation, Philip IV was secretly preparing a supreme blow against the papacy. In June he assembled thirty court-bishops and several barons and jurists in the Louvre of Paris. First there was read to them a list of accusations against the Pope. These were the calumnies which the king's sinister agents, Flotte and Nogaret, had been circulating through France, and which his Italian allies, the Colonnas, had been disseminating in the peninsula. In these outrageous slanders Boniface was charged with heresy, witchcraft, idolatry and unbelief. Then the king and, at his orders, the assembly raised an appeal against the Pope to a future General Council and to a future *legitimate* Pope. This was the first time in the history of the Gallican Church that such an appeal was ever made. Later the charges and the appeal were spread everywhere among the people. Royal commissioners were dispatched over the country to obtain assents from the clergy and the laity. Hard pressure was used upon those who would not voluntarily sign.

But Boniface stood firm. He prepared to excommunicate Philip IV by name on September 8. Only by brutal force would the intrepid Pope be overcome. Nogaret arrived in Italy and, with Sciarra Colonna, organized a body of French men-at-arms and Italian Ghibellines. On September 7 the lawless band appeared before Anagni where the Pope was staying. Admitted into the city by treachery they forced their way into the papal palace. Boniface arrayed himself in full pontifical vestments, seated himself on his throne and commanded the doors to be opened, saying: "Captured by treason like Christ, I shall die like a Pope." He calmly awaited his enemies. Nogaret and Colonna seized the Holy Father, a venerable old man, and dragged him into prison, where he was loaded with indignities, and even deprived of food. On the third day the people of Anagni rose, drove the aggressors from the city, and liberated the Pontiff. The old Pope, prostrated in body but unbroken in mind, was carried to Rome, where on October 11, 1303, he died. The Sacrilege of Anagni spelt the earthly defeat of Boniface VIII; his heroism there has inspired Christians ever since and has signalized the eternal triumph of his Church.

Philip IV was an incipient secularist. His separation of politics from morality and religion developed through the ages into today's world-wide, all-pervading secularism — the system that excludes God and religion from life. Philip also may be considered the founder of Gallicanism, that particularist movement that more than once led the French Church to the brink of total schism, that servile system of clerical subordination to the monarchy that could only be destroyed in the cataclysms of the French Revolution.

The English conflict, if it were not as dramatic as the French, had many similarities. There was an extremely able monarch, Edward I. He also used clerical grants for his secular wars. He too was rapacious; in 1294 he demanded and obtained one half the Church's revenues; in the following year he imposed burdens almost as heavy. The Bull *Clericis laicos* was directed also at Edward I; and he more than deserved it.

Archbishop Winchelsey stood forth as the champion of ecclesiastical rights in England. Armed by the bull, just mentioned, in 1297 he declined to grant a money supply. Edward in a great rage seized all fiefs, goods and chattels of the clergy for the benefit of the crown. Long and bitter was to be the English conflict. The archbishop for a time had to subsist on the meager alms of an obscure parish. However, Archbishop Winchelsey found support from the barons and merchants, who also had suffered grievously from the rapacity of the king. At long last the archbishop was to effect a royal concession that for all taxation the consent of the nation represented in Parliament must be asked by the king. Thus one of the greatest principles of English law was established, owing in great part to the heroic constancy of the Primate of Canterbury, Archbishop Winchelsey.

Anticlericalism

ST. PETER'S BARQUE often is assailed at one and the same time by storms raging from different quarters. This was markedly true in the Middle Ages. During the several conflicts with the power-lusting monarchies, the Popes had to combat many other grave evils: ignorance, superstition, moral license, arrogance and pride. From such malignant forces two sinister movements emerged, first anticlericalism and then heresy.

Opposition to unwarranted clerical action is understandable. Since bishops, priests and monks remained human, it was to be expected that among them would be the haughty and the avaricious, and that some of them would interfere in matters where they had no rights. When the antagonism went beyond the cleric to his sacred office, or when it was aimed at the clergy as a class, then it became undoubtedly evil. Its harmfulness increased when it was nourished by false historical ideas, pride, personal hatreds or resistance to reform. If it finally culminated in false individualism, disobedience to lawful spirituality and abstension from the sacraments, then anticlericalism became a most hostile force against religion.

Anticlericalism was a very potent fact in medieval life. It varied from mere resentment to bitterest enmity. There was widespread disgust with the lower clergy because of their ignorance, superstition and failure to give religious instruction. There was the sharpest resentment for the higher clergy because of their greed, worldliness and interference in the non-religious aspects of lay life. Scant remembrance was

175

had of the worthy shepherds. It must always be borne in mind
that the opposition was not always single-minded but that
very often it sprang from injured self-interest. There was
loud impatience with the slowness and ineffectiveness of
reforms, even of the most devoted Popes and bishops. No
allowance was made for the times, the encroachments of kings
in ecclesiastical affairs, the lack of zeal and spirituality on
the part of the royal appointees in the episcopacy, and the
anarchic confusion of the interminable feudal wars.

This oppositional spirit, only too often justified by the
derelictions of clerics, gave rise, at the end of the twelfth
century, to several lay-inspired movements which aimed at
moral regeneration. The leaders proposed a new, simpler,
higher moral life, such as they imagined the primitive Christians led, such as they were convinced our Lord had designed.
They were sincere, but also stubbornly opinionated. Since
their knowledge of history was sketchy and their knowledge of
theology no better, the danger was serious that they might
drift into fanaticism and heresy.

The first of these anticlericals to gain prominence were
the Waldensians. Their movement was named from its
founder Peter Waldo, a wealthy merchant of Lyons. About
1176, having disposed of all his goods, he embraced a life of
strictest poverty and began preaching to others that the one
really good work was to live without owning, that this was the
way to perfection. His enthusiasm and sincerity gained him
a following which was organized into a kind of penitential
brotherhood bound to practice poverty and to preach it to
others. The Archbishop of Lyons, however, forbade the
organization and expelled the members from his diocese. In
1179 they appealed to the great Pope, Innocent III. He
approved of their life of consecrated poverty; but he still
forbade them to preach in any diocese against the wish of its
bishop. The Waldensians refused to honor this prohibition of
the Pope. Lay fanatics were placing themselves above the
divinely appointed magistracy of the Church.

The movement began to drift towards heresy. The drift
quickened as the Waldensians came in contact with other
anticlerical movements which were definitely heretical,
such as the Humiliati of Lombardy. After the first decades

of the thirteenth century the Waldensians were teaching that the sacraments were invalid if the officiating priest were in mortal sin (the teaching of the Church is that the value of the sacraments does not depend upon the state of grace of the priest who administers them). Other errors of theirs were: the power to forgive sins depends on a life of absolute poverty; confession to a layman is as good, is even better than to a priest; prayers for the dead are useless; oaths are unlawful; any layman, in case of necessity could, without ordination, say Mass, provided he led a life of apostolic poverty. The Waldensians failed in importance in the fourteenth century. But they remained a serious, if minor, problem for the bishops of southern France and northwestern Italy down until the Protestant Revolution. Then the Waldensians were absorbed into Calvinism.

Contemporary with the followers of Peter Waldo, but far more evil, was a sect that developed in southern France. Its adherents were called Manicheans, or Cathari, or Albigensians. The first name arose from their descent from the dualistic heresy of the ancient Manichees (the divine good principle and the divine evil principle). The second derived from their rite of purification. The third came from their chief center, the city of Albi in Languedoc. By whatever name they were known they were the medieval Church's most malignant foe. They aimed at nothing less than a new anti-Christianity. In their active hatred they never ceased their efforts to destroy Catholicism. Their fundamental dogma was that there were two gods, one supremely good, the other supremely evil. By this doctrine they sought to explain the ever difficult problem of evil as the struggle between the two deities. They drew a further conclusion that matter was the creation of the evil god and hence matter was essentially evil. Some of them went so far as to maintain that the human body of our Lord was an essentially evil thing. The ultimate objective of these sectaries was to obtain the victory of the spiritual, as they conceived it, and the destruction of the material.

The Albigensians (the more popular of their three names) had their own ecclesiastical organization. They had also a very distinctive purification rite, the "consolamentum," imposed by the hands of their ministers, called "the Perfect." The ceremony freed the soul from the power of matter and the guilt of sin without any requirement of penance or restitution. If, however, the consolamentum was lost by relapse into sin it could not be regained.

The Perfect were one of the two classes of the sect. They were bound to perpetual chastity, to most severe fasts lasting through most of the year, to complete abstinence from meat and dairy foods, and to a common life. In practice they were a sort of religious order leading a life of the severest self-denial. The second class were "the Believers"; they were by far the greatest number. The Believers shrank from the rigoristic asceticism of the Perfect. All that was required of them was to accept the Albigensian doctrines, to revere the Perfect and to promise to receive the consolamentum before death; meanwhile they were bound to no restraints of their passions.

Many, fearing to lose the consolamentum by moral backsliding, or dreading the frightful austerities of the Perfect, underwent the "Endura," a process of obtaining death by deliberate starvation. Such suicides were venerated as martyrs by the Albigensians. The body, being matter, was thoroughly evil; its destruction then was a holy act. Similarly they held that life was the greatest evil and to communicate life was the greatest of crimes. The Albigensians condemned marriage, nothing was to be shunned more than pregnancy. Yet the Perfect tolerated in the Believers extramatrimonial relations, since they considered sexual immorality a less serious obstacle than honest marriage to the transition from Believer to Perfect. Albigensianism was anti-social; its opposition to birth would have wiped out the human race. It was horribly immoral, since it permitted to the Believers, the great majority of its membership, full liberty to sin and still promised them salvation if they received the consolamentum at the very end of life, even without penance and restitution.

How did this abominable system obtain its unshakable hold on enormous numbers of souls? First there was the zealous, ubiquitous preaching of the Perfect; and their main doctrine, false as it was, offered an easily apprehended solution of the problem of evil. The average Catholic priest did not preach at all. The Perfect lived lives of great poverty and austerity; fanatical they were, but evidently most sincere. The Catholic clergy often were notorious for wealth and luxurious living. The Perfect were generous in almsgiving, often perhaps for proselytizing, in maintaining schools for the children of the Believers, in subsidizing the industries of their disciples. The large sums dispensed came chiefly from the Believers who were powerful nobles or wealthy merchants. Finally it was a very easy system for the Believers. It offered liberation from the difficult struggle against concupiscence, and at the same time it did not impose new commandments. Until his reception of the consolamentum the Believer was limited only by his appetites and his opportunities. Even if he lost the consolamentum he faced no punishments such as the Catholic did—the sufferings of purgatory or the eternal agonies of hell. He was taught that his crimes would be expiated in a future existence, or in a state of future trial. It was from an endless series of possibly difficult lives that the consolamentum delivered him. The body would finally be destroyed. There was no final resurrection; for the body, being material, was essentially evil. How the Church overcame this horrifying heresy of the Albigensians will be treated in the next chapter.

Manicheism—
Its Growth
and Death

MANICHEISM, AN ANCIENT sect, appeared in Asia and in Europe as early as the middle of the third century. So evil were its doctrines and practices that it was soon proscribed by the pagan emperor Diocletian, by the Buddhists in India and China, and by Christian rulers, lay and ecclesiastical. By the fifth century it had apparently been stamped out, although remnants continued to exist, lurking in remote regions of the Balkans. Six centuries passed, and about 1022, this sinister heresy emerged again in Western Europe. By another hundred years, 1125, Manichean groups, strongly established in southern France and in northern Italy, were waging destructive warfare against Catholic faith and Catholic morals.

The chief center of disaffection was Languedoc, that wide district which included most of south-central France. Here nature so abundantly provided for the necessities and the luxuries of life that there was afforded ample leisure for the pursuit of a refined, but also corrupt and licentious civilization. This civilization was also wealthy and orientalized. There were many non-Christian elements in the life of Languedoc. The traditions of the Moors, who once held the region, still remained; indeed many Moors were living in the area. Numerous also were Eastern, non-Christian merchants; these by accumulating great riches achieved positions of importance in the towns of the region. For any attack on Catholicism that developed in this over-refined and licentious culture there would be powerful supporters: corrupt Christian nobles who embraced the immoral position of "Believer" in the Manichean sect; and non-Christian opponents who would sustain any contrary movement.

The Church in Languedoc was in poor condition to meet such an attack. The lower clergy were woefully ignorant. Because they never preached, their flock knew very little about the teachings of Christian faith and morals. Far worse liabilities were the wealthy or the lax among the higher clergy, the prelates who disgraced their office by luxury, pride, lust and avarice. Their scandalous lives were sharply criticized. Such criticisms grew in number and bitterness as the lay-ascetical movements, like the Waldensians, developed in the rising commercial towns. Under these circumstances tinder was plentiful to be ignited by the Manichean sectaries from the East, to produce the conflagration of the Albigensian heresy. This heresy threatened the very existence of Catholicism in Languedoc and in adjoining areas of Spain, eastern France and northern Italy.

The Catholic counter-offensive, and there was one, assailed ineffectually the overwhelming power of the heresy and its supporters, until the great Innocent III ascended the papal throne. In 1198 he appointed two local Cistercian monks to be his agents to the princes, prelates and people of Languedoc. He raised them to the rank of papal legates in the following year. When they made little headway, either against the heresy or the evil-living clerics, Innocent replaced them as legates by other Cistercians, among whom was the courageous and vigorous Peter de Castelnau. Still other Cistercians were added including the very abbot of Citeaux. Thirty Cistercians, twelve of them abbots, worked in the Languedoc conflict. An active anti-Catharist campaign was launched; it consisted of instructions, sermons, disputations and pamphlets. Innocent was using the most learned and the best disciplined religious of the times, the sons of St. Bernard. Despite numerous individual conversions, the monks made little progress; the Count of Toulouse, Raymond VI, the principal ruler, refused to cooperate and so the heresy remained strongly entrenched.

A new impetus was given the Catholic cause by the advent of two Spaniards, Diego, Bishop of Osma, and Dominic de Guzman, prior of his cathedral chapter. Innocent III sent them to Languedoc. Diego suggested that the legates relinquish the pomp of their office and live like the seventy-two disciples, with neither scrip, nor staff, nor money. In this way they would offset the prestige of the Perfect for austerity and they would rebuke the worldliness of the clergy. Diego eventually resigned his see to become a Cistercian. Dominic remained a canon, but within a decade founded the Order of Preachers, the Dominicans. The papal legates accepted the recommendations of Diego of Osma. The mission was worked by small groups (three or four in a group) who toured the countryside, living in apostolic poverty, preaching and instructing, and holding debates with the heretics. Several more Cistercians joined the work, which was blessed by Innocent III and which won back many converts.

Yet, after ten years of most zealous efforts the Albigensians still held firm, with their prestige unshaken. More than a thousand villages in southern France were infected; probably the majority of the nobles were Believers, and the Count of Toulouse, Raymond VI, virtually the prince of Languedoc, supported them with his most powerful protection. Rallying to the aid of the heretics were the armed forces of the freebooting barons, lawless marauders known as the Brabançons. Many nobles, not heretics, aided the Albigensians politically as counterpoises to the rising royal power of the kings of France at Paris.

The supreme crisis was reached when the papal legate, de Castelnau, was assassinated. The legate had determined on one last effort to win the Count of Toulouse to cooperation against the Albigensians, which he had twice sworn to do, or to compel him to move against the heretics. The Count formally refused. The legate excommunicated him and put his possessions under interdict. Three months later, January 5, 1208, de Castelnau was murdered by one of the Count's officers. Raymond VI was generally held responsible for the deed. Europe remembered St. Thomas à Becket's martyrdom, just forty years before. The assassination called for drastic action.

Innocent III summoned the king and barons of France to a crusade against these Manichean infidels, "worse than

Moslems." There followed the twenty years of the Albigensian Wars, marked in the beginning by bloodshed and massacre on both sides. After the first seven years the heretics
lost the protection of the Counts of Toulouse. But the wars
had also been developing into a feudal struggle between the
kings of France and their vassals, the Counts of Toulouse.
The battles of the last ten years were simple conflicts of
national unity against divergent feudalism.

The campaign of preaching and discussion still persisted
though hampered by the continual fighting. St. Dominic
assumed the leadership of this purely religious movement.
He and his small band established themselves at Toulouse;
Archbishop Fulk recognized them as official preachers. In
1216, when the community numbered sixteen, St. Dominic
and the Archbishop petitioned for their establishment as a
religious order. Since the Fourth Lateran Council would
not encourage new religious orders, Dominic, on the advice
of Innocent III, chose the rule of St. Augustine. In the same
year the new Pope, Honorius III, gave papal approbation to
the new venture, as an order of canons dedicated to preaching
and to intellectual work for the salvation of souls. Its austerities were the equal of the Cistercians; its poverty was taken
from St. Francis; its organization was centralized on its Master
General; its stability was vowed to the order as a whole. Each
convent, usually consisting of twelve members, was to
have at least one doctor to give a daily lecture on theology,
from which not even the prior was excused. St. Dominic's
sons, going about in two and living solely on alms, were to
combat the Catharist heresy by their learning as well as by
their holy, mortified lives. The Order of Preachers spread
rapidly throughout Christendom. Within sixty years they
had 394 convents, of which 180 were in the lands once infested by Manicheism.

The Dominican Friars played an important part in teaching at the University of Toulouse. This institution, founded in
1229, by Pope Gregory IX, was supported by Count Raymond VII in consequence of a treaty with Queen Blanche,
regent of France for her son, St. Louis IX. Its object was
to prevent, by higher theological studies, a recrudescence
of Catharism. Raymond VIII had to maintain at his own ex-

pense for ten years a certain number of masters of theology, law, and grammar. The university became a chief means of restoring the Faith in the south of France.

To root out the malignancy of Manicheism, the bishops at the Council of Toulouse in 1229 established the Inquisition — a tribunal to inquire into the existence of heresy. It was to seek the conversion of the guilty and only to hand over to the secular power the completely recalcitrant. In medieval times religion and society were so intermingled that heresy was also a civil crime, equivalent to high treason. Four years later, 1233, Gregory IV entrusted the conduct of the Inquisition to the Dominicans. Their decisions would be the fairest because they were learned theologians, men of evident sanctity and most disinterested judges (in view of their vow of poverty which embraced their order as well as themselves).

From then on the Inquisition was called the "Papal" or "Monastic Inquisition." Contemporary records are scanty; but an indication of the conduct of the Dominican Inquisitors may be gained from the record of Bernard Gui. In sixteen years (1307-1323) he pronounced 920 sentences; 139 were acquittals, 791 condemnations of which 42 ended in execution (an average of less than three a year). His record was a mild one considering the savage criminal codes of European countries, which lasted down to the opening of the nineteenth century. The Monastic Inquisition succeeded, Albigensianism disappeared completely.

Shafts of Light

THE HISTORY OF medieval Catholicism is more than a repetitious chronicling of conflicts with royal despots, stubborn heretics, or evil-living Catholics. It must also be a reporting of marvelous achievements in extending the Faith, ruling the flock, intensifying spirituality, begetting saints, enlarging education, developing theologians, and fostering art and literature.

The medieval Church pursued her divine Founder's charge to bring His truth to all men. In the twelfth century the consolidation of the Faith in the Scandinavian lands was completed. A new mission was begun among the Pomeranians on the Baltic Sea. In the thirteenth century missionaries reached the heathens of Prussia, Lithuania and Livonia. For the protection of the Christians, the Knights of the Sword and the Teutonic Knights were established in these regions. The Christians of far-off Greenland were provided for by the Archbishop of Trondheim in Norway. Even the conversion of the Tartars, whose vast dominion stretched from the Japanese Sea, all over central Asia as far as the Dniester River in the Ukraine, was envisioned. The Popes sent missionaries to Jeughiz Khan and later to Kublai Khan. Among the missionaries who made the lonely, far-distant journeys were the Franciscans, John of Carpini and William of Rrubruquis. The effort was barren of results, although in the next century John of Monti Corvino established an archbishopric in Peking. A more hopeless task was attempted by Franciscans and Dominicans in the thirteenth century: the conversion of the

Mohammedans of Syria. But at least, in both cases, the zeal of the papacy and the friars was heroically demonstrated.

For the internal life of the Church, the Popes of the High Middle Ages summoned and presided over six ecumenical councils. In the twelfth century they assembled the First Lateran (1123), the Second Lateran (1139), and the Third Lateran (1179); in the thirteenth century they brought together the Fourth Lateran, "The Great Council" (1216), the First of Lyons (1245), and the Second of Lyons (1274). Almost all of the councils were largely attended. On the whole these councils were concerned with the government and discipline of the Church, with such problems as clerical laxity, clerical education, the conditions for valid marriage, and the rites of the sacraments. There were some definitions of the truths of Faith, especially in regard to the Holy Trinity and the Blessed Sacrament. There were clear condemnations of schisms and heresies, especially of Waldensianism and Catharism. Strong steps were taken to assert the rights of the Church against the ambitious tyrannies of emperors and kings. More than one council actively promoted the crusades. An immense amount of good for morals and church organization was achieved by numerous local councils held all over Europe. The medieval Church was a vigorous Church — it had to be, under the leadership of Alexander III, Innocent III, Honorius III and Gregory IX.

The state of religious orders affords a good idea of the Church's spiritual life in a given period. By this criterion Catholicism in the High Middle Ages appears to have been flourishing. Of course there were plenty of defects and abuses, sometimes of very grave character. Such unfortunate conditions were usually owing to the lay influence in the nomination of abbots, or to monasteries' amassing of enormous estates, the management of which took the religious from the strict adherence to primitive spirit, especially their ascetical practices. But in the overall picture of monastic life there was so much that was inspiring the numerous vocations to the monastic life in the twelfth century, and the far greater movement into the friar orders in the thirteenth century. Then there must be added the missionary labors among the heathens, the vast charitable care for the poor, and the educational

ST. THOMAS AQUINAS AMONG THE DOCTORS OF THE CHURCH. *Francisco Zurbaran, the Museum, Seville.*

work of the friars in the university. The story of the monks, nuns and friars of the Middle Ages has already been discussed in previous chapters.

A few additions may be made. One was the institution in the twelfth century in the Low Countries of the Beguines. They were lay women who lived together in small communities, leading a life of chastity, prayer and caring for the poor. Some took all three vows of religion (they were free to do so). Eventually all took the vow of chastity. Their settlements were called after them "beguinages." Some lived always in the beguinage; others went out daily to work in the industries of the towns, returning in the evening to the beguinages. The movement was very popular; thousands of single women joined it. In the thirteenth century similar institutions were started for men, who received the name Beghards. They were not as successful as the women; several communities of Beghards became involved in heresy. When the congregations for religious sisters engaged in external apostolic works of teaching and nursing were founded in the seventeenth and eighteenth centuries, the appeal of the beguine life passed. There are still a few beguinages in Belgium; the one at Bruges and the one at Ghent are notable. A striking and over-dramatic type of penitential life was exhibited by another type of semi-religious group, called the Flagellants. These latter, men and women, marched in procession, especially during the penitential seasons, publicly scourging themselves. Sinister elements of politics, to say nothing of fanaticism, damaged the good accomplished; the Holy See in 1261 forbade the processions of the Flagellants. Finally it must be noted that the monks never obtained their former primacy in religious life; the popularity of the friars, especially in their labors for souls in the new towns, and their achievements for higher education definitely placed them first. The monasteries regained their religious spirit; but, because they were rural institutes their spiritual apostolate remained local and their educational works for the most part were restrained to their schools for educating their own novices or the secular clergy of the nearby areas.

The extraordinary number of saints who lived in these times proves the mighty force of spirituality which the medieval Church generated. Only a few names can be cited; they must serve as types of the multitude of holy men and women of medieval Catholicism. In the twelfth century heading the list are St. Bernard of Clairvaux; St. Thomas à Becket; St. Leopold, ruler of Austria; St. Hugh, bishop of Lincoln; and St. Hildegard. In the thirteenth century the outstanding names are: St. Francis of Assisi, St. Anthony of Padua, Saint Clare, St. Dominic, St. Hyacinth (the great Dominican missionary), St. Simon Stock (general of the Carmelites), St. Edmund Rich (Archbishop of Canterbury), St. Albertus Magnus, St. Thomas Aquinas, St. Bonaventure, St. Gertrude the Great, St. Elizabeth of Hungary, and the two Popes, St. Gregory X and St. Celestine V.

Universities and Cathedrals

THE FOSTERING of learning has always been of special concern to the Church. It was never more so than in the High Middle Ages. In the twelfth century a strong current of intellectual progress set in. Aristotle's works, translated in Latin from the Arabic versions used by the Moors in Spain, found warm welcome in the schools of France and Italy. Among the chief centers were the French schools of Chartres and Laon. Philosophy, with special references to religion, was more deeply studied and debated. In writing, greater accuracy and more precise expression were aimed at. During the same period historical chronicles were multiplied and broadened; even initial steps were taken in the physical sciences. These advances the Church encouraged by academic foundations and by seeking solutions in the controversies arising from the interpretations and applications of Aristotle's ideas, or in the conflicts over the rights of reason and the values of devotion. With the Church's support the first universities, Paris, Bologna, Oxford, Salerno and Montpellier, made their appearance.

In the thirteenth century the universities developed into great centers of learning, and their number was increased to twenty-three. In this growth and development the Church took a major part. The principal faculty in almost all universities was that of theology; even where it was that of law, the canon law had a special importance. The Church then had a special interest in the universities. It was in these seats of learning, Paris especially, that brilliant Catholic thinkers brought to perfection "Scholasticism," the great system of Catholic theology and philosophy. The Church developed an extraordinary array of thinkers and writers whose labors gave this period a conspicuous place in the annals of human learning. Among such mighty intellects were: St. Anselm, St. Bernard, Abelard, Peter Lombard, St. Albertus Magnus, St. Thomas Aquinas, St. Bonaventure, Roger Bacon, John Duns Scotus, Ramon Lully, Robert Grosteste and Alexander Hales.

During the thirteenth century the following universities were established: Cambridge, Orleans, Angers, Toulouse, Lerida, Valencia, Valladolid, Salamanca (one of the greatest), Seville, Lisbon, Vercelli, Piacenza, Siena, Arrezzio, Naples, Padua, and Vicenza. It might be noted here that up to the religious revolution of the sixteenth century eighty-one universities were founded in Europe. Of these thirteen were of gradual development, later receiving papal privileges; thirty-three by papal charter alone; fifteen by imperial or royal charter, later receiving papal privileges; and twenty by both papal and regal charters.

Medieval religious poets composed works that are among the richest treasures of world literature. Foremost is Dante Alighieri's *Divina Commedia,* the tremendous account of his imaginary journey through hell, purgatory and heaven. The Florentine poet treats of such overwhelming themes, produces such vast conceptions, draws such vivid and powerful descriptions, expresses so intensely all emotions, delivers such powerful decisions, and unites so effectively the sound of words with the sense of their thought, that the *Divina Commedia* truly merits the judgment of being the greatest epic poem ever written. Because of Dante's vast range of religious thought in his masterpiece, the *Divina Commedia* has justly been described as the *Summa Theologica* of St. Thomas in poetic form.

The religious poets of the Middle Ages raised the Latin hymn to the status of great literature. So may be numbered: *Jesu, Dulcis Memoria, Alma Redemptoris Mater, Salve Regina, Pange Lingua, Adoro Te Devote, Stabat Mater,* and the *Dies Irae.* These hymns have been treasured by men in all subsequent ages — simple men, and men of letters,

Catholic and non-Catholic. Many of the best modern poets, some of them non-Catholics, have given of their genius to translate into the best literary forms of their own languages these lovely, poignant hymns of the medieval Church. One must not forget that it was in the medieval churches that the first steps were taken which led to the miracle plays, the mystery plays and the morality plays of the late middle ages and of modern times. How lovely is the tradition that the first step was the Christmas crib that St. Francis made for the church in Assisi.

"Cathedral and Crusade" were the two words used by Daniel-Rops to summarize the Middle Ages. The Crusade is a memory eight centuries old; the Cathedral still rises to heaven, admired and used by men. At the opening of the twelfth century Romanesque architecture was still the exclusive style. Even today its simplicity, solidness and strength attracts the modern as he examines from outside the sturdy walls, the simple rounded arches, the square belfries; or in the interior he examines the massive piers whose strong rounded arches support the great galleries or triforia. The abbeys of Caen in Normandy, and the cathedrals of Durham, Peterborough and Norwich in England retain their appeal to this day.

About the middle of the twelfth century there began a transition to a new style, the Gothic. The snows of northern winters called for steeper pitched roofs; gray days brought the need of greater light. The answer was found in the pointed arch that could reach to any height and span any distance, in the rib-vaulting that united the lofty arches, and in the buttresses that caught the thrust of the roof arches at certain points in the wall. If the thrust was still great, an arm of masonry was shot from the attached buttress through the air to point of thrust in the roof; this arm of masonry was the flying buttress. Since the spaces between the attached buttresses no longer bore the weight of the roof, these spaces were used for the vast and high windows; thus the problem of greater light was solved.

These structural features endowed the Gothic cathedrals with their inspiring height and their tall gracefulness. Stained

RHEIMS CATHEDRAL. Facade.

DISPUTATION ON THE SACRAMENT. *Raphael, the Vatican.*

glass, brilliant in multicolors, filled the vast window spaces; on a bright sunny day a Gothic cathedral shone and sparkled as a mighty casket of glowing jewels. These colorful windows unfolded the story of the lives of our Lord, of the Blessed Virgin and of the saints, both of the Old and the New Testament. Unlettered medieval peasants knew their faith well; they saw it so strikingly displayed before their eyes every day they entered the Gothic churches. The stained-glass windows of the Gothic cathedrals have been called "The Poor Man's Bible." Other pages of that "Bible" he would find in the sculptured west fronts and side portals, where carvings depicted the life of our Lord and of our Lady, where countless niches were filled with statues of the saints: the statues may be elongated to fit into the architecture, but the faces are real, lively and perfectly executed. Gothic sculpture reached its apex in the statue of Jesus, known as "Le Beau Dieu of Amiens."

The erection of a Gothic cathedral was a great communal project. Of course architects were brought in, and skilled craftsmen were paid. Yet a goodly part was freely contributed, even to the peasant lending his oxen to haul the stones, or his good wife cooking the meals of the laborers. The financing of the construction and decoration arose from the gifts of the bishop, the canons, the clergy, the companies of the merchants, the guilds of the artisans, even from the pittances of the unskilled laborers. When the glorious cathedral was completed, it stood as a monument of religious zeal, civic pride, technical skill and aesthetic understanding. So it stands today, whether it be Notre Dame of Paris, Chartres, Amiens, Rheims, or Bourges in France; Canterbury, Lincoln, York or Wells in England; Burgos or Toledo in Spain; Cologne or Ulm in Germany; Milan or Siena in Italy; or the hundreds of other Gothic cathedrals or churches that still grace the European lands.

With all their trials, amid all the wars and intrigues, in the face of all disasters, the medieval Christians were a happy people. With cheerful terms they described their homelands: Merrie England, Gay France, Song-loving Germany, Happy Spain and Fortunate Italy. And well they did for behind it all was holy Rome, of St. Peter and St. Paul, and of the Pope.

Late
Medieval
Crosscurrents

THE TERM, the Late Middle Ages, applies to the four-teenth and fifteenth centuries. The period opens with the Papal Residence at Avignon, 1309-1377, and closes with the start of Luther's Religious Revolution in 1517. Vast changes occurred during these two hundred years. So overwhelming were these changes, and so often were they marked with grave excesses, that men's minds were in constant and deep-seated confusion. Christendom's unity was being frag-mented into intense local nationalisms. Numerous wars, several of long duration, not only were pushing on the process but were developing the new national governments into highly centralized states ruled by autocratic monarchs. Great increases of wealth among the merchants and the new class of capitalists raised these moneyed-men into high importance in the new states, of which they were strong sup-porters. With the excessive pursuit of riches by many of the bourgeois, materialism spread far and wide. More sinister still, owing to the pretensions both of autocrats and of capi-talists, was the growth of secularism. The whole picture was further complicated by insurrections of the peasants or of the town artisans. Both of these classes had suffered griev-ously in the terrible plagues of the times, of which the Black Death was but one of several. The new economy was pressing heavy burdens upon them. They reacted in agrarian revolts and town tumults. Not only the sanguinary violence, but the wild theories of these uprisings compounded the general unrest and confusion.

The political problems and social evils of the Late Middle Ages grievously affected the Church. It could not have been otherwise since almost all Europeans were still adherents of Catholicism. But the Church in the fourteenth and fifteenth centuries had far graver problems to contend with; it was during this period that the seeds of the Protestant Revolution of the sixteenth century were sown and cultivated.

First there was the weakening of the authority of the Holy See, resulting from such disastrous occurances as the Papal Residence at Avignon, the rivalries of the claimants to the supreme pontificate during the Great Western Schism, and the complaints against administrative and fiscal abuses in the papal court. The worldliness of many and the licentious-ness of some in the highest ranks of the Roman clergy, affected by evil elements in one sector of the Renaissance, tarnished the image of the papacy. The lack of thoroughness in reforms only multiplied sharp criticisms. Weakening of the authority of the highest office resulted in a weakening of ecclesiastical authority at all levels.

Powerful heresies arose in the fourteenth and fifteenth centuries against most fundamental dogmas of the Faith. Foremost were the false teachings about the primacy of the See of St. Peter. Some denied the very idea; others would have made the state supreme in religious matters; others still, backed by a numerous following, proclaimed that a general council was superior to the Pope both in authority and in the teaching of faith. There were heretics also who denied Transubstantiation, or who taught a novel theory of predestination, or who held the Bible to be the sole rule of Faith. The ideas of the great heresies of the next century were developing.

Caesaropapism, the dominance of the Church by the State, was revived on a vast scale by the new autocratic rulers. They encroached so far in ecclesiastical affairs as to threaten seriously the independence at least of the national churches. Kings and oligarchs controlled almost completely the nominations to the local hierarchies. Too often they forced on the episcopal sees prelates who were opportunist politicians, or characterless incompetents, or unworthy, even vicious clerics. Further, these lay princes sought in their realms to fashion religious policies, to manage church finances and to interfere in ecclesiastical discipline. No wonder some local clerical bodies came to have more dependence on their sovereigns than on the Pope. Monarchs frequently nullified the reform programs, alleging such specious pleas as that such reforms were invasions of national rights or, more frankly, royal prerogatives.

The most painful problem confronting the Church in the Late Middle Ages was the moral delinquencies of large numbers of the clergy from the lowest ranks to the highest. Allowing for great exaggerations and much over-emphasis, it must be confessed that the contemporary clerical record contains an abundance of sad pages. But far graver evils afflicted the clergy: widespread theological confusion ending at times in heresy; false mysticism, deceiving pious and simple souls; strange dogmatic solutions aired by shallow-minded, popular preachers, drawing poorly-educated priests from the solid truths of the Faith. The moral deficiencies among the clergy afforded an abundant armory of striking arguments to the enemies of the Church; the dark clouds of dogmatic confusion lowered overwhelmingly as the period ended.

A closely related problem, the sad spiritual condition of large sections of the people, constituted one of the heaviest woes of the Church in the fourteenth and fifteenth centuries. The ravages of wars, insurrections and plagues begot in large numbers of the populace a morbidity of spirit and a pessimistic outlook on life. The worldliness of the upper classes spread widely through the lower strata of society. The current immoralities and scepticism added their baneful effects. But far and away the worst affliction was the widespread ignorance of countless numbers of the people, an affliction that rendered futile some of the best remedial efforts of the Church. There was a deep ignorance of the truths of the Faith, and in this darkness superstitions flourished and multiplied. There was a comparable ignorance of the nature of worship, which led to a false emphasis on externals and ended in empty formalism for many. Here were fertile fields for the seeds of religious revolt.

All the above presents a very dark picture. But it would be a great mistake to imagine that such a picture was the complete portrait of the Church in the Late Middle Ages. In that period the Church gained most glorious triumphs. The dark aspects have been listed at great length to enable the reader to follow the discussion of these problems in future chapters.

In future chapters, too, the bright glories will be described. Such triumphs of the Church in the fourteenth and fifteenth centuries include the wonderful flowering of saints in numbers and holiness; the piety and charity of vast numbers of the faithful, a source of perennial inspiration; the founding of most of the medieval universities; the glorious paintings and sculptures of the Christian artists of the Renaissance; the completion of the Gothic cathedrals. The dark episodes will report the storms that assailed the barque of Peter; the bright accounts will manifest Peter's barque riding out the storms. Peter's barque is the Catholic Church; Christ is always in it.

Seventy Years
and
Seven Popes

THE CHURCH'S TRIBULATIONS in the Late Middle Ages make distressing reading indeed. The listing of sad incidents becomes a doleful task. But for the complete picture, which is the true one, it is necessary always to keep in mind the good that was being achieved contemporaneously. The doctrine of the Church despite many attacks was maintained in its purity. Ecclesiastical and religious life exhibited in many places vigor and variety; saintly lives were frequent in all parts of Europe; domestic missionaries were many and influential. Numerous beneficent medieval institutions of the Church continued their course uninterruptedly: works of education and charity abounded. Religious art in all its forms had a living force; pious and edifying literature was common and appreciated.

During the fourteenth and fifteenth centuries, most of the causes of the Protestant Revolution were sown. One of the most disastrous was the weakening of the authority of the Holy See, progressing until the day when almost half of the Europeans would repudiate all papal power. One of the first blows was the Papal Residence at Avignon, 1305-1377, which the Italians with understandable exaggeration called "The Babylonian Captivity." Let it be remembered that the Popes at Avignon always claimed and always were considered bishops of Rome. The Avignon residence has often been described, very inaccurately, as the seventy years when seven Popes, all Frenchmen, with a French College of Cardinals, lived in France under the domination of the French monarchs. True, the Popes were French, and the majority of the cardinals were French (the College then numbered about thirty-five). But Avignon, though French-speaking, was not then part of France; it belonged to the Holy Roman Empire whose territory reached to the east bank of the Rhone. The domination of the French monarchs was certainly present in the beginning years. But their continuing dominance has been much over-emphasized. No Avignon Pope was entirely the pliant creature of a French king; some proved strong resisters.

Unhappily appearances more than confirmed the far-spread opinion that the Popes at Avignon were subservient. Philip IV of France had influenced considerably the election of his friend, Clement V. The ruthless tyrant began at once to bring the strongest pressure on the Pope to condemn the deceased Pope Boniface VIII, his strongest enemy, as a heretic. Clement yielded much in reversing the work of Boniface; but this must be said to his credit: he never yielded to the insistent demands that Boniface's memory be disgraced as a heretic. The Pope's saddest yielding was his giving in to Philip's demand that the Knights Templars be suppressed. The sinister ruler, envious of their independence and avaricious for their great wealth, began a mighty campaign of slander, accusing the order of heresy, idolatry and immorality. In the courts influenced by the royal power the Templars were condemned; and several of them were burned at the stake. Clement V finally suppressed the entire order, asserting that he was not condemning the order as such, but suppressing the order as a purely administrative act. Their possessions he declared were to go to the Knights of St. John. Philip IV seized about half for himself.

The world could not know the efforts of Clement V to save the memory of Pope Boniface. The world gave small credence to Philip's calumnious campaign. But what the world saw and what it remembered was that an order which had fought so long and so bravely in the Crusades was now disbanded by a French Pope under the pressure of a French king. It was a flaming incident in the early days at Avignon, and it would be remembered all during the period of the residence. It would give strong color to all the charges of subservience which kings or ecclesiastics in conflict with the Papacy would make in the next seventy years.

Most unfortunately this critical judgment came just when the Church could least afford to bear it. These were the days of rising nationalism, when men were becoming acutely aware, even jealously conscious that they were Englishmen, Frenchmen, Germans, Italians, Spaniards or Portuguese. It was then imperative that the Pope of the Catholic Church be above all national considerations. But large numbers of the men of the times nourished the idea that the papacy had become national too. Truly the Popes were in a false position. Their enemies would press it disastrously.

The conflict between Pope John XXII and Duke Louis of Bavaria over the succession to the imperial throne is the most striking instance. The Pope's position was reasonable enough; but the duke's claim was maintained adamantly. The worst elements in Europe, the most anarchic and the most rabid anti-papalists rallied to Louis with the expression: "You fight the Pope with the sword and we will fight him by the pen."

One of them, Marsiglio of Padua, a former rector of the University of Paris, produced a book *Defensor Pacis*, (Defender of Peace), which was the most revolutionary attack on the Papacy and the Church. It became one of the main foundations of the religious revolution of the sixteenth century. Here are some of the teachings. It maintained the unconditional sovereignty of the people and the absolute democracy of the Church. It held that the General Council, made up of clergymen and laymen, summoned and directed by the state, stood at the head of the Church Universal. It taught that the authority of the Pope was derived not from Christ but from the Council and from the state; that all members of the clergy by divine right have equal power; that the Council has legislative power, the Pope has only executive power; that the emperor, as the representative of the people, has the right of appointing, deposing and punishing priests, bishops and Popes; that the supreme disposition of all ecclesiastical property belongs exclusively to the state. Since the conflict of the German princes with the Pope was of long duration, such anti-papalism reached far and wide. The Pope of Rome would have had a herculean task to oppose it; the Pope at Avignon, under the shadow of the French kings, had an almost impossible task.

The ordinary activities of the Avignon Popes were continually and sharply criticized. Only one, Clement VI, was notorious for his extravagance. He was the one who completed the famous Papal Palace. Although a few of the others were too compliant and were guilty of nepotism, as a body they were humble, austere, upright, pious Popes. One, Bl. Urban VI, has been beatified. Yet the two facts best known today about Avignon are the extravagance of Clement VI and the Papal Palace. In their own day the Avignon Popes could do little that would not be complained about. They achieved much in making papal government efficient, yet they were roundly criticized for doing so. Their use of an undoubted right to impose taxes to meet expenses and also of their undoubted right of nomination to foreign sees and benefices brought floods of recriminations down upon their heads. There can be no question but that there were abuses in both these fields. Certainly some of the complaints were justified. But even the most justified complainant, to say nothing of the host of fault-finders, made their charges with the vision before them of the majority of French cardinals around a French Pope at Avignon.

The most disastrous feature of Avignon was its failure to bring about the sadly needed reform of the whole Christian body. Even before the fourteenth century began, materialism, worldliness and the rash pursuit of riches ruled countless hearts. Cynical secularism and selfish ambition, luxury and immorality appeared everywhere. Monarchs aimed to dominate religion that they might further enrich themselves and increase their power. In clerical ranks the number of the worldly ambitious and the shamefully immoral multiplied. So also increased the ecclesiastical sycophants who furthered their own fortunes by playing up to the ambitions of the kings.

The confusion was complicated by such horrible visitations as the Black Death, by the long wars such as the Hundred Years War in France, the revolts of the Lancastrians in England, the perpetual battlings in Germany, in Italy and elsewhere. But the supreme weakness came in the Popes. If they had been in Rome, they could have spoken freely and none could have ignored their impartial words. But they tried to speak from Avignon, and the evil ones shouted them down as mouthpieces of the French kings. It was all clearly a lie. But an immoral prelate or a greedy monarch would never boggle at a lie.

Who brought the Popes back to Rome? The heroic Pope of Avignon, Gregory XI, a holy visionary who prayed continuously for the event, St. Bridget of Sweden, and the greatest woman of the Middle Ages — St. Catherine of Siena. No one loved or revered her Holy Father more than did the glorious Dominican mystic. Perhaps it was because of her intense devotion that she had the courage to point out to the Pope that his place was not in the quiet fields of Avignon, but in the blood-red streets of Rome, with death, if God so willed. Gregory XI was a great enough soul to listen to and to follow his holy daughter, St. Catherine of Siena.

The
Great
Western
Schism

THE RESIDENCE AT Avignon had hardly ended when the most evil of its fruits appeared—the Great Western Schism. For thirty-five years this division split Catholicism into two parties, and for five more years into three. The confusions and weaknesses which reigned during those forty years whipped up one of the most disastrous storms that had ever assailed the barque of Peter. The Church's survival during the four catastrophic decades proves most strikingly Christ's perpetual presence in Peter's ship. In popular controversy, referring to the Western Schism, the question is often asked: "What about the time when there were three popes?" The answer is: "There never was a time when there were three popes: but there were three claimants, a lawful Pope and two anti-popes." The division during the Western Schism was not on the teaching of the Faith; all factions accepted the dogma of the supreme pontificate of the Bishop of Rome. The conflict came on the *historical* question: "Who is the pos-sessor of the pontificate of Rome; who is actually the Pope?" The nations of Christendom divided not into *sects* but into *obediences*.

The trouble started at the election of a successor to Gregory XI. The conclave consisted of the sixteen cardinals who were in Rome. There were only seven others, six at Avignon and one elsewhere in Italy. The seven, owing to their employments in Church affairs, were unable to come to Rome. Of the cardinals who were to participate in the election, eleven were French, four were Italian, and one was a Spaniard from Aragon. The conclave took place April 7 and 8, 1378, amid scenes of fearful violence. A huge turbulent crowd, made up of the city's mob augmented by thousands of peasants and brigands from the countryside, surrounded the Vatican palace where the cardinals were in session. The rabble repeatedly shouted, "A Roman Pope, or at least an Italian." All through the night they kept up their frightening chant, adding threats of bloody violence. In the morning they began smashing windows and attacking the doors with axes. Massacre became a possible eventuality; mob fury is capable of any atrocity.

The beleaguered cardinals, unable to agree upon one of their number, in the morning chose an Italian prelate, Bartolomeo Prignano, Archbishop of Bari. When a lull came in the turbulence they re-elected him. On the next day, April 9, when complete quiet had been restored, the cardinals announced to the Archbishop his election. Bartolomeo Prignano accepted and chose the name Urban VI. Then the cardinals robed him in the papal vestments and did homage to him as Pope. The electors of the conclave went further. They dispatched letters declaring the lawfulness of Urban VI's election; so they wrote to the cardinals still at Avignon, the king of France and the king of Aragon. And even further still, they sought for and accepted spiritual and temporal grants from Urban VI, which they could never have asked for if they were in doubt as to the validity of his papal power.

And yet six months had not passed when these cardinals, from the safety of Fondi in the kingdom of Naples, proclaimed to the world that Urban VI was not a true Pope, because their election of him had been invalidated by fear. Why did they change? They had made a mistaken estimation of Urban VI. He, whom they and everyone had considered a pious and retiring scholar, now turned out to be a most uncompromising, aggressive reformer, determined upon the most drastic remedies. They had also believed that Bartolomeo

ST. CATHERINE OF SIENA. The saint is pictured at Pope
Gregory XI's return to Rome from Avignon, that return
in which she had been so influential. *Benvenuto di Giovanni,
Hospital of Santa Maria della Scala, Siena.*

Prignano, from his long years of service at Avignon, had become almost French. Now they heard him emphatically declare that he would never bring back the residence at Avignon.

Urban VI, himself, incurred much blame by his violent extremes. He was most extravagant in his denunciations of worldly and immoral clerics. He harshly insulted cardinals in consistory with personal attacks. With rash imprudence he announced that he would create so many Italian cardinals that the French cardinals would never again count for anything. St. Catherine of Siena pleaded with him to moderate his course of action but in vain. Whether his wild words sprang from the long suppressed indignation of a good man, or from a mind unsettled by his unexpected elevation, in no case were the cardinals justified in their revolt. The rationalization of self justification can twist facts to strange conclusions. Their internal guilt must be left to God alone.

Christendom split rapidly into two camps. The Avignon claimants were accepted by France, Aragon, Castile, Scotland, Savoy and Cyprus. The Roman Popes were supported by most of the Italian states, England, Ireland, Portugal, Germany, Hungary, Poland, Sweden and Norway. The divisions were not hard and fast: many adherents of the Roman line were in the areas of the Avignon "Obedience"; and many proponents of the Avignon line were in the areas of the Roman "Obedience." Urban VI was lawfully elected. Since no power, ecclesiastical or lay, could depose a Pope, his three successors were legitimate. Only the third of these, Gregory XII is important; it was his resignation in 1416, that ended the terrible disaster.

The Western Schism throughout its forty years kept all Christendom plunged in frightful confusion. In previous history there had been twenty-seven anti-popes, but they were the creatures of tyrannical monarchs or disreputable factions. Their illegality was so evident and the durations of their schisms so brief that no well-informed person could be in doubt as to the true Pope. But this schism came from the very body that had the right to elect the Pope. People at a distance were at a loss to decide, since so many cardinals who had elected Urban VI went over to Clement VII. Persons of the highest sanctity took stands on either side. St. Catherine of Siena, the greatest woman of the Late Middle Ages, and St. Catherine of Sweden, an eye-witness of what had happened in Rome, supported Urban VI; while St. Vincent Ferrer, O.P., the eloquent missionary, and Bl. Peter of Luxemburg, highly reputed for his holiness, upheld Clement VII.

In many dioceses two bishops claimed the same bishopric; in many abbatial lands two abbots contested for the same monastery. In numerous churches divine services fell into neglect, with a consequent growth of lukewarmness in the religious devotion of the people. The papacy grew more and more subordinate to the civil rulers, as Popes or claimants, to secure the support of monarchs, conceded to them larger controls over ecclesiastical affairs. About reform, so sadly needed at the end of the Avignon Residence, the absence, for forty years of a strong papacy prevented any serious action; nay it multiplied immeasurably the past evils. The absence of a strong papacy also prevented effective opposition to three powerful heresies, antipapal Conciliarism, Wyclifism and Hussitism. In summary the Great Western Schism and the heretical movements accompanying it contributed more than anything else to the great apostasy of the sixteenth century.

How was the great schism solved? So universal had become the desire for reunion that when the University of Paris sought for programmes 20,000 replies were sent in. The best way was by resignation. But when first proposed it was frustrated by the failure of Gregory XII, of the Roman line, and Benedict XIII, of the Avignon line, to meet for a common discussion. Then was tried the decision of a general council. It was a dangerous remedy since it was based on the false theory of the superiority of a general council over the Pope; yet it was rather popular at the time. Several cardinals of both lines, disappointed at the failure of the resignation meeting, joined with a considerable number of bishops and theologians to call a general council at Pisa. It was not a true general council, for it lacked two essentials: the Pope had not called it, and the Pope (or his legate) did not preside over it. Nevertheless, when neither Gregory XII nor Benedict XIII appeared, the pseudo-council proceeded to depose both (something they could never do to the one who was truly Pope). The Pisan assembly then attempted to elect a Pope, Alexander V. The hope of the Pisan gathering that they had solved the schism proved vain, because only a small party accepted Alexander V. The over-all result was only the setting up of a third claimant. The confusion became increasingly worse. The Pisan claimant died after a year, and the Pisan party elected John XXIII.

Five years were to intervene before the final solution. Then the Emperor Sigismund forced John XXIII to call a general council at Constance and also forced him to resign. John XXIII had never been a true Pope, but his resignation cleared the boards of the Pisan claimant. Gregory XII, the real Pope, sent his agent to the council with the offer that if the bishops at Constance recognized him as Pope, he would immediately call them into existence as a general council and he would immediately resign his papacy. The bishops at Constance accepted the proposal and then through his agent, Gregory XII abdicated, in 1415. Benedict XIII had never been a Pope, and as he had already lost his following, his subsequent actions had no effect. In 1417 then, a conclave held at Constance elected Cardinal Odo Colonna as Pope. He took the name Martin V. As he was universally acknowledged, the Great Western Schism came to an end.

The harm of forty years of total weakness and universal confusion produced frightful harvests: Europe accustomed to a divided Christianity, far-spreading false ideas of the papal power, unchecked rise of heresies, frustration of the cause of reform, vaster control of Church affairs by secular rulers. Had Catholicism been merely of human origin and human guardianship, it never could have survived the forty years of complete division. Through all the dark hours of this terrible storm it survived because Christ was always in Peter's barque.

Tinder
for the
Reformation

AMONG THE MOST potent causes of the Religious Revolution of the 16th century were the heresies of the two preceding centuries. In those two hundred years many of the doctrines of the later heretics were anticipated, many of the forces of religious revolt were originated. Among the attacks on Catholic Faith, those particularly powerful and of ominous significance were anti-papalism, Wyclifism and Hussitism. All developed in the widespread confusion that resulted from the weakness of Avignon, the anarchy of the Western Schism, the interminable wars and the disasters of terrible pestilences.

Anti-papalism was the longest enduring of these attacks. Among its first proponents were the Fraticelli, a small group of extremists in the Franciscans, who rejected papal mitigation of the rule of St. Francis, maintaining that such action was beyond the power of any Pope. They were supported by Louis of Bavaria in his conflict with John XXII. Far more serious was the blow delivered against papal power by another ally of Louis, Marsiglio of Padua in his *Defensor Pacis*. There he proclaimed the superiority of the state over the Church in all matters and sought to reduce the Pope to a mere cipher, a head of religion who was deposable by the emperor or the state. Marsiglio's wild theories, gaining wide circulation during the long papal-imperial struggle, sowed many of the seeds that fructified in the future religious revolution.

The peak of anti-papalism came at the end of the Western Schism. As the solution by resignation of the claimants began to fail, settlement by a general council attracted a wide following. One might well note here the three essential conditions for a general council: (1) it must be called by a Pope; (2) it must be presided over by a Pope or by his legate; (3) its dogmatic decrees have value when they are accepted by the Pope and published by the Pope and the general council together. One might also note that a lawful Pope cannot be deposed; only by his own free resignation can he cease to be Pope. The advocates of the conciliar solution overlooked the essential considerations. Before long a large number of them were maintaining that a general council was superior to a Pope, could amend or reject his dogmatic teachings, and finally could depose a Pope. Such a theory was called the Supremacy of a General Council over the Pope. Many worthy people, desperate because of the continuance of the schisms, grasped at this plausible solution. Further, since it was the days of the growth of parliamentary government in civil affairs, some sought the establishment of parliamentary government in religious affairs. Such proponents of conciliar superiority forgot that our Lord had founded the government of His Church on St. Peter, the holder of the keys. Christ could not be a parliamentary president whose office and works would be regulated by a majority vote; neither could His vicar.

Acting upon the conciliar theory, a general pseudo-council convened at Pisa and deposed the two claimants of the papacy. Its only result was the production of a third claimant. Pisa was not a general council; it was neither called nor presided over by a Pope. Five years later another attempt to assemble a general council took place at Constance. In the fourteenth session (1415) Gregory XII, the true Pope, recognized Constance as a general council. Seemingly the conciliar theory had triumphed. Its proponents had dominated the earlier session; in the fifth they had proclaimed the superiority of every general council over every Pope. Later the council ordered the holding of a general council within five years, to be followed by another council after seven years, and after that a council at intervals of every ten years.

But the conciliar theory, with its substitution of an oligarchy of bishops as rulers of the Church instead of the Pope, failed within three decades. Its earlier decrees proclaiming the superiority of a general council were valueless; they were enacted before Constance became a genuine general council, by the recognition of Gregory XII. Its program of regularly held councils also failed. The first had to be adjourned for lack of participants. The second, that of Basle, became the prey of quarrels and ended as a schismatical assembly, which elected an anti-pope who received but the scantiest support; the orthodox part was transferred by Pope Eugene IV to Ferrara and then to Florence; it is known as the Council of Ferrara-Florence. This council witnessed the triumph of the Pope's supremacy over this superiority of a general council. The conciliar movement was dead, though its theories still influenced many and contributed to the universal attack on the papacy by revolutionaries of the next century.

In the last half of the fourteenth century, John Wyclif (1320-1384), launched his hostile attack on the Church. It was medieval England's only heresy. Wyclif has been considered by many as one of the chief progenitors of the Reformation. In the Luther-Memorial at Worms, a life-sized statue of him sits at the foot of the column which supports the principal statue, that of Martin Luther. Wyclif did anticipate many doctrines of the Protestants. He held the Bible to be the sole rule of faith. He rejected the papacy, the hierarchy and the priesthood. He denied the sacraments, confession, the Mass and especially Transubstantiation. However he did not teach Luther and Calvin's main doctrine that man had not a free will and that his good works were inefficacious. On the other hand, the Reformers did not teach one of Wyclif's principal doctrines, that of Dominion (that mortal sin destroyed the rights to rule and to hold property).

What influence had Wyclif on the English Revolution? Practically very little. He left a determined body of followers, known as the Lollards. They pushed his doctrines to extremes he had not contemplated; stirred up by agitators, the *poor priests* (most of whom were not priests), the Lollards became involved in agrarian uprisings. Their revolts were finally suppressed about 1420. By 1430, Lollardy disappeared; it had never attracted even any considerable minority of Englishmen. The few Lollards who managed to exist secretly in the sixteenth century had no influence on the revolt of Henry VIII. Indeed this monarch, after his separation from Rome, put Lollards to death as heretics. The only direct influence in England of Wyclif and his followers was to multiply the oppressive confusions of the times.

There was one place in Europe where Wyclif's heresy obtained a numerous and powerful following. It was Bohemia. At the end of the fourteenth century close relations with England had developed and in their course Wyclif's doctrines were brought to Prague. They were adopted by a formidable party, headed by John Hus, the rector of Prague University. Hus had established a reputation as an eloquent advocate of reform; but he was intemperate in his preachings and fanatical in his proposals. Emile de Bonnechose, a Protestant admirer, admits that "in his language one recognizes the frenzy of a sectary rather than the wisdom of an apostle." A numerous and powerful following made him a national hero, especially after his death. He so enlarged upon Wyclif's teachings that his movement must be called the Hussite Heresy. He was condemned by the Council of Constance and executed as a heretic in 1415. The Hussite Wars which followed were only terminated in 1485. The first half were crusades to suppress the heresy. Unfortunately, they became also German and Czech nationalist struggles. The second half were internal battlings between Hussite factions. The seventy years of the Hussite heresy kept alive his heretical ideas, and spread them across the Bohemian border. In the adjacent regions of Saxony in 1483, Martin Luther was born.

Luther more than once acknowledged the influence of Hus' doctrines on his mind and conduct. Hus' anticipations are clearly evident: he taught that Faith alone, not good works, is the means of salvation; he denied the primacy of St. Peter and of the Pope; he attacked violently bishops, priests, monks and especially mendicant friars; he rejected all doctrinal authority in regard to the Holy Scriptures and the law of Christ; he proclaimed the supremacy of private judgment; he advocated the free interpretation of the Bible by anyone; he insisted, as a doctrinal necessity, on communion under both kinds; he denied Transubstantiation; he protested against auricular confession; he attacked the veneration of relics; and he repudiated the existence of purgatory. Certainly John Hus was the immediate precursor of Luther and the Religious Revolution of the sixteenth century. So, but more remotely, was John Wyclif. When Cranmer and the continental heretics got control of the English revolution, Wyclif's teachings, at least the fruition of them, arrived back in England.

Moral Disasters

OF THE FIERCE gales lashing the barque of Peter in the late medieval times scarcely any were more disastrous than the deterioration of morals. Vices of unchastity, avarice and pride penetrated far and wide among the clergy, secular and religious, of lowly rank or of high estate. The same vices infected large areas of the laity. The terrible evils led many to account immorality as the foremost cause of the Religious Revolution, the "Reformation." The conclusion is incorrect; the fundamental cause was the heresies developing during the fourteenth and fifteenth centuries. Yet it must be admitted that these monstrous evils were the most effective means of gaining adherents for the revolutionaries.

The first causes of the deterioration arose out of the dolorous times. Frequent and interminable wars — national, civil, or against the Turks — engendered a bitter heritage of violence and passion. The frightful epidemics, of which the Black Death was but one of six, left vast gaps in the clergy. To fill the depleted ranks there were often only scantily educated and poorly disciplined candidates for the priesthood. The Residence at Avignon and the Western Schism not only begot overwhelming confusion, but hampered and eventually stopped the desperately needed reforms of conditions spawned by secularism and materialism. Heresies, whether of the Lollards, the Hussites or the Conciliarists, unsettled men's minds in questions of morals as well as of faith. Papal reform plans were negatived by pressing political problems, or by the desperate urgencies of defense against the Turks. In the mounting anarchy of these last two centuries moral values were bound to be obscured and moral practices shattered.

But there were far more sinister forces rising up against Catholicism. These were the evil writings and the vile lives of pagan humanists in the Renaissance Movement. An explanation of terms is needed. The Renaissance was a cultural movement enthusiastically accepted by all of Europe in the fourteenth and fifteenth centuries. Its goal was the rebirth of the Classical Civilization of ancient Greece and Rome. The revival was to be complete, and in all areas: literature, art, law, politics, philosophy and life itself (hence morality). Now in the Greco-Roman world there was much that was good and noble; but there was much that was evil and shameful. Among the proponents of the Renaissance very shortly emerged two schools or trends: one, those who imitated the good or, in a Christian spirit, the indifferent; the other, those who adopted the evil as well as the good and the indifferent, the last two frequently in an evil spirit. The first group was called Christian Humanists; the second group was called Pagan Humanists. The word "Humanist" was used because of the stress both groups placed on the *human* both in literature and in philosophy. So the schools were known in Italy, where the Renaissance originated, and in most of the rest of Europe. In the German lands the Christian party was called the Elder Humanists, while the pagan party was called the Younger Humanists, or the Poets. This chapter must deal exclusively with the Pagan Humanists. However it is only fitting that a brief remembrance be made here of the many Christian Humanists and their glorious achievements for God and His Church.

The Pagan Humanists must be considered the chief instigators of the collapse of morals. First of all they corrupted themselves by steeping themselves in the vilest writings of the pagans. Then they adopted the evil maxims of the pagans. Finally they led their own lives in close imitation of the licentious careers of the ancients. Worse than all this they disseminated their corruption through the literate public, especially the youthful students. The means they employed were their own evil writings and their own evil lives — writings and lives that matched the vilest books and deeds of the ancient libertines. The usual horrible harvest which bad literature and bad example produces in men's souls followed; the contaminated appeared in all walks of life: the litterateurs, the scholars, the merchants, the princes and the clergy.

How did the Pagan Humanists rationalize their immoralities? To begin with, they were poor philosophers. They were sceptical about the power of reasoning, and they could not abide the strongly thought out medieval theology and philosophy. The medieval system promoted a program of moral restraint that was a most effective barrier to their viciousness; hence they waged unrelenting war against medieval theology and philosophy. The neo-pagans set up man as the final goal of all human endeavor. Holding that man was essentially good of himself — without reference to God — they argued that man, to be perfect, must be free to indulge his every impulse, his every desire. They maintained that all which was possible to him was lawful for him. In their system sin had no meaning. It was but to be expected that such unrestrained license spawned scepticism in faith and a wholesale flouting in word and deed of Christian morality. Nor is it surprising that Epicureanism and Pantheism, with all their horrible consequences, soon made their reappearances. One cannot but notice the parallels with modern decadence.

The propagandists of the Pagan Renaissance, some to discredit the Christian ideals of moral restraint, some to derogate the Christian Faith itself, employed the vilest weapons: obscene writings, caricatures, satires and absolute lies. They attacked sinful clerics not to excoriate them but rather to ridicule holy monks for their "folly" in following the Christian rules for religious life. Poggio made the sins of priests and monks the butt of his filthy *Facetiae* to stir up prejudice and hatred against the whole class. The neo-pagan writers made a literary glorification of vice; there was scarcely one whose works were free from dirt; their own vices exemplified their vile pages. Needless to say, sexual sins were not the only vices stressed by the Pagan Humanists. They glorified the ancient pagan exemplars of selfish pride, earthly fame, greedy accumulation of riches and personal power, unfaithfulness and violence in public life, materialistic motivation.

What has so far been described were the evil deeds of the Pagan Humanists of Italy, where the Renaissance originated and where it reached its highest glories and sank to its lowest depths. In the German lands the Younger Humanists proved themselves to be sinister rivals. The great majority of them produced wanton attacks upon the Holy See, the faithful in religious orders, the doctrines and practices of the Catholic Faith. One of the most infamous of their works was the *Epistolae obscurorum virorum* (Letters of Obscure Men), a book replete with slander, impiety and blasphemy. They ridiculed and rejected the whole learning of the Middle Ages. They displayed a disgusting pagan immorality in their writings. These Poets, to give them their other name, in their school work read the most profligate pagan poetry with their young students and introduced in universities, such as Erfurt, a reign of unrestrained license. All this degradation came on the very eve of the Religious Revolution; the Younger Humanists were vigorous protagonists of that Revolution.

In summary, who can measure the effects of this frightfulness of evil writings and licentious lives? The faith and morals of all who could read were jeopardized. Especially endangered were the men of letters, the younger intellectuals, the princes and the priests, for these comprised the larger sectors of the reading public. One of the earliest indications of the harm to be expected was the creation of the fashion or craze for reading lewd books; another was the all-too-liberal toleration of notorious evil personages. The state absolutism favored by the revival of the Roman Law and of the Roman political practices promoted a pagan materialism and secularism among rulers and politicians. Here were found the pretexts for arbitrary interference in church affairs. Later there would be found the justifications for royal pronunciamentos about the "Reform of head and members," often only excuses for the secularization of ecclesiastical authority. Machiavelli's *Prince* is the mirror of the Pagan Renaissance's politician: no morality, no justice, no scruples. Among the new capitalist bourgeoisie there were many who, resentful of a morality that lessened their opportunities for high profits, gave strong support to the attacks upon the Church which formulated that morality.

The most deleterious effects were to be found among the clergy. In the higher ranks there was an alarming increase of worldly ecclesiastics. Such were prelates who were avid for riches and power, who flaunted earthly magnificence, and practiced nepotism in the advancement of their kindred. They were managers of unscrupulous civil policies and scandalous appointers of the unworthy clerical officials. Some did not draw back from simony; others lived disgraceful, immoral lives. Contemporaries had an expression, "Renaissance Prelates," for the worldly or recreant ecclesiastics. In the lower ranks there was a frightening increase of priests or monks contaminated by lewd reading and licentious morals, by cynical scepticism and heretical doctrines. Perhaps a brief summary of the sad conditions might be this: the evildoers, lay or clerical, were the wretched souls corrupted by the vile writings and the immoral lives of the Pagan Humanists.

Time of Contrasts

THE PRECEDING CHAPTER treated moral disasters in the upper classes of the clergy and the laity. The account is a shocking one, and justly so. But one must be mindful of exaggerators and calumniators. In the scenes where the delinquents acted their parts, there appeared also holy and noble prelates, princes and litterateurs. It is well to remember that evil is loud, vulgar and sensational, and that good is humble and retiring — often escaping the notice of the superficial. Let it also be recognized that reformers in their fiery zeal are often swept into exaggerations. As for the defamers, as was noted in the last chapter, their diatribes were aimed at the worthy prelates, priests and monks, since their lives exemplified the Christian morality which the calumniators strove to destroy.

The unfortunate pontificate of Alexander VI is mentioned everywhere; but the names of the worthy Popes of his century are known to scarcely anyone. In the last years of the fifteenth century the majority of the College of Cardinals were worldly prelates ("worldly" does not necessarily imply, "immoral," though some lived disgracefully). Yet at that very time a significant minority were saintly and zealous ecclesiastics. Doctor von Pastor lists about a dozen holy and devoted princes of the Church. The College of Cardinals was not the numerous body of today. If at times national episcopates were disgraced by worldly, avaricious, or evil-living bishops, often apathetic and sometimes ignorant, these were the nominees of kings or the younger sons of princes. The same hierarchies were blessed by many saintly bishops, true heirs of the apostles. Gian Matteo Giverti so reformed his diocese of Verona that it was chosen as the model diocese by the reforming Council of Trent. The martyred St. John Fisher was widely renowned for his zealous government of the diocese of Rochester.

The lower clergy, especially the rural priesthood, were made the butt of the most lurid charges; they were depicted as grossly immoral and ignorant, of being disgustingly lazy and completely devoid of zeal. Unfortunately too many instances could be cited to bolster the accusations of widespread evils. But the charges must be examined in their own circumstances. The tumultuous and continual wars, the frightfulness of vast epidemics, the utter confusion of contemporary heresies, all these bore down heavily upon the simple priests. Most of the rural clergy lived close to indigence. In some places the priests were too numerous; there were instances where five priests lived on one benefice which hardly guaranteed a frugal existence to a single priest. Many priests could find little employment. An idle brain can be the devil's workshop for a cleric as well as for a layman. The education and the ascetical training of sacerdotal candidates, owing to contemporary evils, left very much to be desired. Finally the rural priests, almost all of peasant stock, were affected by the social conditions and the intellectual shortcomings of their fellow peasants. Yet the Catholic reformers of their times, often their sharpest critics, found much good in these simple priests, not only morally but even intellectually. The worthy Geilar von Kaysersberg, perhaps the most stringent of the critics, paid a most glowing tribute to the numerous saintly and learned priests to be found in the three bishoprics of the Rhine. A modern historian has declared that many, perhaps the majority, of the clergy faithfully discharged their duties.

No group was more venomously assailed than the religious: the monks, the friars and the nuns. The pagan humanists, in their campaign against Christian morality, attacked them because they were the exemplars of the Christian ideals.

The religious revolutionists denounced them because their lives were based on the Catholic doctrines of good works and of the freedom of the will. Avaricious princes abetted both nefarious campaigns because they coveted the monastic lands and properties. No one will gainsay the facts of evils committed by numerous religious. But some observations are justified. Many monasteries were unable to recover the losses in religious ideals suffered during the catastrophes of the Black Death and similar plagues. Many in the friar orders lost both vigor and integrity in the turmoils of wars and in the confusions of heresies. Other members of these mendicant orders alienated the faithful laity by their venality and their rapacity. The nefarious system of *abbots-in-commendam* by which kings conferred the abbatial title and the revenues of monasteries on their royal favorites (very often not monks at all) robbed zealous priors, who were the acting superiors, of all authority. The good reputation of all religious suffered grievously in the calumnious campaigns against monastic life.

Yet the fifteenth century witnessed in Italy and elsewhere the eloquent preachings of reforming friars, Franciscans, Dominicans, Servites and Augustinians. Late in that century, several decades before the Religious Revolution, there began to appear reformed groups among the monks and friars; such were the Benedictine Congregation of St. Justina, the Benedictine Congregation of Bursfeld, and the Reformed Congregation of the Canons Regular of Windesheim. The martyrdoms of the English Carthusians and of the three mitered abbots of Glastonbury, Reading and Colchester evidenced the value of the monastic revivals. The reform of the friars was similarly witnessed by the martyrdoms of the Franciscans in England and in the Low Countries.

Convents of nuns were often contemptuously dismissed as homes for the unmarried daughters of nobles. True, there were at the time nuns who never had real vocations; many of them welcomed the invitation of the revolutionists to flee their convents. One such was Katherine von Bora, who later became the wife of Martin Luther. Yet the most striking answer to the mean and vile insults against the nuns was the loyalty to the old Faith of the Poor Clares of Nuremberg, under the heroic leadership of their noble abbess, Caritas Pirkheimer. Their faithfulness was not singular among the German nuns. The silent loyalty of the dispossessed nuns of England and Ireland could only have sprung from holiness of life. It was during this fifteenth century that Italy was blessed with St. Frances of Rome, foundress of the Oblates of Tor'Specchi and with St. Angela Merici, foundress of the Ursuline Nuns.

One of the saddest of the moral disasters was the ignorance, superstition, immorality and indifference of large areas of the common people. It is listed among the chief causes of the Religious Revolution. A frightening picture has been painted in darkest colors of conditions among the peasants and the town laborers. A very large part were illiterate. They were borne down by wars, plagues and oppression. They were, above all others, confused by the fanatical preachers of heresies. They were induced to immoral indulgence by the bad example of concubinate priests. Many lapsed into indifference when they received neither guidance nor spiritual comfort from ignorant and lazy pastors. They were hopelessly superstitious; they exaggerated the cult of the saints almost to idolatry; and they were completely swept into the witchcraft delusion.

Such was the appalling picture the apologists of the Religious Revolution painted. It was certainly effective, because so many of the harrowing details were undeniable. But it was a partisan cartoon after all, emphasizing the somber evils, disregarding the bright excellences. Doctor von Pastor gave a more balanced account of the ordinary people in Renaissance Italy. He opened the Fifth Volume (English translation) with two long chapters: the first on the good aspects, the second on the base features. In the first chapter he describes with a wealth of facts the worthy lives of the everyday people: their purity of family life, their constant self-sacrifice, their genuine piety in their devotional life, their treasury of books of solid spirituality, their warm-hearted solicitude for the unfortunate, their numerous charitable institutions and confraternities, their educational endeavors for the poor.

A similar noble Christianity could be found in all parts of Europe. In Germany religious instructions were not omitted, good works were not neglected and there was a

ST. JOAN OF ARC. *Jean A. Ingres, the Louvre, Paris.*

healthy detestation of evil priests. The new printing presses brought out, from 1479 to 1500, twenty-four German editions of the Bible, besides innumerable devotional books and leaflets, confessional manuals and catechisms. Thomas à Kempis' *Imitation of Christ,* translated into various languages, passed through fifty-nine editions before 1500.

How could it have been otherwise when one considers the religious art of the period? The Italians cherished Giotto, the Sienese School and the beloved Fra Angelico. The Germans and the Flemings gazed on van Eycks' "The Worship of the Lamb," Memling's "The Pilgrimage of St. Ursula" and the many paintings of the anonymous masters. The French and the Spaniards had numerous anonymous masters too. These were the times when the mystery plays and the morality plays reached their height of popularity in England, France, Germany and Italy. In Italy the religious drama culminated in the Roman Passion Play, acted in 1490, on the greatest religious stage, the Colosseum of the martyrs. In no field was genuine piety more evident than at the pilgrimage shrines. True, there were abuses, but the overall practices were reasonable and sincere. Thus, great throngs celebrated the Jubilees of 1450, 1471 and 1500 at Rome. Of the great shrines one can only cite here a few as typical: Santiago de Compostella, Canterbury, Einsiedeln, Le Puy and Ste. Anne d'Auray. But at these and a hundred other shrines the prayers and hymns of the throngs afforded unmistakable evidence of their spirit of faith, devotion and loyalty to the Church. Remember that the revolutionists stressed the abuses as an attack on the doctrine of good works. Remember also that the kings and princes forced the new teachings upon the common people by the swords of their soldiery.

Recurrent Attacks Upon the Faith

OF ALL CAUSES of the Reformation the fundamental one was the attack upon the Faith, persisting all through the Late Middle Ages. Scandalous abuses were sensational, but heretical movements were basic. In its last analysis the great catastrophe was a gigantic struggle between two mutually exclusive systems: traditional Christianity based upon the Church's authority, and a new type of religion created by individual interpretation of the Bible. The term "Reformation," is an inaccurate usage; the correct designation is "Religious Revolution," for it was a revolt against the dogmatic teachings of the Church which the "Reformers" launched. And the way for the revolts of Luther, Zwingli and Calvin had been prepared by the heresies of Wyclif in the fourteenth and of Hus in the fifteenth century. Similarly the way for Henry VIII's Royal Supremacy and for the popedoms of the North German princes had been marked out by the anti-papalist theorists of those two centuries.

The constant attacks on the papacy up to this period aimed at the domination of the Popes by kings or civil factions. The new anti-papalist theorists sought to weaken, some even to destroy, the Pope's primacy of government and of teaching. In the sixteenth century, all the leaders of the Religious Revolution, no matter how much they differed in doctrines, were united on one point: the denial of the Pope's religious and spiritual primacy. Each one of them strove mightily to abolish the primacy entirely.

The new anti-papalism became apparent in the struggle between Louis of Bavaria and Pope John XXII.

The *Defensor Pacis*, written by one of Louis' supporters, Marsiglio of Padua, and based on a crude pagan conception of the State, was actually an heretical assault on the Church's constitution. It influenced the ideas of Wyclif and Hus; and through radical factions of the Hussites it was carried down to the reformers. Just at the dawning of the Religious Revolution, the first printed edition appeared in 1517. It was much sought for and eagerly read. One of the first moves of Thomas Cromwell, Henry VIII's chief agent in his campaign for the royal supremacy, was the publication of an English edition in 1535.

During the Western Schism the papal primacy suffered much from the advocates of the Conciliar Theory, some of whom were very devout Catholics. According to this theory a general council was superior to a Pope, it could amend or revoke any of the Pope's decrees, whatsoever, and it could depose a Pope. Such proposals would have reduced the holder of the keys to a mere honorary figurehead. Yet the theory obtained a great following in the theological schools, especially at Paris, whose theological faculty enjoyed universal prestige. It also received wide support from civil rulers, from the clergy and the laity. Its adherents summoned the Council of Pisa and dominated much of the Councils of Constance and Basle. But the theory was a malign panacea for the evils of the Schism. It was subversive to the essential organization of the Church by which Christ gave the offices of governing and teaching to the apostles and their successors, the bishops, with a definite superiority to Peter and his successors, the Popes, as Christ's vicars on earth. Some of the proponents of the theory would have fashioned the Church into an oligarchy, or even a democracy where canon lawyers, doctors of theology, or even laymen would shape the rule and teaching of the Church. Such was not the Church Christ had founded.

The Conciliar Theory reached its zenith when Constance passed its anti-papal decrees. Since this action was taken before the council became legitimate, the decrees were valueless. The Conciliar Movement began to decline; Basle ended in a fiasco, and Ferrara-Florence (1431-1449) brought about its permanent defeat. The theory had damaged men's loyalty to the Holy See during this confused period. Its ideas did not wholly disappear. They were strongly maintained by Gallican ecclesiastics in France and by like-minded clerics elsewhere. But definitely Peter's successor was now master of the barque as it sailed into the gathering hurricane of the Protestant Revolution.

The Religious Revolution of the Sixteenth Century

THE MOST DISASTROUS tempest that ever lashed the barque of Peter was the Religious Revolution of the 16th century. Its violence raged calamitously for a century and a quarter (1517-1648), depriving the Church of at least a third of the people of Europe west of Russia. During two centuries more it continually darkened the skies with ominous clouds which on occasions poured down frightful storms on Peter's craft.

This revolution has been termed "The Reformation." But the expression is incorrect. The ultimate aim of its proponents was the destruction of the Catholic Church. They used the sad, moral lapses in the contemporary Church to launch attacks on the very foundations of Catholicism. For them, the papal abuses which they aimed to liquidate were the institution of the papacy itself, especially the primacy of the Pope, the hierarchy of bishops, the distinct priesthood with its function of offering the Sacrifice of the Mass, general councils and the magisterium of the Catholic Church (its divinely appointed office to teach faith and morals). When the Reformers spoke of corruption of the Gospel of Christ, they meant the doctrine of the necessity of good works for salvation; the seven sacraments (some accepted a few sacraments; others denied all of the seven); the Sacrifice of the

Mass; Transubstantiation—the complete and permanent change of the bread and wine into the body, blood, soul and divinity of Jesus Christ; the honoring and invocation of the Blessed Virgin Mary, the Mother of God; the veneration and invocation of the saints, the existence of purgatory and efficacy of prayers for the Holy Souls in purgatory. The new preachers rejected any divinely appointed, infallible interpreter of the Sacred Scriptures (the Catholic Church); they insisted, on the contrary, that each person had the right of private interpretation of the meaning of the Bible. They maintained that the Holy Writ was the sole source of faith, repudiating entirely the Tradition of the Church as a source of faith. The Reformers would do away with the old Catholic Church and substitute new systems based upon their own revolutionary ideas. Harnack, undoubtedly the foremost of modern Protestant theologian-historians, says: "In Luther's Reformation the old dogmatic Christianity was discarded and a new evangelical view substituted for it." And again Harnack says: "The formal authorities of dogma were swept away; thereby dogma itself, i.e., the inviolable system of doctrine established by the Holy Spirit, was abolished.... The history of dogma, which had its very beginning in the age of the Apologists, (second century), nay, of the Apostolic Fathers, was brought to an end." Clearly the movement was not a reform of contemporary moral laxities but a fundamental revolution in religious systems. Common usage for four centuries, however, has sanctioned the employment of the term Reformation as a general expression describing the movement in all its phases.

The Reformation was started when Martin Luther posted his ninety-five theses on the door of the castle-church of Wittenberg, Electoral Saxony, on the eve of All Saints' Day, 1517. Martin Luther was an Augustinian friar and a professor of theology at the University of Wittenberg. The castle-church served as the university church. Such a posting of theses was routine in university towns; the proponent listed a number of propositions which he offered to defend against any objectors who might seek to deny them or to point out how they would have to be modified. It was a method of probing for truth by academic disputation. The occasion of Luther's theses was the preaching of the indulgence of Pope Leo X, by which funds were to be raised for the building of St. Peter's Basilica in Rome. An indulgence by itself is truly a holy and pious thing, an exercise of the power of the keys; it is the remission of the temporal punishment due to sin in reward for the performance of a good work. The donation of money for the building of churches certainly was a good deed. But indulgences, owing to grave abuses connected with their promotion, especially where donations of money were concerned, had incurred an evil reputation. Furthermore, indulgences are dependent on the performance of good works; now good works, as a part of the process of obtaining salvation, were greatly disfavored by Luther. Some of the ninety-five theses were directed against real abuses in the matter of indulgences; but others were inimical to the whole penitential system of the Church, to the power of the keys, and to the very roots of ecclesiastical authority.

For some time before the controversy over indulgences, Luther had been developing a theory of salvation which from the standpoint of Catholic dogma was heretical. The Church holds two requisites for salvation: God's grace and man's co-operation with God's grace. God's grace is absolutely essential; man by himself is incapable of achieving salvation. But since God has endowed man with a free will, God has made the efficacy of His grace dependent on man's voluntary co-operation with it. This co-operation man gives by performing good works: prayer, penance, virtuous deeds and the positive avoidance of sin. Luther as a young priest had become overwhelmed by two concepts: first, God, the just Judge and awesome punisher of sinners; second, the total corruption of man's nature in consequence of original sin. According to the second concept, man can do no good; indeed every act, because of the corruption of his nature, is a sin. As for salvation, Luther maintained that God chooses some souls for the happiness of heaven; the others He condemns to hell. Man has no part in the choice; he has no free will, hence he can merit nothing. The apparent good deeds of the condemned are of no avail. The Church rejects the idea of total corruption of human nature.

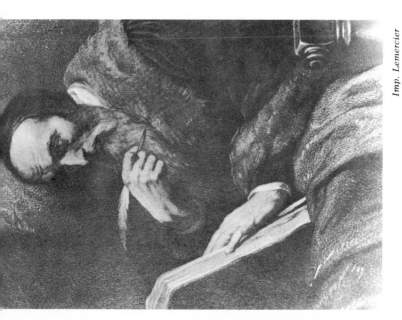

JOHN CALVIN. *Ary Scheffer, Paris.*

MARTIN LUTHER. Portrait by Lucas Cranach. *Uffizi Gallery, Florence.*

Luther was tortured by the fear that he was among the reprobate. He multiplied his prayers and pious practices. But he got no relief, for he would not accept the rational explanations that were offered to him. He would not be at peace unless he had a feeling, an emotional consciousness, that he was of the elect. It is a teaching of the Church that no one can be certain in this life of salvation, unless it has been revealed to him; and it has been revealed only to a few very holy saints. One solution finally satisfied Luther; he claimed that it was revealed to him. It was that God imputes Christ's merits to the man whom He chooses to save — man's nature remains sinful but Christ's merits cover and hide the sinfulness as by a cloak (the metaphor is Luther's). Since man himself, having no free will, can do nothing in the process of salvation, any good works of his are useless. Luther put it strikingly, "Good works are of no avail." What is left for man? Let him have faith (that is, confidence or trust) that he is chosen for salvation. Luther puts this strikingly too, "Salvation is by faith alone." Luther called for confidence in God the Savior. He did not propose salvation as a reward for the good act of confidence; for with Luther good acts were of no avail.

Revolutionary ideas about good works, free will and subjective faith were not new with Luther. During his four years as a professor of theology at Wittenberg he had been developing such ideas, as his lecture notes on two epistles of St. Paul, "To the Romans" and "To the Galatians," reveal. In a disputation (September, 1516), he had one of his students defend theses along such lines. Again in a disputation (September, 1517), he had another student uphold similar views. Luther himself for a year or more in his office of University Preacher advanced his propositions during his sermons on the Ten Commandments and on the Our Father. In 1516, he began to teach his doctrine on faith in Christ's Redemption without regard to good works. Certainly for a year before the eve of All Saints, 1517, Luther was teaching doctrines which, from a Catholic viewpoint, were heretical. In the ninety-five theses he denied the Power of the Keys.

Luther had now become the outstanding figure in Germany. Many rallied to him, believing him to be the long-hoped-for leader of the Reform. Others gave support from mixed motives: nationalistic and absolutistic princes, timorous bishops or clerics with confused ideas of papal power, large sections of the common people stirred by Luther's great eloquence, younger humanists enthusiastic for a monk who would assail the Pope. Very few at first perceived the fundamental religious revolution. The war of theses and counter-theses heaped confusion on confusion. The Pope's efforts to bring Luther to reconciliation or to trial were frustrated by the protection offered to Luther by the Elector Duke, John Frederick of Saxony.

The air was cleared by the Disputation of Leipsic held in the summer of 1519. Luther who was moving back and forth between defiant attacks and promises of submission to papal or conciliar decision, repeatedly sought a public debate on his ideas. He was granted one at Leipsic. His opponent, Johann Eck, vice-chancellor of Ingoldstadt University, pressed Luther on his doctrine of good works and on what course he would take if he could get no favorable decision either from present or future Popes or from a general council. Luther in answer rejected the epistle of St. James (which stresses good works), the primacy of the Popes and the infallibility of general councils. By these denials Martin Luther was openly repudiating the *magisterium* of the Church — that is, the Church's office and power to teach infallibly. No one could make such an open denial and remain a Catholic. Many who sincerely desired reform withdrew their support from Luther, recognizing that his movement was a revolt against revealed truth and divinely founded institutions. Luther now proclaimed the Pope as antichrist and himself as a true evangelist, commissioned by an immediate revelation of God to preach the new gospel as the only means of salvation. Shortly he followed with a rejection of Catholic doctrines on the sacraments, the sacrifice of the Mass, the hierarchy and the priesthood. Further he declared Christianity to be an invisible church with a universal priesthood governed by evangelical liberty — all heretical according to the teachings of the Catholic Church.

Wittenburg
and After

AFTER REPEATED EFFORTS to bring Luther to reconciliation, Pope Leo X felt obliged on June 15, 1520, to publish a bull condemning Luther's teachings, citing forty-one of them as heretical. Sixty days were given him to accept the decision and sixty more to assure the Pope that he had done so. Luther replied with a gesture of open defiance. He attended a riotous celebration at Wittenberg on December 10, and witnessed the casting of the papal bull and a copy of canon law into a bonfire. On January 3, 1521, Leo X issued a second bull definitively excommunicating Luther.

Even before this excommunication, Luther had risen in permanent revolt against the Catholic Church. During 1520, he brought out three clearly heretical pamphlets: *An Appeal to the Christian Nobles of Germany, The Babylonian Captivity of the Church,* and *The Freedom of the Christian Man. The Appeal,* permeated with exaggerated nationalism, vigorously maintained that Germany for centuries had been drained of its resources to provide money for the Popes. Luther proposed most revolutionary counter-actions. He urged the princes to destroy every power of the Popes in Germany and to obliterate every connection with Rome, devotional as well as doctrinal. Declaring that all believers were priests and that the ecclesiastical hierarchy and the clerical state were merely human inventions, he insisted that the princes were the ones who must preside over the believers. He recommended that the princes take over the "usurped" properties of the ecclesiastical powers. Luther went further: he advocated that monks free themselves from their vows and that priests marry and live like laymen. In *The Babylonian Captivity*, Luther attacked the Catholic sacramental system as a popishly-devised corruption of the Faith. He declared that there were only three sacraments: Baptism, Holy Eucharist and Penance. He rejected the idea of *sacrifice* in the Mass, branding it as simply devilish wickedness. Later he would drop Penance as a sacrament. In the pamphlet, *On the Freedom of the Christian Man*, Luther gave an exposition of his fundamental teaching that salvation was by faith alone and that good deeds were useless for the obtaining of salvation. This pamphlet he wrote in a gentler style. It was a simple explanation in devotional language of his doctrine, albeit the thought-content was distinctly heretical.

In the civil law of those days, heresy was counted a capital offense, hence excommunication by the Church was followed by outlawry by the state; on May 21, 1521, the Imperial Diet, the national assembly of Germany, placed Luther under the Ban of the Empire (the legal term for outlawry). The sentence was never carried out. In the complex anarchy that was the Holy Roman Empire of the Germans (more than 200 sovereignties, of which only a dozen were strong states), there existed no national force to implement the sentences of the Diet. Any powerful prince could frustrate a decree of the Diet. So now acted the Electoral Duke of Saxony, Luther's protector. He had his troops carry off the condemned friar to a remote castle of his, the Wartburg, and there guard him with secure protection. In this safe haven Luther remained for almost a year.

During his stay on the Wartburg, Luther advanced considerably the revolution by his writings. Foremost was his translation of the New Testament. This eminently readable version was supremely important for the Lutheran creed, which made the Bible the sole source of belief. Luther, who had a powerful command of the language of the common people, produced in his new version one of the greatest masterpieces of German literature. But from a dogmatic point the work does not merit similar praise. It was not always a faithful translation, for Luther at times manipulated texts so as to fit his own tenets. In the retreat Luther also produced the following Latin tracts: *On Confession*, in which he abandoned the sacrament of Penance; *On the Abolition of Private Masses;* and *Opinion on Monastic Life*, one of Luther's most important writings. This work was an attack on celibacy, especially on the religious vow of chastity. *The Opinion on Monastic Life* went far to depopulate the sanctuary and the monastery not only in Germany but wherever the Religious Revolution triumphed. The most striking repudiation of monastic celibacy was made June 23, 1525. On that day Luther married Katherine von Bora, an ex-nun.

Luther left the Wartburg in early March, 1522; by that time the condemnation of Worms was quite evidently a dead letter. He hurried to Wittenberg to address himself to problems of propagating his doctrines there and elsewhere. Germany was living on a politico-religious volcano. In the anarchy of powerful principalities and numerous small sovereignties, ambition, avarice and unrest permeated all classes. Luther's denunciations of Popes and clergy intensified nationalistic and religious animosities. During the next few years, Luther had relations with various social classes; the results were of momentous consequence to the destiny of his revolution.

The Knights of the Empire were the first group. Large numbers (by no means all) banded together under Franz von Sickingen and Ulrich von Hutten "to make an opening for the gospel" of Luther. The former was a ruthless soldier of fortune, possessing three castles and a private army of 6,500 veteran soldiers; the latter was the leader of the pagan humanists. For a long time the minor nobles had been planning to recoup their financial and political power by overthrowing the prince-bishops and, that accomplished, by assailing the secular princes. In 1522, von Sickingen laid siege to Trier, whose bishop, one of the Electors, was an energetic opponent of Luther. The siege failed and the freebooter's army was driven away by the local princes. A second war in 1523 ended more disastrously; von Sickingen was mortally wounded in the siege of his castle by the Rhenish

princes; von Hutten died a fugitive. The support of Luther
by the Imperial Knights was a complete failure.

Next came the Rising of the Peasants. Their lot was
deplorable: destitution, depression, devastation, extortion
and injustice. Numerous unfrocked priests and run-away
monks moved among them, preaching strongly on their
legitimate grievances. These sparks were fanned into fierce
flames by Luther's writings, which were avidly read by the
peasants. They looked upon the "son of a peasant" not only
as an emancipator from Roman impositions but as a precursor
of social utopias. Luther's invectives against the clergy rapidly
bore bitter fruits: sacking of monasteries, looting of churches,
smashing of sacred images and horrible desecrations of the
Blessed Sacrament. The revolt involved lands from the southern Alps almost to the Baltic Sea. Only when the tumult
threatened the princes did some of the powerful princes
move to its suppression.

In its beginning Luther published a pamphlet condemning the uprising. But his language was as yielding and conciliatory to the peasants as it was violent and insulting to the
bishops and the Catholic princes. Later, when the princes
were ruthlessly crushing the rebels, he issued another
pamphlet in which he urged the princes on with the adjura-
tions: "Strike, slay front and rear; nothing is more devilish
than sedition. There must be no sleep, no patience, no mercy;
they are the children of the devil." The clashes became more
massacres than battles. Frightful were the effects of the
Peasants' War: more than a thousand monasteries and castles
were levelled, hundreds of villages were burned, the harvests
of the nation were destroyed and 100,000 persons slain.

The most significant after-effect was that Luther and his
supporters ceased to be men of the people and became men
of the princes, henceforth defenders of princely absolutism
and preachers of passive obedience. The anarchy in religion
forced them to put religious authority into the hands of the
temporal lords. The civil powers would now regulate all
church affairs, even to deciding controversies among the
preachers and to putting down religious dissensions with
arms. The lay rulers would also have the disposition of the
vast possessions of the old Church. All that was requested

of the princes was the pledge to accept the new doctrines and to introduce them as the territorial religion. The new protection could be embarrassing, as when Philip of Hesse demanded a document permitting him a contemplated bigamous marriage. Luther and three other divines finally signed the permissive document, which said: 1) a general law that a man could have more than one wife could not be handed down, 2) a dispensation could be granted Philip, 3) this marriage should be kept from the public by absolute silence.

The princes, with a few exceptions like the Austrian Hapsburgs and the Dukes of Bavaria, eagerly took over the Reformation Movement. As absolutists they already had completely dominated the political liberties of their subjects; now as lay-popes they controlled as completely their religion. They quickly confiscated the lands and revenues of the old Church. The princes set up territorial religions. Each in his own lands proscribed the Catholic Faith, abolishing its doctrines and its rites, especially the Mass. They banished all faithful priests and lay people, allowing only the alternative of emigration. Nor did they tolerate any form of Protestantism except the one they themselves headed in their particular territory. The princes tore from Catholicism at least two-fifths of Germany. Their example was followed by the rulers of the Scandinavian lands. Finally in the Religious Peace of Augsburg (1555), the princes obtained the decision that the prince alone determines the religion of his territory. And so there was freedom of religion in Lutheran territories for no one but the territorial prince.

John Calvin

OF ALL THE STORMS lashing against the barque of Peter during the Religious Revolution, the most potent and the most far-extending was Calvinism. This was due firstly to the extraordinary personality of its founder, secondly to the development of his "Reformed Church" into the major force of Protestantism. John Calvin was an intellectual giant. He was at once a keen philosopher, a deeply versed theologian, an expertly trained lawyer and a master of French prose. John Calvin was also a good man. As a layman and later as a minister (he had never been a priest), he lived his moral life without blemish. John Calvin was, in his own rigoristic way, a devout man. One of his chief aims was to be the master of the spiritual life for his followers, leading them to what he considered was the perfect service of God. His followers, in their thousands, accepted his leadership with passionate fidelity. In less than three generations the Calvinists were the strongest and the most uncompromising body in the Religious Revolution. Calvanism had become the dominant Protestantism in seven European countries, and the vigorous rival of Lutheranism in Germany and of Anglicanism in England.

John Calvin was born in northern France, at Noyon, Picardy, in 1509. His father was a successful lawyer, who, though a layman, had his practice in the ecclesiastical courts. He was also a capable administrator, managing the nonclerical business of the bishop of Noyon. It was not strange that such a man should destine his second son, John, for the Church. By his connections the father had some clerical benefices bestowed upon his son, the revenues of which would support him in his studies.

Calvin's university career covered ten years, five at Paris, three at Orleans and Bourges, and two again at Paris. A dedicated student, he earned a reputation for great scholarship in humanities, philosophy and law. But also during these years he became involved in the Religious Revolution. In the universities he encountered Lutherans secretly propagating their doctrines. He found fellow-students perusing and discussing Lutheran books, ignoring the prohibitions against reading such works. At length Calvin abandoned the Catholic Faith, most likely before 1534. In that year he wandered about France preaching to various Lutheran groups. Also in May, 1534, he resigned his benefices. In October he came back to Paris, only to encounter the storm aroused by the "Affair of the Placards." The Placards were printed sheets filled with blasphemous and scurrilous attacks on the Mass and other Catholic teachings. One morning they were found pasted on the walls of public buildings in Paris and other French cities. The Catholics, the vast majority of the French people, were outraged. Raids, arrests and numerous executions followed. Calvin managed to escape from the city, and in December he fled from France forever.

Calvin reached Basel, in Switzerland, in January, 1535. In that now Protestant town he devoted eight months to composing the first draft of his famous work, *The Institutes of the Christian Religion*. In later years he frequently revised and enlarged *The Institutes*, into four books, containing a complete presentation of Calvinistic theology and church organization. It is the greatest literary production of Protestantism. Calvin, continuing on his journeyings, arrived in August, 1536, at Geneva, a city of the French-speaking section of Switzerland. He originally intended to spend but a night passing through. But on the vehement urgings of Farel, a French refugee minister, he agreed to stay and help the Protestant cause. On September 5, the city officials appointed him to lecture on the Sacred Scriptures in the cathedral. This was the turning point in the reformer's career, the first step towards his becoming the major prophet of the Religious Revolution. Calvin was only twenty-seven years old.

Geneva at the time had a population of 13,000. An oligarchy of prosperous merchants and lawyers, at the most 1,500 voters, elected the council which governed the city. From 1518, Geneva had been a place of endless turmoils, political at first but religious after the appearance of religious revolutionaries in 1532. In the next few years French refugees led by the Lutheran Farel worked strenuously to make the city-state Protestant. The chief attacks were against the Mass, but there were also the smashing of holy statues and the destruction of sacred paintings in iconoclastic riots. The council sided with the innovators in spite of the opposition of the Catholic majority, who were too insignificant socially to control affairs. On May 21, 1536, the assembly voted to adopt the new doctrines and to abandon "all Masses and other ceremonials and papal abuses, images, idols and all connected with these things." This action was taken ten weeks before Calvin's arrival.

Farel and Calvin went to work in earnest. Their extreme program, however, aroused such opposition from the loose-living libertines and from the council, jealous of its governing prerogatives, that both were expelled in 1538. Three years passed and Calvin was brought back, pretty much on his own terms, except that the council held closely to its governmental powers. Calvin dedicated himself to establishing complete control of the religion and morals of Geneva. He found himself in frequent conflict with the governmental opposition. Twelve years were to pass before he achieved the complete establishment of his theocracy (a state directed and controlled by his religious ideas). Calvin never held political office, but after 1553, and until his death in 1564, he controlled those who did.

For his "Reformed Church" Calvin completed two master-plans. The first was his *The Institutes of the Christian Religion*, and the second was the theocracy of Geneva.

In the four volumes of the *Institutes*, Calvin explained his dogmatic teachings, his directives for sacred worship, and his plan of church organization. He made Luther's fundamental doctrines his own. Like the Wittenberg theologian, Geneva's pastor held: the total corruption of man's nature, resulting from original sin; the utter powerlessness of man to do good; the justification of man by faith alone; the impossibility of man's being able to merit anything. For neither reformer did free will exist.

Calvin accepted Luther's teaching on absolute predestination; but he developed it further to logical and terrible consequences. He maintained inflexibly that God created some men for the enjoyment of everlasting happiness in heaven. They were the elect. He maintained just as inflexibly that God created other men for the suffering of everlasting misery in hell that by damning them He might show forth His justice. They were the reprobate. Elect or reprobate, men shall not be so because of the lives which they will lead, but by a positive act of God. Predestination, even to hell, was for Calvin an aspect of divine Providence. How numerous are the elect? How numerous are the reprobate? Calvin, or at least his followers, held that the elect were few, and that they would have some intimation of their election. The reprobate then would include the rest of mankind. This terrible teaching has long since been abandoned by modern Calvinists. But for two centuries the gloomy belief was preached.

Calvin on some vital points was far more radical than Luther. He rejected all the sacraments—the outward signs instituted by Christ to give grace. For him the sacraments had no connection with grace. Calvin retained a few sacraments, but only as external signs of initiation or, as in the case of the Eucharist, as a memorial commemorating the Last Supper. Though Calvin's ideal was a weekly participation in the Lord's Supper, in the Holy Communion of that commemorative rite there was not a vestige of the Real Presence. Luther at least taught the temporary Real Presence in the unchanged bread and wine. Calvin vehemently rejected the Mass as an imposture.

In the ritual which he designed for the Reformed Church Calvin's principle was: whatever finds no mention in the Scriptures must be cast out. Consequently he directed the destruction of all crucifixes, statues, sacred paintings, stained-glass windows depicting the saints, vestments, altars and confessionals—all were idols or pertained to idols. Iconoclasm became the distinctive practice of the Calvinist troops and rioters of the first hundred years. Worship in the cold, barren churches consisted of sermons on Calvinistic doctrine, lectures on the Sacred Scriptures, prayers, and the partaking of Communion at the commemorations of the Lord's Supper. There was one heart-warming feature, the communal singing of devout and beautiful hymns.

Calvin's most revolutionary change was made in his plan for the government of the Reformed Church. The church organization was simple and democratic. There were three grades in the ministry: pastors, deacons and elders. God's call to the ministry was indicated through the voice of the people. Each Calvinistic congregation was independent of all others and was the final authority in faith and action. The only bond of unity between the individual churches was found in the synod of the local or national area.

Like Luther, Calvin held that the Bible was the sole source of faith. He devoted much of his busy life to its complete explanation, producing many massive commentaries. Though he never claimed a specific inspiration on the part of God, as Doctor Luther did, yet Pastor Calvin was convinced that he was God's messenger and as such had the right to demand assent to the message he delivered.

Theocracy in Geneva

IN THE PRECEDING CHAPTER it was noted that Calvin produced two master-plans for his "Reformed Churches." The first was *The Institutes of the Christian Religion,* his complete theory of dogma, morals, organization and worship. It has been discussed in the last chapter. The second was the model community of Geneva, where his ideas became realities in actual and full observance. Calvin transformed the Swiss city-state into a theocracy completely dominated by himself. The reformer attained this pre-eminence only after sharp struggles with the secular government. The civic council always retained its right of officially issuing the decrees of dogma. One such was its declaration that Calvin's *Institutes* was a holy doctrine against which no man might speak. Even to the last the council alone exercised the secular arm, punishing the delinquents, imprisoning the recalcitrants and executing the heretics and atheists. Eventually, however, Calvin became so influential that he determined who were to be the councillors, choosing those who were favorable and blocking those who were unfavorable. Then Calvin could realize his teaching that the state was under the church. No advocate of the medieval papacy upheld more strongly the supremacy of the spiritual. He made the holiness of God's law one of the chief tenets of his teaching. Indeed he considered himself to be God's prosecutor against the law's violators whether in faith or morals.

Calvin deemed the worst of all violations the crime against religious doctrine. So he wrote: "Whatever crimes can be thought of, do not come up to this (heresy)." He also wrote: "What, indeed, can be more peculiarly belonging to God than His own truth?... Now to corrupt pure doctrine, is it not the same as if to put the devil in God's place?" He had no time for religious toleration. Once he declared: "If authority and liberty of judging the law be left to private man, there will never be any certainty set down, but rather all religion will become doubtful." To the Earl of Somerset, the Lord Protector, who was assisting the foundation of the Reformed Church in England, his advice was: "Beware of all moderation; it is the bane of all improvement."

In Geneva the repression of religious liberty was thorough and ruthless. Not the least expression of the old Catholic creed—"now completely liquidated"—was permitted. It was forbidden to say a prayer in Latin, to hint disbelief in the Pope being antichrist, or even to repeat that the Pope was kind to the poor. Protestant proponents had to submit their writings for rigorous censorship; each page of the manuscript had to bear the author's initial, and also the counter-initial of the censor. Contradicting Calvin was swiftly and decisively punished. Some very distinguished Protestant theologians were condemned to exile. Anabaptists were banished with the accompanying threat of execution if they dared return. The atheist (the term embraced a denier of the inspiration of the Scriptures, or of the immortality of the soul) was tortured and beheaded. The most celebrated victim was Michael Servetus, an eccentric Spanish Unitarian, who was burned at the stake in 1553. Calvin was responsible for the condemnation, though later he stated that he sought mitigation of the extreme penalty. Calvin did not shrink from the death penalty for heretics; he was a man of his age. At one period of five years during Calvin's domination of Geneva, fifty-five people were executed and seventy-six driven into exile; most, if not all, were heretics. In 1559, Calvin translated into French his favorite disciple Beza's work which argued violently that heretics ought to be persecuted.

Morals were as much regulated as beliefs in Geneva. Calvin induced his model city to judge and punish all the human sins and frailties. Serious crimes were mercilessly dealt with; a special prison was established for sex-offenders. And there was a tremendous number of punishable small offenses, even trivialities. Sternly forbidden were playing cards and dice, light songs, and dancing. Restraints were placed on such minute matters as the dress and shoes of men and women, even on feminine hair styles. No protection was afforded by social position; ladies were sent to prison as easily as their maids. Numerous were the punishments inflicted for failures in church-conduct: non-attendance at the sermons (five weekly), playing games during church-time, leaving church during the sermon, saying that Calvin was not a good preacher, protesting the giving of only biblical names at Baptism. There was scarcely an aspect of life that was not affected by edicts of the council. Officials pried into men's intimate affairs, dogmatic and moral, making Geneva a city of glass. Twice a year a commission of ministers and elders inspected every home to see if all things were kept godly: no papist holy pictures, no wrong religious ideas, diligent attendance by all at the sermons and in the participation of the Lord's Supper. All findings were listed in a huge book, with such notes as "pious," "lukewarm," "corrupt" beside each name! Further information was brought in by hosts of volunteers, the pious who spied upon their neighbors. A harsh doctrine, a cold worship, a straight-jacket existence, a bleak outlook—what a somber place Geneva must have become!

Yet from such dour components developed one of the master forces of Protestantism. How so? First there was the appeal of Calvin's vast doctrinal system. He convinced his followers that his special way of righteous living was the exclusive way to God, the way which God demanded. He convinced them too that faithful living according to such high ideals produced a happiness that made a mockery of materialistic pleasures. Calvin looked upon himself as the master of the spiritual life; his disciples accepted him as such with passionate fidelity. They were totally secured when he buttressed his every step with biblical allusions. They came to believe that they, and they alone, were God's people. Secondly, their minds were captivated by Calvin's powerful logic in his reasoning on justification. Mistaken, as he was, about the mysteries of God's relations with man, they had eyes only for his brilliant argumentation; in consequence they readily accepted his mistaken conclusions. Thirdly, the certainty of eternal salvation tremendously attracted the citizens of a pessimistic world, terrified by continual sermons on hell and the tortures of the damned. How reassuring was the conviction that the elect, no matter what their human frailties or sins, could never lose their salvation! Fourthly, the equation of rigorism with righteousness, of severity with godliness, of sadness with sanctity won countless dour personalities, those especially who suspected all human joyousness.

To propagate his teachings, Calvin founded at Geneva his great college. Ex-Catholic priests flocked there, along with dissatisfied Lutherans, dissident Anglicans and his own young zealots. From his lips they received the dogma, morality, worship and church organization of the *Institutes.* They observed the practical living of the Calvinistic system in the controlled iron morals of the model city, Geneva. They accepted the harsh regime completely. Thoroughly imbued with Calvin's spirit they came forth, the most militant, the most uncompromising force in Protestantism, to gain thousands of converts to his way of life. They attacked other Protestant sects hardly less vigorously than they did Catholicism.

Calvinism became the most powerful force in the religious revolution. Calvin's "Reformed Churches" reigned supreme among Swiss, French, Dutch and Hungarian Protestants. So it was in Scotland, where almost the whole nation embraced Calvinistic Presbyterianism. In England, Calvin's Puritans almost captured Anglicanism. When they failed, some formed the independent Congregationalist Church; others, content to remain Anglicans, wielded an influential part theologically as the Low Church Party. Irish Protestants were largely Presbyterians; even the official government church was controlled by the Low Church Party.

Of all the religious revolutionists the Calvinists inflicted the worst losses upon the Catholic Church. Fanatical Calvinist armies and mobs massacred priests and Catholic lay people, destroying thousands of churches, monasteries and convents, with horrible blasphemies desecrating the Blessed Sacrament, smashing in iconoclastic fury sacred statues, paintings and stained-glass windows. Unfortunately Catholics made dark records too as sanguinary persecutors. The Sixteenth and Seventeenth centuries were not tolerant times. The Calvinist persecutions are cited here to explain the finality of some of the Catholic losses and the tremendous over-all threat to the very existence of the Catholic Church in those centuries.

The Eve
of the
English
Religious
Revolution

THE SEPARATION of England from the Catholic Church was the last storm that broke upon the Barque of Peter during the Religious Revolution. The obliteration of the Pope's authority in England was so thorough that by the end of the century almost the entire nation was Protestant. From the beginning there was only one primary doctrine in the revolt: the Bishop of Rome has no powers—either spiritual, or dogmatic, or jurisdictional—in England; but all these powers are possessed solely by the king of the realm. This doctrine is summarized in two words, "Royal Supremacy."

During seventy years (1534-1603), something of greatest significance emerged: England became the champion of Protestantism, not so much in dogmatic matters as in external conflicts with Catholicism. In the three centuries following, as England developed into the most powerful of empires, she also grew into the most powerful of all the supporters of Protestantism. Without England's support the Religious Revolution in Europe would have died out. And more, England propagated her own type of Protestantism far and wide in the new colonies and states beyond the seas. Protestants in the old and new worlds all looked to England as the great Protestant state. So also did Catholics consider England.

And yet such eventualities could not have been imagined in 1520, when the English king, Henry VIII, published his

Defense of the Seven Sacraments against Luther. The work not only vindicated the Church's dogmatic teaching on the sacraments, but also maintained in unequivocal terms the supremacy of the papacy. Furthermore there were few places in Europe where conditions were less conducive to religious revolution than in England. Disturbing elements, of course, did exist, which under certain stimulations might lead to revolt. But such elements were in every European country.

Relations between the clergy and the laity were, on the whole, very good. There was hearty cooperation in the work of the guilds and in the healthy parish life of the period. There was an abundance of bequests and legacies by the lay people for the embellishment of shrines and the establishment of foundations for Masses for the departed souls. Such gifts were intended in part for the support of the clergy. Catholic generosity was strikingly manifested in the great church-building of the late fifteenth and the early sixteenth centuries. It was the "Tudor Gothic" period of English architecture. The cathedrals were completed with splendid west fronts and glorious central towers. Well nigh every town or village built or finished its parish church in this style of high-pointed arches and strong square towers. All Englishmen took part in the common achievement, the country folk and the town people as well as the great churchmen and the powerful nobles.

A Venetian visitor in the beginning of the sixteenth century recognized things even more fundamental, when he expressed his admiration for the universal observation of Catholic practices and the general manifestation of English piety. A modern English scholar, Cardinal Gasquet, declared that from the literature of the period it was quite certain that the rise of the anti-Catholic spirit in England dates from about five years before 1533, the five years of Henry VIII's conflict with Pope Clement VII, about the annulment of the monarch's marriage. It was during those years that the new teachers, the crypto-revolutionists, began to stir up the popular mind against the clergy.

Of course there was friction between the English monarchs and the Popes, as there had been all through the Middle Ages, over ecclesiastical appointments or royal claims upon

HENRY VIII. Portrait by Hans Holbein the Younger.
Borghese Gallery, Rome.

the management of the material affairs of the Church. Ever since the Residence at Avignon there were resentments against the taxing policies of the papacy. But these frictions were no greater on the eve of the Religious Revolution than in the earlier days.

The contemporary evidence is overwhelming that, despite complaints and criticisms over material affairs, there was always full acceptance by the English nation of the Pope's spiritual supremacy. As late as 1520, Dr. John Clarke, who presented Henry VIII's work against Luther to Leo X, attested to "the devotion and veneration of the king toward the Pope and his most Holy See"; and he continued on to say that Luther had declared war "not only against Your Holiness but also against your office — against the See and the Rock established by God Himself." Later a more learned and holier witness, St. Thomas More, in the shadow of the gallows, could assert, "The doctrine of the Royal Supremacy has never been held in England."

The morals of the clergy were better in England than anywhere on the continent, save Spain. The old accusations of wholesale immorality have been rejected by Brewer, the foremost authority on the times of Henry VIII. The intellectual standards of the lower clergy, unhappily, were not high. Still felt were the deleterious effects of the great plagues and the long wars. Seminaries did not exist; they were to be creations of the future. Yet the clergy were not illiterate. The regulations about preaching made by Archbishop Neville, in 1466, for the synod of the province of York took for granted the capacity of country clergy to explain the principal doctrines and practices of the Faith. Of the books issued from the new British press during four decades around 1500, the great majority were of a religious character. The clergy, far from discouraging the use of such books, actively helped in their distribution. Evidently a large portion of the laity were literate and also well instructed in the Faith.

Abuses among the higher clergy were graver. True, gross scandals were comparatively unknown; the one glaring exception was Cardinal Wolsey. Pluralism (the holding by one bishop of two or more sees) was less flagrant than in earlier times; again Wolsey was the one glaring exception. But of really grievous harm were absenteeism, preoccupation with affairs of state, accumulation of wealth. Because of superior training in law—civil and canon—prelates were employed by the king in government and diplomacy. There were too many court bishops in England. Such shepherds did not give their flocks the proper pastoral guidance; rather they relegated this important task to suffragans or commissioners of spiritual affairs. Since bishops owed their sees to the king (his nomination to every English see was almost invariably followed by papal confirmation), they were the king's men. As they received their elevation from the monarch, so they depended on him for their future prospects. No wonder that, dwelling in the worldly atmosphere of the court, many of these bishops became unduly ambitious for higher places in the Church and for the greater wealth involved. In their civil positions they incurred the rivalry and envy of the new nobility, who were quick to turn against them when Henry VIII apostatized. But it must be said that these court bishops despite their shortcomings were not small copies of Cardinal Wolsey. That most powerful and most worldly ecclesiastic was not typical of his order. He was neither a scholar, nor a theologian, nor a canonist, but a most skilled politician. He was vulgar, ostentatious, utterly secular, avid for wealth, and dishonest. He was the all unique example of moral turpitude, as he was also the sole pluralist. Yet upon these prelates was visited some of the widespread hatred for Wolsey, a hatred not only of sincere men, but of envious politicians and of the promoters of the coming revolution.

Doctrinal revolution was not a probability in the early years of Henry VIII. A hundred years before, Lollardism had faded into obscurity. The few secret Lollards in no way influenced Henry's revolution. More significant was the small group of Cambridge students who, about 1520, adopted Lutheranism. Years later some of them would strongly influence the theology of the Anglican Church; but that was after Henry VIII had died. In this third decade only one of them, Tyndale, achieved importance. He published an English translation of the New Testament—liberally furnished with explanatory notes—and some anti-Catholic pamphlets. The notes and pamphlets were completely Lutheran. His works and similar ones by his colleagues, all written in an anti-clerical and an anti-Catholic spirit, began to be secretly imported and circulated in England about 1528. A great assembly at Westminster of bishops and civil officials, in 1530, condemned all such pamphlets. However some of the bishops had misgivings that Henry VIII was abetting the circulation of these works in order to embarrass the bishops and the Pope; in 1530 he had suffered a decided setback in his struggle for the annulment of his marriage. But Henry never accepted the doctrines of the secret English Lutherans; even after his separation from the Church, Henry VIII would have condemned to death a professing Lutheran.

One force existed which could bring England to a repudiation of the papacy. It was Tudor Absolutism. The first two monarchs of the Tudor line, Henry VII and Henry VIII, complete absolutists, ruled without restrictions. The powerful check of the medieval families had been swept away when the old nobility were wiped out in the War of the Roses. The Tudors filled the government and parliament with peers, minor nobles and officials who were all parvenus, without any sympathy for the best traditions of the past. Such creations and appointees were largely place-hunters and political adventurers, ever ready for their own gain, to further any royal plan, always eager to profit by any disturbance—social or religious. As for the common people, they still had vivid remembrances of the long enduring War of the Roses. The recollections of its horrors inclined the average Englishman to endure any tyranny rather than imperil the peace of the country by open resistance to the king's will. The catastrophe came when Henry VIII, failing to obtain the annulment of his marriage from Clement VII, repudiated all papal power whatsoever and made himself the sole source of spiritual and sacramental power in the Church in England. He brought about his revolt and made it a success by Tudor Absolutism.

Royal
Supremacy
in England

SO NUMEROUS WERE the important persons involved in the English Religious Revolution, and so many were the significant events occurring in its course that in a brief treatment only a summarization is possible.

The conflict began with Henry VIII's efforts to obtain from Pope Clement VII an annulment of his marriage with his queen, Catherine of Aragon, who had been the widow of his elder brother, Prince Arthur. The king's pretext was that the dispensation, given by Pope Julius II, removing the impediment of marriage with his sister-in-law, was invalid. Contrary to an oft-repeated but false assertion, Henry never sought a divorce (the dissolving of a real marriage). What he wanted was an annulment (a declaration that, because of an essential defect, no marriage ever existed). His real reason was the freeing of himself from his wife, Catherine, that he might marry Anne Boleyn, a lady of the Court.

Six years followed in which Henry VIII ruthlessly pressured, intrigued against and threatened Clement to force his compliance. In 1527, the Pope allowed the trial to be held in England. But on the appeal of Catherine to Clement VII for his personal judgment the trial collapsed. The failure ruined one of the trial's chief promoters, the ambitious Cardinal Wolsey. Henry had more success intimidating the English clergy. His menacing forced from the Convocation (the assembly of the bishops and clerical delegates) an acknowledgment of him as "the supreme head of the Church and the clergy of England." Archbishop Warham of Canterbury, the Primate, was able only to insert a saving qualification, "as far as the law of Christ will allow." On the death of Archbishop Warham in 1532, King Henry named as his successor in the primatial see of Canterbury, Thomas Cranmer, a chaplain of the Boleyn family, a secret heretic and a pliant servant of Henry. Early in 1533, Henry and Anne Boleyn were secretly married. Four months later Cranmer pronounced Catherine of Aragon's marriage invalid and Anne Boleyn's marriage lawful. In July the Pope declared Cranmer's decision null and void. On March 23, 1534, Clement VII solemnly pronounced the validity of the marriage of Henry VIII with Catherine of Aragon, and the nullity of the marriage of Anne Boleyn.

Even before the news of the papal action had reached England, Henry VIII and his parliament, completely dominated by him, achieved the separation of the country from the Catholic Church. In the spring of 1534, a whole series of laws was passed placing all ecclesiastical offices, procedures and revenues under the king's control. For instance, bishops were not only appointed solely by the monarch, but they owed the temporalities and even the spiritualities of their sees to his bestowal. The November session passed the formal Act of Supremacy: "Be it enacted by the authority of this present parliament, that the king, our sovereign lord, his heirs and successors, kings of this realm, shall be taken, accepted and reputed the only supreme head on earth of the Church of England called Anglicana Ecclesia." The royal supremacy was made to extend to faith, worship and discipline. A formal renunciation of the Pope followed in 1535. Henry now demanded of the clergy an acceptance of Royal Supremacy entirely and without any qualifying phrase. A majority of the clergy bent before the storm. All the bishops repudiated the primacy of the Bishop of Rome and accepted the new English lay-papacy; all, except one, St. John Fisher, who was to be martyred, after a year's harsh imprisonment, for his loyalty to the Pope.

ST. JOHN FISHER. *Hans Holbein the Younger, Windsor Castle.*

ST. THOMAS MORE. *Hans Holbein the Younger, the Frick Collection, New York.*

The bloody years which followed the Act of Supremacy are cited only to show that the majority of the nation was sincerely attached to the old Faith and that only a policy of terror forced from them an external acquiescence. This will be made clear by citing a few of the Englishmen who carried their loyalty for the Roman Pontiff to ultimate martyrdom. Their memory today is honored by all Englishmen, whatever their creed may be. There were the two noblest men of the realm, St. John Fisher, the venerable old Bishop of Rochester, formerly the chancellor of Cambridge University; and St. Thomas More, the learned lawyer and the brightest wit of the whole Renaissance; the more than fifty Franciscans who were put to death; the eighteen Carthusians of London, with their abbot, St. John Houghton; the three mitered abbots of Glastonbury, Reading and Colchester; the hundreds of simple peasants and country-gentlemen of the North Country slaughtered after the failure of the Pilgrimage of Grace; and Bl. Margaret Pole, the aged Countess of Salisbury, the last of the Plantagenets and even the cousin of King Henry VIII. Along with Catholics the ruthless tyrant sent to death Lutherans, Zwinglians and Lollards. A fine legal distinction was made. The Catholics, under the pretext that they were traitors for denying the royal prerogatives, were beheaded, or hanged, drawn and quartered with all the barbarous cruelties of the punishment for high treason. The Reformers, as heretics, were burned at the stake. In either case death was horrible.

Almost of equal importance to the rejection of the Papal Supremacy was the suppression of the monasteries. Their destruction riveted the Religious Revolution on England, because it furnished the basis of the wealth of the new aristocracy which was to dominate England until the nineteenth century. There were some 600 monasteries, 125 of which were convents of nuns. In total they possessed large areas of land, the accumulation of gifts of pious Catholics during more than six centuries for religion, education and poor-relief. Abuses appeared from time to time, but on the whole the monks and nuns faithfully carried out their obligations for Masses and prayers for the souls departed. But the doom of the monasteries was sealed. First they did not fit into the contemporary religious revolution which was entirely hostile to monastic life; in England they formed a possible rallying point for a return to Rome. Secondly it was estimated that their dissolution might turn over to the royal treasury a gross annual income of 300,000 pounds. In 1535, an investigation was launched against the monasteries, with the avowed purpose of blackening their reputations. The visitation was a farce: there were only six investigators — at least some of them were of shadowy reputation; they made investigations of only a third of the religious houses; and after only six months they presented their findings to parliament. They claimed that so vile were the moral conditions of the smaller monasteries that their immediate suppression was a duty. The hypocrisy of the report was clearly evident from its reference to the larger houses: "the great and solemn monasteries of this realm, wherein, thanks be to God, religion is right well kept and observed." Within three years these great monasteries were also dissolved. Even the sycophant parliamentarians gagged at the prospect of voting the suppression of the monasteries. Henry assembled them, and addressed them thus: "I hear that my bill will not pass. But I will have it pass, or I will have some of your heads." The bill of suppression was passed.

Tremendous confiscations swept into the king's hands not only the lands and the revenues of the monasteries, but also their treasures: chalices, reliquaries, vestments, libraries, even the lead on the roofs. To the enormous sums realized must be added the incalculable wealth of the many English shrines (sixty wagons were needed to carry away the loot from the glorious shrine of St. Thomas of Canterbury). The wealth was spent on governmental projects, for diplomacy, or for military expenses. Henry lavishly handed out abbey lands to his favorites, or sold them far below their value. Speculation in abbey lands became quite common. The *nouveau riche* nobility plunged into the amassing of vast holdings. A most important result followed: the confiscated abbey lands and church wealth became the basis of the fortunes of the new nobility; and this was the class that was to rule England until the nineteenth century. In the first century, at least, the new proprietors were men of no deep religious convictions. Their first purpose was to hold on to their newly acquired fortunes; they easily changed their religious views to be sure that their hold would not be lessened. Thus they supported every whim of Henry's religious policies; then they shifted to the continental heresies of Edward VI, or rather of Cranmer; they even swung back to Catholicism, uneasily, of course, and only when Mary assured them that they would not be disturbed in their possessions. Naturally they welcomed the revival of the Royal Supremacy under the more congenial reign of Queen Elizabeth, and they worked with her to establish the Anglican Church. Lord Cecil, one of their leaders, wore a rosary in his belt during Mary's reign, but discarded it when Elizabeth chose him for her great minister of state. Cecil was the co-author with Elizabeth of Anglicanism. The greatest barrier for three hundred years to any return of England to the fold of Peter was the opposition of the English aristocracy.

There was much rivalry between the various Protestant groups to control the doctrine of the new Church of England. Henry alternated his using and his rejecting of the various factions: the Catholic-minded who wished to return to Rome, and the Lutheran-Zwinglian groups who strove to have him adopt the continental revolution. Always he remained the master. In 1539 Henry compelled parliament to adopt the Six Articles: Transubstantiation, Communion under one species, Masses for the dead, Confession, vows and celibacy. His reason was that in him alone resided the power to determine the religious faith of England. Henry VIII was not only the organizer and protector of the Church of England, but in his opinion, he was also its divinely-appointed teacher of faith and morals.

England Becomes Protestant

WITH THE ACCESSION of Edward VI came the second phase of the English Revolution. Henry VIII's Council of Regency for his heir, a sickly child of ten, was overthrown by its two leaders, the Duke of Somerset, the boy's uncle, and the Archbishop of Canterbury, Thomas Cranmer. Somerset became Lord Protector and sole ruler of England. He rewarded Cranmer for his assistance by giving him a free hand in religious changes. The archbishop, even before his consecration, had been a secret heretic of the continental type; and so he had remained for fifteen years under Henry VIII. Now openly he addressed himself to magnifying Henry's revolt (principally a denial of the Pope's authority) into a Lutheran-Calvinistic religion.

Parliament was quickly brought to repeal Henry VIII's *Six Articles* of belief, two of which insisted on Transubstantiation and Masses for the Dead, and also to abolish the laws against heresy. Then was inaugurated a campaign to establish the new doctrines and to root out the remains of the old Faith. From the continent, leaders of heresy, like Peter Martyr and Martin Bucer, were brought over to teach in the universities the new creed and to propagate it by their publications. Proclamations of innovations, settled between Cranmer and Somerset, were continually issued in the name of the boy king. Great public sermons against Catholic beliefs were authorized by the government. The country was flooded with translations of the writings of foreign "reformers," and with similar works composed in England. Cranmer published his

THE FORTY MARTYRS OF ENGLAND AND WALES.

translation of a Lutheran catechism, annotated by his own comments. He also produced *The Book of Common Prayer*, (first edition in 1549 and second in 1552); in both he embodied his own religious ideas.

Against the Mass, in particular, a veritable war was carried on. Sermons authorized by the government denounced "the idolatry of the Mass." The translations of foreign heretics and compositions of native ones were filled with blasphemies and profane abuses of the Blessed Sacrament. The Act of Uniformity (1549), which introduced *The Book of Common Prayer*, swept away the essential parts of the Mass. The Edwardian Ordinal (1550) deleted from the prayers conferring the priestly and the episcopal orders all words that conveyed the sacrificial powers of the priest and the episcopal power of creating sacrificing priests. The second version of *The Book of Common Prayer*, introduced by a new Act of Conformity (1552), destroyed the last vestiges of the Sacrifice of the Mass and of the Real Presence. Altars were destroyed as "useless" and were replaced by "decent tables" set in the midst of the congregation. Such actions were to emphasize that the service of the "Lord's Supper" was not a sacrifice but merely a commemorative act. Even the altar-stones were placed in the thresholds of the churches, so that the people by trampling on them would manifest their repudiation of the Sacrifice of the Mass. Bishops who adhered to the Catholic doctrine of the Holy Eucharist, like Gardiner of Winchester, Bonner of London, Tunstall of Durham and others, were either cast into prison or deprived of their bishoprics. In such manner was the Blessed Sacrament swept out of the "Church of England by law established."

The religious innovations encountered strong opposition in several parts of England. There were popular risings; but these the government ruthlessly suppressed with the aid of foreign mercenaries. Cardinal Gasquet, a modern historian, declared that the imposition of the new services was only effected by the slaughter of many thousands of Englishmen. The fall of Somerset and the rise to power of the Duke of Northumberland did not bring any interruption in the religious program of Cranmer. But its abolishment would come in a year or two with the accession to the throne of the Catholic Queen Mary. The six years of Edward VI were of major significance for the Religious Revolution. During that short time Calvinism was so irradicably sown that Puritanism, its English manifestation, would become and remain for three centuries the most vital factor of English Protestantism.

The new ruler, as provided by the will of Henry VIII, was Mary, the daughter of Catherine of Aragon. An ardent Catholic, Mary moved promptly to restore the old Faith. Judging from the popular rally to her when Northumberland plotted to keep her from the throne, she had most of her subjects with her. Mary re-invigorated the hierarchy. Bishops who had suffered in the previous reign for the Mass and Catholic doctrines were restored to their sees. Excellent ecclesiastics were nominated to replace heretical appointees of Cranmer in other sees. All Edwardine enactments concerning religion and public worship were repealed. England was united to the Pope in 1554; in the following year, Cardinal Pole was made Archbishop of Canterbury. The wide popular rejoicing at these events proved that the great majority of the English people were still Catholics in heart and soul.

The holders of the monastic lands, who were scarcely enthusiastic for the new Queen, supported Mary's religious program, especially when Pope Julius III, recognizing the accomplished fact, confirmed the past alienations of church properties. During Mary's reign, this landed gentry became Catholics again. Only the proponents of the Religious Revolution stood in absolute opposition. Some of their leaders were executed (they were not only heretics but also rebels). By no means a numerous group, they carried on from hiding or exile an unrelenting war not only against the Queen, but against the Mass, the Holy Eucharist and Catholicism as a religion.

After a reign of five years Mary died. Five troubled years were too short a time to solidify the Catholic position against the forty years' attack that was to come. Yet Mary's work was not in vain. Without her reign the Catholic religion in England would probably have been entirely destroyed. Mary's efforts produced that small heroic minority that kept the old Faith alive through two hundred and fifty years of darkness and persecution.

The third and final phase of the English Religious Revolution was achieved during Queen Elizabeth's long reign, 1557-1603. At the end, most of the nation was Protestant; only a small persecuted minority clung faithfully to the Catholic Faith. The new religion was known as Anglicanism. Its authors were Elizabeth and her aide, Lord Cecil; both were extremely able, and in full control. The Parliament of 1559 reimposed the oath of royal supremacy on the clergy and several classes of officials. It also abolished the Mass, decreed uniformity of prayer and administration of the sacraments, and enforced these statutes with grievous penalties. The bishops officially condemned these attempts to suppress Catholicism, and all but one refused the Queen's demands. They were deposed, sent to prison or forced into exile. The bulk of the priests at first followed the hierarchy's example. But later about half of the lower clergy, to retain their livings, took the oath of supremacy. The majority of the laity passively acquiesced, as they had done under Henry, Edward and Mary.

The problem facing Elizabeth and Cecil was this: most of the nation and the lower clergy wanted the old religion, but, through self-interest or lack of knowledge, were not prepared to face the consequences of opposition; only a small minority were willing to endure persecution and death for the Catholic Faith. On the other hand, there was another minority that pressed vigorously for, and would accept nothing but, a Calvinistic religion. To hold the larger portion it was decided to retain the old organization and the old ceremonies and vestments. To gain the Puritan minority it was decided to have a Calvinistic theology, or at least one slanted towards Geneva.

In the first decade the establishment visited upon non-compliant Catholics fines, confiscations and imprisonments, and prevented any public celebration of Catholic rites. It aimed not to make martyrs, though in 1569, it ruthlessly suppressed a rising of northern Catholics. Then its policy changed in 1570 when Pope Pius V excommunicated Elizabeth. In view of the fact that Elizabeth had fought the Catholic Faith in every country, dragged a Catholic sovereign (Mary, Queen of Scots) from prison to prison against the law of nations, and butchered her own Catholic subjects in the Northern Rising, St. Pius V excommunicated her and absolved her subjects from the oath of allegiance.

The Pope's action has been criticized because it was the signal for all-out war against Catholicism, but it did draw a much-needed line between loyalty and disloyalty to the Catholic Faith. No longer would priests secretly say Mass for Catholics in the morning, and officiate openly as Protestant ministers in the evening, thus saving their livings. No longer would Catholic laity try to rationalize their participation in non-Catholic worship in order to save their properties. Many failed in courage, but a heroic minority, very small at times, faced the rack, the rope and the axe. They were the nucleus that kept the Catholic Faith alive.

As the persecution of Catholics took a bloody turn, actions were made treasonable which had no element of treason. In 1571, Parliament made it treasonable to introduce into the country any papal document, to absolve or reconcile with the Church any person, to be so absolved or reconciled, to call the queen a heretic. In 1581, Parliament established a fine of 200 marks and a year's imprisonment for saying Mass, a fine of 100 marks and a year's imprisonment for hearing Mass, a fine of 20 pounds a month for absence from Anglican services. It also made an act of high treason the giving or receiving of absolution. In 1585, Parliament ordained the penalty of high treason for any Jesuit, or seminary priest, or other priest who remained in England over forty days, or for any English subject who studied at a foreign seminary, ordering such seminarians to return within sixty days and take the oath of supremacy. After 1573, the pretext for persecuting Catholics was the Catholic Faith alone; apostasy was the one thing demanded of Catholics.

At the end of Elizabeth's reign 189 priests had been executed; 90 had died in prison; 62 distinguished Catholic laymen and 3 women had been martyred. Hundreds of the Catholic gentry and thousands of the lower classes were fined into poverty, imprisoned, whipped or tortured. Who kept the Faith alive in the Catholic remnant? Heroic priests from the continental seminaries — Jesuits, Benedictines and Friars — and the constant Catholic lay people in England. But a second generation was coming along in England whose only knowledge of Catholicism was the horrible caricatures of it put forth by the propagandists of Elizabeth and Cecil. England now was thoroughly a Protestant land.

The
Catholic
Revival

THE CATHOLIC REVIVAL in the sixteenth century forms a most assuring chapter of the Church's history. In that long record no other movement vindicates more clearly the promise of Jesus Christ to be with His Church "all days even to the consummation of the world." The Catholic Revival was active in four fields; they were, in order of emphasis and of time: the revival of the faith, the intensification of religious devotion, the reform of abuses and the defense against Protestantism.

The movement is often called the Counter-Reformation. The term is inexact, especially if it implies that the Revival came only after the launching of the Religious Revolution, and that it was but a defensive rallying of Catholics against the Protestant Reformers' attack. Now, there can be no question that much of the Catholic reform was actuated by these attacks and by the spectacle of the Church's disastrous losses. But the Revival's beginnings had already appeared during the century preceding the Revolution. It must further be noted that some important projects and many outstanding participants of the Catholic movement had little, if any, connection with opposition to Protestantism. However, common usage has given the term "Counter-Reformation" the wider sense; hence it can be used.

Among the antecedents of the Catholic Revival were the efforts of Popes and councils during the hundred years from 1418 to 1519, to draw up and carry out programs of reform. Nine out of the twelve Popes labored for the amendment of conditions — some on a wide scale, others on a narrower field. Three councils, Constance, Ferrara-Florence and Lateran V, drew up definite reformatory programs. Unfortunately these papal and conciliar efforts were not crowned with wide successes. The wisdom of hindsight can perceive the reasons: old methods, when new remedies were needed; half measures and superficial attempts to carry out salutary reforms. But the chief causes were the sinister external forces which checkmated the best plans of able Popes and devoted clerics. Such were: the "conciliarists," who strove to make general councils completely superior to the Popes; the absolute monarchs who wielded almost full dominance over the Church in their states; the unending European wars, especially the conflicts of the Roman factions; the worldly clerics in high places; and the continual lack of funds in the papal office.

But everywhere in the Church through that dismal century there were sincere promoters of faith, devotion and moral reform. Just to name a few among many, there were: in Italy, St. Antoninus of Florence, St. Bernardine of Siena, St. John Capistran, Bl. Niccolo Albergati and Cardinal Cajetan (former Master General of the Dominicans and second only to St. Thomas as a theologian); in Germany, Cardinal Nicholas of Cusa, Geiler von Kaisersberg, Abbot John Trithemius and Denis the Carthusian; in the Low Countries, Gerard Groote and Thomas à Kempis; in France, Cardinal d'Estoutville and Jean Standonck; in England, St. John Fisher and St. Thomas More; in Spain, Cardinal Ximenes, Francisco de Vittoria and Dominic de Soto.

Pastor, the great historian of the Popes and a pre-eminent authority on the doleful fifteenth century, pays a special tribute to these clerical and lay champions of the Faith. He cites their numbers, their holiness and their intense devotion to eradicating the evils which beset the Church. And he points out that in their dedicated labors for a wide and deep reformation, they kept well within the bounds of strict

ISABELLA THE CATHOLIC. Monument erected in Madrid.

loyalty to the Church. But, however hard they worked and however bravely they spoke out, their end-results fell far below the programs they had planned. The relatively poor results were not due to any faults or faintheartedness of these devoted bishops, priests, religious and laymen. The clerical and ecclesiastical abuses had spread too far and had sunk too deeply for individual or local reformatory programs. Pastor emphasizes this fact.

The first great restoration was accomplished in Spain. There the Catholic Revival was begun in the last decades of the fifteenth century, and it was brought to full success in the second decade of the sixteenth century. Its first three objectives—deepening of the faith, intensification of devotion and reform of abuses—were in a great human measure achieved. There was no organization of a counter-opposition to the Religious Revolution because the revolt had not yet been started in Germany. This last fact is the reason why the Spanish renewal is classified as an antecedent of the general Catholic Revival.

The Catholic Revival in Spain was largely the work of Cardinal Ximenes, Archbishop of Toledo and Primate of Spain. A Franciscan, he brought to the restoration of the Church the ardent dedication of the Saint of Assisi. Armed with papal approval he advanced determinedly in his task. He conducted visitations of monasteries and convents; abolished useless privileges; transferred excessive resources to needy churches, schools and hospitals; and drove into banishment incorrigible monks. Other Spanish bishops associated themselves with Cardinal Ximenes in his labors for deep and permanent reform. The total result was a moral regeneration of the Spanish people, both clerical and lay. The reforms achieved by the Cardinal and his fellow bishops may be traced in great measure to the heroic labors of the Spanish Franciscans, Dominicans, Augustinians and Jesuits in the mission fields just about to be opened in the New World and in the Far East. To the same source likewise can be ascribed the origins of the spiritual forces which produced the profound mysticism of St. Teresa and St. John of the Cross. Nor should the influence of Isabella, the Catholic Queen of Castile, be overlooked. She invariably backed projects of reform with her powerful support. She used her privileges of nomination, excessive though they were, to secure for the Spanish episcopacy the learned and pious prelates who brought about the great reform.

The resurgence of Catholicism in Spain was mightily aided by the universities of Salamanca and Alcala in their revival of Scholasticism, the system of theology and philosophy developed in the Middle Ages by St. Thomas Aquinas. The revivalists were led by two brilliant thinkers of the Dominican Order, Francisco de Vittoria and Dominic de Soto. They and their collaborators, casting aside the debris of two centuries of subtle but useless refinings of thought, brought back St. Thomas' clear perception of truth and his accurate reasonings about truth. As a result, men could now, moving in the light of these truths about God, His Church and His moral law, organize a program of solid recovery; and they could by accurate thinking shape the correct methods for its accomplishment.

Thus these Spanish thinkers had produced the philosophy of their own Catholic Revival. Before long their work was brought to Rome, the center of Catholicism, there to become the philosophy of the entire revival. All this philosophical endeavor was worked out in Spain before the Religious Revolution; hence it is another reason for classifying the Spanish Revival as an antecedent of the universal Catholic Revival.

The Papacy Preceding Trent

THE CATHOLIC REVIVAL will be treated under five headings: The Papacy (immediately preceding the Council of Trent); Religious Orders, Old and New; The Council of Trent; The Papacy (after the Council of Trent); The Saints of the Revival. It would be well here to recall the four elements of the movement: revival of faith, intensification of religious devotion, reform of abuses, and defense against Protestantism.

Pope Adrian VI, 1522-1523, was the forerunner of the Catholic Revival. Born at Utrecht of humble Dutch parents, he became a leading theologian of Louvain University and eventually its Rector. His learning was equaled by his prayerfulness and strictness of life; he was revered as a holy priest. Emperor Maximilian chose him as the tutor of his grandson, the future Charles V. His appointment as Bishop of Tortosa in Spain made Adrian a close associate of Cardinal Ximenes in the Spanish Revival. In 1517, he was elevated to the cardinalate, and in 1522, he was crowned Pope. Adrian brought to Rome the vigor of the Spanish Revival. Immediately he revealed himself as an outspoken and uncompromising reformer. Numerous and grave problems confronted him, and none harder than the opposition of worldly eccle-

siastics. But undauntedly he set himself to the work of rejuvenation. Unfortunately after a pontificate of little more than
a year, he died, his health shattered by disappointments
and by his own unrelenting activities. Adrian's achievements
amounted actually to little. His true significance is to be found
in his aims. He laid bare the evils, and with clear understanding he suggested the right cures to be employed. It was upon
the principles formulated by Adrian VI that at a later date the
internal reform of the Church was achieved.

Reform went on developing during the pontificate of
Clement VII, 1523-1534, despite tremendous hindrances. The
new Pope planned remedies for evils in clerical and monastic
ranks, and he encouraged efforts of reforming bishops and
superiors. But the early promise did not produce correspond-
ing fruit. Clement's attention became absorbed in political
disturbances. He must not be blamed too severely. The great
war between France and the Hapsburg Dominions held grave
threats for the freedom of the Papacy. The dangers were compounded by the pretensions of both monarchs, Francis I and
Charles V, in ecclesiastical affairs. And more, there was the
disastrous conflict with Henry VIII. Clement VII was a diplomat; but under pressure he was apt to be timid and procrastinating. This was unfortunate, for the crisis demanded a
strong direct-actionist. Still, even during the most distress-
ful years Clement did his best to make the Catholic Reformation possible, notably by supporting the reforming Bishop
Giberti and Bishop Sadolet. Towards the end of his pontificate he made provision for the reform of priests, in a number
of Italian dioceses, and of religious orders in Italy, outside
of Italy, and even in Poland.

Clement VII has been criticized for not convening the
general council demanded so widespreadly. But he had good
reasons for putting off the calling of the council. There was
hopeless disagreement among the proponents about its locale, composition and program. In some minds the antipapal
theories of the councils of Constance and Basle were still
nourished. Secular sovereigns, for their personal advantages,
were seeking to dominate the council; and they were not
above threatening schism. Protestant princes, who had already denied the magisterium of the Church, demanded the

admission of their ministers; that would have been the legitimatizing of their religious revolution. Further, they proclaimed their refusal to comply with any conciliar decrees contrary to their dogmas and their church-organizations. There was also the opposition of worldly ecclesiastical officials; these could seriously impede the implementing of reformatory decrees. Finally, the times were most unpropitious; a great war was raging in most of western Europe. Clement strove earnestly for peace so that a general council could be held. But in the whole problem of the council, Clement VII was overimpressed by its difficulties, and was lacking in foresight and enterprise. True, he always wished for a council; but his procrastinating gave the impression that the papacy did not want a council. One of his last acts was his best, his recommending the election of the strong Cardinal Farnese for his successor. His advice was followed.

Many scholars begin the Catholic Revival with the new Pope, Paul III, 1534-1549, because he set up the great Commission of Reform, officially approved the Society of Jesus and launched the Council of Trent. He began his pontificate by immediately inaugurating reforms on a far grander scale than had yet been attempted. One instance was his ordering absentee prelates to return to their dioceses. Similar orders manifested his determination for a thorough removal of abuses. How effective were his methods was soon shown by the opposition that rose against them. It was strong enough to cause some hesitancy in the Pope. But the improvements were so marked even in a short time that the pontiff was strengthened to proceed on his course.

Paul III called to his assistance a number of dedicated reforming bishops and organized them into an advisory council. One, most outstanding, was Cardinal Giberti, whose reform of his diocese of Verona was to serve later as the model for the Council of Trent. The Pope followed a strict policy in his many appointments to the Sacred College. Seldom has a sovereign pontiff been served by so many cardinals who were noteworthy for their wisdom and goodness. A few among the many were: Contarini, Caraffa, Sadoleto, Pole and Morone. These were either activists in the reform movement, leaders in the Council of Trent, or papal diplomats in Germany, France or England.

The first of the three great achievements of Paul III for the Catholic Revival was his creation of the Commission for Reform. Its business was to study the whole problem of contemporary evils and to propose remedies. It comprised four cardinals and eight bishops, with Cardinal Contarini as president. The members were given the most complete freedom. Late in 1537, they submitted their report. It is one of the greatest documents of its kind ever published. Severe, outspoken, objective, honest, detailed, it spared no one from the lowliest cleric even to the members of the papal household. Protestant propagandists quickly seized upon it for justification of their revolt. It was a drastically practical document, because its recommendations, attached by way of conclusion, had been given the force of law. This fearless report became the blueprint for the Tridentine Reform. Paul III's official approval of the Society of Jesus brought into existence the religious order which was to supply a dedicated body of workers for the Catholic Revival. His launching of the Council of Trent was the inauguration of the supreme fact of the Revival. Both of these achievements will be treated at length later.

No consideration of the papacy previous to the Council of Trent can be made without mention of the Catholic defenders in Germany. Papal legates and nuncios, such as Cardinal Aleandro, Campeggio, Cajetan, Contarini and Morone, served the Popes with conspicuous sincerity, vigor and prudence. No one must ever forget the German champions of Catholicism, men of eloquence and zeal, of tireless labor and undying loyalty, such as Johann Eck, Emser, Pflug, Cochlaeus and Gropper. For many of them it was a lonely battle, isolated as they were in the midst of entirely hostile populations. It was a hopeless struggle too, for they had no sign of a turning tide. But they never yielded. It must also be recorded that Charles V, with all his blunders and intrigues, never deserted Catholicism; nor did his brother, the Archduke Ferdinand of Austria, nor the Dukes of Bavaria. At times the Catholic cause was saved from annihilation only by the armies of Austria and of Bavaria.

For the papal reform projects to be vital they had to have a spiritual basis. This was furnished largely, though not entirely, by small groups of the faithful who for some time had been uniting themselves for prayer and holy studies. Typical and most important of all was the Oratory of Divine Love, begun in Rome shortly before 1517. Its members included clerics and laymen, pious merchants and classical scholars; its numbers were never large, fifty at the most. Their purpose was to initiate the reform of the Church by first reforming themselves. They worked for this objective by prayer and exhortation, by frequent Communion and confession, by studying the Scriptures and the writings of the Fathers, by discussing problems and projects of reform, and by devoting themselves to works of charity. Among the participants in the pious exercises were great reformers, or those who later would be leaders of the Catholic Revival. Such were St. Cajetan and Cardinal Caraffa, co-founders of the new Theatine order; Cardinal Giberti of Verona; Cardinal Lippomano, a future presiding officer of the Council of Trent; and two famous reforming Cardinals, Sadoleto and Fregoso. The Oratory of Divine Love at Rome and its counterparts elsewhere furnished the leaven for the Catholic Reformation.

The Council
of Trent

THE COUNCIL OF TRENT was the supreme event of the Catholic Revival. It did away with all fluctuations in doctrine which the Protestant controversy had induced, and it created a system of reforms which has been singularly effective down to modern times. And yet no other council struggled against such tremendous obstacles as those which faced the Tridentine assembly.

It was a miracle that Trent was ever brought into existence; it was a miracle also that it kept in session; and it was still another miracle that it was successfully completed. Never was a general council more interfered with by civil rulers seeking personal advantages in their conflicting ambitions or fighting any diminution of their almost total control of the Church in their respective dominions. Conciliarist theologians, encouraged by the monarchs, actively sought to checkmate the papacy. And always Protestant princes and divines opposed the effort.

The course of the council illustrates its perplexed history. The first assembly, called by Paul III, was held at Trent, 1545-1547 (Sessions I-VIII); then on the outbreak of an epidemic it was transferred to Bologna, 1547 (Sessions IX, X). But since Charles V forbade his bishops to go to

Bologna, little was accomplished and the council was suspended. The second assembly, called by Julius III, was held again at Trent, 1551-1553 (Sessions XI-XVI). But the approach to the Alpine passes by the Lutheran cavalry, victorious in the Smaldkald War, forced another suspension. There was no assembly held during the next ten years. Paul IV, 1555-1559, the stern and over-rigoristic reformer, had little use for the council. The last assembly, called by Pius IV, was held in Trent, 1562-1563 (Sessions XVII-XXV).

On his election to the papacy, Paul III set for the great goal of his pontificate the long-desired council. After a conference at Rome with distinguished prelates and the representatives of Charles V and his elected successor, Archduke Ferdinand, the new Pope decided on holding the council. His nuncios announced the decision to the rulers of France, Spain and Austria, to the Electors of the Empire and to the other German princes — Protestant as well as Catholic.

In June, 1536, Paul III issued the call for a general council to be held at Mantua, opening on May 23, 1537. Issuing a document was no guarantee of its fulfillment. Nine years, replete with frustrations, were to roll by before the council was started, and then only in a city that was the third choice.

Pope Paul possessed a strong personality. But it took all his iron determination to persevere through the welter of disappointments, delays, postponements and regal intrigues that filled up those nine years.

One of the obstacles hardest to overcome was the widespread scepticism that the Popes and the curia really wanted a council, or that they were laboring for practical reforms. Many doubted that the council would, or could, produce any extraordinary benefits. Such suspicions did not disappear until the last assembly was summoned by Pius IV. Threats of non-attendance of their bishops were made loudly and often, by monarchs who opposed a chosen location for the council.

Before the opening, there was considerable talk, both in the Empire and in France, of national councils. Such

THE COUNCIL OF TRENT IN SESSION. Italian engraving by Antonio Lafreri. *The Metropolitan Museum of Art, New York. Harris Brisbane Dick Fund, 1941.*

gatherings would have decisively hampered and impaired the Church universal. Only to be expected was the opposition of the Protestant princes and theologians. Their absolute rejection of the authority of the Holy See and their insistence on "pure Scripture" as the sole basis of all discussion made any understanding impossible.

Negotiations for the council were hampered, at times completely prevented, by two wars between Charles V and Francis I, involving most of western Europe, and by the revolt of the Lutheran Smaldkaldic Confederates. Belligerent powers frequently employed pressures and intrigues to control the council or to further their own personal interests. Conciliar planning was hardly possible amid the alarms of wars.

The council was never assembled at Mantua. The objections and the demands of the Duke of Mantua made action impossible. Then a choice was made, in 1538, of Vicenza in the Venetian Republic. But no council was held in Vicenza. Besides the legates, only six bishops appeared. Later the Republic of Venice refused its support. In the desperate situation, the choice of the locale was given over completely to Paul III. Finally he decided on Trent, May 22, 1542. But delays kept the opening back for three years until December, 1545. During nine years Paul III, due to forces beyond his control, was compelled to postpone the council six times.

The second miracle was the council's continued existence. Consult its schedule: two years at Trent, a half year at Bologna, four years' suspension, another year at Trent, nine years' suspension, and finally two years and a half at Trent. Almost to the end, its sessions were plagued by oppositions, pressures and intrigues, such as have already been described. In addition new difficulties were always appearing.

In the very beginning, the emperor and king of France insisted that only reformatory programs be considered and that dogmatic discussions be barred, or postponed, lest the Lutherans and the Calvinists be alienated. Paul III was adamant that dogmatic decisions be given priority, because reforms would be superficial gestures unless based on solid theological foundations. A compromise was effected: each session would treat and publish two programs: one dogmatic, one reformatory.

The decree on Justification, owing to two strongly defended theories, produced most acrimonious debates. Especially difficult was the decision on the contrasting rights of the papacy and the local hierarchies. The conclusion arrived at was that the bishops possess their episcopal powers immediately from God, but their particular jurisdictions, the limits of their dioceses, come to them mediately from God through the Pope as Christ's Vicar on earth.

Any other solution would have made each bishop a pope in his own diocese (a solution strongly favored by the monarchs who made all the nominations). Such a solution too would have rendered the Pope a shadowy, impotent figure and the term, Vicar of Christ on earth, would have been rendered meaningless. Christ had made Peter the Rock and had given to him the Power of the Keys.

These are but samples of the problems which occupied the fathers of the Council of Trent; and they, with all their human frailties, proved themselves devoted sons of the Church.

The third miracle of the Council of Trent was its successful completion. This was owing especially to three men: Pope Pius IV, who summoned and made possible the last assembly; St. Charles Borromeo, Papal Secretary of State, who from Rome, through daily correspondence with the legates at Trent, guided the course of events to a successful conclusion; and Cardinal Morone, whose skillful negotiations averted, near the end, a fatal rupture with the Emperor Ferdinand I.

The last sessions had their difficulties. But they were the best attended and the most harmonious of the entire council. The compelling force of utter necessity, and even more, the contagious enthusiasm of holy idealism carried the fathers to the happy completion.

Only one serious failure marked the last sessions; it was the reform of the princes. A program was prepared; it had the support of a large number of the fathers, but it was striving for the impossible. This was proven by the princes' reception of the Tridentine decrees.

Immediate and full reception was given only in the Republic of Venice, in the principal Italian states, in Portugal and Poland. Philip II published them in Spain, Naples and the Low Countries, adding the clause: "without detriment to the royal prerogatives." In 1565, they were received by the Catholic princes, lay and ecclesiastical, of Germany, and by Maximilian II and the Diet of Augsburg for the Empire. In France, though the dogmatic decrees were accepted without qualification, the monarchy rejected the decrees on discipline; only gradually did the individual bishops, without government support, succeed in introducing them. Of course the Tridentine decrees were never even acknowledged, much less accepted, in the Protestant lands, or in lands controlled by Protestant rulers.

From the standpoint of faith, the Council of Trent was monumentally important. True, it did not achieve the reunion of the Protestants. That was impossible as long as the fundamental doctrines of Catholicism were rejected. But the council's dogmatic decrees furnished the unerring basis of any reunion in the future.

Each decree was made up of a chapter in which the particular Catholic teaching was clearly and simply defined, followed by an enumeration in brief, clear and dispassionate sentences, called canons, of the opposite errors. There could remain no doubt as to what the Church taught and to what she was opposed.

Almost every controverted teaching was so treated. Thus the council declared holy Scripture and Tradition to be the norms of faith. It vindicated the necessity of good works and the freedom of the human will. It defined the following doctrines: the seven sacraments, in general and in particular; Transubstantiation, and the Real Presence; the Sacrifice of the Mass; the sufficiency of holy Communion under one species. It vindicated purgatory, indulgences, the veneration of the saints, of relics and holy images.

Trent did not explicitly treat the papacy. The supremacy of the Pope and the magisterium of the Pope and the bishops were of the most ancient Christian teaching. Even those fathers who retained conciliarist ideas referred final decision to the Pope, especially in the late sessions of the council. And all the fathers at its conclusion begged the papal confirmation of all dogmatic and reformatory decrees as necessary for their validity. These recourses to the Pope were equivalently a public acknowledgment of the papal power.

In Denzinger's collection of all the creeds, conciliar decrees and papal pronouncements on dogma from the Apostles' Creed to Pope Paul VI (833 pages of small print), the dogmatic decrees of Trent fill 64 pages, or 8% of the book. That is the largest contribution by far.

A New
Springtime

THE COUNCIL OF TRENT is best remembered for its reforms. Because of them, in four centuries, there has been no need of a general reform, such as existed prior to the council. True, evil conditions occasionally developed, but the instances were few and usually in areas where the Tridentine decrees had never been introduced or had been suffered to lapse. The enforcement of Trent's reforms remedied the unhappy situations. The long and widespread effectiveness of the great council's reforms seems all the more remarkable when one remembers that the mass of Catholics, clerical and lay, during these four hundred years, were but ordinary mortals.

The reforms of Trent began with the court of Rome and worked down through all grades of the hierarchy and the priesthood to the whole Catholic people. All—cardinals, bishops, priests, religious and the faithful—were again subjected to the discipline of the Church. Enumerating all the decrees and explaining their significances would require a vast space. A few will be cited to indicate the nature of the total body of reforms.

The bishops were strictly held to their duties as shepherds of their particular flocks. Pluralism and absenteeism were forbidden them. In consequence, a bishop could possess only one diocese; and he was obliged to remain constantly in it. Enjoined on the bishops was the careful superintendence of their clergy, which involved constant visitation of parishes, the holding of annual diocesan synods, and participation in regional and national councils. Similarly religious superiors were held to yearly visitations of the houses subjected to them. This constant visitation maintained zeal and discipline at a healthy point, and destroyed evils in their incipience. All bishops had to bind themselves solemnly to a special confession of faith, signed and sworn, to observe the decrees of the Council of Trent, and to submit to the Pope, whose primacy of jurisdiction, as instituted by Christ, was recognized by the universal Church. In relation to the diocesan clergy the bishops had to regulate the parishes anew, and to draw up and enforce ordinances regarding the administration of the sacraments and the office of preaching. One reform which gained considerable historical notice was the council's defense of the sanctity of the sacrament of Matrimony. All common law marriages were forbidden by making the validity of all marriages depend on the presence of three witnesses, one of whom must be the parish priest. (If within a reasonable time a priest could not be present, as might happen on a frontier, two witnesses sufficed.)

The most valuable legislation of the Council of Trent concerning priests was its provision for the education of candidates for Holy Orders. Few evils in the preceding period wrought more harm than clerical ignorance and clerical immorality. This was but to be expected considering how sadly inadequate was the formation of future priests. Some had only the meager instruction of a rural parish priest, himself poorly educated. Others fared scarcely any better in small schools attached to cathedrals. Only about ten percent attended the universities; but this fact by no means guaranteed them either requisite knowledge or good moral training.

To remedy such woeful conditions the council proposed the establishment of an institution, called the seminary, which would be devoted exclusively to the thorough training of aspirants for Holy Orders. Its course of study would take four years and would embrace dogmatic theology, moral theology, canon law, liturgy, and Church history. Also the seminary during all four years would impart a solid training in the spiritual life by prayer, practice of devotions and self-discipline. The seminary was to be a proving grounds, where the aspirant should test his vocation. If he concluded that God had not called him for the sacerdotal state, he could in all honor leave. But if he were convinced that God had chosen him for the altar, then he must strengthen himself to encounter the trials and temptations which he was sure to meet. (Philosophical and literary studies were prefixed at a later date to the four years of strictly sacerdotal learning.)

Originally Trent ordered the establishment of a seminary in every diocese. This was found impractical, especially in the case of small and impoverished dioceses. Regional seminaries were permitted where conditions warranted them. But from now on every candidate for the priesthood had to be trained in a seminary. The fact that for four hundred years there was no need of a general reform, and little need of local reforms, is owing to the seminary. This institution guaranteed to the Church a well instructed and a holy priesthood. The seminary is the greatest single achievement of the Council of Trent.

It was providential that a succession of strong Popes followed after the Council of Trent. Their strength was needed to guarantee the carrying out of the Tridentine decrees. Stern men undoubtedly they were. But stern men were called for. One had but to remember the belated acceptance of the reformatory decrees by certain rulers, which was noted in the preceding chapter. That there were also prelates, priests and religious who did not welcome the reforms, or who procrastinated in applying the regulations to themselves, goes without saying. There had to be adamant insistence on acceptance. By their own example these Popes further proved themselves worthy pastors of the flock of Christ. They fostered religious fervor and they devoted themselves to the protection of the spiritual interests of Christendom. Under them Rome again became the center of piety and learning.

POPE ST. PIUS V. Detail of the portrait by Federico Zuccari.
Stonyhurst College, Blackburn, England.

The first and the greatest of the post-Tridentine Popes was St. Pius V (1566-1572). As a Dominican friar and as a cardinal, Michael Ghislieri had been one of the most dedicated protagonists of the Catholic Revival. St. Pius, the Pope, was as unwearying in admonishing the clergy, high and low, to do their duty, as he was fearless in punishing transgressors. His government and his life of prayer and mortification infused a new life and vigor into the whole Church, and earned him the veneration and obedience of the Catholic world. By his bull, *In Caena Domini,* he strove for the independence of the Church and of churchmen everywhere against the dominance of secular powers. He inaugurated the movement which under his successors re-established the faith in a great part of Europe. He reorganized the College of Cardinals, the Roman clergy and the religious orders. True to his Dominican traditions he fostered the devotion of the rosary. He organized a crusade against the Turks, which resulted in the victory of the papal fleet under Don Juan of Austria at Lepanto in 1571, a victory which destroyed the naval supremacy of the Mohammedans in the Mediterranean.

Gregory XIII (1572-1585) vigorously carried on the works of his predecessor for the Catholic Revival, principally the reforms of Trent, the defense of the faith against heretics, and the deepening of Catholic devotional practices. He strongly supported the educational works of the Jesuit colleges which had become citadels of the defense and restoration of Catholicism. Thus Gregory XIII founded and entrusted to the order the Roman, German, Hungarian, English and Greek Colleges in Rome. Similarly he gave most generous financial help to the Jesuits conducting the seminaries of Vienna, Prague, Gratz, Olmutz, Braunsberg and Dillingen, and the universities of Wilna and Pont-a-Mousson. To the new missionary labors in Latin America, Japan and China, this Pope gave such interest and financial assistance that his contemporaries called him by a title which then was a new one, "The Pope of the Missions." These new evangelical labors in fields far from Europe were glowing indications of the revitalizing spirit aflame in the Church.

The energetic Sixtus V (1585-1590) was prominent as a spiritual and temporal ruler and as an administrator and a reformer. He carried on successful reform programs in Germany, Switzerland, Poland and the Netherlands. Though Sixtus reigned but five years he is universally ranked as one of the ablest of the Popes. Clement VIII (1592-1605) was another outstanding pontiff. Although he is remembered chiefly for his handling of most difficult diplomatic problems regarding the position of the Church in the conflicts between France and Spain, he could as well be recalled for his labors in the Catholic Revival. The celebration of the Jubilee of 1600 by an immense concourse of people in Rome, under Clement VIII, marked the high level of the Catholic Revival, a level which was to be maintained through the coming seventeenth century.

Religious Orders, Old and New

VITALLY IMPORTANT FOR the Catholic Revival were the reforms in the old religious orders. The monks and friars, by their example of renewed spirituality and by their increase of zealous apostolates, profoundly influenced the diocesan clergy and the lay people to splendid renewals of faith and devotion. The reform of the religious orders was achieved by a return to the primitive spirit of each order. This involved an earnest rededication to God and to His Church, a complete reassumption of the two essential practices of religious life, prayer and penance, and a strict observance of the vows of poverty, chastity and obedience, as set down in the ancient rules. It called for the rooting out of abuses, a sweeping away of luxuries and an abandonment of worldliness. Eventually men once more beheld prayerful and mortified monks, friars and nuns, tirelessly promoting solid piety and true devotion for the salvation of men's souls. The reformed religious nourished two great motives: an intense personal love of Jesus, and an unswerving loyalty to His Vicar on earth, the Pope of Rome.

The reform of the orders had been started, in several instances, before the Revolution. The reform developed considerably during the years between the pontificate of Leo X and the Council of Trent, and it was brought to completion by Pope St. Pius V and his immediate successors. The methods were: visitation, legislation by general chapters, determined government by abbots and general superiors, directives from the Holy See, and the examples and exhortations of saintly religious.

Reformation, it need scarcely be said, was not readily accomplished; in many areas powerful and long-protracted opposition blocked the way. First there was the bitter resistance of recalcitrant religious. On a few occasions even troops had to be called in to smash down barricaded entrances. But often the only recourse left against willful intransigents was expulsion from the orders. A serious hindrance was the practice of monarchs nominating abbots and abbesses. There were rulers who zealously supported the reforms; but there were other rulers who gave only lip-service. No monarchs, however, relinquished their "rights" of nomination. The best that the reformers could do was to persuade emperors and kings to nominate only worthy abbatial superiors.

The greatest obstacle in the reforming of the orders was the Religious Revolution. It halted promising reformatory programs begun before 1517. It destroyed numerous monasteries and convents and obliterated many provinces of the old religious orders. It waged in pulpit and press unremitting war against even the idea of religious life. This last hostility has been regretted by Harnack, one of the greatest of modern Protestant theological scholars. In recent times devout souls among Anglicans, Lutherans and Calvinists have begun to found religious institutes. The Religious Revolution gravely affected some members of the old religious orders located in the parts of Europe that had remained Catholic. It took years of most strenuous efforts to eradicate heretical ideas and even heretical members from the ranks of two of the greatest Catholic religious orders.

A detailed account of this reform cannot be given here. Some names and facts will emphasize its reality. The Benedictines, the oldest of the orders, may be considered first. In Germany the beginnings of the reform came in the last half of the fifteenth century with the labors of Cardinal

Nicholas of Cusa (almost two hundred monasteries) and the work of the Bursfeld Union (one hundred and thirty monasteries). The Revolution swept away nearly all these zealous communities, except those in the Rhineland and southern Germany. In Italy, reform was assured when early in the sixteenth century all monasteries were placed under the presidency of Monte Cassino. In France, revival followed the visitation of all French monasteries by three Benedictine abbots on the directive of Pope Alexander VI. Earlier, between 1481 and 1486, the Cluniac monasteries had reformed themselves. In England, widespread reforms had been achieved in the early part of the sixteenth century; but the good results were wiped out by Henry VIII's destruction of all the English monasteries. In Spain the reform was accomplished before 1517; one notable example of the Spanish revival was the monastery of Montserrat, the work of Gracia de Cisneros. After Trent St. Pius V and his successors completed the reform of the Order of St. Benedict.

The Dominicans at the opening of the sixteenth century were effecting a promising revival under the leadership of Thomas de Vio (later Cardinal Cajetan) and other learned and pious superiors. But the progress was seriously halted by the Revolution, during which seven provinces were lost and several hundred convents destroyed. After a few years, however, the Dominican revival was again a most active movement under the direction of excellent leaders, such as Thomas Badia (later the great reforming cardinal). In two visitations, 1543 and 1547, the Friars Preachers cleared their ranks of any heretically-minded members. Once again Dominican theologians were leaders of Catholic thought, notably at the Council of Trent. No stronger evidence of the Dominican revival need be sought than the glorious missionary apostolate of the friars in Mexico and Peru. Under St. Pius V, himself a Dominican, the renewal among the Order of Preachers was completed.

Quite similar was the history of reform among the Augustinians. Before the Revolution they had developed reformative movements: in the fifteenth century the Windesheim Congregation (one hundred houses), and in the early years of the sixteenth century the widespread revival achieved by the father general of the order, the celebrated Giles of Viterbo. The disasters caused by the Revolution to the Augustinians were very great, and most painful of all was the fact that Luther and many of his followers were from the order. But let it be noted that among the strongest opponents of the new teachings were Augustinians and that the order spared no effort to rid its membership of heretics and heretical doctrines. In 1539, the father general, Girolomo Seripando, instituted a thoroughly successful visitation of all the Italian, French, Spanish and Portuguese houses. The zeal of the Augustinian missionaries in the New World witnessed the profound values of their order's reform.

The Carmelites too achieved reforms in the fifteenth century, especially those of Bl. John Sorith. Like the other orders, the Carmelites suffered grievously from the Revolution. But during the Catholic Revival the Carmelites produced great reformers and mystics: St. Teresa of Avila, foundress of sixteen convents of nuns; St. John of the Cross, doctor of mystical theology; and St. Mary Magdalene de Pazzi, restorer of the Italian Carmelites. Carmelite missionaries in New Spain and in the Near East produced glorious chapters in the history of Catholic Missions.

The Franciscans numerically were the largest of the religious orders. For more than a century before 1500, they had been organized into two autonomous branches: the Conventuals and the Observants. Both branches experienced revivals in the fifteenth century, suffered terribly in the Revolution, and were thoroughly strengthened by the Catholic Reformation. Both produced many saints, scholars, and an extraordinary number of heroic missionaries. The Franciscans' apostolic labors, especially in Latin America and in the Far East, form the most inspiring records in Catholic missionary endeavors.

A unique development appeared among the Franciscans about 1525; it was the formation of a third autonomous branch, the Capuchins. It was a reform within a reform, for its members came from the Observants. They sought a stricter following of the ideals of St. Francis, particularly in poverty, simplicity of life, greater emphasis on prayer, and the evangelizing of the poor. The leader was Matteo de Bassi. The movement spread rapidly, but incurred very strong opposition from worthy men. The Observants felt that the existence of their branch was jeopardized; reforming cardinals were against any new religious orders; sincere clerics were suspicious of novel religious projects. The fears of the last were not unreasonable; the Religious Revolution in Italy was an underground affair, often propagated by some eloquent, popular preacher who, while apparently orthodox, was secretly heretical. The Capuchins, however, did not lack strong supporters in Rome; one, for example, was the iron-willed reformer Cardinal Caraffa. A terrible blow descended upon the harassed Capuchins when Ochino, their father general and the most popular preacher in Italy, apostatized and fled to Calvin in Geneva in 1542. That the Capuchins survived such a disaster evidenced that God's blessing was with them.

Indeed the Capuchins were to become one of the greatest forces in the Catholic Revival. They won the hearts of all Catholic Europe by their eminent virtues, their penitential lives, their heroic charity in the midst of pestilences, and their love of the poor. Their greatest work was done by their fiery, fearless, yet simple, sermons. Their preaching safely guarded the common people from heresies, and won back many who had been led away from the Catholic Faith. They had their martyrs, like St. Fidelis of Sigmaringen. The Capuchins were the most vigorous champions of the Faith among the older orders in the Catholic Revival.

New Power
for Good

THE CATHOLIC REVIVAL produced a new type of religious order, the clerks regular. "Clerks" indicated that they were clergymen; "Regular" meant that they lived under a rule (Latin, *regula*). They were not to supplant the older orders. There was then, and there always will be, the widest need for the monks, the canons regular and the friars. The new orders aimed to serve by new methods the changed society of the Renaissance, methods more direct and external than would be possible in cloistered monasticism.

The clerks regular combined the life of a religious with that of a secular priest. They took the vows of poverty, chastity and obedience; they dwelt in communities under constitutions approved by the Holy See; and they performed fervently the two essential practices of religious life, penance and prayer. At the same time they lived like diocesan priests. They wore the same black cassock, and they engaged in the parochial apostolate of preaching, hearing confessions, administering the sacraments and dispensing charity to the needy and the unfortunate — always with the same sovereign purpose of saving souls for God. Indeed they aimed to be the assistants of the diocesan priests and to encourage them to aspire to holy lives. The clerks regular were reformers; and since they were convinced that thorough reform could come only from the Popes, they made themselves dedicated servants of the Holy See. The first three orders of the clerks regular were the Theatines, the Somaschi and the Barnabites; the fourth, more numerous and influential, was the Jesuits.

These new orders shared a common Christian ideal, but they differed in points of emphasis. The Theatines, Somaschi and Barnabites subordinated their many activities to personal sanctification. They were persuaded that they could best help the Church first by their own self-conquest and prayer. The Jesuits did not reject this view. They, however, did not encumber themselves with monastic obligations, such as the chanting of the office in choir or the detailed program of penitential practices. They wished to hold themselves alert in bodily and intellectual strength for the task of serving God, His Church and His people.

The Theatines were founded at Rome in 1524, by Saint Cajetan of Thiene and Bishop John Paul Caraffa (later Pope Paul IV). The two differed markedly in temperament. Saint Cajetan was a cultured humanist, a learned theologian and a gentle mystic; Bishop Caraffa was an energetic prelate and a combative, rigoristic reformer. Yet in spite of their differences they combined harmoniously for the Church's recovery. Their order was called Theatine from Theate, the Latin word for Bishop Caraffa's diocese of Chieti. Caraffa resigned the bishopric in order that he might rank as a priest with his co-laborer.

The Theatines did not become a large order. St. Cajetan did not seek numbers; he aimed rather for chosen vocations from which leaders would be produced. His communities were said to be not "seminaries for priests," but "seminaries for bishops." The number of bishops who came from this small order is astonishing. People soon recognized that the Theatines represented a new spirit; any strict moralist or determined reformer was called a Theatine.

Always the Theatines' objective was the elevation of the priesthood. They strove to convince priests of the excellence of their priestly vocation and, hence, of the need of their adopting a rule of virtuous conduct. The rule was not to be unduly strict or monastic, but it was austere in regard to poverty, actual and spiritual, and in regard to personal morality. The Theatines urged priests to seek a deeper knowledge of God, to be intensely God-centered. Nor did they neglect the laity, recalling them to the practice of virtue, notably of frequent Communion. St. Cajetan advocated daily Communion, certainly a novelty in his day. The spirit of the Theatines was stern, but it mightily influenced the clergy to lead holy lives. By inculcating strong religious feeling and deep spirituality, the Theatines brought the priests, and also the laity, to strong reaction against the sensuousness and decay of the pagan Renaissance. They influenced priest and layman to struggle determinedly against their lower tendencies so that they might remain unsullied in the midst of corruption and heresy. The Theatines confirmed their arguments by the example of their own disciplined lives.

The Somaschi were founded about 1528, by St. Jerome Emiliani. Formerly a Venetian army officer, brilliant and dissolute, after two remarkable escapes he turned his mind to God. Henceforth he devoted himself to caring for the sick, the orphans and fallen girls. He gathered about him some pious laymen and established his headquarters in the village of Somascha, near Bergamo. It was from Somascha that his small company derived their name; officially they were called the "Clerks Regular of San Maiolo," from the church in Milan given them by St. Charles Borromeo. The work of the Somaschi centered mostly on the relief of the poor; during the famine of 1528, they won universal admiration.

The Barnabites were founded by St. Anthony Maria Zaccaria in 1530. Their name came from their church of

St. Barnabas in Milan, though officially they were the "Clerks Regular of St. Paul." Their founder aimed to repair the material and moral disasters of the times. The Barnabites preached, catechised, heard confessions, gave popular missions, ministered in the prisons and hospitals, educated youths and devoted themselves to the exposition of the Epistles of St. Paul. They achieved wonderful results in reviving the spirit of the clergy. St. Charles Borromeo held them in high affection. St. Francis de Sales called them "the coadjutors of the bishops." They spread through most of the Catholic countries of Europe. They were largely responsible for the return to the Catholic Faith of the French province of Béarn. In the pursuit of Christian learning, the Barnabites produced several able theologians and church historians.

The Jesuits came into existence when Paul III, in 1540, established them as a religious order and authorized their founder, St. Ignatius Loyola, to write their constitutions. It took the saint fifteen years; but he fashioned for the Popes their powerful body of assistants in the Catholic Revival. The Society of Jesus is the order's official name. It has but one purpose, the total service of the Holy Father, as the Vicar of Christ on earth. Thus the constitutions say: "The Society of Jesus and each single member, especially the solemnly professed, is bound to campaign under a special bond of obedience to the Roman Pontiff." The solemnly professed bind themselves by a fourth vow to go to whatever mission the Holy See sends them, even if no means of support are given them. St. Ignatius planned the Jesuits to be a disciplined, mobile body of spiritual warriors, learned and dedicated to the Holy See for whatever the Popes wished to use them in propagating and defending the Church. They were not founded merely to oppose Protestantism, or to be a teaching order, or even to be a missionary order. Such employments, however important they later became, were of secondary concern. This dedication to the Holy See accounts for the bitter opposition visited upon the Jesuits by all enemies of the Roman Pontiff, not only Religious Revolutionists, but Gallicans, Jansenists and Legal-Absolutists. The one purpose of the Society of Jesus was, and is, the total service of the Holy See.

ST. IGNATIUS LOYOLA. Portrait by Sanchez Coello, after restoration. *Professed House, Society of Jesus, Madrid.*

Only a few indications can be given of the first campaigns of the Ignatian spiritual warriors. They expanded with greatest rapidity; at the death of Aquaviva, the fifth general superior, in 1610, they numbered 13,132, maintaining 372 colleges and 123 residences, and operating in 14 foreign missions. They engaged in every phase of the Catholic Revival. Four of them participated in the Council of Trent, Laynez, Salmeron, Canisius and LeJay—the first three as papal theologians. Later several Jesuits were sent by the Popes through Europe to arrange for the implementing of the Tridentine decrees. Many more struggled for the Popes against absolute rulers in the Empire, France, Spain and the Venetian Republic; the latter suppressed the Society for a considerable time. For deepening the faith and intensifying devotion, numerous Jesuits spent themselves in spiritual and temporal works of mercy: nursing the sick, caring for prisoners, preaching missions, catechising children and peasants in neglected rural areas, reforming lax religious and reviving priestly ideals.

The most striking labors of the Jesuits concerned their conflict with the Religious Revolution. They produced many books, three of the most famous being Bellarmine's *Controversies*, Canisius' *Catechism* and Pazmany's *The Guide to Divine Truth*. Jesuits gave their lives as martyrs in England, France and Hungary. But their colleges were their most effective instrument, especially the German College in Rome; the colleges on the frontier; and the colleges in Spain, Rome and France for the preservation of the English, Irish and Scotch priesthood. The Jesuit colleges educated, along with lay students, the young religious of the older orders, as well as their own, and candidates for the seminaries. Dr. Pastor says that a new era dawned when the first generation came from the Jesuit colleges, for they possessed a strictly Catholic education, were solidly instructed, and were trained to a strong character, vigorously determined to struggle for the spread of the Church.

That the Jesuits stopped the tidal wave of the revolution and drove it back in many places is acknowledged by several Protestant historians—von Ranke and Macaulay for instance. Their successes were true not only in Germany, Belgium, the

Slavic lands and Hungary, but in Italy, where they nullified the underground attack, and in France where they defeated the Calvinists. In summary the spiritual warriors of St. Ignatius served the Popes with complete devotion, fighting in every part of the far-flung battlelines of the Continent, strengthening the faithful Catholic remnant in England and Scotland, and preserving by their heroism at home and their educational labors in their schools abroad the sterling loyalty to Catholicism of the Catholics of Ireland. St. Ignatius had given his sons a motto: "For the Greater Glory of God." They had fulfilled it.

The Flowering of Sanctity

A VERY STRIKING feature of the Catholic Revival was the great number of saints who belonged to it. In few periods of her history has the Church been served by so many and such able champions. They offer the strongest evidence of the depth and value of the Revival. They were products of the movement, participants in its activities and, by their own lives, exemplifiers of its ideals. Only a few of the saintly legion can be treated in a few brief chapters, but they will typify the rest.

At the head of the list are the saints who worked in close cooperation with the papacy. First of all is the strong Pontiff, St. Pius V. His labors, treated in previous chapters, can be but summarized here: he launched the program by which he and his successors made the Council of Trent a reality; he personally achieved much in the reform of the Cardinals, the diocesan clergy and especially the religious orders; he published the bull, *In coena Domini*, to protect the whole clerical body from interference and domination by the secular powers; he acted vigorously against heresies; and he inaugurated and financed the crusade against the Turks which resulted in the victory of Lepanto.

The apostle of Rome was St. Philip Neri. For the sixty years of his residence in the Eternal City, and especially for the forty years of his priesthood there, this lovable and cheerful saint influenced countless souls to sanctity of life and to loyalty for the Faith. He so affected all classes, high ecclesiastics of the Curia, important lay leaders, simple people, the youthful, the middle-aged and the old, that he became an outstanding leader of the whole Catholic Revival. His gentle guidance filled out the strict moral legislation of the Popes. Because he achieved so much to make the central city of Catholicism a worthy city in the eyes of the world, St. Philip has been called the "Reformer of Rome." To serve the crowds that frequented his church and oratory of San Girolomo, St. Philip founded the Oratorians, a congregation of secular priests living a common life. Services at the Oratory, besides Masses and confessions, consisted of discussions, familiar talks and learned lectures on sacred subjects. St. Philip enhanced the gatherings by heartwarming devotions and by the playing and singing of stately musical compositions, the origins of the oratorios of sacred music. But the guidance of souls he made the most important function of the Oratory. For forty years St. Philip himself, from his obscure room at San Girolomo, directed innumerable souls.

St. Ignatius Loyola and his work, the founding of the Society of Jesus, has been treated in the previous chapter. Here two points may be reconsidered. One is his unflagging zeal for the welfare of the Church. It inspired all that he said, wrote or did. One instance will suffice; he concluded the last pages of his spiritual classic, *The Book of the Spiritual Exercises,* with eighteen loyal directives, which he entitled "Rules for Thinking with the Church." Those rules were of the utmost importance in the day of the Religious Revolution; they have as strong a value in our confused times. The other point is his sole purpose in founding the Jesuit order, namely the total service of the Holy Father, as the Vicar of Christ on earth. St. Ignatius' life as the first Father General was an implementing of that dedication.

Add to the names of St. Pius V, St. Philip Neri and St. Ignatius Loyola, that of St. Charles Borromeo, and one enumerates the four outstanding leaders of the Catholic Revival. St. Charles Borromeo proved emphatically the practicableness of the reformatory decrees of the Council

of Trent by putting them into successful operation in the grave
conditions of his own great archdiocese of Milan.

Prior to this reform St. Charles had become a potent figure
in the Catholic Revival. Pius IV, his uncle, had elevated him
to the cardinalate and had made him his secretary of state.
When the pontiff decided on reconvening the Council of
Trent he entrusted all the negotiations to his secretary. It
was a most difficult assignment, owing to adverse political
and ecclesiastical interests. Further, during the two year
session he had to maintain and, at times, to direct the enormous correspondence between Rome and Trent. His was also
the task of exercising skillful diplomacy to offset the maneuvers of civil rulers; on one occasion there was danger that
the emperor might abandon the council. And always he had
to be extremely vigilant for the faith, since in this last session
some of the most vital doctrinal and reformatory decrees were
to be finally settled. He did not spare himself in the least.
To St. Charles Borromeo, more than to anyone else, were
owed the successful results of the third and last session of
the Council of Trent.

With the Council completed, St. Charles began to apply
to himself its regulations. Trent had definitely legislated
against absentee bishops; Milan for eighty years had not seen
a single one of its archbishops! St. Charles, hastening to
relinquish the office of secretary of state, sought permission
to take up residence in his own archdiocese of Milan. Pius IV,
still feeling a great need for his services, refused the request.
Two years later St. Pius V, who also valued St. Charles
greatly, reluctantly permitted him to depart for Milan.

The archdiocese of Milan was second only to Rome in
importance. Its population was almost 900,000. Its territory
spread over most of the plain of Lombardy and reached up
into Alpine valleys to include Ticino, the Italian-speaking
canton of Switzerland. The faithful of the archdiocese of
Milan were Italian-speakers; but there was a significant
number in the Alpine areas who spoke German. Milan was
one of the top-ranking cities of Europe, ever since Diocletian
had made it the western capital of the Roman Empire. But its
long history was a turbulent one of domestic strife and foreign invasion. Milan, in 1566, had about every contemporary

ST. PHILIP NERI. Portrait by Vecchietto. *Vallicella, Rome.*

ST. CHARLES BORROMEO. Portrait by Giuseppe Crespi. *Milan, Ambrosian Gallery.*

problem. The Church was afflicted by the deep ignorance of
many of the clergy and the lay people; religious practices were
profaned by abuses and superstitions; and some of the monasteries were filled with disorders. Immorality was rampant
in clerical and lay ranks. Heresies, seeping down from the
North, were establishing secret conventicles. Finally, the
liberty of ecclesiastical leaders was seriously hampered by
the caesaro-papism of the Spanish governors of the Duchy of
Milan. Nowhere in the Catholic world was there a greater
need of the reforms of Trent. And yet nowhere were the prospects of accomplishing them more meagre.

St. Charles Borromeo began the task by assembling at
Milan a great provincial chapter for the introduction of the
reformatory decrees of Trent. His ten suffragans assisted him.
During his twenty year episcopate he held seven provincial
councils and eleven diocesan synods. Two years before his
death the legislations of these assemblies were published
in a work, *Acts of the Church of Milan;* it became the pattern
for synods held all over Europe. One of the chief objectives
of these assemblies was a virtuous and capable clergy. For
this end the archbishop founded three seminaries and established annual retreats for clerics. But his most effective
contribution was the example of his own holiness and complete dedication to the priestly apostolate. He was indefatigable in the visitation of parishes, undeterred by heat or cold,
storms or disasters. He called to his aid the Barnabites and
the Jesuits; and to increase the number of his co-workers
he founded the Oblates of St. Ambrose, a congregation of
secular priests, bound by a single vow to serve him in any
apostolate.

To dispel the appalling ignorance in matters of faith,
St. Charles Borromeo founded a confraternity of Christian
Doctrine, which numbered 2,000 teachers, instructing 40,000
children in 740 schools. For the education of girls, the archbishop organized the Ursulines of his diocese into a single
community; for boys and young men he supported several
schools, colleges and seminaries. One of the seminaries was
for Swiss youths. St. Charles visited Switzerland three times
to establish the decrees of the Council of Trent. He held
jurisdiction over Ticino as archbishop of Milan, and he was

Apostolic Visitor for the whole country by appointment of the Holy See. His main efforts were centered on the seven Catholic cantons. In these he preached and catechised, and made conversions from Protestantism. He replaced unworthy clerics with saintly and capable pastors, and he restored discipline in the monasteries.

The vigorous reforms of St. Charles Borromeo of course raised powerful opposition. Anticlericals, an ancient force in Milan, resisted violently and uncompromisingly. The Spanish governors, agents of Philip II's caesaro-papism, seriously blocked freedom of action. But the worst antagonism came from worldly or unworthy ecclesiastics. The canons of the church of Santa Maria della Scala strongly resisted visitation by the archbishop, slamming and locking the door in his face. Three priors of the degenerate order of the Humiliati hired one of their own priests to assassinate St. Charles. Fortunately he was only wounded by the assassin's gunshot.

St. Charles Borromeo faced every trial with uncompromising heroism. His courage was never more manifest than in the terrible plague which raged in Milan from the summer of 1576 to the beginning of 1578. Most of the important people fled the stricken city, but not St. Charles. His notable charity to the poor surpassed itself as he organized the daily feeding of 60,000 to 70,000 starving unfortunates. His own health had always been delicate and he suffered frequent illnesses; but he ignored his own danger to nurse personally the victims of the plague and to minister to the dying.

The plague came a little more than half way through the episcopate of St. Charles. In the two decades of his rule of the archdiocese of Milan, he proved that the Church could reform herself. When some critics dismissed the reform program of Trent as fine theory, the Popes had but to cite their successful actuality in the populous and problem-beset archdiocese of Milan. That was the supreme achievement of St. Charles Borromeo.

Great Pens
in Defense
of the
Church

MANY WRITERS CHAMPIONED the Catholic cause during the Religious Revolution. Four were pre-eminent: St. Robert Bellarmine, Ven. Cardinal Baronius, St. Peter Canisius and St. Francis de Sales. Although all four participated in various activities of the Catholic Revival, their literary apostolates were their most important work.

The foremost Catholic controversialist was St. Robert Bellarmine who was born at Montepulciano in 1542, and died in Rome, 1621. He possessed vast learning, a keen mind, and a friendly disposition, which he strove always to manifest towards his opponents. He became a Jesuit in 1560. Some years later he was sent to the University of Louvain to complete his studies. After his ordination he was appointed a professor at the university. His lectures on grace, free will and the papal authority attracted crowds, including many Protestants. In 1576, he was called to Rome to occupy the chair of Controversial Theology at the Roman college. For the next eleven years, St. Robert labored tirelessly, lecturing and preparing his famous three-volume work, *Disputation on the Controversies.*

The *De Controversiis*, to give it its Latin term, was the greatest literary defense issued by Catholics during the period of the Reformation; in whole or in part it has gone through at least forty editions. It became the handbook of Catholic controversialists on every front of the Religious Revolution. Not only did those of the opposite cause forbid the reading of it, but in over one hundred books they strove to answer it. In some of their universities, professorships were founded for its continual refutation. Even three hundred years later, Hefele, the noted Catholic scholar, praised it as "the most complete defense of Catholic teaching yet published."

Clement VIII, in 1598, raised St. Robert to the cardinalate. During the next thirty years Bellarmine played an important part in the government of the Church. However, he did not cease his literary apostolate: writing two catechisms; a controversial work against the apostate friar Sarpi, who had supported the Venetian encroachments on the rights of the Holy See; two controversial works against King James of England; a commentary on the Psalms; and five devotional books. Cardinal Bellarmine was canonized in 1930, and declared a doctor of the Church in 1931.

Venerable Cardinal Baronius was the foremost defender of the Church in the arena of historical controversy. He was born in Naples in 1528, and died in Rome in 1607. He early became an Oratorian and was a great favorite of St. Philip Neri. It was St. Philip who directed Baronius to his great historical works.

In 1559, there appeared in Basel, a Protestant center, the first volumes of a work whose long title may be summarized, *A History of the Church...according to the centuries...done at Magdeburg by some learned and pious men.* It was called briefly, *The Centuries,* and its authors were known as the *Centuriators of Magdeburg.* The work was never completed. By 1574, the thirteenth volume was published; it was the last. *The Centuries* had some very good features: a plan for the critical treatment of Church history, a seeking of original sources, and a marshalling of vast collections of materials. But the execution cannot merit the same praise. The exercise of the critical faculty was limited by anti-Roman controversy, and no attempts were made at a calm and impartial survey of the Church's history. It was fundamentally a polemic work.

ST. PETER CANISIUS WITH THE EMPEROR FERDINAND AND
CARDINAL OTTO TRUCHSESS VON WALDBURG. Painting by
C. Fracassini. *The Vatican Gallery of Modern Art, Rome.*

ST. FRANCIS DE SALES. Portrait by an unknown artist.
Visitation Convent, Turin.

The Centuries did much harm. The immensity of its scope and the vast apparatus of its scholarly method initially made a tremendous impression. The Catholics, not prepared for this new type of attack, were dismayed. Several replies were attempted, but all were inadequate until Baronius produced his *Annales Ecclesiastici* (The Ecclesiastical Annals).

The *Annales* were published from 1588 to 1607. They consisted of twelve folio volumes, and reached down to 1192. Baronius died in the very year he had completed the twelfth volume. Almost three decades had passed from the day when St. Philip appointed Baronius to answer the Centuriators until the appearance of his first volume. The *Annales* were a work of painstaking and conscientious erudition. Baronius' transparent intellectual honesty was acknowledged by his most scholarly critics in the bitter controversies around the early volumes. His work was not without errors, but they were the mistakes of a pioneer in the new science of historical criticism. The *Annales* completely superseded the work of the Centuriators. Clement VIII, in 1596, created Baronius a cardinal. In 1607, the great historian died, in his sixty-ninth year. Benedict XIV, in 1745, raised Cardinal Baronius to the rank of Venerable; during his lifetime he possessed the reputation of profound sanctity.

If anyone, observing St. Peter Canisius, S.J., on a wintry day in 1549, riding through the Brenner Pass on his way to Germany, had greeted him with, "Here comes the Counter Reformation," nobody would have laughed more heartily than this modest and friendly Dutch Jesuit. Yet if ever a man was movement, it was Canisius. He was the chief inspirer, the leading director and the greatest participant of the German Catholic Revival. He has been called the Second Apostle of Germany. St. Peter was born at Nymegen in 1521, entered the Society of Jesus in 1543, started his German apostolate in 1549, and died at Fribourg, Switzerland, in 1597. The following summary will help one to appreciate St. Peter Canisius' multitudinous labors for the Catholic Revival.

He took a leading part in seven public disputations with foremost Lutheran theologians. He was the special advisor of the Catholic princes for the defense of the Faith. He founded nine Jesuit colleges, and once served as the rector of the Catholic University of Ingolstadt. For thirteen years he was the provincial of the Upper German province of the Society of Jesus, directing and extending its works in the Revival. He was constantly in the pulpit; in seven cathedrals at different times he was the official preacher (for seven years, almost daily, at Augsburg). He devoted himself to evangelizing abandoned districts and also to catechizing children, servants and peasants in at least a half dozen rural areas. He took part as an official theologian in the Council of Trent three times (once as the papal theologian). Pius IV sent him as his special agent to the Catholic princes and the bishops of Germany to deliver the decrees of the Council of Trent, especially to urge the establishment of seminaries. Father Brodrick, his great modern biographer, has estimated that St. Peter in thirty years traveled 20,000 miles on foot or horseback in the interest of the Catholic Revival.

St. Peter's greatest service for the Church was his literary apostolate. His supreme work was his *Catechism,* published in 1555. It was in three editions, one for schoolmasters, one for lay people, and one for children. Canisius' *Catechism* was reprinted two hundred times and was translated into fifteen languages.

It is well to note that St. Peter never attacked his opponents with rudeness or violence, either in his *Catechism* or in his instructions. St. Peter Canisius' *Catechism* was a most important book on the faith for the ordinary Catholic people. But it was not the only work he wrote for the Catholic cause. He composed books on theology, devotions (especially about Mary, the Mother of God), asceticism, apologetics, prayer-books and sermon outlines. In the listing of the Jesuit writers, the books and their editions written by Canisius fill forty-nine columns — and the list is incomplete. Pope Pius XI, in 1925, canonized St. Peter Canisius and on the very same day declared him a doctor of the Church.

St. Francis de Sales is considered the chief of the popular spiritual writers of the Catholic Revival. He was born of one of the oldest families of Savoy in 1567. After a brilliant university career he chose to be a priest. He was ordained in 1593 to work in his native country. One of his first labors as a priest was to bring back to the old Faith most of the inhabitants of the canton of le Chablais. It was a difficult and dangerous task (twice attempts were made to assassinate him). But after five years his moderation, kindness and priestly zeal were successful. To reach the people he wrote numerous leaflets explaining the Catholic teaching as opposed to the Calvinistic doctrines. These leaflets he later published in a book called *Controversies*.

After his election, in 1602, as bishop of Geneva (he had to reside at Annecy), St. Francis organized catechetical instructions and enforced the Tridentine decrees. He wrote a number of remarkable spiritual works. The most famous was *An Introduction to a Devout Life*, which was translated into many languages, has gone through many editions, and is still one of the masterpieces of devotional literature. Another important work of his was the *Treatise on the Love of God*. Others of his writings were: *Defense of the Standard of the Cross, Spiritual Conferences, Sermons, Letters* and a large number of small treatises.

Not only in Savoy but in many parts of France, St. Francis became one of the most sought-after preachers. With St. Jane Frances de Chantal he founded the Visitation Order of Nuns. All his written works introduced a gentle, beautiful spirituality, but also a very practical one, into the Revival movement. He brought the virtues of religious life to the lay people and mingled with them a sanctified human conduct. Francis de Sales died in 1622. He was beatified in 1662, canonized in 1665, and declared a doctor of the Church in 1877. Pius XI declared St. Francis de Sales to be the patron saint of journalists.

Unflinching Witness

NONE EMPHASIZE MORE the strength of the Revival than the martyrs of the Religious Revolution. Their number and their constancy are the most inspiring aspects of the Catholic Reformation. It is not the purpose of this chapter to rekindle bitter memories of religious strifes long past. Outrages disgraced both sides. The sole consideration is the heroic fortitude of the martyrs in suffering and dying for the Faith. Their sacrifices are the most glorious fruits of the Revival.

The Church has raised to her altars as martyrs of this period 64 saints and 206 blessed. It will be helpful to recall some of the conditions which the Church insists upon, when canonizing or beatifying a martyr. First, there must be the free and unresisting acceptance of death for the refusal to abandon a doctrine of the faith. A soldier, killed in battle while fighting for the faith, is not strictly a martyr, though he may be honored as a Catholic hero. Secondly, there must be clear proof that the proposed martyr was put to death out of hatred for the faith. If the motives were primarily political, his cause is not considered. Thirdly, there must be clear-cut documentary evidence, assembled in legal form, before any movement may finally be inaugurated towards beatification.

It should be remembered that the Church does not attempt to canonize or beatify all her innumerable saints and martyrs. The task would be impossible. She must content herself with choosing outstanding personalities, or those in whom there is great interest. Oftentimes nothing can be achieved because of the lack of authentic documents; sometimes interest wanes and a cause of beatification dies out. Daniel-Rops' remark that there were countless unknown and forgotten martyrs in the first centuries' persecutions is applicable to the martyrs of the Religious Revolution.

Ireland illustrates the point. There is only one Irish martyr listed, Bl. Oliver Plunkett, Archbishop of Armagh. Yet the popes often have hailed Ireland as a "martyr nation," because of her constancy in all-out persecutions during the Religious Revolution, and these papal tributes have been endorsed by Catholic peoples everywhere. The principal explanations of this apparent discrepancy are: first, the historical situation of continual warfare for more than two centuries, the complete denial of education to Catholics, and the vast social disasters—especially recurrent famines; secondly, the great lack of authentic documentation, owing to the wholesale destruction of Catholic documents by the religious revolutionists, and to the practical impossibility of records being kept by hidden priests whose lives and possessions were in constant jeopardy.

What might have been accomplished under even half-better conditions, may be judged by the investigations of the Irish hierarchy in 1904 and 1905. After two years of difficult studies, the bishops were able to draw up a list of persons who lived during the persecution times and who might be ranked as martyrs. The list counted 340 such persons. Yet in almost all cases the sources of information were so meager as to leave little hope of eventual beatification.

Similarly in France, Poland, Hungary, Bohemia, Germany and the Low Countries, there were many Catholics whose deaths during the religious conflicts might be considered martyrdoms. But the vital records that might have established the heroism of their sacrifices were lost in such disasters as the Huguenot Wars, the Thirty Years War, the destruction of Poland, and, above all, the French Revolution.

All these martyrs, officially canonized or not, died for their beliefs in the doctrines of the Catholic Faith, especially the primacy of the Holy See, the magisterium of the Church, the absolution of the confessional, the truth of the sacrifice of the Mass and the real and perpetual presence of Christ in the Eucharist. Life, freedom and, in the case of clerics, religious preferments were offered to them if they would abjure the doctrines of their Faith. But heroically they made their choice to stand fast by their ancient Catholic religion: "come rack, come rope," as the martyred St. Edmund Campion proclaimed it.

Only a few of the martyrs can be cited here. They will exemplify the unflinching sacrifices of the rest. The two hundred English martyrs included one Cardinal, St. John Fisher, priests and religious — Franciscans, Carthusians, Benedictines, Dominicans, Jesuits and, more numerous, secular priests. There were four laymen, including St. Thomas More, and four lay women.

Among the priests the most striking figure is St. Edmund Campion, S.J. While a young professor at Oxford he had conformed, but shortly afterwards, he repented, fled to the Continent, was reconciled and entered the Society of Jesus. In 1580, he came back to England as part of a secret mission to strengthen Catholics and to bring back lapsed ones. Though obliged to move about in disguise, with priesthunters hot upon his trail, Campion, together with his colleague, Father Robert Parsons, S.J., converted or reconciled at least 10,000 in a period of eight months. During furtive journeys St. Edmund wrote, and managed to get published clandestinely, two valuable pamphlets explaining his mission.

At last he was captured, exposed to the insults and taunts of a London mob, imprisoned, tortured and, after a disgraceful trial, was hanged, drawn and quartered at Tyburn Hill. Edmund Campion's heroism, intelligence, gaiety, energy and chivalrous conduct eventually gained the admiration of all Englishmen.

The courage of two of the women martyrs deserves notice. St. Margaret Clitherow, "the Pearl of York," unflinchingly endured being pressed to death rather than reveal her harboring of priests and her hearing of Mass. St. Anne Line devoted her life, though always in extreme ill-health, to maintaining her London home as a secret refuge for hunted priests. At her trial she was so ill that she had to be seated in a chair. When she was asked if she pleaded guilty to harboring a fugitive priest, she cried out so that all could hear her: "My lords, nothing grieves me more but that I could not receive a thousand more." When Anne was brought to Tyburn she kissed the gallows and knelt in prayer until her execution.

The martyrdom of Bl. Oliver Plunkett crowned a career associated almost entirely with the Catholic Revival. He was trained for the priesthood in the Eternal City and in two institutions conducted by the Jesuits, the Irish College and the Roman College. For twelve years following, he taught theology in the College of the Propaganda, and acted as the Roman agent for the Irish hierarchy. All the while, he lived with the Oratorians at their church of San Girolomo della Carità and participated in their priestly apostolate. In 1669, he was appointed Archbishop of Armagh and Primate of Ireland.

Bl. Oliver's episcopacy, which lasted another twelve years, was in very truth a prolonged martyrdom. Religious conditions could hardly have been worse; the Irish Church lived in the shadow of persecution. The archbishop had to move about in disguise. He was forced to live in direst poverty, and he had to endure the most painful physical hardships. Since most of the Irish hierarchy were dead or in exile, he was obliged to do the work of several bishops. Enormous crowds came to him in remote valleys to receive the sacrament of Confirmation.

Finally he was made a victim of the infamous Titus Oates' plot; he was accused of planning a foreign invasion against the king, Charles II, and the Protestants. So evident was the innocence of the archbishop that no jury of Irish Protestants would condemn him. He was brought over to London and imprisoned in the filthy, noisome Newgate dungeon for nine months. After a farcical trial, in which two of his accusers were evil priests, he was sentenced to death. The presiding judge admitted openly in court that the basic reason for the condemnation was the primate's Catholic religion. Bl. Oliver Plunkett was hanged, drawn and quartered on Tyburn Hill, 1681.

A number of the martyrs chose death rather than repudiate the Holy Eucharist and the Real Presence. Among these were the Martyrs of Gorcum, nineteen Dutch priests, religious and secular; the Martyrs of Aubenas in France, Bl. James Salès, a priest, and Bl. William Saultemouche, a lay brother, of the Society of Jesus. All these and the following gladly died for the spiritual supremacy of the Pope: Bl. John Ogilvie, in Scotland; Bl. Ignatius Azevedo and his forty young novices, who bravely gave their lives when their ship, on its way to the mission of Brazil, was attacked by Huguenot corsairs; Bl. Canon Mark Crisin, Bl. Stephan Pongracz and Bl. Melchior Grodecz, all three who died together for the Faith in Hungary.

We must also include St. Andrew Bobola, S.J. and St. Josaphat, Archbishop of Polotsk; both heroically endured frightful deaths for the sake of the reunion of Ruthenian Catholics with the Holy See.

All these martyrs of the Catholic Revival proved conclusively the deep and lasting effects of the Catholic Reform. No man can do more for the Catholic Church than to die for it.

Spiritual Resurgence

ONE OF THE STRONGEST foundations of the Catholic Revival was the resurgence of spirituality. It provided the inspiration of all activities, it made the movement holy, and it guaranteed the solidness of the results. Old systems of prayer and piety, of mysticism and asceticism experienced vigorous revivals. New schools of holiness and devotions provided fresh approaches to the practices of saintly living, which corresponded well with the current intellectual and spiritual tendencies. Here was a section of the Catholic Revival which was not a counter-movement to the Religious Revolution. It was a domestic development in and for the household of the Faith.

The spiritual resurgence was thoroughly in the spirit of the Council of Trent. It was a movement against the new religions only by its theological bases, which were completely Tridentine. It was in contrast with the revolutionary teachings on the unworthiness of man, the denial of his free will, the impossibility of his doing good deeds, the denial of his power to cooperate with God, and the denial of his power to merit. The optimistic spirit of its holiness was in contrast with the pessimistic outlook of the revolutionists just because it insisted on trust in human nature, in the beauty of the human soul and in the fruitful value of man's good works.

The Catholic ascetical and mystical writers were all dedicated reformers. St. Ignatius Loyola, St. Philip Neri, St. Cajetan, St. Teresa, St. John of the Cross, St. Francis de Sales, all aimed at the rejuvenation of the Church. They are typical of the numerous other writers and teachers of prayer, penance, God's love for us and our love for God. Every one of the holy cloistered nuns of the period, like St. Mary Magdalene de Pazzi, daily besought God for the amendment of the clergy. The great mystics strove untiringly to improve prayer and spiritual life in religious houses, and to inspire the parish clergy to a love and practice of the ideals of the priesthood. The almost perpetual theme of St. Vincent de Paul's preaching to the clergy was the sanctification of the priesthood, the excellence of the sacerdotal dignity and the sacredness of the sacerdotal duties.

The protagonists of the spiritual resurgence — sometimes directly and, more often, indirectly through zealous priests — influenced the lay people. And so all people, high and low, rich and poor, great and simple, each according to his capacity, learned the ways of God: the purgative, the illuminative and the unitive. All were urged to self-knowledge and self-conquest. All were warned against formalism, and of the necessity of sincere action. The hearts of men were reached and moved; hence the reforms of the Catholic Revival would not be merely finely drawn plans.

The three outstanding leaders of the spiritual resurgence were St. Ignatius Loyola, with his *Book of the Spiritual Exercises*, St. Philip Neri, with his apostolate of the Roman Oratory, and St. Francis de Sales, with his *Introduction to the Devout Life* and his *Treatise on the Love of God*. But they were important in so many ways to the Catholic Revival that the totality of their contributions had to be mentioned in previous chapters. Hence the nature and value of their writings and counsels for prayer — mystical and verbal — for devotional life, for self-discipline and for the interior service of God have already been treated.

But St. Ignatius, St. Philip and St. Francis de Sales were only in the van of numberless writers on the mystical and devotional life. Since most of these brought fresh approaches and fresh insight into the spiritual life, they have been

Alinari

ST. TERESA OF AVILA. Portrait of the saint at the age of sixty-one. St. Teresa herself sat for this portrait at Seville in 1576.
Friar Juan de la Miseria.

ST. VINCENT DE PAUL. Likeness based on a portrait by Simon Francois of Tours. *Motherhouse of the Congregation of the Mission, Paris.*

considered as forming a new school of prayer and devotions, although their teachings were always thoroughly in the spirit of the Council of Trent. A different and a more definite classification has been given these new writers. Because their works reveal clearly their national origins, they have been divided into three schools: the Spanish, the Italian and the French. The differences were largely of emphasis and arose from national characteristics and local viewpoints. The writings of all three schools were the same in fundamentals, and were securely grounded in the ancient Catholic principles of faith and morality.

The sanctity developed by the Spanish was deeply stamped with the intense loyalty, romantic chivalry and strong determination of that warrior nation which produced crusaders, explorers, conquistadores, missionaries and theologian-champions of the Faith. It was marked, too, with a practical realism that seemed to be drawn from the rugged hardness of the peninsula's mountains.

The greatest representative of the Spanish school was St. Teresa of Avila (1515-1582). She is one of the most extraordinary women in all of history. To reform the Spanish Carmelites she founded the austere Discalced Carmelites. From 1562, when she established the convent of St. Joseph at Avila, almost until her death in 1582, she trod the highways of Spain making other foundations, despite ill health, bodily pains, and hostile criticism. St. Teresa established seventeen convents of Carmelite nuns. She assisted her countryman, St. John of the Cross, in his reform of the Carmelite Friars and helped him to found fifteen monasteries.

St. Teresa is one of the foremost writers on mystical prayer, especially because of her *Letters* and her *Autobiography*. Her writings, combining practical efficiency with the most sublime devotional ideas, have had a profound spiritual influence upon every generation down to the present day. Paul VI, in 1970, proclaimed St. Teresa and St. Catherine of Siena, Doctors of the Church; they are the first women to be so honored.

St. John of the Cross (1542-1591) almost equals her as a representative of the Spanish school. He, too, deserves the same rating among the great spiritual authorities, because of his mystical writings: *The Ascent of Mt. Carmel, The Dark Night of the Soul, The Living Flame* and *The Spiritual Canticle.* The Church has officially declared St. John of the Cross a Doctor of Mystical Theology. The works of these two Spanish Carmelites are the classical sources of mystical theology.

The origins of the Italian school of spirituality have been described in previous chapters where the Oratory of Divine Love, St. Cajetan and the Theatine Order, and St. Philip Neri and the Roman Oratory were treated.

The Italian school was more inclined to action than the Spanish. In the midst of the sensuousness and moral decay of the Pagan Renaissance, it sought for each man the means of struggling against his depraved tendencies and also the means of remaining unsullied amid the surrounding corruption, and later the surrounding heresy.

The Italian masters of the spiritual life labored for the reform of the Church, particularly for the improvement of the priesthood. They drew up rules of conduct which, if hard, were neither unduly strict nor monastic. They urged on the clergy and laity a fuller devotional life which, although austere, stressed the beautiful and comforting in Christian teaching. The Italian mystics were the first to revive the practice of frequent Communion; they invigorated the veneration of our Savior, of the Madonna and of the saints. Sixteenth-century Italian devotional life inspired numerous charitable works and brought countless volunteer helpers into the hospitals. Due to this impulse, St. John of God and St. Camillus of Lellis founded their religious orders for the nursing of the sick.

The French school, which flourished in the seventeenth century, was graver in expression and temper than the Spanish and the Italian. It laid great emphasis on the sovereignty of God and took a severe view of men. It was not Jansenistic. The leader was Cardinal Pierre de Berulle (1575-1629), the founder of the French Oratorians. According to him, the first duty of the Christian is to worship God, and not so much for His kindness to man, as for His sovereign majesty. Humiliation and abnegation were two very important duties for man. Berulle possessed an intense devotion for the person of Christ, which he communicated to the whole French School. One great occupation of the cardinal was the spiritual training of worthy priests.

Another leader was Jean Jacques Olier (1608-1657), the founder of the Seminary of St. Sulpice and of the Sulpician Fathers for the conducting of seminaries. Monsieur Olier vigorously promoted the Catholic Revival, organizing religious instruction for old and young, rich and poor, great and simple. Olier emphasized in spirituality the virtue of abnegation, the necessity of mortification and the dignity of the priesthood. In the most beautiful terms he described the relations between the priest and Christ.

St. Vincent de Paul (1581-1660), the beloved apostle of charity, the founder of the Vincentian Order and of the Sisters of Charity, was the third leader of the French School. St. Vincent's spirituality combined Berulle's austerity, French common sense and Salesian cheerfulness. Two of his goals were: training worthy priests in seminaries, and bringing piety and faith down to ordinary people by means of the parish mission. Another leader was St. John Eudes (1601-1680), founder of the Eudists, a congregation for conducting seminaries. St. John introduced the first liturgical celebration of the feast of the Heart of Jesus and of the Heart of Mary. The attachment of the French School to the person of Jesus produced many devotions to the Blessed Sacrament, to the divine nature of Christ, and to the glorious union of the Lord's divine and human nature.

One must be careful not to overstress the national characteristics of these schools. There was unity in the fundamentals, and the differences were unimportant. All the contemporary spiritual writers — mystical, ascetical and devotional — strove with all their souls for more zealous religious orders, holier secular priests and more truly devout lay people — in brief, the Catholic Revival.

The Huguenot Wars

THE STRUGGLES BETWEEN the Catholic Church and the Religious Revolution may be said to have ended in the Wars of Religion. These conflicts determined what areas of Europe were to be Protestant and what areas Catholic. It is regrettable that the religions of men should have been decided by the arbitrament of arms. But such was the historical fact. Those parts of Europe where Protestantism was predominant at the end of the Wars of Religion remained Protestant until modern times; and those parts where Catholicism was predominant remained Catholic until modern times.

The Wars of Religion were fought with extreme bitterness, and outrages were committed by partisans of both sides. It must be said to the credit of the men of those days that religion was their supreme good. To avoid being deprived of it, or to resist attempts to force them into another, they were prepared to fight to the death. Such motivation would be incomprehensible to millions of the modern unchurched for whom religion has little, if any, meaning.

There were four Wars of Religion; actually there were four series of wars. They were: the Huguenot Wars in France, 1562-1593; the Revolt in the Low Countries, 1559-1592; the Struggles for the British Isles, 1561-1603, 1649, 1689-1691; the Thirty Years War in the Holy Roman Empire of the Germans, 1618-1648. While all these wars were fundamentally religious conflicts, they were all hopelessly complicated by secular politics, programs for predominance, dynastic ambitions, nationalistic and linguistic clashes, greed for landed possessions and, finally, commercial rivalries.

To make confusion worse, all four struggles reacted on one another, as the fortunes of the two great forces flourished or weakened. Yet through all the cross-purposes, the primary questions stood out emphatically: "Shall this area be Protestant or Catholic?", "Shall that area be Catholic or Protestant?" Needless to say the Church suffered grievously. In some lands it ceased to exist; in other lands it was forced back into the furtive life of the catacombs.

In the Huguenot Wars the question was whether France would remain Catholic or become Calvinist. France was the most populous and the most powerful of all the European kingdoms. She was the most strategically placed, with her long Atlantic seaboard and her protective barriers of the Alps and the Pyrenees. Whatever triumphed in France might determine the religious future of most of northern Europe. Further, France was already moving into the cultural leadership of Europe, a position which she maintained through the next three centuries. It was of vital importance whether this predominance would be Catholic or Calvinistic.

There were three parties in the French conflict. First were the Calvinists, unalterably determined on making France completely Protestant. They were not numerous, constituting only about three percent of the total population. But they were very powerful in the character of their adherents: they had a few princes of royal blood, very close to the throne; they counted about a third of the nobility, who with their castles and retainers made up no insignificant force; and they held several walled cities. With help from Germany, Holland and England, they might well have been able to achieve their ultimate objective. They possessed first class leaders in Henry of Navarre, a possible future king, and Admiral Coligny.

Their opponents were the Catholics, the vast bulk of the nation, passionately loyal to the old Faith, whose leaders were the Dukes of Lorraine, of the House of Guise. They were able and devoted Catholics, although their advocacy was mingled with personal ambitions (as was also true of the other side). Though they were of royal descent from the kings of France, they were looked upon by some as foreigners; they had come into France with the annexation of French Burgundy. Their masterful role near the throne, which they had quickly begun to play, aroused the enmity of certain Catholics. However, this enmity dissolved, and such Catholics joined the Guise when it became evident that the struggle was to decide the very existence of Catholicism.

The third party was the "Compromisers," a group of politicians who sought to prevent the predominance of either Huguenots or Catholics by throwing their influence on the side of the group temporarily weakened. They were headed by the Queen Mother, Catherine de Medici, an unscrupulous woman of few religious convictions. Her sole purpose was to keep the kingship in the hands of one after another of her weakling sons: Francis II, Charles IX, Henry III, and Francis, Duke of Alençon.

The Huguenot struggles lasted for thirty-one years and were contested in eight cruel and sanguinary wars, marked by assassinations, treacheries and massacres. The massacre of St. Bartholomew's Eve was but one of several horrible events; because the victims were Calvinists it received wide notoriety in England and Germany. Actually it was a political plot of Queen Catherine de Medici to destroy Coligny who had obtained ascendency over Charles IX. It had religious overtones because it took place during the Huguenot Wars. The Church had nothing to do with it.

Both in Paris and in the provinces, many Huguenots were saved by the humanity of officials and the charity of priests and religious. The Archbishop of Lyons, the bishops of Lisieux, Bordeaux, Toulouse, and other bishops sheltered the fleeing Huguenots and restrained the popular violence. Well before St. Bartholomew's day, priests and religious had been massacred in thousands. Wherever the Huguenots triumphed, they sacked churches and ruthlessly destroyed their works of art, stained glass windows, statuary and sacred vessels. More than 20,000 churches in France were thus ravaged and despoiled. What outraged Catholics the most were the constant sacrilegious desecrations of the holiest of mysteries, by trampling on the Sacred Hosts or feeding them to the horses.

As the danger of foreign aid to the Huguenots was still great and the supineness of the government was still helping them, the Catholics formed the Holy League, under the leadership of Duke Henry of Guise. Henry III so hated the Guise that he joined Henry of Navarre, the Protestant leader, in the siege of Paris, which was a stronghold of the Catholic cause. The duke of Guise appealed to Philip II of Spain. With the latter's assistance, he successfully defended Paris. Henry III then caused Duke Henry of Guise and the Duke's brother, the Cardinal of Lorraine, to be assassinated at Blois, only to meet the same fate himself, shortly afterwards, at the hands of a crazed religious. What the Catholics feared the most had now come about, a Huguenot prince, Henry of Navarre, was to mount the throne of St. Louis.

Knowing how in Germany such a succession usually brought about the end of Catholicism in a great principality, the Holy League determined to fight on. They lost many supporters, for numerous Catholics, followers of the rights of legitimacy, went over to Henry of Navarre, now claiming to be King Henry IV.

The new monarch, convinced that he could not rule France as a Calvinist, sought absolution (for a short while in the past he had been a Catholic) and made his profession of the Catholic Faith at St. Denis in 1593. The royal action practically ended the Huguenot Wars. In 1598, Henry IV published the famous Edict of Nantes. By the edict the Catholic churches which had been devastated were restored, freedom of religion was given to the Huguenots and a very large measure of freedom of worship was also accorded to them. As they were allowed to retain many fortified places and some walled towns, the Huguenots continued to be a menacing force—a state within a state. However, the Catholicity of France was assured.

Henry IV's successor, Louis XIII, was a devoted Catholic; the vast bulk of the French nation was more loyal to the old Faith than ever, because they had suffered so much for it; and by the capture of La Rochelle, in 1628, Cardinal Richelieu ended French Calvinism as a political organization. Richelieu granted the Huguenots religious liberty and civil equality.

Catholicism in France was safe. It was a complete victory; and it was owing to the strong faith and simple patriotism of the Catholic majority.

The
Low
Countries

THE RELIGIOUS WARS of the Low Countries lasted from
1559 to 1592. The issue was whether this region of northern
Europe was to be Calvinistic or Catholic. Closely entwined
was another issue, whether this territory was to become an
independent nation or remain a principality ruled by the
Hapsburg kings of Spain. Today the area includes Holland,
Belgium and a small portion of northern France. In the
Late Middle Ages, and down even to the French Revolution at the end of the eighteenth century, the region was
called the Low Countries, or the Netherlands. Its inhabitants
were divided into three linguistic groups: the Dutch, in the
north; the Flemish, in the center; and the Walloons, French-
speakers, in the south.

These Netherlanders were thrifty people; by their
flourishing agriculture, commerce and industries—the principal of which was weaving—they had made their territory
one of the richest in Europe. They were also a very populous
group, possessing in their small area 200 walled cities, 250
open towns and over 6,000 villages. Among the leading cities
were Brussels, Bruges, Ghent, Antwerp, Amsterdam, Utrecht
and Rotterdam. The Low Countries were divided into seventeen provinces, each with a legislature, called an estate.

The central government was located at Brussels; there dwelt the Stadtholder (Viceroy); and there met the estates-general to legislate for the whole country.

The ruler of the Netherlands was the Hapsburg prince who possessed the Burgundian inheritance, the lands of the Duchess Mary of Burgundy, of which the most important parts were the Low Countries. At the outbreak of the Religious Revolution, this prince was the Emperor Charles V, who was the grandson of the Duchess Mary and of her husband, the Emperor Maximilian of Hapsburg. When Charles V retired in 1555, he passed on to his son Philip II his two great personal inheritances, Spain and the Low Countries.

Charles V had been popular with the Netherlanders. They looked upon him as one of their own. He had been born in Ghent, he spoke Flemish, and he participated in their games and festivities. Moreover, he gave the nobility many important positions — military in his wars, and governmental in his vast dominions. Philip, on the other hand, was unpopular. He was a stranger; he had been born in Spain, he could not speak Flemish, he was reserved and averse to warlike exercises and athletic sports. And what is more, he did not give the nobles lucrative positions, neither military nor administrative in his larger dominions, and only a limited share in the governments of the local provinces. Such a program bore hard on the nobility, many of whom had been impoverished by the wars or by their own expensive living.

The first stirrings of opposition came principally from such nobles, who hoped to retrieve their shattered fortunes by political changes. The presence of 3,000 Spanish soldiers, guarding the southern frontier from the French, increased the discontent. These troops were paid partly by Spain and partly by the Low Countries, and by both very irregularly; hence several riots by the soldiers broke out, which only further inflamed the national antipathy between the Netherlanders and the Spaniards. Philip was induced to withdraw the troops to Spain, which he did shortly after his own departure. He had hardly been two years in the Low Countries; he never returned, but strove — not very successfully — to rule from Spain the turbulent events which followed, by means of regents acting on his instruction.

Religious conditions in the Netherlands, at the beginning of Philip's reign, were better than in Germany, France and England. However, evils existed which could be fanned into revolution. Although clergymen of irreproachable life were numerous, there were bad priests and religious, lax monasteries and convents, and clerical scandals connected with the abuse of wealth. A minority among nobles, merchants and other citizens were affected by anti-clericalism, due to the so-called "Guilds of Rhetoric," which in pamphlets, lampoons, plays and popular festivities ridiculed the Pope and monks, indulgences, pilgrimages and other religious institutions in the cynical spirit of radical humanism. Further the geographical position and the commercial connections of the Low Countries opened the region to emissaries of English Protestantism, German Lutheranism and French Calvinism.

Charles V, in 1522, checked religious agitation somewhat by anti-heretical edicts. They were harsh in the texts, but much milder in their application; and they had the approval of the great majority of the people. These edicts of Charles V would never have caused the Revolution without the political revolt which used them as a means of agitation.

What kept the mass of the people loyal to the Church was the extraordinary influence of the University of Louvain. It sent out its devout and well-trained scholars, writers, preachers, parish priests and religious into every part of the Low Countries as so many defenders of the Faith. All the faculties of the University were united in the cause of Catholicity. The humanistic studies in particular were cultivated on conservative lines. As a result, in spite of the radical humanists and the foreign preachers, not a single organized heretical community was formed before 1560.

The explosive crisis came in the agitation against the new hierarchy established by Pope Paul IV, which provided for three archbishops and fourteen suffragan bishops. The measure was urgently needed for the instruction of the people. The densely populated seventeen provinces had only three bishops and no archbishops; and at that, a great part of the country was under the jurisdiction of German and French prelates, who often neglected their charges. Objections to the new hierarchy were made by abbots and nobles on economic, political, or legal grounds. To stir up opposition among the people the new establishment was decried as the introduction of the *Spanish* Inquisition, although nobody thought of introducing the Spanish Inquisition. Philip II positively denied any intention of this kind.

The principle cause of the disturbances and the eventual wars was the ambition of William "the Silent," Prince of Orange, to be the ruler of the Netherlands. To achieve this he put himself forward as the champion of Protestantism. Actually religion sat lightly on the shoulders of William of Orange; he was Catholic at the court of Philip II, Lutheran in dealing with German Lutheran princes, and Calvinist when political interest suggested the change. He made himself the leader of the Protestants without losing the political support of such prominent Catholics as Count Egmont and Admiral Horn. When Philip II departed from the Netherlands in 1559, William was given the government of several provinces, though he thought himself entitled to the regency of the whole country. He took, however, the oath of allegiance to Philip II.

The revolutionary wars were not long in breaking out. They lasted for thirty years and deluged the Netherlands in blood. There was hardly a section that was not frequently overwhelmed with frightful excesses and terrible cruelties. Anarchy was so prevalent that it would be impossible within the limits of this chapter to trace the shifting alliances, the intrigues, the battles and sieges in the conflict of these political and religious wars. Only a few outstanding facts can be touched upon.

The first was the development of the Religious Revolution. Once the government broke down, countless English Radicals, German Lutherans, and French and Genevan Calvinists hurried over the border. Eventually the latter predominated and the Protestantism of the Low Countries became Calvinistic. All, including the formerly secret Anabaptists, were bitterly hostile to the old religion. They launched several iconoclastic campaigns. The first, typical of the rest, broke out on the eve of the Assumption, 1566, when 300 people broke into the churches of St. Omer and destroyed all they could lay their hands on. The devastating mob of image-breakers swept through many cities in the vicinity of St. Omer and thence on to the northern cities.

Over 1,000 churches and monasteries were sacked in less than two weeks. Manuscripts, statues and paintings were destroyed in the fury. Yet far surpassing all this were the horrible desecrations of the Blessed Sacrament. In 1572, similar iconoclastic furies took place, including the execution of nineteen priests, who have since been raised to the altars of the Church as the Martyrs of Gorcum. After the defeat of the Confederates' army at Gembloux, a third general attack was made against churches and monasteries, religious and priests.

The second important fact was the terrible rule of the Duke of Alva, 1567-1573. Instead of supporting the regent, Margaret of Parma, who had at last shown strength and was achieving considerable success, Philip II sent his Captain-General to restore peace. It was Philip's greatest mistake. Alva was a great soldier, but also a most iron disciplinarian. His orders were to restore religion by strict enforcement of the severe laws of Charles V. He followed them completely. He began at once by arresting many of the leaders of the late disturbances, Catholic as well as Protestant. He instituted the "Council of Troubles" which, from its undoubted severity, was called the "Council of Blood." Punishments by death, exile or imprisonment were numerous.

Because the Queen of England forcibly detained 80,000 ducats sent to him by Philip, Alva had no money to pay his troops. The soldiers were terrorizing the towns by robberies and lawless violence. He decided to make the Netherlands pay for the occupation. He imposed the heaviest taxes, which soon brought grave disasters to this commercial country. In his warfare against the rebellious forces of William the Silent, the Captain-General was usually successful, but his campaigns were fought with a terrible fierceness. At length all parties petitioned the recall of the Duke of Alva, which Philip did in 1573.

The third fact was the final division. Alexander Farnese, the greatest general of his time, managed to gain back the larger part of the Low Countries. The population, more than half Catholic, realized that the final question was not of

Philip II or William of Orange, but of Catholicism or Calvinism. Already in 1578, seven northern provinces in the Union of Utrecht combined into an independent state, which eventually became the Dutch Republic under the restricted rule of the House of Orange. Though there was a small Catholic minority, the vast majority of the Dutch were Calvinists. In 1579, by the Union of Arras, ten provinces, mostly in the south, formed the Spanish Netherlands. They were Walloons and Flemings, and they were convinced that they could only save their faith under the protection of Spain. Philip II reserved the sovereignty to himself, but gave the actual rule to his daughter Clara Eugenia and her husband, the Archduke Albert.

So the religious wars in the Low Countries resulted in division: the Calvinist Dutch Republic in the north and the Catholic Spanish Netherlands in the south.

The British
Isles in
Turmoil

WHEN THE WARS of Religion began, the British Isles
included three countries: England, Scotland and Ireland.
The conflicts in these regions lasted for about forty years,
the years of the reign of the English Queen Elizabeth, 1559-
1603. The major struggle was to be in England. That country
had emerged as a leading European state. It was also becoming a great naval power on the western coasts of Europe;
already it dominated the North Sea and the English Channel.
By this last fact England was wielding a powerful influence in
the affairs of the Netherlands and of France. On what side
of the religious struggles was the might of England to be
ranged? The outcomes in the two smaller states, Scotland
and Ireland, would spur or check the English course.

Scotland's struggle will be treated first; it ended much
earlier than the conflicts of the other two countries. In the
turbulent Scottish affairs the nobility, not the monarchy,
was the major power. A very large party among the nobles
had gone over to the Religious Revolution. They aimed at
self-enrichment through the plunder of the Scottish churches
and monasteries. They employed inflammatory preachers,

343

such as John Knox, to gain large followings among the town populations. They sought and received powerful support, financially and militarily, from Queen Elizabeth, who for ten years strove to undermine the rule of the young queen of Scotland, Mary Stuart, who possessed a strong claim to the throne of England.

Mary, Queen of Scots, had not pursued this claim. The Scottish Catholic party was weak and scattered. Only the strong stand of the regent, Mary of Guise, the mother of Mary Stuart, protected her daughter's throne and the Catholic cause. Mary Stuart herself was in France; she was the wife of the French King, Francis II. On the death of her husband the young queen, only eighteen years of age, returned to Scotland in 1561. The situation was ominous for her; the regent was dead, and the nobles, her enemies, were in the ascendency. The young queen could obtain no tolerance for Catholics, only a grudging permission for the private practice of Catholicism by herself and her entourage. The prospects for the survival of Scottish Catholicism were extremely dubious.

Four years before, the Protestant lords had signed a document, the "First Covenant," in which they bound themselves to do all in their power to maintain the "Congregation," and utterly to forsake and renounce the Catholic Church. Wherever they were able, they drove out Catholic priests and installed their own ministers. John Knox came back, in 1559, to support the Lords of the Covenant. A wave of iconoclasm, the breaking of sacred images, the sacking of churches and the demolishing of monasteries, swept over a great part of the land.

Foremost among these lords was James Stuart, half-brother of the Queen; he was her worst enemy and her most traitorous confidant. In 1560, a parliament, irregular but powerful, under the domination of the Lords of the Covenant adopted a Calvinistic profession of faith, abolished the jurisdiction of the Pope, repealed all former statutes in favor of Catholicism, made the hearing or saying of Mass a crime, with the death penalty for the third offense, and confiscated the property of the Church.

For seven turbulent years, the young queen tried vainly to preserve her rule and the existence of the Catholic Faith in the midst of plots, betrayal, violent deeds, murders and and threats of her own imprisonment and death. She managed to practice her religion, but only by stealth. Often she was forced to sit in her room and listen to Knox thundering his personal diatribes at her. She was swept into a whirlwind of plots. Her enemies denounced her for marital infidelity and murder. Those seven years gave rise to unending controversies about Mary, Queen of Scots, which persist to the present day. At length, when her supporters suffered their last defeat in 1568, she fled to England. She asked Elizabeth to allow her to live in England, or to have free passage to France, or to return to Scotland. Elizabeth answered by imprisoning her for nineteen years, although Mary, Queen of Scots, was a foreign ruler and not an English subject.

With Mary's flight the religious war in Scotland terminated. Scotland eventually became almost completely Calvinistic, or Presbyterian, as it was termed in Scotland. Fundamentally the result was brought about not by the people but by the aristocracy. The attachment of the people to the old faith was unmistakably shown. Thirty years after the Parliament of 1560, half of the parish churches were still in the hands of the Catholics. For years, Mass continued to be said in the burnt and blackened ruins of churches and monasteries. In 1580, a few Benedictine monks still kept watch by the shrines of St. Margaret and St. David at Dunfermline. But it was in vain that the people tried to stem the tide of force. Gradually all the churches were put into the hands of Calvinist preachers. The time came when no priests were left to offer Mass, hear confessions and instruct the children, and most of the people were absorbed in the new system. Only remnants of Catholics remained in the Highlands and out on the Hebrides. There, Gaelic-speaking priests from Ireland ministered furtively to their Scottish Gaelic brethren.

In England, Elizabeth refused all requests of Mary Stuart for passage to France or Scotland until the Queen of Scots should clear herself of alleged complicity in the death of her husband, the Scottish Lord Darnley. Commissioners were appointed by Mary, Elizabeth and Moray to sit in conference on the allegations. The conference proved a judicial farce. Moray presented a mass of forgeries against his sister, but Mary was not allowed the privilege of the lowest criminal: confrontation with the proofs of supposed guilt. Through her agent Cecil, Elizabeth closed the conference with this remarkable decision: "that nothing had been sufficiently produced by Moray and his party whereby the queen of England should conceive or take any evil opinion of the queen, her good sister." On the other hand, the statement declared that Elizabeth was "equally convinced of the unimpaired honor and allegiance of Moray himself" and his adherents!

Mary Stuart, prisoner though she was of Elizabeth, came to be looked upon by the persecuted English Catholics as the chief hope of the old religion. Her claim to the throne of England was at least as good as Elizabeth's. During the first decade of the latter's reign, the Catholics had endured every type of persecution except bloody martyrdom: their bishops exiled, imprisoned and replaced by heretics; their faithful priests deprived of their livings; their Masses prohibited; their lands and possessions burdened with crushing fines if they absented themselves from new official worship, when they were not jailed for their non-attendance.

In 1569, a rising took place in the north, where the old faith was strong; it was a second Pilgrimage of Grace. The demands of the insurgents were: the Catholic religion must be restored; Cecil was to be driven from power; Elizabeth was to acknowledge Mary as her heir and successor; the Duke of Norfolk (a Protestant but a party to the rising) was to marry the Stuart Queen. Under their banner of the Five Wounds, the insurgent army restored the Mass to Durham and wherever they passed on their march south. But the Catholics of the midlands and the south were not ready, and the promised help from the Spaniards in the Netherlands failed. The rising was crushed by a Puritan army levied in the south.

Terrible was Elizabeth's vengeance. Martial law was proclaimed in Northumberland, Durham and Yorkshire; 900 peasants and yeomen were executed in summary fashion. The gentry were tried for high treason, either by local courts or by the Star Chamber in London. The Earl of Northumberland died for his faith in 1572.

The searching and ransacking of homes by priest-hunters at any hour of the day or night began in 1574. Notwithstanding, hundreds of priests, secular and regular, wandered in disguise from hiding-place to hiding-place, risking imprisonment, torture and execution, to strengthen Catholics in their faith. Their constancy and that of their people was the inspiration for the grand old hymn, "Faith of Our Fathers."

Mary, Queen of Scots

THE WARS OF RELIGION continued through the second part of Elizabeth's reign. They were prosecuted through internal intrigues and by a long naval war against the Spaniards. Among the intrigues two plots stand out. The first was the Ridolfi Plot of 1572, which planned to free Mary Stuart, marry her to the Duke of Norfolk and eventually raise her to the throne. These objectives were to be achieved by a rising of the English gentry, aided by a Spanish invasion.

The agent of the English Catholics with the continental powers (Pius V, Philip II and Alva) was Ridolfi, a Florentine merchant residing in London; the plot was named after him. The agent was indiscreet in his talk and no match for the wily Lord Cecil. The plot was discovered; the Spanish ambassador was driven from England, and the Duke of Norfolk was beheaded.

The second plot was the Walsingham Conspiracy, named after its leader, Elizabeth's chief-secretary. Its objective was the death of Mary Stuart, whom many Englishmen considered the lawful heiress to the throne. Its plan was to implicate Mary in a plot directed against Elizabeth's life, and thus to obtain a pretext for her execution. Walsingham organized a complete system of secret communication between the imprisoned queen and the outside world; his spies and forgerers through fraudulent recommendations insinuated themselves completely into Mary's confidence.

The most notorious among the spies was Gilbert Gifford, a seminarian, who afterwards got himself made a priest in order to carry out his deceit with less suspicion among Catholics in England and on the continent. He was the chief contriver of the channel of correspondence, and so efficiently did he operate that every letter that was sent to or from Mary passed through the hands of Elizabeth's decipherer Thomas Phillips, and was copied by him. The chain of treachery around the unfortunate queen was complete before the first sign of the "Babington Plot."

Babington was a young, enthusiastic supporter of Mary Stuart, but a naive one. With five associates he entered into a plot to liberate Mary. He was being used, and he had no suspicion of it; two of the associates were agents of Walsingham from the very beginning, and the real director of the plot was Gifford. The suspicion is strong that these undercover agents suggested Babington's letter to Mary inquiring whether she would reward the associates if they dispatched Elizabeth and freed her. However, as yet no positive proof of such a suggestion has been found.

On May 17, 1585, Mary wrote her answer, an elaborate instruction on how an insurrection might be organized and war made against the queen of England. She promised to reward those who aided her escape; but she wrote nothing about assassination. Mary, as an independent sovereign detained against her will and in violation of the law of nations, had a right to issue such an instruction.

The instruction was not what Walsingham wanted; it would not have justified the execution of a sovereign queen. So he and his agents inserted a clause in which Mary Stuart was made to approve the assassination of Elizabeth. Part of the letter, still preserved, shows the erasure and the incriminating sentence written on the erasure. The falsification is so clumsy that the sentence contains a most ridiculous contradiction.

Babington and his companions were executed. Mary was tried on October 14 and 15, 1586. The Babington letter and the forgeries of her reply were used against her. Not a witness nor an original document was produced in evidence against her. Mary freely confessed that she always had sought and always would seek to escape. As to plotting against the life of Elizabeth, she protested "her innocence, and that she had not procured or encouraged any hurt against Her Majesty." Father J. Hungerford Pollen, S.J., one of the leading modern authorities on the question, has declared that her statement "was perfectly true."

Mary walked to her beheading, piously, bravely, even with a pleasant word for her executioners. The Earl of Kent, after delivering the death warrant, told her: "Madame, your life would have been the death of our new religion, while your death — God grant it — will be its life."

The English religious wars were contested to a large extent outside the British Isles in conflicts with the Spaniards. Elizabeth intermittently supported the Netherlandish revolts. For many years English seamen such as Raleigh, Hawkins, Grenville, Drake and a dozen more — often with the encouragement of their queen, though England was at peace with Spain — attacked Spanish shipping and ravaged Spanish towns in the New World with piratical raids. Elizabeth, who shared in the spoils, ridiculed the protests of the Spanish king. When Philip II launched the Spanish Armada in 1588, he had many reasons besides his declared purposes of avenging Mary Stuart's execution and of claiming the British throne as the descendant of the younger son of Edward III.

Most English Catholics, not accepting the last claim, rallied to support Queen Elizabeth. In the running fight up the English Channel, the better equipped and better manned English fleet was victorious. The fleeing Spanish ships, encountering a mighty storm in their efforts to sail back to Spain by rounding Scotland and Ireland, suffered tremendous losses. This English victory and two others later secured the naval supremacy of England, which now became the greatest champion of European Protestantism.

Elizabeth died in 1603. In her long reign of forty-four years, she made the English a thoroughly Protestant nation. The second generation now knew nothing of Catholicism save the caricatures of the hostile propagandists. This generation was Anglican to the core in worship, education and life; they gloried in their national religion as they did in the brilliancy and prosperity of their Elizabethan times.

Here and there, in remote spots in the north and in a few of the towns, there still existed the pitiful remnants of the Catholics, furtively living the old faith, aided by hunted priests. But they were scarcely known at all, except during occasional outbursts of fanaticism against them. A *gens lucifuga*, "a people in hiding," they did not count. England was now a Protestant land.

The wars of religion came to Ireland in 1562, the third year of Elizabeth's reign; she bore the title, Queen of Ireland, as an inheritance from her father, Henry VIII. Elizabeth had a single policy for the people of Ireland; it was their total Anglicization. This meant above all else the destruction of their Catholic Religion. To the minds both of the Gaelic majority and of the Anglo-Irish minority, this would be ultimate catastrophe, so passionately loyal were both groups to the old faith.

Elizabethan Anglicization entailed for the Gaels also the eradication of their language, laws, customs and social life. This eradication was but another war upon their religion, for all these elements of their Gaelic culture were intermingled most closely with their Catholicism. The policy of Elizabeth could only be successful if it were imposed by total military conquest and complete legal suppression. The Catholics of Ireland only too clearly saw these fearful consequences to their faith and to their country. That is why they fought so desperately in three revolts against the Elizabethan policy.

The first struggle was the Insurrection of Shane O'Neill, Earl of Tyrone and the leading Irish prince in Ulster. It took place in the northern province from 1562 to 1567, and was an entirely Gaelic enterprise. The second was the Desmond Rebellion which occurred in the south and southwest, from Tipperary to the Atlantic coast of Kerry. It was fought by the Anglo-Irish followers of the Earl of Desmond, allied with neighboring Irish chiefs. The third was the War of the Two Northern Earls, Hugh O'Neill of Tyrone and Hugh Roe O'Donnell of Tyrconnell. It lasted from 1594 to 1603, and was carried on in all parts of Ireland by Gaelic chiefs aided by many Anglo-Irish lords. All three insurrections failed; the Irish Catholic forces never approximated the number of soldiers and the strength of armor possessed by their more powerful opponents.

However, it was not the superiority of their enemies that brought down the Catholic forces into overwhelming defeat. It was the war of extermination waged by the Elizabethan generals; they systematically butchered men, women, children, the sick and the aged. Their most efficacious weapon was planned starvation. Year after year, all means of subsistence were steadily destroyed, so that famine would result for the fugitives fleeing from the Elizabethan armies. Military forces would leave their bases, armed, not only with swords and guns, but with sickles and scythes to destroy the crops as well as the cattle.

According to a high English official, in the year 1582, during six months, 30,000 people had been starved to death in Munster. With terrible significance the *Book of the Four Masters* describes the plight of this province: "neither the lowing of a cow nor the voice of a ploughman was heard from Cashel to the farthermost parts of Kerry." Long before the wars were terminated, Elizabeth was assured that she had little left to reign over but ashes and carcasses.

And yet of the three kingdoms of the British Isles, Ireland remained Catholic. How did this happen? For one thing the passionate loyalty of the Gaels and of the Anglo-Irish for the old faith was deepened more than ever by their sufferings for it. Another reason was the fact that the priesthood was kept alive by the Irish seminaries established in Spain, Portugal, the Low Countries, France and Rome, and was supported by all classes of Catholics from kings and grandees to peasants and fishermen. In these schools boys, smuggled out of Ireland, were trained, ordained and smuggled back to administer the sacraments as hunted priests to persecuted flocks.

Still another cause was the charity of continental Catholics — Spaniards, Portuguese, Flemings, French, Germans and Italians — for their persecuted brethren in Ireland, for those living as exiles among them. Symbolic of this affection are the graves of Hugh O'Neill, Earl of Tyrone, and Rory O'Donnell, Earl of Tyrconnell, buried by the order of the Pope in the center of the main aisle of the church of San Pietro in Montorio, in Rome.

The Thirty Years War

THE LAST OF THE WARS of religion was the Thirty Years War. It determined the final religious divisions of the Holy Roman Empire of the Germans, that loosely connected jumble of principalities, duchies, prince-bishoprics and free cities — over 300 sovereignties in all — which sprawled over all of central Europe. This vast state had been called "Holy" because its principal aim was the protection of the Holy See and Catholic Christendom. It had been designated "Roman Empire" because, though founded in 961 by Otto I, it was looked upon as the descendant of the ancient Roman Empire of the West. It had been named "of the Germans," not because it was mostly German in population, but because the German princes had the right of electing the emperor and of presenting him to the Pope for imperial coronation.

A witty French writer once remarked that it was neither Holy, nor Roman, nor an Empire, nor even German. Certainly by 1618, half at least was decidedly anti-papal, and for over two centuries, it had had little influence in Italy, except for the efforts of the Hapsburg emperors to secure a position of political influence in northern Italy. It could scarcely be called an empire, except as an historical relic — its emperors had only a nominal suzerainty, except in their own archduchy of Austria. Although largely so, it was not entirely German, because within it were Slavic states such as Bohemia, Moravia and Croatia. True, the imperial crown had been worn by the Catholic Hapsburg Archdukes of Austria for more than a century, but their possession of the imperial office was soon to be challenged by a combination of Protestant princes. In fact this challenge of setting up a Protestant emperor was to be one of the proximate causes of the Thirty Years War.

The Thirty Years War, the most fiercely contested of the four wars of religion, did not begin until 1618, twenty years after the other three wars were over. It lasted until 1648, fifty years after the termination of the wars of the Huguenots, the Dutch Calvinists and the Elizabethan Anglicans. There were several causes of this postponement. The first was the Religious Peace of Augsburg (1555). It had left the Lutheran princes in the possession of the ecclesiastical lands which they had confiscated. It had sought by an Ecclesiastical Reservation Clause to prevent future apostate prelates from taking with them the territories and resources of their former dioceses or abbeys. It finally confirmed the rule that the prince, and the prince alone, determined the religion of the subjects of his particular territory. The Religious Peace of Augsburg gave the German world an uneasy peace for sixty years. There were several violations of the Ecclesiastical Reservation Clause, in which the Church lost some bishoprics and several monasteries. The weak emperors who succeeded Charles V were unable to protect Catholic interests.

A second cause for the postponement of the German conflict was the quarreling among the Protestants themselves. The Peace of Augsburg had been made between Lutherans and Catholics; the Calvinists, unimportant at the time, were not included. But in the subsequent twenty years, the Calvinists had become a strong party in southwestern Germany, especially in the Palatinate. Bitter doctrinal controversies between the Calvinists and Lutherans only increased mutual antagonisms. The Calvinist princes insisted that they be allowed to "reform" Catholic districts, which meant the obliteration of Catholicism. The Calvinist princes also demanded the right to change Lutheran districts, which they had taken over, into Calvinist states, according to the principle that the prince determines the religion of his subjects. Such demands gained them few supporters among the Lutherans, but many strong opponents.

A third cause of the postponement was the strong revival of German Catholicism. The publication of the decrees of the Council of Trent, numerous popular missions, the reforming labors of the Capuchin friars and the Jesuits, inspired the Catholic people with fresh vigor. Immensely effective were the works of St. Peter Canisius at the diets, in the pulpits, in the universities and in his *Catechism* and other religious publications. The many Jesuit colleges sent forth a constant stream of youths dedicated to the Church and well-trained to defend her. The German College in Rome and the new Tridentine seminaries in all the Catholic sections furnished the Church with holy and able prelates and intelligent and devoted priests. Zeal, learning, devotion, self-sacrifice and enthusiasm marked the now-fervent German Catholics.

Supporting the revival were the three zealous Bavarian dukes, Albrecht V, William V, and Maximilian, and the pious Archduke Ferdinand of Styria. The advance of the Protestant revolution was not only stopped, but several areas were gained back to the old faith. For one example, at Cologne the combination of the clergy and the laity, aided by Duke William of Bavaria, frustrated the attempt of the Archbishop Gebhard, an apostate to Calvinism, and his wife, an apostate nun, to turn the Archdiocese of Cologne into a lay, Calvinistic principality. Equally successful in recovering their rights were the Catholics of Strasbourg, Aachen and other cities.

The conflict could not be postponed much longer. In 1608, the Calvinists withdrew from the diet of Regensburg when they failed to gain the sanctioning of their confiscations of bishoprics and monasteries and the free hand they demanded for future destroying and confiscating of other Catholic bishoprics. Under the leadership of the Prince of the Palatinate, they formed a military league to obtain their demands by force of arms. Though they were Calvinists, they called their league the Evangelical Union in order to attract Lutherans. No important Lutheran prince joined the Union; but several wealthy imperial cities, such as Nuremburg, Ulm and Strasbourg did. The Union was supported by England and the United Provinces.

A year later, 1609, to counteract the Evangelical Union, Maximilian, Duke of Bavaria, formed a defensive Catholic body, known as the Catholic League. Maximilian was joined by the three ecclesiastical electors, the Bishops of Mainz, Trier and Cologne, and a number of prince-bishops and abbots. The Pope and King of Spain contributed financial support.

Only the briefest outline can be given of the Thirty Years War. It had five phases: the Bohemian, 1618-1620; the Palatine, 1620-1623; the Danish, 1625-1629; the Swedish, 1630-1635; and the Franco-Swedish, 1635-1648. The first three phases were struggles of the Calvinists and their allies with the Catholics and the Imperialists. The Catholics and the Imperialists, who entered in the third phase, were universally victorious. Had the conflict ended then, Germany probably would have come out more than two-thirds Catholic.

In 1629, however, Emperor Ferdinand II issued the Edict of Restitution, by which Protestant princes, in conformity with the Ecclesiastical Reservation Clause, were ordered to restore bishoprics and monasteries seized in violation of the Religious Peace of Augsburg. The measure was legal and strictly in keeping with the Peace of Augsburg. But it was unrealistic and was bound to rouse the strongest opposition among the Protestants; most of the property had been in their hands for two generations, and some of it had been sold. The Edict of Restitution made a continuation of the war inevitable.

The Swedish phase witnessed a complete reversal of fortunes. The Protestant victory was owing to Gustavus Adolphus, King of Sweden. His aims were to weld the Protestant territories of Germany into an Evangelical Body under his leadership, to subject the Catholic territories of middle Germany to his own scepter and thus to found a great Protestant Empire of the North. During his reign, the practice of Catholicism in Sweden was punished with death.

Gustavus Adolphus was a military genius of the first order, an experienced, brave and unscrupulous conqueror.

He gained the common people by his personal affability and his ostentatious Protestantism, while he bent the Protestant princes to his will by his indomitable energy and unmovable determination. Among his allies was France, which contributed subsidies. The person responsible for this was Cardinal Richelieu, a statesman first, then a prelate. Richelieu rationalized his strange position by his opposition to the Hapsburgs. Thus, the disasters to the Catholic cause in Germany were partially due to a Catholic cardinal. Within two years the Protestant armies, having defeated the Catholic and Imperial forces, were ravaging unchecked far south in Bavaria. Even after the death of Gustavus Adolphus in the battle of Lutzen, 1632, the Swedish forces for years held their preponderant positions.

The Franco-Swedish phase saw the entry of French armies into the conflict, which by this time had become more political than religious. The war was now a struggle between the Bourbons of France and the Hapsburgs of Austria and Spain. The war continued in Germany, assuming a most horrible character. Saxony, Bohemia and Bavaria were reduced to deserts. On both sides all traces of discipline vanished in the dealings of the armies with the inhabitants among whom they were quartered. Outrages and unspeakable atrocities were committed everywhere. The horrors of a town taken by storming were repeated in the open country. Three-fourths of the peasant population of Germany had perished in war or by pestilence.

At last exhaustion forced the Peace of Westphalia in 1648. Despite great losses, Catholicism at the end was stronger in Germany than before the war. After 1648 German prelates had no longer to fear destruction and confiscations. Up to 1618, the Peace of Augsburg had given rise to endless misrepresentations, whereas after the Peace of Westphalia everything was definitely settled. This final religious settlement left Germany divided into two almost equal parts: the north was compactly Protestant; the south and west, with a few exceptions, completely Catholic. That half-and-half division has remained in Germany for the last three centuries.

Jansenism

THE ENDING of the Protestant Religious Revolution at the Peace of Westphalia (1648) brought little peace to Catholicism. Since the beginning of the seventeenth century a new movement was mounting disasters against the Church. It was the secularizing of Europe, the establishment of worldly interests over the spiritual order. Protestant governments barred Catholics completely from their states, which included a third of Europe. Catholic governments dominated the life of the Church in their domains, reaching out even to interfering in the conduct of the papacy itself. The veto of Catholic rulers against a candidate for the papacy during a conclave dated from this time. Threats of a national schism were often raised during powerful anti-papal movements such as Gallicanism. Grave heresies appeared during this period; Jansenism and Quietism are examples. And yet, through all these hostile times the Catholic Church manifested great spiritual strength. She inspired countless of her adherents to lead lives of fervent holiness; she directed hosts of her missionaries to glorious apostolates in the New World and in the far-distant Orient.

French history best epitomizes the seventeenth century. France was the greatest nation in Europe, culturally, socially and religiously. It was also the strongest in its material resources and its military forces. Politically it was the most powerful absolute-monarchy among the European states, all of which were more or less absolute-governments. During the reign of Louis XIV, France reached the zenith of its influence. All other nations, friendly or hostile, acknowledged and imitated its cultural and social pre-eminence. All feared or copied its absolutism. But that absolutism, especially in regard to religion, could have and did exercise much ominous pressure on the freedom of the Church.

One striking aspect of seventeenth-century France was the intense revival of Catholic life. It was a most glorious realization of the Counter-Reformation, as was already noted in a previous chapter. Here let one recall the reference: St. Francis de Sales, his ascetical classics, his sermons, and his founding of the Visitation Nuns; Cardinal Bérulle, the French Oratory, and his devotion to the priesthood of Christ; St. John Eudes, devotion to the Sacred Hearts of Jesus and Mary, his seminaries; Jean Jacques Olier, the Seminary of St. Sulpice; St. Vincent de Paul, the Congregation of the Missions (domestic and foreign), works of charity. To these can be added St. John Baptist de la Salle, education of boys; St. John Francis Regis, rural missions; St. Peter Fourier, domestic missions, education of young women. Among the women saints one can list St. Louise de Marillac, foundress with St. Vincent de Paul of the Sisters of Charity; and St. Margaret Mary Alacoque, promoter of the devotion to the Sacred Heart of Jesus.

These names symbolize a countless host of preachers of retreats and missions, of revivifiers of priestly ideals, of saintly women who restored sanctity in convents and holiness in families. Some of the greatest of Christian orators were heard in the French pulpits; to mention only a few: Bossuet, Bourdaloue and Fenelon. One of the most remarkable organizations for reform was founded and directed by laymen; it was the Company of the Blessed Sacrament. Though bishops and priests belonged to it, it was a layman's movement. One must pay tribute to Abbé dé Rancé, the restorer of the ideals of the Cistercians; by his reform of his monastery of La Trappe, of which he was the abbot, he brought almost the whole Cistercian Order into the Reform of La Trappe.

During this century Catholic France began its wonderful work in the foreign missions. St. Isaac Jogues, St. John de Brébeuf and their companions, the Martyrs of North America, sanctified with their blood the beginnings of the apostolate of their countrymen in North America. It was in this century that the renowned Paris Mission Society was founded, that society which has sent countless of its members to spread the

ST. LOUISE DE MARILLAC. Eighteenth-century copperplate engraving by Gaspard Duchange. *Bibliotheque nationale, Paris.*

ST. JANE FRANCES DE CHANTAL. Portrait. *Visitation Convent, Turin.*

Catholic Faith in the Orient. In this century, practically every French religious order began to send its missionaries into the Near East, the Far East and Canada.

But there were also long enduring attacks of powerful opponents for seventeenth century French Catholicism to withstand. Among these was Jansenism, which put forth a teaching on grace and salvation that was heretical and which produced a "sort of Calvinized Catholicism." Its name came from its founder, Cornelius Jansen, Bishop of Ypres and a one-time professor of Louvain. He had written a book called *Augustinus* in which he elaborated doctrines based on his interpretations of writings by St. Augustine on grace which he professed to have discovered. The *Augustinus* was not published until two years after the author's death. Jansen on his deathbed affirmed that he accepted fully whatever decision the Church would make concerning his book.

The affair would not have gotten beyond academic disputations had not Abbé St. Cyran, a French associate of Jansen, published the *Augustinus* in Paris and there began to apply its theories to morality and spirituality. He attracted a considerable following among priests, nuns and lay people, all influential, and he organized them into an inflexible faction of zealots. Among them were the Arnaulds, an important family of lawyers, and especially their sister, Mère Angélique, the Abbess of the convent of Port Royal. The sect battled the Church for almost a hundred years. They found sympathizers among conscientious people by their severe austerities and their rigoristic ideas, which contrasted with the laxities prevailing in many circles of French society. Later certain Gallican antipapalists encouraged them in their resistance to the Popes.

The most fundamental of the Jansenist controversies dealt with the relations of grace and the free will. The Catholic doctrine is: God's grace is absolutely necessary for salvation; God wishes all men to be saved; God gives to each man sufficient grace to be saved; God, since He endows man with a free will, makes the efficacy of His saving will depend on man's cooperation with it. Against this doctrine the Jansenists taught that God gives grace only to the small minority whom He wishes to save; for God does not will to save all men; nor did He die for all men, but only for the minority that He determined to save. Jansenistic predestination would have killed off prayers for the intercession of our Blessed Mother and the saints.

More striking were the controversies over the usages of the sacraments of Holy Eucharist and Penance. The Jansenists sharply opposed frequent Communion and the Church's practice of absolution in confession. Frequent Communion was one of the great fruits of the Catholic Revival. It was recommended by the Council of Trent, advocated by numerous saints of the Revival, and enthusiastically propagated by the Society of Jesus. The action of the Jesuits aroused the Jansenists to the strongest opposition. The Church taught that one effect of the Holy Eucharist is to purify men from venial sins and to strengthen them against mortal sins. The Jansenists on the contrary held that the Holy Eucharist should only be received when there was a certain proportion of worthiness between the recipient and our Lord; only persons with perfect contrition should receive Holy Communion. There were instances where Jansenists abstained from the Holy Sacrament for long periods of time, two years even, if not more.

The Jansenists also held that without perfect contrition the sacrament of Penance was of no avail. They would revive the ancient severe penances and would not allow absolution until such penances were completed. All this absolutely contradicted the Church's teaching that imperfect contrition sufficed, and with the gentler discipline of the Church, using the Power of the Keys.

The Jansenists were a gloomy lot, apparently more austere than the rest of men. They nourished a certain consciousness that they were an *elite* group among Catholics. Yet in their attitude toward papal decisions, they showed themselves to be the shiftiest of casuists. No heresy ever displayed such readiness in mental reservations and deceits. There is not space to list the papal condemnations, the apparent submissions—which were regularly explained away. The process was repeated time and time again through a century. Near the end, Louis XIV stepped in, not to protect a heresy but to prevent a papal condemnation lowering his prestige as protector of French Catholicism, that is as its master.

Near the close of the century Jansenism began to fade. It lingered on through the first three decades of the eighteenth century. Though the faction had given up the fullness of its creed, it still retained its attitude towards the papacy and also its rigorism in the use of the sacraments. Some of its rigoristic spirit affected many sincere Catholics — bishops, priests, nuns and lay people — who were eminently loyal to the faith and the papacy, but who were inclined to sternness in viewpoints on life and conduct. However, the epithet, "Jansenists" is most unfairly applied to such good people. They have always been most loyal to the papacy and to the doctrines of the Church. Their sternness of view is owing to their own temperament, and that is their own business.

Gallicanism

GALLICANISM WAS THE most harmful of all the storms that raged against the barque of Peter in the seventeenth century. Its attacks were ceaseless during all of that century and through most of the eighteenth century. It was widespread, dominating France especially, but also every Catholic state. Its evils were ever ominous; kings, princes and ministers in all these governments marshalled numerous bishops and theologians in the support of their ultra-nationalistic pretensions. The term, "Gallicanism," was used to lend an aura of antiquity to the movement. "Gallican" held a reference to Gaul, that ancient Celtic land which Caesar had conquered for the Roman Empire. Christianity had come to Romanized Gaul, possibly in the first century A.D., certainly in the second. France, and the Church in France, in the seventeenth century embraced most of the territory of old Gaul.

The antiquity of Gallicanism was vastly exaggerated. Actually it first appeared in France at the beginning of the Late Middle Ages, in 1303, during the conflict of Philip IV with Pope Boniface VIII. This ruthless monarch had instigated an assembly of thirty court-bishops, several barons and jurists to appeal against the Pope to a future general council and to a future "legitimate" Pope. Such an appeal had never appeared before in France. Royal commissioners were dispatched to gather assents from other bishops, and even to force them from prelates who had refused. The method was new, though attempts of civil rulers to dominate local churches was certainly not; such attempts had been going on since the days of Constantine.

Nor was Philip's attempt unique. In his time all the monarchies were nourishing ideas of exaggerated nationalism. Unfortunately in France, when it was emerging from the Hundred Years War as the greatest European power, Gallicanism had developed so that the Pragmatic Sanction of Bourges, issued by Charles VII and accepted by a large assembly of prelates and notables in 1438, brought France perilously near the state of schism. To persuade Francis I to abolish the Pragmatic Sanction, Pope Leo X, in 1516, had to agree to a concordat which gave to this monarch the right of nomination to all French sees and prelacies. The French monarchy had thus obtained that tremendous dominance over the Church in France which lasted until the French Revolution.

The Protestant Revolution indirectly increased the power of Gallicanism — and not only in France, but in all Catholic states. Dr. MacCaffrey, in his *History of the Catholic Church from the Renaissance to the French Revolution*, I, 309-310, states very clearly: "Catholic sovereigns began to understand that the Protestant theory of state supremacy meant an increase of power to the crown, and might be utilized to reduce the only-partially independent institution in their kingdoms to a state of slavery.... They urged the bishops to assert their independence against the Holy See.... Men like Bossuet, carried away by the new theories of the divine right of kings, aimed at reducing the power of Rome to a shadow.... Their whole policy tended to the realization of the system of national churches."

The Catholic Revival was able for a time to restrain the pretensions of Gallicanism and to strengthen the bishops and priests in France who opposed it. In spite of the royal court's rejection of the Tridentine decrees on discipline, the clergy of France, by 1614, brought about a general acceptance of these papal decrees. The Dominicans were strong opponents of Gallicanism; and so too were the Jesuits, whose opposition earned for them the enmity of the powerful legalistic class, which helped in their eventual suppression. The local council of Aix-en-Provence, in 1612, censured the Gallican works of Edmond Richer. Twenty French bishops condemned Pithou's book on the so-called rights of the Gallican Church.

However, the growth of absolute monarchy, fostered by Henry IV, Cardinal Richelieu and King Louis XIV, brought about a powerful revival of Gallicanism. Besides royalist politicians and court bishops, very forceful protagonists of Gallicanism were to be found among the judges and lawyers of the parliaments, as the higher courts were called, especially of the parliament of Paris. From every side, appeals were heard for the "Ancient Liberties of the Gallican Church." Heavy tomes were produced to bolster these shadowy pretensions. Attacks were levelled unremittingly against the French bishops and theologians who stood loyally for the Holy See, and particularly against the Jesuits, the vowed defenders of the Pope of Rome.

The climax came in 1682, at Paris, when an assembly of French clergy issued the *Declaration*, a document concerned with the extent of papal power in France, and to which the assembly annexed the celebrated Four Gallican Articles. The assembly had been called by Louis XIV, and consisted of thirty-four court bishops and thirty-seven theologians or canonists, all adherents of the so-called "Gallican Liberties." These "Gallican Liberties" were nothing less than an attempted transfer of Church jurisdiction to the state, and the sacrifice of papal rights and authority to the secular power.

The Four Gallican Articles were: (1) the king is independent of the Pope in all temporal matters; (2) the Pope is inferior to the general council, and the decrees of the fourth and fifth sessions of the Council of Constance are still binding; (3) the exercise of pontifical authority should be regulated by the ecclesiastical canons; (4) the dogmatic decisions of the Pope are not irrevocable until they have been confirmed by the judgment of the whole Church.

In regard to the first article, the Gallicans by "temporal matters" understood many ecclesiastical and some even purely spiritual rights. In regard to the second article, the superiority of the general council over the Pope was a rejected heresy of two centuries before. Further, Constance was not a general council until its convocation by Gregory XII; the fourth and fifth sessions predated that call, and hence their decrees had no binding force. In regard to the third article, the practical meaning was that the Pope was bound to respect the "Gallican Liberties." In regard to the fourth article, that statement was a clear denial of the Pope's infallibility.

Louis XIV ordered that the Four Gallican Articles must be taught in all seminaries in France, and that they must be accepted by all who were to take theological degrees in the universities of the kingdom. There was strong opposition. It was only by royal edict and by main force that the clergy were compelled to subscribe and the Sorbonne to register the Declaration and the Four Gallican Articles.

The Popes vigorously protested these schismatical maneuvers. Innocent XI condemned the usurpations and threatened to use against Louis XIV "the remedies which God has placed in our hands." He annulled all the proceedings of the assembly. He refused to appoint to vacant bishoprics anyone who had participated in the adoption of the Articles. The king, who had the right of nomination, on his part persisted in presenting none but members of the condemned assembly. The vacant sees in France mounted to thirty-six.

The conflict lasted until 1693 when Innocent XII induced Louis XIV to disavow the Declaration of 1682, and to withdraw the edict imposing the teaching of the Four Gallican Articles on the seminaries. In return the Pope appointed all the bishops nominated by the king for the vacant sees.

But Gallicanism did not die with Louis XIV's disavowals. It lived on for more than a century until it all but perished with the monarchy in the French Revolution. Some echoes of it were heard in the nineteenth century. The Four Gallican Articles, concrete and explicit formulations of old vague anti-papal theories, continued to be taught to a considerable section of the French clergy. The spirit of Gallicanism was kept alive by politicians and court prelates. Hence in many circles there continued to exist a distrust of Rome, manifesting itself in the royal nomination of bishops and in the occasional refusal to allow the publication of papal decrees.

However, the Gallicanism of the French clergy certainly has been exaggerated. One can recall the number of French bishops who stood by the Jesuits when they were being suppressed by the government of Louis XV. Their special champion was the Archbishop of Paris, Christophe de Beaumont.

But the greatest witness of the true and basic loyalty of the French clergy to the Pope of Rome was their rejection of the Civil Constitution of the Clergy during the French Revolution. This was a document whose Gallicanism far exceeded anything dreamed of by Louis XIV or his advisers. Out of 130 archbishops and bishops, only four took the Constitutional Oath. Out of the 70,000 priests, nearly 50,000 refused the Oath. And of those who first took the Oath, thousands repudiated their action once Pope Pius VI had condemned the Constitution of the Clergy and its Oath. God alone knows the number of these prelates and priests of France who for their loyalty to the Holy See were guillotined or massacred during the Reign of Terror.

Continuing
Religious
Conflicts

ALTHOUGH THE WARS of Religion had set the geographical boundaries of Protestantism and Catholicism, they did not end armed religious conflicts. Such conflicts occurred frequently during the seventeenth century. Actually the fourth of the Wars of Religion, the Thirty Years War, the bloodiest and the most devastating, was fought from 1618 to 1648. The position of Catholicism worsened in most of the northern sections of the Empire during the seventeenth century. In the Peace of Westphalia there were many violations of the rights of the Church. These came in the concessions of church lands belonging to the bishoprics ceded by the treaty to Protestant princes. Such alienations spelled the annihilation of Catholicism in the conceded areas, for the prince alone determined the religion of his subjects. There were a few exceptions; but practically the only remedy left to Catholics was emigration. Pope Innocent X vigorously protested the concessions. But his protest was ignored. In fact, a policy of ignoring future papal protests was established. Secularism was becoming predominant in European religious affairs. The immediate result of the Westphalian concession was the almost complete extinction of Catholicism in the former ecclesiastical lands of northern Germany.

In the Scandinavian countries — Denmark, with Norway and Iceland, and Sweden, which held a considerable stretch of the Baltic lands of Germany — Catholicism had long ceased to exist. The death penalty was inflicted on Catholic priests who said Mass and performed their sacramental ministrations; confiscation of properties and banishment were forced on converts to Catholicism. Poland, then a large kingdom on the northeast frontier of the Empire, was one of the Church's few consolations in the seventeenth century; the Polish priests and people were thoroughly Catholic. Yet through the first half of the century Poland had had to endure conflicts and wars that were at least partially religious. In the second half, the nation had made itself completely and devotedly Catholic; heresy was practically ended within its borders. Unfortunately, politically Poland was ceasing to be a great power. The weakness of the Polish monarchy and of the Polish legislature, the Diet, was drawing the country into anarchy. Russia, barbaric, despotic, and only partially emerged from oriental seclusion, was an enigma to western states. The Popes had high hopes of religious reunion. But their hopes were shattered by the Tsars, who by harsh laws and savage cruelties forced the Uniates under the rule of the Russian Orthodox Church.

Along the northwest frontier of the Empire, on the southern shores of the North Sea, stood the Dutch Republic. It had been organized as the Union of Utrecht in 1578; it finally was recognized a national sovereignty by the Peace of Westphalia in 1648. The Dutch Republic from its very beginning, when it made Calvinism its state religion, was aggressively Protestant. It visited on the Catholics of the country the most severe persecutions, forcing them to lead a practically underground existence. There were no bloody repressions, it is true; but in every other way the Dutch Catholics were as oppressed as their fellow Catholics in the British Isles.

With admirable courage the Dutch Catholics stood firm. Faithfully they attended their hidden Masses; they solidly taught their children the catechism; and they kept up their race of priests by sending their young men across the frontier into the Catholic Rhineland to be trained and educated for the priesthood. They held their ranks; it has been estimated that the Dutch Catholics numbered about 300,000 in 1715, which indicates that they were not a pitiful handful, but a strongly united and devoted minority. The Dutch Republic was just as aggressively Protestant in foreign affairs. Its military forces were active in every religious war of the seventeenth century. The Dutch fleets wrought havoc and destruction in several Catholic missions in the Far East.

In France the Edict of Nantes (1598) restored Catholicism throughout the nation and gave Calvinism a wide measure of tolerance. However, its provision allowing the Huguenots the holding of a hundred garrisoned cities scarcely guaranteed lasting peace. The Huguenots were thus constituted a state within a state, certainly a serious threat to the unity of the realm. A formidable revolt centering about the important port of La Rochelle, one of the Huguenot strongholds, broke out in 1620, and lasted until 1628, when the city surrendered. Cardinal Richelieu, the actual ruler of France, was the one responsible for the capture of La Rochelle, the last bastion of political Calvinism. When his chief purpose—the ending of this grave threat to the unity of France—was achieved, he granted the Huguenots liberty of worship and civil equality. Cardinal Richelieu was not a religious persecutor.

Louis XIV, from the time of his accession to actual rule, began to curtail the privileges of the Huguenots, as inimical to his conception of the royal power. In 1681, he turned to more severe methods, offering special privileges to those who renounced Calvinism, and depriving Huguenots of many rights and privileges. Insurrections broke out in several districts, causing terrible sufferings to both Calvinists and Catholics. The insurrections were put down with merciless severity by the dragoons of Louvois. Finally, in 1685, Louis revoked the Edict of Nantes, destroyed the churches and schools of the Huguenots, banished their ministers, and ordered the forced Catholic Baptism of their children.

Louis XIV's motives were largely political; like all contemporary rulers, Protestant or Catholic, he identified religious uniformity with the unity of the state. The chief promoters of the revocation were the Chancellor, Le Tellier, and the Minister of War, Louvois. Pope Innocent XI and the French Jesuits were strongly opposed to the revocation, and to any policy of coercion. However, the king's action was favored by some court bishops, the Supreme Court of Paris and the Sorbonne. Despite the strict prohibitions against emigration of the Calvinist laity, far more than 100,000 Huguenots, many of them solid and talented citizens, emigrated to Prussia, the Dutch Republic, Switzerland, England and America. The Revocation of Nantes held direst results for Catholicism. In Germany it put a stop to a widespread movement for religious reunion. In the Dutch Republic it led to retaliations and local persecutions of Catholics. In England it filled the Protestant mind with suspicions against James II's efforts for religious tolerance. In Ireland it was the much-used justification for the iniquities of the Penal Laws, even long after the French Protestants' affairs were ameliorated.

For English Catholics, the seventeenth century was an unbroken period of persecutions, sometimes erupting into wholesale executions. Even in the rare relaxations, the terrible anti-Catholic laws remained, an ominous threat of future terror. Only a few Catholics, and these in blank desperation of the revival of the Elizabethan persecutions, resorted to arms, in the Gunpowder Plot, 1604-1605. Their foolhardiness brought down on their fellow Catholics the most terrible legislation and the execution of eighteen priests and seven laymen, *solely* for their profession of the Catholic Faith.

The Stuart kings — James I, Charles I, and Charles II — did not relish persecution, but they were forced into it by the monumental hatred for Catholicism of the Puritans, the Cromwellians, the Calvinists, and even the Anglicans. The various Test Laws passed by Parliament prove that. Heavy fines were forced on those who abstained from Anglican services; later it was prescribed that no one could hold office who did not under oath deny Transubstantiation. Cromwell said that he would tolerate any man's religion, but that he would never let the Mass be said in the British realm. All Catholic priests were banished from the kingdom. Catholic lay people were forbidden a Catholic marriage and also the Catholic baptism of their children. Catholics were denied all civil rights and liberties.

The climax of the sufferings of the English Catholics came in the Popish Plot, in 1678. A clique of powerful and bigoted politicians, headed by the Earl of Shaftesbury, con-

CONTINUING RELIGIOUS CONFLICTS 375

cocted a false plot alleging that English Catholics were to bring on a French invasion during which all prominent Protestants were to be killed. There was not one iota of truth in the whole tale. The clique hired a band of the most disreputable perjurers to arouse the fury of the London mob. All historical scholars reject the plot. The leader, Titus Oates, has been called "the greatest liar in history." Yet judges, members of parliament and other leaders availed themselves of the impostures to send to their deaths thirty-eight priests and laymen, all innocent, for a plot that never existed. The conditions of English Catholics remained so poor until the nineteenth century that, as Newman said, they had become so weak they could safely be pitied.

The lot of the Irish Catholics was even worse than that of their English brethren. Not only was Catholic worship totally proscribed and all bishops and priests exiled, but some prelates and several priests were put to death. All education, even the most elementary, was forbidden to Catholics. Catholics were driven from the lands that their ancestors had held from time immemorial. This was achieved by "Plantation," a process by which large areas were cleared of all Catholics without compensation, and these lands were distributed among speculators who were to plant the districts with garrisons of English and Scotch Protestants. These were to establish Protestant colonies and hold the land for England. More than once genocide occurred in the clearing off of the Catholic population.

In the early part of the century, James I planted the northeast corner of the province of Ulster. The effects of his actions are felt to this day. Half way through the century Oliver Cromwell descended on Ireland. His one-year campaign brought the horrible massacres of Drogheda and Wexford. Cromwell planned the biggest of all the plantations. One third of Ireland was to be entirely Protestant; another third was to have Catholic servants whose children must be brought up Protestants; the last third was to be made into a vast prison camp for the Catholics of Ireland: it was the rocky, barren province of Connacht and the County of Clare. Cromwell's plantation failed only because it was too vast. It did achieve one thing: from then on the lands of Ireland were owned by the Cromwellian adventurers.

After Cromwell's invasion Ireland lay void as a wilderness. At the end of the century came the Williamite War, and as an aftermath the long night of the Penal Laws, for more than seventy years. The Penal Laws violated every right or liberty of the human race. Their main purpose was to enslave the Irish Catholics, eighty percent of the population, and eventually to obliterate the Catholic Faith. They were voted by the Irish Parliament, which represented only the Cromwellian-landlord class (less than twelve percent). As one of their judges said, they presumed that the Catholic eighty percent did not exist, except to be taxed and legislated against. The Penal Laws only drove the priests and the people closer together in their common poverty and in their undying loyalty to the Pope of Rome.

New
Missionary
Apostolates

THE VAST LOSSES in the ranks of the European Catholics during the Reformation were counterbalanced by the multitudes of conversions to the Faith in the Far East and in the New West. In fact, the two and a half centuries from 1500 to 1750 witnessed one of the greatest missionary expansions of the Church. Just before the period opened, the voyages of two sea captains changed the world. In 1487, Dias, a Portuguese, rounded the Cape of Good Hope and opened the sea route to the ancient Orient; in 1492, Columbus, an Italian in the service of Spain, discovered in the unknown western seas the continents of the Americas.

Then followed the epics of discovering, exploring, conquering and colonizing, the first century of which was almost entirely Spanish or Portuguese. True, the two nations had their mundane ambitions, which at times were only too sadly evident. But the peoples and the kings of these two nations very definitely always nourished the motivation of the spreading of the Faith and the conversion of the natives.

Fortunately the new fields for the preaching of the Gospel were opened just when the Catholic Revival was beginning. It may be recalled that the Revival was an accomplished fact in Spain before 1500. The monasteries and convents of the older religious orders were filled with zealous, saintly and disciplined monks and friars dedicated to the ancient spirit of their orders, above all to the apostolic work of spreading God's kingdom and of saving souls. The newer religious orders, Jesuits, Capuchins and Vincentians, were made up of priests eager to engage in the holy tasks of evangelizing the heathen.

The Popes encouraged the zealous missionaries, sanctioned their labors and often financially supported them. In the next century the Congregation *De Propaganda Fide* was founded in 1622, and in 1627, the Urban College was established in Rome for the education and training of missionary priests. In the same century the renowned Society for the Foreign Missions was founded at Paris to train secular priests for the missionary apostolate.

The missionary monks, friars and priests (regular and secular) of these two hundred and fifty years constitute one of the holiest and most courageous groups that have ever glorified the history of the Catholic Church. The many canonized and beatified martyrs from their ranks testify to the completely dedicated and sacrificial lives of the thousands and thousands of these heroic proclaimers of the kingdom of God.

They had to be heroes to face the obstacles and the oppositions that confronted them. There was the absolute remoteness—it took at least two years for a ship, which sailed as part of the annual Great Fleet, to reach Goa. From Goa, in western India, the vast ancient East reached for thousands of miles farther. The annual Great Fleet of the Spaniards, sailing from Cadiz, took much less time in reaching Vera Cruz or Panama; but these were only depots for the hundreds and hundreds of miles of travel through jungles and over extremely high mountains to Lima, or to Acapulco, where the ship lay that was to carry shipments across the wide Pacific to Manila.

The lands of the missions afforded terrible hardships: thickly-matted jungles, impenetrable forests, burned plateaus, and the rocky gorges of the Andes and the Sierras. The climates of these varying terrains proved most difficult for Europeans; the steaming dampness of the lowlands, the burning heats of the plateaus, the frigid blasts in the mountain heights, and the snow and bitter cold of the northern forests took a frightful toll of life from the missionaries.

Greatly discouraging obstacles arose from the natives themselves. The barrier of languages was one. The missionaries found that the peoples of Asia, of Africa and of the New World spoke languages which in words and structures differed entirely from those spoken in Europe. There was one exception: the Hindus in India spoke Hindi, an Indo-European language deriving from the same sources as those of European tongues. There were great differences, but the basic words and structures were the same. The intellectual classes of the rest of India and of the highly cultured Chinese, Malayans and Japanese possessed well-developed written languages which Europeans could learn.

In the African continent there were whole series of languages which were completely different from the Asiatic tongues and from each other. Most of them were still in the oral state. In the continents of the New West the American Indians had a large number of quite disparate languages. None of these had been written down, except in a few instances of some pictographs. The greatest differences often existed between proximate languages.

The missionaries started with interpreters; but at the same time they began to collect word-lists and make vocabularies, and finally to discover the grammatical structures of the various tongues. They then reduced the native speeches to written languages. Their first purpose was to explain Christianity to the aborigines of the forests. Here lay an extremely difficult and exacting task. The natives had very small vocabularies, 300 to 500 words at the most. And all their words were the results of sense-perceptions alone. How explain to them the true idea of God, of the Holy Trinity, of the redemption, of sanctifying grace, of the sacraments, of the Holy Eucharist, of the essential good and the essential bad, and of so many other spiritual concepts?

The missionaries had to invent terms and produce circumlocutions of words and ideas — and always to be sure that they were perfectly orthodox. What a martyrdom of holy patience! Yet they succeeded. In a remarkably short time they were directing saintly and, possibly, mystical souls. Their simpler converts knew their Faith solidly.

The Christianization of the natives stirred up bitter hostility towards the missionaries, which often broke out into cruel, bloody persecutions of the fathers and of their converts. The missionary apostolates revived the age of the martyrs. The virulent opposition of the pagan priests, the bonzes, the witch doctors and the medicine men is understandable. St. Paul experienced it. The rural and forest heathens, whose beliefs were a mixture of dark superstitions and ancient myths, a mixture that mingled in every phase of their lives, stubbornly refused the missionaries a hearing. St. Martin of Tours had encountered the same hostilities. Hatred of foreigners easily fanned superstitious terrors into sanguinary massacres.

Perhaps the greatest cause of antagonism against the missionaries was the very moral code of Christianity. Heathenism at the best was indifferent to morality; at the worst it was an incentive to immorality. Proofs could be found in the legends, in the fertility rites and in the boundless sex license.

An intelligent heathen chief could recognize the logic of God's existence and His oneness; he might even commence Christian instructions. But when he was told that he must abandon his harem and choose but one wife, when he was warned against immoral license, he lost all interest. On many occasions such a leader turned into the cruelest of persecutors. More than once in the early part of this period Rome was filled with glowing reports of the coming conversion of some pagan king and his people, only later to receive disastrous reports of the ruler driving Christianity from his kingdom and murdering his Christian subjects. Almost invariably the explanation was summed up in one word, polygamy.

Probably the worst hindrance to the missionaries was the cruelties, the scandals and the malevolent opposition of some white colonists. It must always be kept in mind that the same boat carried to the colonies the hero and the villain, the good-hearted settler and the vicious reprobate. The colonizing record of Spain during this period, despite some truly black pages, is by far the best of all the powers. The Spanish monarchs generously supported the Church and the missions; and they issued many decrees to protect the Indians and to forbid their enslavement. The Spanish people bestowed their rich Renaissance civilization on the majority of the Indians. They erected ninety great cities in Latin America and founded at least two first-class universities.

The darker aspects must be considered to illustrate the heroic constancy of the missionaries. One great obstacle to their evangelizing labors was the hatred of the Indians for some of the first conquerors who waged such horrible wars and inflicted such cruel slaughterings on the natives. Then another cause for bitterness was the raids of the slave hunters from Brazil who carried so many poor wretches into bondage. Having far worse effect upon the Indians were the scandalous lives of some white colonists. Abandoning the practices of their religion, these degenerates sank to the vilest debaucheries of the effete East or the savage West; they even pandered to the worst native vices. Such debased white men were living contradictions of the preachings of the missionaries to their neophytes.

Lastly, greedy politicians and venal officials blocked or slowed down the excellent decrees of the Spanish kings in defense of the Indians. Boldly and cynically, these unworthy administrators checkmated the labors of the missionaries for the Faith. Perhaps it was miraculous that such mission priests somehow circumvented the nefarious schemes of such impious rascals. Modern Latin American Catholicism has survived the numerous and most destructive persecutions of the secularism of the nineteenth and twentieth centuries because of the solid foundations laid by the monks, friars and priests of the colonial days.

Francis Xavier

When the news of Vasco de Gama's epic voyage reached Lisbon, the Portuguese began sending out missionary friars to India. The Franciscans arrived in 1500, and the Dominicans in 1503. The friars made many converts and established relations with the "Thomas Christians," who claimed descent from St. Thomas the Apostle. In 1533, a bishopric was set up in Goa, and nine years later a seminary for native priests was established there. But tremendous obstacles thwarted the zealous efforts of the friars: the vastness of the sub-continent of India, the density of population in its numerous kingdoms, the complete absorption of the natives in very ancient pagan cults, the hostility of local kings, the enmity of the highly-cultured intellectual classes, and, very much, the cruelties and the vicious lives of many newly-arrived Europeans.

But then, in 1542, there disembarked at Goa St. Francis Xavier, one of the first companions of St. Ignatius Loyola. He came as a special agent of Pope Paul III and of King John III of Portugal for the conversion of the heathen. Yet so scandalous were the examples given by very many Portuguese colonists that Xavier immediately had to devote himself to renewing completely their lost faith and to remedying their immoralities. After five months of tireless labors he

ST. FRANCIS XAVIER. Portrait in the Church of the Gesu.
Cappellette di San Ignazio, Rome.

wrought such changes that he was able to address himself to his primary task, the spreading of the Gospel among eastern pagans.

St. Francis Xavier has been called "a saint in a hurry," and for ten short years he traversed back and forth from India to Japan and through many lands on the way bringing countless souls into the fold of Christ. On October 24, 1542, Xavier entered upon his tremendous journeyings. First he went to Travancore in Southern India and strengthened the purely nominal Christians of Pearl Fishery Coast, and also converted thousands of the heathen. Then he continued on to Ceylon, and finally at the end of three years he reached the city of Malacca on the Malay Straits, which was the second center of importance in the Portuguese Empire of trading posts. Conditions were the same here as those which Xavier had first encountered in Goa; nevertheless he made the trading town his headquarters. After some months Francis started off on several missionary journeys still further eastward to the numerous Molucca Islands, known also as the "Isles of Spice." Some hold that he even reached the isle of Mindanao in the Philippines. Everywhere he tried to learn the native tongues. Possibly he received the gift of tongues; certainly he was granted many mystical favors, and he was endowed with miraculous powers on several occasions. His kindness, charity, indefatigable zeal and simple straightforward teaching of Catholic doctrine brought uncounted converts. Scholars aver that Xavier baptized something like a million persons. He himself wrote that his arms used to become so weary from baptizing that he could scarely move them. He often wrote letters to Europe, excoriating the cruelties and the immoralities of the colonists, though he took good care to praise the worthy officials. He did not hesitate to address pointed warning to King John III if he should neglect his responsibilities in the evil conditions.

In 1547, Xavier was back in Malacca, and while there he met with a Japanese, who aroused his interest in the conversion of Japan. Problems in India called him back to Goa in 1548. It must be remembered that Francis Xavier was no romantic wanderer, even though he flashed across the Far East like a meteor. He always provided for successors to follow him. He appointed several, and sometimes he had them accompany him. This last journey to India was to provide for assistants from Europe, and also for the establishment of a novitiate and a house of studies for European and Indian Jesuits.

At the end of June, 1549, St. Francis set sail from Malacca for an entirely new world, Japan. He was accompanied by Father de Torres, S.J., and Brother Fernandez, S.J., and also by three Japanese whom he had met and converted. After a month and a half of sailing, the party landed at Kagoshima, Japan, on the feast of our Lady's Assumption. Xavier spent the first year in learning the Japanese language. With the aid of a convert he translated into Japanese the principal articles of faith and composed short treatises which were to be employed in preaching and catechising. When he began evangelizing, the ill will of the bonzes (pagan priests) obtained his banishment. Moving towards the center of Japan he succeeded in preaching the Gospel in some of the southern cities. Then he conceived the idea of going to Meaco, then the imperial city, and seeking permission to preach from the mikado (the emperor). The journey, made in an unusually bad winter of great snowstorms and bitterest cold, was a frightful experience for St. Francis, lightly clad, quite impoverished, unwelcomed everywhere as a foreigner. And, at the end there was the crushing realization of failure. Xavier had misjudged completely the state of affairs. The mikado was but a powerless puppet; and the whole country was torn by the baronial wars of the daimios. It was the anarchy of the seventh-century Merovingian Frankland all over again.

After two and a half years Xavier departed from Japan. He left in the charge of Father de Torres and Brother Fernandez several Christian communities, totaling about 2,000 Japanese Christians. St. Francis had great confidence in the fidelity of the Japanese Christians, a confidence that was vindicated in growth and in heroic martyrdom during the next one hundred years.

Urgent domestic problems required Xavier's presence in Goa. When these were settled he turned his thoughts to a project far greater than any he had hitherto labored upon, the conversion of China. He had heard much in Japan about the greatness of the Celestial Empire, and he had heard the Japanese admiring it as the source of their own high culture. With the help of friends he arranged an embassy to the Emperor of China; the Viceroy of India appointed him an ambassador, and the Holy See made him a Papal Nuncio. He left Goa in 1552. But he encountered the stiffest opposition in Malacca. However he was able to obtain a passage in a Portuguese vessel sailing to a small, desolate island, Sancian, a trading post, six miles off the southern coast of China and a hundred miles west of Canton. China was absolutely closed to foreigners; immediate execution was meted out to any who gained entrance. Xavier remained onboard the ship, but kept seeking for some Chinese smuggler who would on a dark night place him on the forbidden mainland. But as he waited he was seized with violent fevers. Even the motion of the boat caused him painful agonies. The sailors brought him onto the island's shore and placed him in a rude hut. He suffered terribly for five days more, mostly in a delirium. Only two persons watched over him, a converted Chinese servant and an East Indian boy. On December 2, 1552, St. Francis breathed his last. He was only forty-six years of age.

Father Astrain, S.J., one of the foremost of modern Jesuit historians, writing in the *Catholic Encyclopedia,* thus sums up St. Francis Xavier's work in the Orient: "It is truly a matter of wonder that one man in the short space of ten years (May 6, 1542 – Dec. 2, 1552) could have visited so many countries, traversed so many seas, preached the Gospel to so many nations, and converted so many infidels. The incomparable apostolic zeal which animated him, and the stupendous miracles which God wrought through him explain his marvel, which has no equal elsewhere.... St. Francis Xavier is considered the greatest missionary since the time of the apostles." St. Francis Xavier was canonized together with St. Ignatius Loyola in 1622. In 1904, St. Pius X made St. Francis Xavier the patron of the works for the Propagation of the Faith; in 1927, Pius XI declared him together with St. Thérèse of Lisieux the patron of all missions of the

Catholic Church. The still-incorrupt body of the great missionary is venerated at Goa; his right arm, however, is venerated at the altar dedicated to his intercession in the Church of the Gesù in Rome.

Missionary activities in India continued to follow the progress of Portuguese conquest; but they also extended far beyond it in the south and west, and even tried to reach into the center and the north. There were several martyrs and much heroism. The tide of missionary enterprise reached its highest point some years after 1600, by which time vast numbers had been enrolled in the membership of the Church. The needs of such large communities tended to limit further missionary expansion. It must be kept in mind that still the bulk of the tremendous population of the Indian subcontinent remained pagan. Moreover, as the power of Portugal began to decline, there was a falling off in the supply of missionaries. English and Dutch inroads into the overseas Portuguese empire meant the end of Catholic missions in the areas where they established themselves. Through the two succeeding centuries grave problems beset the Indian Catholic Church. The first was the involved question of the methods to be used in the conversion of the powerful upper-class Brahmins. The second was the arising of sharp conflicts over jurisdiction among the missionaries themselves. Both problems will be treated in the next chapter.

India
and
Japan

AS WAS NOTED in the preceding chapter, the leading opponents of Indian Christianity were the Brahmins. They were the priestly caste, the highest of the four leading Hindu castes, and the most powerful. As priests of the ancient polytheistic paganism of India, they wielded tremendous influence over the countless multitudes of the subcontinent. They shared in the reverence paid to their holy men for the latter's fastings and ascetical practices. The Brahmins were also highly cultured from constant perusal of the venerable holy books, some of which were literary masterpieces. Finally, they were possessors of a strong intellectualism, by which they had developed their own personal esoteric religious beliefs into a formidable philosophical system.

The most difficult aspect of Brahmanic opposition was the seeming impossibility of any conversions from their ranks. Unless there were some measure of conversions, the establishment of Christianity would not be realizable for centuries. The zealous Portuguese missionaries during the first century had gained numerous converts, but they were from non-caste peoples who were relatively non-influential among the vast population of India.

A break came in the Brahmin opposition when Robert de Nobili, S.J., arrived in South India. Within a year he mastered the local languages, Tamil and Telegu, and the ancient classical Hindu language, Sanskrit. De Nobili came to the conclusion that the failure among the Brahmins was due to the contempt of this high caste for the missionaries as Portuguese, or as friends of the Portuguese, and especially as associates of the casteless pariahs. The Brahmins detested the Portuguese not only as intruders, but as contemners of their Hindu gods and goddesses, and spurners of their Hindu dietary customs and practices. And the Brahmins considered the pariahs as little better than animals.

Robert de Nobili proposed to gain a hearing for Christianity by approaching this most influential caste in the role of a Christian Brahmin. He planned no deception, always professing himself to be a Catholic priest, who was following, as far as his religion permitted, the Brahmanical customs. He wore the garb of a Hindu holy-man; he led a life of similar austerities, especially abstaining from animal foods forbidden to the Brahmins. De Nobili let it be known that he was a Roman noble, who respected the Indian customs and caste divisions. In consequence he condemned himself to a lonely existence for a long time, for he had to avoid every contact not only with the Portuguese and the pariahs, but even with his own brethren.

When finally inquirers entered his hermit's hut they found a holy ascetic, speaking their own language perfectly, and quoting their ancient classical literature better than they could. Then they listened intently to his explanation of Christianity and to his demonstration of how its truths realized completely the highest of their philosophical and religious ideas.

The new method soon proved its worth as hundreds of converts were brought into the fold. Yet de Nobili did not minimize or corrupt any Catholic truth. In the difficult task of adaptation, he manifested a prudent regard for the caste system and for certain rites connected with it, which he treated as partaking of a national rather than an essentially religious character. Several Jesuits were sent to learn his methods and to work with him. However, others of de Nobili's fellow Jesuits in Madura objected strongly to his method as countenancing superstitions by allowing pagan rites, and as encouraging schism and dissension by permitting no intermingling between Brahmins and pariahs in the churches. (De Nobili and his companions did not like the caste system. They hoped under the influence of Christianity to make it disappear, just as slavery had died out in the early Church.) The archbishops of Goa and of Cranganore approved of de Nobili's methods.

The controversy was waged for a hundred years until a condemnation came from Benedict XIV. Mitigations were made later, and the problems have practically faded out of existence. Today the authoritative *Catholic Mission History* of Schmidlin-Braun hails Robert de Nobili as one of the greatest stars in the firmament of mission history. The canonization, in 1947, of the martyr St. John de Britto was the Church's final approval on the work of de Nobili, for St. John was one of his most faithful assistants.

Unfortunately the progress of the Indian Catholic Church was slowed during the seventeenth and eighteenth centuries. There were several causes. The growth of membership outstripped proper priestly care. The long conflict between Portugal and the Holy See over jurisdiction in areas not under the scepter of Lisbon brought grave confusion. The new colonies of the Dutch Calvinists and the English Protestants prevented the existence of Catholicism in their spheres of influence. The suppression of the Jesuits (1759, in the Portuguese dominions) involved the destruction of the colleges and religious houses which supplied laborers for the missions. Finally, other religious orders in Europe suffered similarly during the French Revolution, with disastrous effects for Indian Christianity.

But in the overall view these religious orders, missionary societies and the native Indian clergy produced, all through these two hundred and fifty years, a race of heroes, saints, martyrs and dedicated apostles. Not only do those canonized and beatified compare well with the best traditions of the Church in all ages, but so also do the rank and file of the devoted priests, devout laymen and pious laywomen of the Indian Church.

The Japanese Christians numbered over 2,000 in 1551, the year of St. Francis Xavier's departure. They increased astonishingly. Within thirty years (1582), they counted 200,000. In that year the Christians sent an embassy of three

Japanese princes to Rome (arriving in 1585). The feudalism of Japan, which was quite similar to that of the eighth-century Frankland, contributed to the growth. Several of the semi-independent feudal lords were favorable to Christianity; some even embraced it. Affairs would continue well as long as the shogun (the Japanese Mayor-of-the-Palace) remained favorable. But the worst could be expected if this supreme ruler changed.

So it was with the Shogun Hideyoshi, who, in 1587, began the era of persecutions. Originally favorable, his mind was prejudiced by the bonzes to believe that the missionaries were spies of Portugal and Spain. He proscribed Christianity, though he refrained from slaying its adherents. The missionaries went into hiding and continued their apostolates; within ten years they baptized 65,000 persons, making a total of 300,000 Japanese Christians served by 134 religious, native as well as foreign, of various orders. Even the shogun seemed about to become favorable again.

But the foolish remark of a stranded sea captain that the missionaries had been sent to prepare for the conquest of the country, aroused his fear and anger again. Religious were arrested and orders were given for a listing of the Japanese Catholics. On February 5, 1597, twenty-six martyrs were crucified at Nagasaki; they died either preaching or singing hymns to the end. Pius IX, in 1862, canonized these martyrs. Twenty of the twenty-six were Japanese.

After the death of Hideyoshi in 1598, an interval of peace was granted the Japanese Christians. It was to last for fifteen years, and during the brief period their numbers and their works of faith and charity multiplied. Then, in 1614, a new shogun published a decree abolishing Christianity; two years later his successor renewed the edict. Now came the complete persecution, and it was horrible. On September 2, 1622, at Nagasaki, the "great martyrdom" took place. Fifty-two Christians were martyred on the same day; twenty-seven were decapitated and the rest were burned alive. In the following year the persecution waxed still more furiously and was extended throughout the empire.

The sufferings of the Japanese martyrs and their clergy, European and native, rival anything in the annals of the

Martyrs of the Catacombs. The Japanese martyrs were from all classes: clerical and lay, native and European, men and women; old people and little boys and girls, rich and poor, learned and humble. They were laid on beds of burning coals, cast into sulphurous waters, hanged head-downwards over sulphurous pits. These and worse horrors failed to shake the constancy of these Oriental heroes and heroines. The exact number will never be known. On July 7, 1867, Pius IX beatified 205 martyrs, far more than half of whom were natives. These beatified heroes are a small token of the rest.

From 1614 to 1640, the persecutions were carried on in a systematic manner, so that eventually all the missionaries were either dead or banished, and the young communities they had formed were obliterated. Thus Japan was closed, and remained closed for two centuries, during which the persecution did not cease. A price was set on the head of any Christian, native or foreign. Each year every Japanese was called upon to trample on the cross, or on a plaque of the Blessed Mother and her Divine Son. The three attempts to enter Japan, two by Jesuits and one by Dominicans, ended in the execution of each group after torture. One other attempt was made in 1708, by an heroic Italian missionary, Sidotti, who was forty years of age and all alone; it ended in his perpetual imprisonment until his death in 1715.

But God cannot be circumscribed. On March 17, 1865, fifteen Japanese came into the new church which the French Government had been allowed by treaty to build in Nagasaki. They revealed to the priest who spoke with them that they were Christians, that they represented other Japanese Christians, who secretly from generation to generation had handed down the Catholic Faith, and that their numbers amounted to 50,000. There were three marks by which these descendants of martyrs had recognized the new missionaries as the successors of their ancient fathers: obedience to the Pope of Rome, veneration of the Blessed Virgin, and the practice of celibacy by the clergy. Two hundred years of fierce waves of persecution had pounded in vain upon the Rock of Peter!

Behind
the
Great Wall

THE MIGHTIEST POWER in the Far East was China. It was the oldest, going back in its origins to at least 1500 years before Christ. Its three vast river valleys constituted the most fertile regions in the Orient and supported teeming populations. Chinese culture, with its ancient literature, its exquisite art and its philosophical thought, held dominance over the countless peoples who dwelt along the far-flung borders of the Chinese Empire. It was the declaration by the Japanese that they owed their civilization to the Chinese that prompted St. Francis Xavier to attempt at any cost an entrance into the Celestial Empire.

But China presented most formidable obstacles to Christianity. First there was the exclusion of Europeans from its empire. Much more formidable were Chinese religious concepts. China's paganism, with its ancestor worship and nature cults, traced back roots through thousands of years of Chinese history. It was raised by Confucius, a philosopher and teacher who lived about five hundred years before Christ, to its highest form of an ethical system which stressed ancestor worship, family loyalty and noble principles of justice and truth. The Chinese thus had worship and an ethic given them by their noblest sage. They were convinced that they needed "no inferior system."

Following St. Francis Xavier's death, several abortive attempts were made to bring Christianity into China. But lacking any adequate training in the Chinese languages, or any knowledge of the characteristics of the Chinese peoples, the zealous pioneers were bound to fail.

The founder of the Catholic missions in China was Matteo Ricci, an Italian Jesuit, who, in 1583, was able to set up a permanent residence in Canton. He was remarkably learned in mathematics, physics and astronomy, and he planned to use his competence to gain a hearing from the Chinese intellectuals, who possessed an especially powerful position in the Celestial Kingdom. But Ricci was also a very prudent man. He introduced himself and his companions as wise men from the West who wished to live in China and to practice there their own religion. He knew well that any declared intention of inducing the Chinese to accept a foreign religion (Christianity) would have brought immediate banishment, so convinced were the Chinese scholars of their complete superiority over foreigners in any field, especially in religion.

Following his plan of using science to open the way for the apostolate of the Gospel, Father Ricci wore the costume of Chinese intellectuals and spoke the Mandarin dialect of the scholars and the officials, dispensing with interpreters as soon as possible. He made his residence at Canton a veritable museum, filling it with mathematical and astronomical instruments, prisms, small clocks, musical instruments, oil paintings, prints, illustrated printed books and maps. Attracting special attention were a prominently displayed painting of the Madonna and her Child, and an extra large map of the world.

Ricci's companions, dressed as he was and also speaking Mandarin, courteously answered all inquiries. They overcame much antipathy and distrust. But the missionaries never hid their Faith; they respectfully answered all questions about their religious beliefs, their moral principles and their ethical doctrines. More, they edified the Chinese whom they met, with their strict lives, disinterestedness, charity and their patience under the persecuting oppositions which they occasionally experienced.

Father Ricci moved northward, establishing residences in three important cities, Saochow, Nanch'ang and Nanking. Finally, after some difficulties, he entered Peking, the capital, to which he was admitted on the summons of the Emperor Wan-Li. This ruler then showed much good will to "the holy wiseman from the West." Ricci lived in Peking for nine years, during which he won approving hearings from the Chinese savants for his lectures on science and astronomy. He also gained a number of converts from the ranks of these scholars. Among his most fruitful works were his writings in Chinese on the Catholic Faith. The most valuable was his *The True Doctrine of God*. It was a masterpiece of apologetics and controversy which then and long afterwards led countless numbers to Christianity. And among the readers whom it did not convert, it aroused a great esteem for the Catholic Religion. He wrote several other works of high importance for the new Christian converts.

As the founder of the Chinese mission, Father Ricci had to invent formulas capable of expressing Christian dogmas and rites clearly and unequivocally in a language which had hitherto never been put to such use. It was a difficult and dangerous task, yet it formed only a part of the heavy burden which the direction of the mission was for Father Matteo Ricci, particularly during the last years of his life. Always he devoted himself to the training of his assistants to follow the courses which he had set. When he died in 1610, five residences had been established; the last one was in Shanghai. The numbers of the baptized had reached something over 2,000. This may seem a small figure, but, as Father Ricci well said in his *Memoirs*, considering the obstacles to the entrance of Christianity into China, this result was "a very great miracle of Divine Omnipotence."

An ever-present threat to the missionaries was banishment. To forestall it, they strove to form a native clergy and to design a liturgy in harmony with Chinese customs. Rome granted their petitions, substituting Chinese for Latin in the ceremonies and providing for a Chinese translation of the Sacred Scriptures. A formidable persecution in 1617 did banish all the priests to Macao, but peace in 1622 enabled them to return. A period of forty flourishing years followed; whereas, in 1617, the Christians numbered 17,000, in 1664, they counted 237,000. Even the conquest of China by the Manchus, in 1644, did not destroy the growth, though for a short time it caused great suffering to the Christian Church. Thus, Father Johann Adam Schall, the superior of the Catholics, was at first cast into prison, but soon he regained favor with the first Manchu Emperor.

Father Johann Adam Schall von Bell, S.J., a native of Cologne, was the outstanding priest-scientist who continued the program of Matteo Ricci. For years he held the presidency of the Mathematical Tribunal at the Imperial City (its membership comprehended 200 scholars whose chief task was the rectifying of the official calendar). Father Schall was made a Mandarin of the First Class. He was one of several Jesuit scientists and scholars who taught and wrote in Chinese on a wide variety of subjects, from astronomy to music and religion, aiming to acquaint the Chinese with Western culture and religion. One other who ought to be remembered is Ferdinand Verbiest, from Flanders, who constructed the astronomical instruments still seen and admired in Peking. The work of these priest-scientists was of the utmost importance to the advance of Christianity, for its success won the good will of the emperor and of his high officials throughout China towards the new religion. Nor did these priests neglect the more evident apostolic labors.

Yet destruction was always threatening. During a severe persecution, 1664-1665, Fathers Schall, Verbiest, Buglio and Megalhaens were condemned to be strangled for their "revolutionary, evil learning and false astronomy." The sentence was nullified by the new emperor, the celebrated Kang-Hi. Schall, old, worn out and suffering from almost complete paralysis, died shortly; Verbiest and his companions were restored to their positions.

The half-century reign of the favorably-inclined Kang-Hi witnessed remarkable growth in the Chinese Church. New missionaries arrived, Dominicans, Franciscans, Augustinians, Lazarists, Paris Foreign Mission Fathers and Jesuits from the Province of France. The converts, which included several princes and princesses, mandarins and scholars, entered the Church in large numbers. In 1692, the emperor issued an edict of complete toleration. Before the renewal of persecutions in 1724, the Chinese Catholics counted 800,000.

However, during the years 1687 to 1742, an internal storm, the controversy over the Chinese Rites, almost wrecked the Chinese mission. It arose from the always difficult problem of accommodating the local traditions and practices of converts from paganism with the Christian Faith. The Chinese question concerned the ceremonies paid to ancestors and the honors given to Confucius, as well as the words used to designate the Deity. To prohibit this honoring of ancestors and of Confucius would have put an end to all hope of conversion, at least of the mandarin and official classes, and to tolerate these rites looked like tolerating paganism. Father Ricci and his Jesuit brethren, with hardly an exception, believed that the rites could have a secular significance, and hence they permitted their converts to use them. Furthermore, for want of a better name for the Deity, Ricci allowed the use of Tien-tschu (Lord of Heaven), Tien and Shangti (Supreme Emperor), words that had been used hitherto in an idolatrous sense, but which in themselves and as explained by the Jesuit missionaries were orthodox enough. Later missionaries, especially Dominicans and Paris Foreign Mission Fathers, rejected both the honors to ancestors and the names of the Deity as purely pagan. Both parties in the controversy meant well and could adduce very convincing arguments in favor of their own views.

There is no space here to detail the appeals and counter-appeals to Rome and the different papal decisions. The final decision came in 1742; in it Benedict XIV condemned the Chinese Rites and ordered all missionaries to take an oath against further discussion of the question. It must be noted here that in modern times Pius XI and Pius XII, after careful inquiries among modern Chinese officials as to the present-day changes in the meanings of the practices, due to modern cultural changes in Chinese thought and expression, have permitted the usages of the rites as solely political actions.

Back also in the dark eighteenth century, Chinese Christians were subjected to three fearful persecutions. Moreover, the suppression of the Society of Jesus in Portugal, Spain, France and the rest of the Catholic world — begun in 1759 and completed in 1773 — brought irreparable damages to Chinese Christianity. Catholic China was deprived of so many devoted missionaries whose places could never be filled. Nevertheless, at the end of this dismal century, Chinese Catholics actually numbered 300,000. That fact alone is an eloquent testimony to their faithful loyalty to Jesus, a loyalty which the Chinese Catholics still carry on in their present night of persecution.

Southeast Asia and Africa

THE ACCOUNT of Catholic missions in the Eastern hemisphere during the period of the 16th through the 18th century may be concluded by considering the propagation of the Gospel in Southeast Asia, Indonesia and Africa. The first region to receive the Faith was Indo-China, which included Burma, Siam (now Thailand), Cochin-China (now Vietnam, Laos and Cambodia) and Malaysia; and secondly, the great islands of Borneo, Sumatra, Java, Moluccas, Celebes and New Guinea.

The inhabitants ranged from primitive savages to highly cultured town dwellers. Most, however, were simple agriculturists or lonely fishermen. They spoke a wide variety of languages. Their chief means of communication were their fishing vessels — frail crafts that normally hugged the coast lines, but also ventured way out on the boundless, unchartered seas seeking islands far below the horizon. In religion many were primitive animists; but far more were sophisticated idolaters who worshiped deities of ancient agricultural cults. Mohammedans, converted more than a century before by Arabs, were numerous, powerful and strongly opposed to Christianity.

Such were the obstacles confronting the first Christian missionaries, Dominicans and Jesuits, who preached the Cross tirelessly, some even at the cost of their lives. The foremost among them was St. Francis Xavier; he set the standard of their works. As a result they baptized hundreds of thousands of people. They continued their ceaseless labors all through the 17th century, but with setbacks. Franciscans and Jesuits from Macao established a mission in Siam. Similar missions were founded in Cochin-China (Vietnam) during the first half of the century. But in the second half a violent persecution destroyed churches, murdered Christians and expelled priests. Other missionaries at the same time introduced the Gospel into Ceylon, Sumatra, Java, Borneo, Celebes and New Guinea.

A new and very potent persecution began when the Dutch started to supplant the Portuguese in Indo-China. As early as 1596, they drove the Catholic priests from Java, and two years later from Sumatra. In 1643, they closed the Franciscan and Dominican missions in Formosa. Moreover, much harm was done to the Catholic cause by moral corruption among the Portuguese traders in Molucca, their principal city.

In the 18th century the greatest blow was dealt the Catholic missions in these regions by Portugal's suppression of the Society of Jesus. There were practically no replacements for their abandoned mission stations. However, despite persecutions, local wars and other evils, Indo-China at the end of this century had more than 300,000 Catholics who were served by 300 priests. The failures were more than balanced by the countless baptisms of three centuries; infinite is the value of the baptized soul of a child.

The greatest missionary achievement in this area was the Christianizing of the Philippine Archipelago; almost the entire population of the more than 1,670 islands was converted to Catholicism. The only exceptions were the Mohammedan Moros of the large southern island of Mindanao, and some remote heathen tribes. The outstanding figures of the movement were Legaspi, the first governor; Salazar, O.P., the first bishop of Manila; and Sanchez, S.J., who was sent to Spain to persuade Philip II not to abandon the colony. To these pioneers is due the fact that the Philippines eventually became, and is even today the only Catholic nation of the Orient.

The chief co-laborers in this Far-Eastern vineyard were the friars — Augustinians, Franciscans, Dominicans, Recollects — and the Jesuits. All these orders were set up in islands within the first forty years, and they continued to labor during the entire colonial period. They taught the natives farming, textile manufacturing, road construction and bridge-building. They directed the erection of churches, hospitals and schools. The foremost educational institutions were the Dominicans' University of Santo Tómas (1611) and the Jesuits' College of San José. In their principal work, the conversion of souls, these apostolic priests baptized two million souls within a hundred years. They also established a native clergy.

During the first half of the 17th century, the colony and the missions had to struggle against internal and external foes: the Dutch, in particular, the Japanese, the Chinese, the Moros and other native opponents. In spite of the difficulties, the work of evangelization went rapidly forward. The friars and priests with rare heroism penetrated farther and farther into the interior of the country, and established their missions in what had been the centers of paganism. The natives were won by the self-sacrificing lives of the missionaries, and accepted the teaching of Christianity in great numbers. Schools were established everywhere, and books were published in native dialects. The Augustinians were especially active in the apostolate of printing; by 1780, they had produced 200 volumes, including even works in Chinese and Japanese. The missionaries made every effort for the material and moral improvement of the people. From the times of the fearless Salazar, these apostolic priests espoused the cause of the natives against the injustices and exactions of rapacious officials and landholders.

In the 18th century the best days of Spain were over; the great nation declined to a second-class power in politics, economics and military strength. Nowhere was the decline more effective than in the far-distant, isolated colony of the Philippines. The islands' economy and commerce were almost completely ruined; and shorn of adequate military and naval defense, they were at the mercy of powerful pagan neighbors. The Moros multiplied their attacks; the English held Manila for two years.

In the dangers and confusions, morals deteriorated sadly; Manila was given a reputation of being a home of corrupt and quarrelsome people. Religion was hampered by clashes between clerics and bishops, and by strife between bishops and governmental officials. The worst blow came with the suppression of the Jesuits through all the Spanish dominions in 1767. The Spanish government's efforts to replace the Jesuits by secular priests became but a futile gesture; there were hardly any available. In spite of all the disasters and turmoil, the Filipino people remained loyally the only Catholic nation in the Orient.

The Catholic missions in Africa, whatever the causes, were not productive of much fruit. The missionaries were confronted by almost insurmountable obstacles: unhealthy climate, vast deserts, impenetrable jungles, enormous distances linked only by primitive trails. The Christian evangelists had to contend with jealous pagan priests, frightening sorcerers, angry natives provoked to reprisals by the infamies of the slave-trade, and bitterly hostile Mohammedans (Negroes as well as Arabs). The entire history of the African missions is an unvarying tale of heroic laboring, utterly discouraging failures and appalling mortalities.

Among the first projects were the efforts for a return of the schismatic Abyssinian Christians to the fold. The negotiations inaugurated by the Emperor of Abyssinia with the Pope and the King of Portugal were for a long time fruitless, owing to the impossibility of effecting the arrival of the papal delegates in Ethiopia. Finally an entrance was made, and an emperor was converted with some of his people. But the succeeding emperor launched a bloody persecution, and all the good hopes were permanently wiped out.

Most of the missions, because of lack of personnel, supplies and any knowledge of the interior, were restricted to the long, thin coast of the Dark Continent. On the west coast were established the missions of Congo, Angola and Guinea. The priests were Portuguese friars and Jesuits. They had some successes and some failures, but lack of replacements prevented great growth. On the east coast the missions were erected in Mozambique, along the Zambesi River, and on the island of Madagascar. There were some French missioners on the island; they were sent out by St. Vincent de Paul. The successes and failures were about the same as on the west coast; however, in 1674, a frightful massacre almost wiped out the Christians of Madagascar.

In summary, the Catholic missions in Africa during the three centuries between the Protestant Reformation and the French Revolution seemed to have yielded a very small return for all the labor and sacrifice put into them. Such is true from a purely human consideration. But it must be remembered that God's values are otherwise. The exhausting toil on the hot sandy beaches and in the steaming jungles, the martyrdoms of priests and lay people, and the countless baptisms are exceedingly precious in God's sight. In His own good time, the eternal God will use these treasures for the welfare of the peoples of Africa.

Spreading
the Gospel
in the
New World

BY FAR the Catholic Revival's greatest missionary success
was the conversion of native races in the Spanish and Portuguese dominions of North and South America. But, as will
be shown, this success was achieved in the face of continual
opposition from powerful enemies, native and European.

The propagation of Catholicism throughout their far-
extending possessions was a prime goal of all Spanish monarchs, but especially of the great ones, Charles I (called
Charles V in the Empire) and Philip II. This ideal of the sovereigns was supported wholeheartedly by their Catholic-
minded subjects: they gladly sent their missionary sons in
thousands to carry the cross to the aboriginal tribes. From the
beginning, priests were dispatched with every Spanish ship
bound for the west. They were mostly from religious orders:
Dominicans, Franciscans, Carmelites, Augustinians, Mercedarians and, after their founding, Jesuits.

The Spanish rulers made most generous provisions
for the support of the clergy, secular and religious, as well
as for the maintenance of religion. They erected splendid
cathedrals, churches and shrines much admired to this day.
They founded and endowed archiepiscopal and episcopal
sees. They established at least two great universities and a
hundred or more colleges, besides numerous technical
schools for Indian boys. They built large, spacious hospitals

for the sick, in which all races were cared for. The ancient royal hospital of Mexico City is still in use, and is still highly praised. In the course of less than a century, the Catholic Church had gained in the New World about as many as she had lost in the Old World by the Religious Revolution.

The Spaniards endowed their native Indian subjects with their own rich culture, the Spanish version of the Renaissance. They erected ninety colonial cities, and they made them in size and in value — even in the number and qualities of institutions — replicas of the cities in their Spanish homeland. Much could be said of the labors of thousands of missionaries in exploration, education, committing the native languages to writing, teaching and training the Indians in agriculture and in technical crafts. They made it all part of their apostolate of souls, for the primary purpose of the missionaries was the gaining of souls for God.

In the history of Catholic missions few, if any, encountered such tremendous obstacles and such embittered opposition as the Spanish padres had to endure continually. First there were the obstacles of nature: the excessive heat and cold, the fever-ridden jungles, the pathless grass-plains, the dense forests, the mighty rivers and tumultuous cascades, the arid upland plateaus, and finally the massive mountain ranges of the Andes, with their towering heights and their frightening abysses. All these the missionaries were penetrating and crossing interminably.

Then there were the barriers of totally different cultures, the Greco-Roman-Christian civilization of the missionaries and the Late Stone Age customs of the aborigines. Most of the natives were hunters and food gatherers, though some were agriculturalists. A relative few had built massive stone forts, cities and temples. None of them had a written language. Their sparse collections of words and their expression of them were unlike any tongues known to Europeans. Communication was extremely difficult. Since their words expressed only sense-perceptions, there was nothing to express speculative thoughts. One of the hardest tasks for the missionaries was the making of words that would convey even the simplest religious and spiritual ideas.

In religion the native tribes were animists, the most primitive type of idolaters, who worshipped the spirits which they imagined lived in the animals, birds and forces of nature. Their worship locked them in almost universal superstition. At times the adoration of their fearful idols was carried on by the bloodiest, wholesale human sacrifices, as witness the rites of the Aztecs. The ministers of their cults were sorcerers, or "medicine men"; they kept the simple savages in an iron grip by their superstitious incantations and wizardry. The "medicine men" were bitter and formidable enemies of the Christian priests.

In large part the aborigines were wanderers of the forest, existing in the lowest living standards. It took dedicated heroism for the missionaries to live with them, to be content with their primitive habitations and food. Supreme courage was called for to penetrate among the natives who were burning with savage hatred for the new conquerors who had cruelly slaughtered, enslaved and oppressed them. Their hatred for the Spanish strangers was one of the chief obstacles to the missionaries' labors for their conversion.

Here it must be noted that not all Spaniards were guilty of the outrages. Despite bloody massacres and harsh oppressions, greatly falsified and exaggerated in the Black Legend and in writings of the Voltarian Encyclopedists, the Spanish regime was less cruel and destructive to the native races than that of some of the other colonial powers. The Spanish clergy, bishops and priests, made it their special task to defend the rights of the Indians.

First among the champions of the red men was Bishop Bartolomé de Las Casas, of Chiapas, who crossed the Atlantic fourteen times to obtain freedom for the Indians. He induced Ferdinand of Aragon to issue in 1512, "The Laws of Burgos" for their protection. Cardinal Ximínes and Cardinal Adrian (later Pope Adrian VI), both advisers of the future Charles V, encouraged him in his charitable attitudes towards the Indians. In 1537, Pope Paul III forbade under pain of excommunication enslaving and plundering of Indians. In 1542, Charles V issued decrees which embodied all the measures proposed by de Las Casas; Charles V made the natives of all the Spanish possessions in America free vassals of the Crown. Philip II confirmed all his father's decrees. In Mexico, 130,000 Indians were freed under the law of Charles V.

From the beginning, bishops and priests, with rare exceptions, sought education and social welfare for the Indians. Bishop Juan de Zumárraga, the first bishop of Mexico, heads the list of countless priests, and especially religious, who founded schools for the Indian youth. It was not long before secondary schools of the best classical traditions were established throughout the Spanish conquests. In the sixteenth century two great universities, Mexico and Peru, were the first in the whole New World by over a quarter of a century.

The glories and adversities of the Spanish missions are exemplified in the Jesuit "Reductions of Paraguay." These were settlements of Guarani Indians who, while directly subject to the crown of Spain, enjoyed complete home rule under the guidance of the missionaries. The reductions were established far from white settlements so that the natives would be isolated from the repressions and the vices of the colonists. By royal decree all whites, except the missionaries, were forbidden to visit the Indian settlements.

The Reductions prospered after heartbreaking initial failures with the nomads. Religion was the all-pervading motive. There were two priests and at least four lay brothers in each settlement; every morning and evening the natives met for divine worship. Schools flourished; the Guarani language was written down, and all were taught to read and write it; later, in the eighteenth century, Spanish was taught. The Indians chose their own civic officials, magistrates and judges. Punishments were light, serious crimes were unheard of. For protection against the terrible slave-hunters, from São Paulo, Brazil, Spain allowed the Indians to maintain a native military force, armed with guns and officered by their own chiefs. It was a well-drilled militia of 30,000 soldiers.

The missionaries, besides deepening the faith of their flocks, taught them grazing and farming. Each reduction had its common herd, land and granary. When the natives became advanced enough, each family was given its own herd and its own fields, which they worked three days for themselves; the remaining three days they worked on the common lands. These natives, whose forefathers were cannibals, were trained by the priests to be carpenters, masons, iron-workers and practicers of every industrial craft of Europe. So the Indians built their own homes, simple but strong and commodious; and hospices for widows, which also were used as industrial schools for girls. Eventually they built magnificent churches and public buildings, the ruins of which still excite the admiration of travelers.

Thus in a century and a half, from 1610 to 1767, in thirty-two reductions, over 700,000 Guarani were Christianized and civilized by Jesuit missionaries to become a free, happy and innocent people. Paraguay was not the only place with reductions. The Jesuits established similar ones throughout the Spanish colonial regime, even up to and including Lower California and the present Mexican state of Sonora. The method was copied successfully by other religious orders; the best known are the Franciscan Missions erected by Fra Junipero Serra, O.F.M., in Upper California.

Unfortunately, all this glorious apostolate of the Reductions was destroyed by selfish and greedy officials and adventurers. First, part of the Paraguay reductions fell when they were ceded by Spain to the Portuguese from São Paulo. Then the rest and all the other Jesuit missions in the Spanish colonies were destroyed as a result of the Spanish suppression of the Society of Jesus in 1767. Finally, the splendid works of the other religious orders were utterly ruined by the anti-clericals of the eighteenth and nineteenth centuries.

Spanish Missions

A GLORIOUS FEATURE of the Spanish Missions was the large number of saintly participants. Just to list their names would require several large tomes; to sketch even briefly their toil for souls would call for an extensive library. Yet outside the Spanish-speaking world, how little is known about this mighty host of bishops, missionaries, parish priests and apostolic lay people, Spanish or Creole, who brought millions of Indians and Negroes into the Catholic Faith, who civilized these converts, and who protected them and their descendants from slavery and oppression.

A few citations would be appropriate. The first American native canonized as a martyr was St. Philip of Jesus, O.F.M., who was born in the City of Mexico in the latter part of the sixteenth century. St. Philip de las Casas, to give him his family name, was crucified in Japan at Nagasaki, on February 5, 1597. He was beatified in 1627 and canonized in 1862.

Though never having labored in Latin America, because of his birth St. Philip of Jesus is honored as the patron of his native City of Mexico. He is commemorated in Guatemala, Colombia, Venezuela and Ecuador. He is also venerated in the United States, in the archdioceses of Baltimore and Los Angeles.

One of the earliest of the Spanish missionaries was St. Luis Bertrand, O.P. He was born in Valencia in 1526, and he crossed over to South America in 1562 to convert the Indians, even, if God willed, at the price of his life. In Spain he had been known for extraordinary sanctity. For several years he had been master of novices among the Dominicans, and St. Teresa of Avila chose him as her advisor in works for reform. He labored among the Indians of the coastal areas of New Granada, especially at Cartagena and Panama, and also in the Leeward Islands among the Caribs.

His apostolate was brief, lasting only seven years; yet it was most fruitful, for he baptized 25,000 pagans. He is said to have had the gift of tongues; he could preach only in Spanish, but he was understood in several languages. He was also credited with prophecies and miracles. Certainly his very evident holiness contributed much to his success. St. Luis was recalled to Spain, where he died at Valencia in 1581. He is the principal patron of the Republic of Colombia, and is venerated also in Venezuela and Chile.

St. Toribio Alfonso de Mogrovejo, the third archbishop of Lima, Peru, may well be considered the most apostolic prelate in the history of the Americas, North and South. It is a pity that he is so little known outside Spanish America, for he measures up to the stature of St. Charles Borromeo and St. Francis de Sales. St. Toribio was born in Leon, Spain, in 1538. He became a distinguished professor of law at Salamanca. Because of his ability and his marked holiness of life, King Philip II nominated him, though he was a layman, for the much troubled archdiocese of Lima. After vigorously opposing the designation, St. Toribio Alfonso acquiesced to the royal nomination with the greatest reluctance. He was ordained a priest in 1578 and consecrated a bishop in the year 1580.

He arrived in his diocese in the following year and immediately plunged into missionary labors. For the next quarter of a century he worked unceasingly, correcting abuses — lay and clerical — defending the rights of the Church, and personally spreading the Faith among the natives. He mastered the Quichua language, the most widespread of the Indian tongues, so that he might fully understand his Indian flock and thus be able to protect them against exploitation, and be better equipped to promote their interests.

St. Toribio spent half his time in visitations of his vast diocese, which lay for four hundred miles along the Pacific coast and reached far into the first high ranges of the Andes. He made three great visitations; the first lasted for seven years, the second took four years; he was on the third when death overtook him. In all these visitations he exposed himself to tempests, mountain torrents, tropical heat and high-plateau cold, fevers, wild beasts and savage tribes. Generally he proceeded on foot, defenseless and often alone. At times his only abode was the wretched hovels of the poorest of his people. St. Toribio baptized or confirmed nearly half a million souls. Among the children of his zeal were St. Rose of Lima and St. Martin de Porres.

Indefatigably the archbishop proceeded, building numerous chapels, schools, hospitals and convents, and even the roads that connected them. In 1591, he founded the first American seminary; it was the seminary of Lima. He assembled and presided over thirteen diocesan synods and three provincial councils.

As has been noted St. Toribio was on a missionary visitation when he was struck down by a fever. He kept laboring to the last, arriving at Sana, near Lima, in a dying condition. Dragging himself to the sanctuary he received Viaticum and then was carried to his death bed. He made his will, bestowing almost his entire revenue on the poor — his "creditors," as he called them. He expired shortly afterwards on March 23, 1606. He was canonized in 1726.

St. Toribio Alfonso is the principal patron of the dioceses of Lima, Trujillo and Cajmarua in Peru, and the diocese of Managua in Nicaragua. His feast day is celebrated all over South America.

The figure of the Franciscan friar has become almost a symbol of the Spanish missions, so numerous were the sons of the Poverello in all areas and from the very beginning. One of the most outstanding of the Franciscan missionaries was St. Francis Solano, O.F.M. He was born in 1549, in Spain, at Montillo in the diocese of Cordova. He entered the Friars Minor in 1568. Such was his spirituality that he was appointed master of novices. During a pestilence at Granada, braving all dangers, he gave abundant proof of his unbounded charity.

In 1587, St. Francis sailed for the New World. From Peru he was sent to the Rio de la Plata, where he worked with great success among the Indians of Tucuman and Paraguay; he attracted many of the natives by the playing of his violin.

His missionary labors extended over a period of twenty years, during which time he spared himself no fatigue, shrank from no sacrifice, however great, and feared no danger that stood in the way of evangelizing the vast and savage regions of Tucuman and Paraguay. So successful was his apostolate that he has been called the Wonder Worker of the New World. Notwithstanding the number and the difficulties of the dialects spoken by the Indians, he learned them in a very short time. It is said that he often addressed tribes of different tongues in one language and was understood by them all. Towards the end of his life he worked without rest for the Spanish colonists in Lima and in Trujillo, Peru.

St. Francis Solano foretold his own death, which came to him on July 14, 1610. His death was the cause of general grief throughout the Vice-Royalty of Peru. In the funeral sermon at the burial of the saint, his eulogist, Father Sebastiani, S.J., said that "Divine Providence had chosen Father Francis Solano to be the hope and edification of all Peru, the example and glory of Lima and the splendor of the Seraphic Order."

St. Francis was canonized in 1726. He is venerated especially in Peru, but also in Ecuador, Argentina, Bolivia and in his native Cordova.

In the Spanish missions there was nothing more glorious than St. Peter Claver's apostolate among the Negro slaves. Peter Claver was born in Catalonia in 1581, and entered the Society of Jesus in 1601. While studying at Majorca he became the friend of St. Alphonsus Rodriquez, the porter of the college. The holy brother, having learned from God the future mission of his young associate, never ceased exhorting him to set out for the Spanish missions in America. St. Peter complied and, in 1610, landed at Cartagena, where for forty years he devoted himself to the Negro slaves.

Cartagena was the chief slave-market of the New World; each month a thousand slaves were landed there. The horrors of the passage in the slave-ships cannot be described. The slave-trade was extremely lucrative. The wretched creatures were sold for 100 times the price paid for them in Africa; even if half the human cargo died en route, the trade remained profitable. Neither the repeated censures of Popes, nor the denunciations of Catholic moralists could prevail against this cupidity. The missionaries could not suppress slavery; they could only alleviate it.

No one worked more heroically than St. Peter Claver. He declared himself "the slave of the Negroes forever." Every month when the arrival of the Negroes was signaled, Claver sailed out in the pilot boat to meet them, carrying food and delicacies. The Negroes, cooped up in the hold, arrived crazed and brutalized by suffering and fear. St. Peter cared for each one, and showed him kindness, and made him understand that henceforth he was his father and defender. Thus he won the slave's good will.

St. Peter Claver's ultimate goal was the eternal salvation of the Negroes. He assembled a group of interpreters of various Negro races, whom he made catechists. While the slaves were penned up at Cartagena waiting disposal, St. Peter instructed them and baptized them in the Faith. His untiring labors in defending the poor wretches from oppressors gained him enemies from the slave-merchants. But this enmity was only part of his trials. He had to suffer from charges of indiscreet zeal and from sharp criticisms of his methods — and some of these criticisms were listened to by certain of his superiors.

Near the end of his life, while a very sick old man, he had to suffer terribly from neglect. Yet St. Peter persevered in his heroic career, accepting all humiliations calmly, adding even rigorous penances to his works of charity. The strength of God was given to him; he became the prophet and wonder worker of New Granada. During his life he baptized and instructed in the Faith more than 300,000 Negroes. He died on September 8, 1654.

St. Peter Claver was canonized by Pope Leo XIII on January 15, 1888. The same Pope, on July 7, 1896, proclaimed him the special patron of all Catholic missions among Negroes. St. Peter is especially honored throughout the United States.

Sanctity
in the
New World

THE PERSONAL HOLINESS of most of its communicants bore witness to the persisting strength of the Catholic Church in the Spanish colonies. Sanctity, an internal quality, is difficult to gauge. The crowds in great churches, at the popular shrines and in the colorful processions were striking manifestations. More significant still was the universal devotion to the Mass and the Blessed Sacrament, the Rosary of the Blessed Mother Mary, and the Communion of the Saints. As astonishing as admirable was the piety of the Indians of the Paraguay reductions, hardly a hundred years from fierce savagery. Twice daily, morning and evening, they gathered in the chapels of the settlements, for divine services and common prayers. No wonder they had become a people of innocence.

The monasteries and convents of the cities and towns evidenced the many holy religious (of various racial origins) who practiced in notable degree the virtues of the contemplative or of the active spiritual life. At the head of these holy souls, two must be considered, St. Rose of Lima and St. Martin de Porres.

St. Rose was born at Lima, Peru, in 1586; her parents were natives of Puerto Rico. From childhood, in imitation of her chosen patroness, St. Catherine of Siena, she gave herself to a life of prayer, heroic virtue and most austere mortification. She lived as a recluse in a shed in the garden of her parental home. When Rose was twenty years of age, she was clothed in the habit of the Third Order of St. Dominic. Tried by spiritual sufferings, external persecution and sickness, she was also glorified by miracles and extraordinary mystical gifts, visions and revelations. One can say with all due reverence, that the fearsome austerities which she practiced and the almost unceasing prayers which she said, rank St. Rose of Lima as one of the most heroic ascetical saints in the history of the Church.

She was also a very practical, apostolic saint. She offered to God all her mortifications and penances in expiation for offenses against His Divine Majesty, for the idolaters of her country, for the conversion of sinners, and for the souls in purgatory. St. Rose died in 1617, after a long and painful illness. She was canonized in 1671. She is the patroness of all Latin America and the Philippine Islands, but she is also greatly venerated in the United States and in Europe.

St. Martin de Porres was born in Lima in 1569, an illegitimate son of a Spanish noble and a free negress. Eight years later his father acknowledged him as his son and made some provision for his education. The young mulatto was never embittered about his unfortunate origin. He was too charitable for that. Rather he was preoccupied with love for the poor; even as a child he shared his meager store with the unfortunate. When he was twelve he apprenticed himself to a barber so that he might give medical treatment to the poor; in those days barbers were accepted as surgeons and pharmacists. A few years later young Martin applied for admission into the Dominican Order; in his humility he sought acceptance as a lay helper. The friars came to realize that God had sent them, in this humble, charitable soul, an extraordinarily holy man of prayer and penitential practice. They admitted him to the full religious profession.

In the succeeding years of his life St. Martin increased his prayers and mortifications and devoted himself even more intently to feeding the hungry, nursing the sick and caring for the outcasts. He became such a master of the spiritual life that his Dominican brethren, priests and religious, made him the director of their souls; yet he was never

ST. MARTIN DE PORRES. Oldest known likeness of the saint. *Lima, Peru.*

formally trained in theology, nor ordained a priest. His severe asceticism was blessed with visions and ecstasies. For his complete dedication to the poor and the wretched, he was universally called the "Father of Charity."

St. Martin de Porres, O.P., died at Lima on November 3, 1639. His body was found incorrupt in 1664. He was beatified in 1837, and canonized by John XXIII in 1962.

As has been noted in a previous chapter, the achievements and problems of Catholicism in Portuguese America of colonial times were quite similar to those in Spanish America of the same period. Yet there were many differences. Brazil, which was Portuguese America, covered an enormous area; it was thinly populated, difficult to explore, and contained fiercely savage aborigines. The Portuguese were less numerous than the Spaniards.

The Franciscans were early in the mission field, bringing the Faith to the natives and protection for them against greedy colonists. The Jesuits arrived in 1549, sent by Saint Ignatius. They opened colleges for the Creole youth and established missions for the natives. They produced the foremost figure among the pioneer missionaries, Ven. José Anchieta, S.J., educator, poet, converter of souls, preacher to the heathen, and worker of miracles. He has been unanimously called "The Apostle of Brazil."

Martyrs were to be found, too. They were Bl. Ignatius Azevedo, S.J., and his thirty-nine young companions, whom he was bringing to finish their studies and be ordained in Brazil. On July 15, 1570, off the Canary Islands, their ship was captured by Soury, a Huguenot sea-captain. In his implacable hatred of Catholic priests, though he spared the crew, he massacred in cold blood Bl. Ignatius and all his young companions, and then cast their corpses into the sea.

Wars with the French and the Dutch, and bitter opposition from colonial officials, angered by the missionaries' protection of the Indians and the Negroes, rendered the work of conversion exceedingly difficult. But the Jesuits, Franciscans, Dominicans and Mercedarians were able in spite of all obstacles to baptize several hundred thousand natives and Negroes. Perhaps the greatest of the Brazilian missionaries was António Vieira, S.J., 1608-1697. As superior of the Maranhão Mission, he fearlessly denounced the crimes of the officials; he was one of the greatest of the European orators of his day. In 1661, he and several other Jesuits were sent as prisoners to Lisbon. When he returned to Brazil, Vieira succeeded in founding 150 Indian villages north of the Amazon River. He was credited with having baptized 60,000 pagans in seven years. Pombal's expulsion of the Jesuits from all the Portuguese dominions in 1759 dealt a particularly disastrous blow to the missions and to the Church in Brazil. The four hundred Jesuits driven from Brazil, most of whom perished in prison dungeons in Portugal, could never be replaced. At the end of the century, less than half of the population of 2,000,000 in Brazil were Christians.

New France was a mighty forest country extending from the Atlantic, across the wide St. Lawrence, up that broad river to the Great Lakes and beyond; later it continued down the Mississippi to the Gulf of Mexico. It also was a land of lonely distances, for its population, native and white, was never very numerous. Its Christian missions began in the early seventeenth century in Acadia, on the Atlantic coast; they were brought to a quick stop by an English raider from Virginia. A few years later Champlain called the Recollects to Quebec to work for the conversion of the Indians. These devoted friars, not having men enough, invited the Jesuits to assist them.

The Jesuits began their explorations and their preaching through the vast regions of Canada and the Mississippi Valley. Their martyrs wrote one of the most inspiring chapters in the history of Catholicism. They were Sts. Isaac Jogues, René Goupil and Jean Lalande (these last two were *donnés* of the Society) who suffered and died in the present New York State; Sts. Jean de Brébeuf, Charles Garnier, Anthony Daniel, Gabriel Lallement and Noel Chabanel who made the supreme sacrifice in the present province of Ontario. The period of these martyrdoms was between 1642 and 1649. The successors of the martyred heroes converted the numerous Algonquins and even many of the Iroquois.

Catholicism in New France was blessed by a holy and great leader, Bishop Laval, the first bishop of Quebec, and by devoted trainers of priests, the Sulpicians of Montreal. It was further blessed by saintly nuns, such as Bl. Marguerite Bourgeoys, Ven. Marie de l'Incarnation, the mystic of Quebec, the Ursuline Nuns and the Sisters of the Hotel-Dieu, both with convents in Quebec and Montreal. The Mohawks can claim a holy virgin, Ven. Kateri Tekakwitha. These and the many devoted priests of the last three centuries produced the solid and splendid Faith of the Canadian people of our present day.

The Age
of the
Enlightenment

THE CENTURY and a half between the Peace of Westphalia, 1648, and the outbreak of the French Revolution,
1789, has been called "The Age of the Enlightenment."
It was a superficial label, standing much less for good than
for evil. The good was to be found in the great discoveries in
the physical sciences — physics, mathematics, chemistry,
biology, zoology and astronomy — made by such renowned
scientists as Newton, Boyle, Malpighi and Halley. The evil,
far more preponderating, was to be found in the far-reaching
pseudo-philosophical movements which had developed from
mere naturalism, sceptical rationalism, materialism, agnosticism and deism.

Such movements were infidel in principle and action;
they rejected religious revelation and they spurned Christian
Theology. Eventually the movements coalesced into a
single force, assumed the name "Philosophism" (Philosophy),
and spread by tremendous literary campaigns to become
the fashion of the shallow thinkers and the accepted doctrine of many among the worldly-minded statesmen in the
cabinets of Europe. "Enlightenment," or "Philosophism,"
plunged into an intellectual war to the death against the
Church.

The Peace of Westphalia in its sessions and in its aftermath inflicted grave evils upon the Catholic Church. By

secularizing a considerable number of ecclesiastical states and by bestowing them on Lutheran or Calvinist princes, it strengthened the Protestant states of the Empire immeasurably, at the expense of the Catholic states. These secularizations threatened ominously the faith of the Catholic populations of the transferred districts. Significantly, the jurisdictions of the Catholic bishops were immediately abolished.

Most disastrous of all was the enforcement of the provision of the Augsburg Peace, 1555, which laid down that the prince alone decided the religion of all in his principality. In consequence, the Catholic subjects of the newly secularized bishoprics and abbey-lands were faced by the alternatives of exile or apostasy.

Pope Innocent X's legate was rigidly excluded from the deliberations of the Peace of Westphalia, even though most vital religious matters were at stake. The fate of Catholicism was being arranged solely by politicians, Protestant and Catholic; neutrality in religion was being fashioned as the future policy of the Empire. When the Treaty of Westphalia was signed, Innocent X strongly protested the injuries done to the Church. He dispatched an epistle to all the rulers. They ignored his letter; only a few would permit its publication.

The Popes and the Church were now excluded from all participation in public affairs, except in the government of the Papal States. Their exclusion was to last until the days of Leo XIII. After Westphalia, a solid mass of Protestant states and nations blocked the further spread of the Catholic Reformation. As for the Empire, it ceased, for all practical purposes, to be the champion of Catholicism.

These one hundred and fifty years under review have also been called "The Age of Absolutism." All the monarchs of continental Europe ruled without restraint of legislative or judicial bodies; in England the aristocratic Parliament followed a similar course. Absolutism in government had a rebirth during the Renaissance. It began to develop in the domain of religion during the Religious Revolution. Most of the successes of the latter were owing to the support of absolute rulers, such as Henry VIII, the Princes of northern

Germany and the King of Sweden, Gustavus Wasa. Thenceforth, these kings and princes became so supreme in spiritual matters that their claim to determine the religion of their subjects was recognized as a first principle of government.

During the religious enthusiasms of the Catholic Revival, Catholic sovereigns, though absolutists with personal ambitions, fought more for the unity of their kingdoms and the defense of the religion of their fathers, threatened as it was with complete overthrow. But the Wars of Religion were now ended, and the stalemate of a Europe permanently half Protestant and half Catholic was an established fact. The first fervor of the Catholic defense had long passed. Catholic sovereigns began to imitate, as far as they could without denying the dogmas of their Faith, the Protestant rulers' supremacy in religion. For the Popes and the Church, this change of policy was fraught with ominous possibilities.

The dangers and difficulties of the Protestant Revolution were not a whit more critical than those confronting the Holy Father and the ancient Faith in the increasing and selfish demands of Catholic monarchs during the Age of Absolutism. The Popes were continually called upon to defend their essential rights to exercise control in purely ecclesiastical and spiritual affairs.

The worst offenders were Louis XIV of France in the beginning of the period and Joseph II, the Emperor and ruler of the Austrian lands, near the end. But their ideas were shared by most of the other Catholic rulers. These sovereigns demanded an overwhelming voice in all ecclesiastical appointments. They insisted upon exercising the *Royal Placet* on papal and episcopal documents; without this official approval no such documents could be published in their territories. They revoked at pleasure the privileges and exemptions admitted by their predecessors in favor of clerics and of ecclesiastical properties.

They controlled education in their own domains, determined the laws and rules concerning marriages and matrimonial dispensations; they fixed the constitutions of those religious orders the existence of which they were willing to tolerate. They claimed the right to dictate to the Pope who should be cardinals, and they likewise claimed the right to dictate to the conclaves whom these cardinals should, or should not, elect to be Pope. This last claim was exercised by placing a *Veto* against the name of any cardinal whom they did not wish to see seated on the Papal Throne. The Veto was by no means infrequently used.

To obtain their demands, these ambitious Catholic monarchs often had recourse to high-handed measures: expelling papal nuncios, breaking off relations with the Holy See (sometimes for a lengthy period), military invasions of papal territories, even of Rome itself. Finally, some of them did not hesitate to threaten withdrawal into schism, or the establishment of national churches.

Dr. MacCaffrey in his *History of the Catholic Church, From the Renaissance to the French Revolution*, Vol. I, pp. 390-391, lists the powerful and widespread support which these Catholic despots received:

"Unfortunately in their designs for transferring ecclesiastical jurisdiction from the Popes to the crown, the princes were favored by many bishops, who were annoyed at the continual interference of Rome and who failed to realize that the king was a much greater danger to their independence than the Pope; by a large body of clerics and laymen, who looked to the civil authority for promotion; by the Jansenists who detested Rome because Rome had barred the way against the speculative and practical religious revolution which they contemplated; by the philosophers and rationalists, many of whom, though enemies of absolute rule, did not fail to recognize that disputes between the Church and the State, leading necessarily to a weakening of the Church's authority, meant the weakening of dogmatic Christianity; and by liberal-minded Catholics of the "Aufklärung" (Enlightenment) school, who thought that every blow dealt at Rome meant a blow struck for the policy of modernizing the discipline, government, and faith of the Church."

Fourteen Popes reigned during this period. Personally they were virtuous and devout men. But all were circumscribed by the pressures of Catholic monarchs. A few resisted strongly, most persevered tenaciously in whatever opposition they could make, and a few were conciliatory—but only because they thought they were making the best of bad situations. Such conciliations at times only led to more outrageous demands, as when the Bourbon Courts badgered and threatened Clement XIV into the terrible disaster of the total suppression of the Society of Jesus. None suffered stronger opposition from many rulers than Pius VI — even to exile and imprisonment in France, where he died during his incarceration. It was the price of his heroism in defying the French Revolutionary fanatics by condemning their iniquitous Civil Constitution of the Clergy.

After one hundred and fifty years of seeking to be dominating masters of the Church in their domains, would it be possible that the Catholic despots might complete their imitation of the Protestant lay-popes? Some rulers and their ministers of state hinted at such an eventuality. But their disastrous threats were drowned out in the fierce cries of the atheists of the French Revolution. The Popes and the Church survived both deluges. Christ, the God-man, had guaranteed the eternal survival of the Church that He built on Peter the Rock.

Anti-Christian Philosophy

AMONG THE MOST harmful movements in the so-called Enlightenment was the widely accepted rationalistic philosophy. It rejected all supernatural religion and divine revelation, basing all religious knowledge on human reasoning alone. Rationalism of this type fostered scepticism, materialism and, with some, even atheism. Most rationalists, however, developed a religion of their own, known as Deism. It was the purely human recognition of the existence of God, the Supreme Being and Creator, the Deity, as they were accustomed to refer to Him. But that was about all. They denied His revelations to man and His Providence; their principal concern almost exclusively was man and his human affairs.

Rationalist sceptics had always plagued Christianity, but they had not assumed widespread influence until the rise of a vigorous sceptical literature in English literary circles, sometime after 1660. The rejection of Catholicism's dogmatic authority, and the propagating of free interpretation of the Bible by each individual person had by now produced its full fruit of religious confusion. This confusion was immeasurably increased by the various changes in religion developed by the English monarchs, by the quarrelings of the Puritans and the High Anglicans, and by the spread of revolutionary principles during the conflicts of the reign of Charles I.

From the days of Cromwell it was the leading object of the English sceptics to reject the Bible, miracles, revelation and Christianity. Such sceptics were first called Deists or Rationalists. Later, those who denied Christianity were known as Freethinkers. Hobbes declared that all religion was a mere human invention; Blount labeled it a crafty device of the priesthood. Locke by his speculations about "thinking matter" became the forerunner of *materialism* which denied all spiritual existence from the human soul upward. Some literary men wrote in a serious strain, but others mocked cynically at religion and morality. A few nourished a diabolical hatred for Christianity. Most restricted knowledge to the exclusive and one-sided investigation of natural phenomena. They rejected every higher truth that could not be found with the dissecting knife; they called this rejection "enlightenment." Knowing little, if any, theology, or intoxicated by their own superficial concepts of science, these litterateurs invented the supposed war between religion and science. Between true religion and true science there can be no real conflict; both are sure paths to truth. These partisans of infidelity went further to substitute Deism, Pantheism, and Atheism for Christianity, and they gave to their substitution the name of "philosophy." In England, by 1740, a reaction set in against sceptical literature, and henceforth most of the freethinkers retired to the secrecy of Masonic lodges.

Freemasonry was one of the chief means of spreading rationalistic philosophy. The first grand lodge appeared in London in 1717, when a moribund medieval guild was revived into a rationalistic society. It was at a time when Deism and Naturalism were rampant in England, and when powerful interests which were exceedingly hostile to supernatural religion existed in most continental states. Actually Masonry was a Deistic sect; its idea of God as the "Grand Architect of the Universe" was a Deistic concept. While the society professed to be non-sectarian in its objects, the whole tendency of its rules and organization in practice promoted opposition to dogmatic orthodoxy and to religious authority. Its modified Christianity eliminated specifically Catholic doctrine. In Catholic lands, Latin or Germanic, Masonry and Rationalism worked together for the overthrow of the established Church and for the spread of rationalistic views. Freemasonry developed most powerfully; within four decades it extended through all European countries, Protestant, Orthodox and Catholic. Royal personages, statesmen and cabinet-ministers, deists and freethinkers, members of the educated and professional classes joined the secret order. Most of the prime ministers of Catholic countries could be classed as members of the lodges, or as influenced by them: Kaunitz in Austria, Pombal in Portugal, d'Aranda in Spain, Choiseul in France, Tanucci in Naples. These all were more or less outspoken freethinkers and conspirators against the Holy See and the rights of the Catholic Church. No wonder that Clement XII, in 1738, and Benedict XIV, in 1751, condemned Masonry as a Deistic religion and as a source of rationalistic philosophy.

France, not England, became the foremost promoter of rationalistic philosophy. France was the cultural leader of the world; if rationalism were adopted by a wide sector of the French intelligentsia, their action would certainly be followed in every European country. So it turned out! Unfortunately French "Philosophisme" assumed a most violent form and had most destructive influences. At the time there was widespread religious indifference in France, due to the long religious wars, the controversies of the Jansenists, the enslavement of the Church by Gallicanism, the flagrant immorality of the court during the regency of the Duke of Orleans and the reign of Louis XV, and finally, a decline of zeal and training among some of the higher clergy. The indifference reached down to the lowest ranks of society. Infidelity became a fashion in the intellectual salons, where rationalism was considered a mark of good breeding, and loyalty to the dogmas of the Faith was sneered at as vulgar and unprogressive.

There were two classes among the freethinkers: one was the "Encyclopédists" and the other was the Socialists.

The first group included sceptical scientists, atheists and materialists. Almost all were indefatigable in propagating the gospel of open impiety, unblushing immorality and deadly hatred against the Church by a veritable Niagara of pamphlets, lampoons, dialogues, parodies, letters, novels and pseudo-scientific treatises, distributed among the higher and middle classes. Countless cheap editions were brought out for the consumption of the lowest classes. Much of the propaganda was patently dishonest; books and pamphlets purporting to be descriptions of customs in most remote lands were but thinly veiled attacks aimed at civil and religious institutions and ideas in France.

The outstanding leader of this rationalist movement was Voltaire, whose real name was François Marie Arouet. For half a century Voltaire turned his brilliant gifts of poetry and wit into weapons of invective, slander, ridicule, buffoonery and malice to wage unrelenting war against the Catholic Church. "Écrasez l'infame" ("Crush out the infamous thing") was his motto, and it possessed his soul. "The infamous thing" was Voltaire's epithet for the holy Catholic Church.

The most powerful work of the philosophical sect was the *Encyclopedia*. It was begun under the direction of the atheist Diderot, and almost all the leading sceptics contributed to it. Ostensibly it was like any other encyclopedia, a handy reference work, with up-to-date articles on all phases of life, literature and science. Actually it was made a vehicle for popularizing the irreligious views then current among the nobility and the literati, by spreading rationalistic ideas among the lowest classes. Much deception was used in the placement and style of the articles; the damage was enormous. The producers of the *Encyclopedia* boasted that it would be an easy thing for twelve philosophers to destroy what twelve fishermen had built up. The extreme fanatics among the sect proclaimed atheism as the supreme duty of mankind.

The second group among the anti-Catholic philosophers were the Socialists. They aimed their attacks directly against the government, society and private ownership. Their leader was Jean Jacques Rousseau, a native of Geneva, a Calvinist, then a Catholic and again a Calvinist. He had scarcely any religious principles, and no moral ones either. He had not the wit nor the literary ability of Voltaire. Yet he wielded a far greater and a far longer influence. His chief work was *The Social Contract*, in which he gave his theories about the origins of the state and the nature of its authority. *The Social Contract* became the bible of the French Revolution and of most of the economic and social revolts which came from it. A small book, yet it has influenced millions. No admirer of Voltaire, Rousseau nevertheless became one of the chief figures in Voltaire's war upon Catholicism.

This has been a discouraging chapter. But it can be ended on an encouraging note. Recall the boasting of the insufferably proud Encyclopedists that it would be an easy task for twelve philosophers to destroy what twelve fishermen had built up. Well, that boast was uttered more than two hundred years ago. Who today can name three of the twelve philosophers? And what of their fine-spun theories? Forgotten! Buried in dusty books on silent shelves. But that ship of the twelve fishermen? It is still sailing the seas, having weathered at least a half-dozen storms, as bad if not worse than the windy onslaughts of the philosophers. Jesus was always in the apostles' ship. He is in there now, and He will be there to its last calm entry into the port of heaven.

Threats
to the
Company
of Jesus

THE WORST DISASTER inflicted on the Catholic Church
by the infidel philosophers of the eighteenth century was
the suppression of the Society of Jesus. St. Ignatius in founding the Society had made its distinguishing mark complete
dedication to the Church, with special emphasis on unflagging loyalty to the Pope. During two centuries and a half,
his sons faithfully carried out these ideals of their founder
in seven hundred and fifty colleges, in countless sermons
and in numerous books and treatises. But hard was the
price they had to pay for their loyalty to Church and Pope.
This was the bitter and unremitting enmity of many, such as
Jansenists, Gallicans and infidel philosophers. Even on the
distant missionary scenes they had to endure harassments
from avaricious colonial officials and plantation-owners.

The Gallicans of France and the Regalists of Spain,
Austria and other Catholic lands frequently tried to dominate
the organizations and activities of the Jesuits in their particular countries. France once expelled the order, and so did
the Republic of Venice. The Jansenists pursued unrelenting
controversies with the Jesuit theologians in France and in
the Netherlands. But under the Providence of God all these
dangers were overcome. In the middle of the eighteenth
century the Jesuits were still vigorous in Europe, and still
vigorous in the faraway mission fields.

Yet it was just at this time that the fatal campaign against the order was launched. The opponents of the Society of Jesus had never relinquished their enmities, no matter how often they were defeated. It remained for the infidel philosophers, busily planning their own war against the Jesuit order, to bring finally the diverse enemies together for one overwhelming campaign against the common foe. They joined into alliance: Huguenots, still mindful of Jesuit successes in the Counter-Reformation; Jansenists, eager to avenge defeats at the hands of the Jesuit theologians; and absolutist monarchs, statesmen and jurists, who feared that the Jesuits might thwart their schemes for dominating the local churches and for immobilizing the Holy See.

The infidel philosophers of themselves nurtured a perfect hatred for the Catholic Church. In consequence these disciples of the Enlightenment had a driving incentive to bring down in total destruction the Society of Jesus, for they had come to recognize that the Jesuits were the ablest defenders of Christianity. Without question, their most skillful opponents were the French Jesuits who published the excellent literary periodical, the *Journal de Trévoux*. For twenty-two years, 1745 to 1767, in the pages of the *Journal* the French fathers battled ceaselessly and brilliantly against "Philosophisme."

Furthermore Catholic education, both lay and clerical, was in a large measure controlled by the Jesuits; it was hoped that, on the expulsion of Jesuit educators, in their vacant posts would be placed educators devoted to the Enlightenment and to the supremacy of the state. Then the future of infidel rationalism in civil life and the future of state-absolutism in ecclesiastical circles would be assured. Voltaire put it succinctly in a letter to Helvetius, another Encyclopedist, "Once we have destroyed the Jesuits, we shall have it all our own way with the *Infamous Thing*." The Infamous Thing, it will be remembered, was Voltaire's expletive for the Catholic Church.

The war of the infidel philosophers against the Society of Jesus began with a mighty propaganda campaign. Books, pamphlets and fly-sheets, a perfect deluge of them, thundered out all manner of charges. No calumny, or scurrility, or intrigue was spared to blacken the members of the order in the eyes of the rulers, the clergy, the nobles, the lawyers, the merchants, even the artisans and the peasants. The Jesuits were proclaimed decadent from their original spirit, scandalously rich, inimical to civil governments. The members of the order were denounced as proud, arrogant, ignorers of authority (royal or episcopal), laxist in the teaching of morals, heretical on the question of God's salvific grace, unscrupulous in criminal intrigues, and adamant foes of liberty and progress.

This farrago of accusations was based on garbled extracts lifted from the writings of individual Jesuits, but presented as the officially adopted opinions of the whole body. Some assertions were just plain lies. Even that old forgery, the *Monita Secreta*, was resurrected for the assault. It purported to be secret, villainous instructions of Father Aquaviva to his subjects, but actually was a piece of revenge concocted by an ex-Jesuit. To refute these allegations would require a library of learned tomes. One document and one fact must suffice.

As for the document: "On January 7, 1767, when the enemies of the Jesuits were sweeping along in the full tide of victory, having encompassed the destruction of the order in Portugal, France and Spain, Pope Clement XIII issued the Bull *Apostolicum pascendi munus* not only to defend the Society of Jesus, but to give it a new and solemn confirmation." Numerous bishops in all parts of the world sent letters of congratulation to the courageous Pope.

As for the fact: "After the suppression, the enemies of the order had in their hands all the archives, all the correspondence and records of the Society of Jesus; they ransacked them for proofs to substantiate their allegations. So far they have never given to the world a justification of their charges. The reason is simple enough: they found none."*

The Society of Jesus had no lack of defenders. The majority of the College of Cardinals, known as "The Zelanti,"

---

*Both quotations are to be found in *The Jesuits in History*, pp. 295, 296 by Harney, Martin P., S.J., New York, 1941.

were their staunch supporters. Hundreds of bishops and thousands of priests, secular and religious, manifested their approval of the fathers in petitions and personal letters. The laity of all classes, but particularly the simple people, held public demonstrations to manifest their esteem for the Jesuits. Later these clerics and lay people were most generous to the exiled religious in the trials and poverty of their dispersion.

But in the contemporary scene the anti-Jesuits held the more powerful weapons. First there were the crowds of pseudo-intellectuals, the very vocal faddists who could dominate the press and could shout down any opposition. Second, and most powerful of all, there were the prime ministers of the leading Catholic governments, Pombal in Portugal, de Choiseul in France, d'Aranda in Spain, Tanucci in Naples and Kaunitz in Austria. All these were disciples of the Enlightenment, all gloried in being called Philosophers, all were enemies of Catholicism and the Papacy. Each was the actual holder of the reins of power in his particular country. Each one had the police, the bureaucracy and the army to enforce his schemes and to crush all opposition.

The suppression of the Society of Jesus by political governments was first accomplished by Portugal, 1759, then by France, 1764, then by Spain, 1767, and finally by Naples, 1767. Pombal, a ruthless despot, employed all sorts of false charges and dishonest intrigues to destroy the Portuguese part of the Jesuit Order. He added cruelties to his evil machinations. By his false accusations he forced the Jesuits from Paraguay and Brazil, and also from India, back to the home country. Then he engineered an ecclesiastical visitation of the Order. It was conducted by one of his creatures, Cardinal Saldanha, who completely ignored the regulations of the Pope for a fair trial. Indeed he permitted the fathers not a single word for their defense. Of course the Society of Jesus in Portugal was condemned.

Pombal's next move was to accuse the Jesuits of complicity in an alleged plot on the king's life. There was not a particle of truth in the charges, but the fathers nevertheless were found guilty. The prominent priests of the order were incarcerated for life in loathsome dungeons; several lost their reason and a number died of illness brought on by the terrible conditions. The majority of the Jesuits were banished to the Papal States. For a while the young Jesuits, novices, and ecclesiastical students, 300 in number, were kept in Portugal. Every inducement and every threat was used to bring them to abandon the Order. Out of the 300, only 6 succumbed. The faithful young religious were banished to join their elder brethren in the Papal States.

The heroic constancy of these young Jesuits illumined the gloomy darkness of the scene. It was dark, not only because of the personal sufferings of the Portuguese Jesuits, but also because of the utter ruining of their splendid missions in Paraguay, Brazil and India.

Next came the turn of the French Jesuits. They had many devoted friends, almost all the bishops of France and large sections of the clergy, secular and religious. But they also had many able and determined enemies: the whole Enlightenment movement, the Jansenists who controlled most of the law courts, and the Gallicans who crowded the royal court. The anti-Jesuits were assisted by Madame de Pompadour, the mistress of Louis XV. This vicious courtesan hated the Jesuits because, it was said, she had been refused absolution by Jesuit confessors. She was a most formidable enemy because of her domination of the weak king.

The financial misfortunes of Father La Valette, superior of the Jesuit mission in Martinique, afforded the Supreme Court of Paris, controlled by Jansenists and Gallicans, the chance to try the Jesuits. It was the opportunity they had long been seeking. The Court condemned officially the Constitutions of the Society of Jesus as godless, sacrilegious and treasonable. (These were the Constitutions which so many Popes had solemnly confirmed and approved.) The Court suppressed the order in France, closed all its schools, and forbade Frenchmen to enter it. This decree was promulgated in 1761.

The Pope and the French hierarchy rose to the defense of the Society. But their actions were in vain. In 1764, the Court left the Jesuits the alternative of foreswearing their society or of going into exile. They took the road to exile. Of 5,000, only 5 abandoned the Order. The heroic French missions too were lost in the destruction.

An observer of the times certainly would have believed that the Society of Jesus would never be destroyed in Spain, so loyal were the Spanish Church and the Spanish people to the Jesuits, especially in these years of their trials. But there was a very active clique among the ministers of the king, Charles III, who were intense disciples of the Enlightenment. Under the leadership of d'Aranda, by lies and false charges, they convinced the credulous king that the Jesuits were behind the riots against his policies and that they were spreading rumors and writing forgeries insinuating the monarch's illegitimacy. Charles III fell into the trap and decreed the abolishment of the Jesuit Order.

By a prearranged plan all the houses and colleges of the Society throughout the Spanish dominions were invaded on the same day, their papers sealed and their properties confiscated. In 1767, without a hearing, without even the semblance of a trial, 6,000 members, provided only with the clothes they wore and their breviaries, were crowded into ships and exiled to the Papal States and to Corsica. The missionaries were brought from Latin America and the Philippines to share the same exile. Perhaps here was the hardest blow: they were forced to abandon over 500,000 native Christians.

In the same year and by the same methods the Jesuits were driven from Naples and Parma. The next goal of the Bourbon Courts — France, Spain, Naples and Parma (all ruled by princes of the Bourbon House) — was the forcing of the Pope to suppress the Society of Jesus ecclesiastically throughout the whole world.

The Suppression
of the
Jesuits

IN 1768, WHEN the Bourbon Courts moved to force the Pope to decree the total ecclesiastical suppression of the Society of Jesus, the membership of the Order had not been noticeably diminished. The almost 14,000 Portuguese, French, Spanish and Neopolitan Jesuits, though dispersed in poverty-stricken exile, were still members of the Order and, as best they could, were carrying on their apostolates. Return to their native provinces was at least a remote possibility. The 10,000 other Jesuits carried on their spiritual and educational works unmolested in Austria, Germany, Poland, northern Italian principalities, Hungary, and the Austrian Netherlands. Over a hundred Jesuit priests were serving small Catholic groups in England and in the American colonies of Pennsylvania and Maryland.

The campaign for total suppression was begun with threats of dethroning the Pope and partitioning the Papal States. French troops took over Avignon and Venaissin; Neopolitan troops seized Benevento and Montecorvo, papal duchies in central Italy. Efforts were made to turn the Empress Marie Theresa against the Jesuits, and pressure was brought on the smaller Italian states to abandon their support of the Order. But in the face of all violence, Pope Clement XIII stood undaunted. He refused even to consider the Bourbon demands that he suppress the Jesuits, against whom nothing could be proved except their ardent defense of the Catholic Church and their unwavering attachment to the Holy See. In January, 1769, the ambassadors of France, Spain and Naples officially demanded the total suppression of the Society of Jesus. The Holy Father refused absolutely. Before the threats could be carried into execution, Pope Clement XIII passed away in February, 1769.

The Bourbon governments swung quickly to dominating the conclave. They encountered most formidable opposition. A majority of the cardinals ardently supported the Jesuits; the most numerous group, called the "Zelanti," determinedly opposed the suppression. Those of the conclave who favored the demands of the monarchies were known as the "Court Cardinals." Some of these were worthy ecclesiastics who sincerely believed that appeasement was the only possible course for the safety of the Church; but others among them were politicians working only for their governments' demands. The conclave lasted through three months of bitter struggle. The ministers and ambassadors of France, Spain and Naples hesitated at no intrigue or threat. Seldom, if ever, have the meetings of the Sacred College for the election of a Supreme Pontiff been subjected to such unwarranted pressure and illegal interference. The solemn prescriptions of secrecy and isolation made by several former Popes were violated time and again, not only by the lay politicians from without, but by a handful of Court Cardinals from within. These latter grossly violated the oaths which they had sworn upon their entrance into conclave.

A policy of deliberate exclusion prevented any of the "Zelanti," or any other cardinal favored by them, from being chosen Pope. If such a cardinal's election approached probability, the insinuation would be made that his election might not be recognized by the ministers of the Bourbon sovereigns. The objecting cardinals talked piously enough about not wishing to force the election of anyone on the conclave, but they never failed to make clear the hidden hint of schism. At length only five cardinals survived the exclusions. The foremost of these was the worthy Franciscan, Cardinal Lorenzo Ganganelli. The "Crown" cardinals decided to support him, even though his attitude towards the suppression was known only to himself. Their questioning of him on the powers of the Pope for suppressing the Society of Jesus, and of the wisdom of favoring the Bourbon kings, if it were for the good of the Church, elicited from him only answers which any good theologian would have given. One thing, most important, must be noted: Cardinal Ganganelli never gave any promise, either in writing or verbally, to suppress the Society of Jesus. He was elected, on May 19, 1769, unanimously. He chose the name of his predecessor, and became Clement XIV.

Hardly had Clement XIV been crowned than the representatives of France and Spain made insistent demands for the suppression of the Society of Jesus. The Pontiff agreed, but asked for time for the consideration of such a momentous step. Then followed two years of delays and mitigating proposals on the part of the Holy Father, who seemed to grow even more reluctant to destroy the order. Several conjectures have since been made to explain the Pope's changed attitude. The most plausible is the one made by a renowned English Jesuit, Father Sidney Smith, S.J., in the *Month* (1901-1902). It is: "First, Clement XIV was convinced, and rightly, that the extinction of a religious order was warranted if thereby the necessary peace of the Church might be achieved. Secondly, Clement XIV in the case of the Jesuits did not hesitate very much, since apparently he was not favorably disposed toward them. Thirdly, after his election he came to a very real appreciation of what terrible disorders their suppression would really entail. There would be the patent contradiction of so many Sovereign Pontiffs, especially of his immediate predecessor and his solemn approval of the Order just a few years before. There would be the ignoring of the wishes of several Catholic princes, and of the very numerous bishops, who were devoted to the Society; as well as the scandalizing of vast numbers of the faithful by condemning as corrupt an Order which up till then the Holy See had recommended to them for their spiritual guidance. There would be the injustice of attaching a stigma to so many individual religious whose entire personal innocence even the Courts had admitted, especially by the Courts' failure to give proof of their accusations. Finally, there would be the destruction of a multitude of schools, missions and other good works, a destruction for the most part beyond remedying. Appalled by the thought of such overwhelming disasters, Clement XIV drew back, determined to postpone the suppression, with the possibility of preventing it, or at least to achieve it in such a form as would obviate the consequent evils."

During the two years, the ambassadors of the Bourbon monarchies relentlessly pressured Pope Clement XIV with intimidations and threats of schism. The Pontiff was ill, especially near the end; but he was given little respite. Most offensive was the Spanish envoy, Don José Monino, a stubborn, hard man and a bully—if he felt the occasion called for it. He was hostile to Rome and to the Pontifical authority, and absolutely determined on the extinction of the Jesuits. Monino's browbeating certainly succeeded. He terrorized the ailing Pontiff with his vehement onslaughts, with his threats of the destruction of all religious Orders in Spain and of the cutting off of the Spanish Church from the Apostolic See. The prospect of Spain, Naples, France and Portugal outside the true fold overwhelmed Clement XIV. He agreed to the total suppression of the Jesuits and to the publication of it in a brief. The Brief of the Suppression was announced officially on August 16, 1773.

The Brief of Suppression, "Dominus ac Redemptor," was not a judicial sentence; there had been no judicial inquiry. It was an administrative measure, which Pope Clement XIV took to restore the peace and the tranquillity so necessary to the Church. The document contains a catalogue of complaints, charges and controversies against the Order, but makes no assessment of guilt. The document does not condemn the Constitutions and Rules of the Society of Jesus; neither does it lay any blame on the personal conduct of its members, nor does it impugn the orthodoxy of their doctrines. The brief was promulgated in a special fashion; it was read to all Jesuits, gathered in their respective houses, and then each one had to sign a document of acceptance. It was not promulgated in the customary way "urbi et orbi" (to the city and the world), nor was it proclaimed in the Campo dei Fiori, nor was it affixed to the gates of the Vatican. These changes later on led to unexpected results.

The Society of Jesus, to the deep sorrow of the great majority of bishops, priests and devoted Catholic laity, was no more. The former Father General, Lorenzo Ricci, a pious and learned old priest, was confined as a close prisoner and treated harshly in the Castel Sant'Angelo. The ex-Jesuit priests generally entered the secular clergy; many became seminary professors, some were given high positions in dioceses, fifty-five were consecrated bishops. During the French Revolution forty-four were put to death; twenty-three of them have been beatified. The recent canonization of St. Joseph Pignatelli, S.J., may be considered a vindication of the Society of Jesus. He led the Spanish Jesuits into exile; he cared for their support in the poverty of their unhappy lot, and he kept their brotherhood together; finally he led a remnant back into the restored Order. This restoration was the greatest vindication. In 1814, forty years after the Brief of Suppression, Pope Pius VII by the solemn Bull "Solicitudo omnium ecclesiarum" restored the Society of Jesus, completely and throughout the world.

The suppression of 1773 did not bring the hoped-for peace and tranquillity. The Bourbon ministers increased their demands upon the Papacy and extended their encroachments upon the Church. The agents of the Bourbon Courts now searched the abandoned colleges and residences of the former Jesuits, seeking proofs for their charges. They ransacked archives, records and offices meticulously. But they found no traces of guilt, and no accumulations of wealth. There were none. One group only profited by the destruction of the Jesuits — the Revolutionaries. Scarcely three decades passed and they were tumbling into overwhelming destruction the Bourbon monarchies of France, Spain and Naples.

After a year of sickness and despondency, Clement XIV died, a truly tragic figure. He was succeeded by Pius VI, who had been a "Zelanti" Cardinal. Pius wished most ardently to restore the Society of Jesus, but given the still great power of the Bourbon Courts, that was impossible. He did quickly ease the harsh imprisonment of Father Ricci. When the old priest died, Pius VI honored him with a tremendous public funeral. There is good reason to believe that Pope Pius gave secret approval to the existence of a small group of Polish and Lithuanian Jesuits. They were not affected by the Brief of Suppression, because the Empress Catherine refused to allow its promulgation in White Russia, where they lived. Thus a small nucleus of the Society of Jesus remained alive. Later in 1801, when the Bourbon power had vanished, Pope Pius VII gave public and vocal approval of this living remnant of the Jesuit Order. It was to become the basis of his universal restoration of the Order throughout the Catholic Church in 1814.

Febronianism

THE ENLIGHTENMENT in the Germanic lands, because of local features, usually is called by its German translation: "Aufklaerung." The Germanic lands meant at this period not only the German sovereignties of the Holy Roman Empire, presided over by the Hapsburg Archduke of Austria as emperor, but also the non-German lands outside the Empire, over which the Hapsburg Archduke ruled as their personal monarch. Such were the Austrian Netherlands, several Slavic principalities, the Kingdom of Hungary, and some North-Italian duchies; in all of them Germanic influence was quite important. Together the Empire and the non-imperial Hapsburg dominions embraced the whole of central Europe.

The anti-Christian Enlightenment gained wide acceptance in the upper and middle classes of the Germanic world. Sceptical professors, deistic theologians, materialistic scientists, and rationalistic writers welcomed the new secular ideas. High prestige came when great political personages like Frederick II, King of Prussia, and Kaunitz, Prime Minister of the Austrian dominions, proclaimed themselves Philosophers. As in France, it became the fashion to pose as a Philosopher.

The Aufklaerung—henceforth this German term for the Enlightenment will be used—was not of sudden occurrence. It had been germinating in German Protestantism for a long time. From the beginning, Lutheranism and Calvinism had been riven with domestic controversies over dogmatic teachings, and over the interpretation of the Bible (though all held the infallibility of the Bible). But after the Peace of Westphalia (1648) had guaranteed the Protestants in their duchies, an aggressive scepticism flared up among the German Protestant intellectuals, the university professors and the men-of-letters, who lectured or published in theology, philosophy and studies of the Bible. As theological rationalists, these men recognized no teaching of religion to be unchangeably true. They sought to revise religious beliefs so as to bring them more in line with what they considered progress, to fashion them into harmony with what they considered the results of science and the necessities of the age.

Naturalistic theology spread rapidly and extensively. First came the rejection of dogma; even the mentioning of the word was scorned openly. The rejection of the authority of the Bible and the proposed rationalistic interpretation of the Bible followed next. Everything supernatural was explained away, and an extremely violent onslaught was made on Biblical miracles, above all, the Resurrection of Christ. Rejection of dogma produced its woeful harvest of religious indifference. Religion was identified only with duty and disassociated from dogmatic definition.

The Aufklaerung received tremendous impetus from the flood of books, pamphlets, and treatises which poured in from France and England. After 1764, it had its own press in Berlin from which books hostile to Christianity were scattered among a large circle of readers. The Protestant Aufklaerung was primarily the concern of intellectuals; large areas of the simple people remained believing and devout. But the intellectuals were to fashion and shape the ideas of countless numbers in the future generations.

The substitution of a naturalistic for a supernatural religion by so many Protestant theologians could not fail to have an influence in Catholic circles. Many Catholic scholars read closely the German rationalists, and even more the French encyclopedists. Such Catholics often rejected Scholasticism (the theology of St. Thomas Aquinas, St. Bonaventure, and a host of medieval thinkers) as out of harmony with modern progress. They went on to advocate that Catholicism be remodeled so that it would be brought into line with the conclusions of modern philosophy. They paid less attention to dogmatic teachings and to controversies; they emphasized rather the ethical and the natural principles contained in the Christian revelation.

Among Catholics the Aufklaerung featured an ominous spreading of Gallicanism. This hostility towards the papacy, so developed by royal absolutists in France, was eagerly adopted by leading rulers and politicians. For a century they had been striving to obtain wide control of the Catholic Church in their dominions. Their present imitation of Gallicanism now gravely weakened the authority of the Pope and of the bishops in the German lands. It helped to break down the defenses of Catholicism, and thus made it easy to propagate rationalistic views, especially among university men, professors and students. Much of the disastrous fruits of the Aufklaerung happened after the destruction of the Jesuits, the only body then capable of resisting its evils— especially at the centers of education.

The curriculum for ecclesiastical students was reorganized completely. The plan drawn up for the ecclesiastical students of the University of Vienna, and later proposed for all Austrian universities, was nothing less than a complete break with the whole traditional system of clerical education. In the plan there were good features, but the principles underlying its administration and the class of men administering it, were enough to render it suspicious. Only professors of "liberal" views were appointed. In the hands of such professors, Scriptural studies began more and more to partake of the rationalism of the contemporary Protestant divinity schools; Church history became in great part an apology for Gallicanism; moral theology was modeled largely on a purely rationalistic system of ethics; and canon law was brought into complete harmony with the anti-papalism and absolutism of Joseph II.

The prince-bishops of Mainz, Trier, and Cologne spared no pains to propagate "liberal" views among their future priests. At the University of Mainz one professor's view on the Holy Scriptures brought him into conflict with the Church, while a professor of dogma denied the infallibility of the Church and of General Councils. A similar state of affairs prevailed to a greater or lesser degree in other Catholic universities, with the notable exception of the conservative University of Cologne. It was by means of the universities and by the publications of various reviews that the "liberal" theories were spread throughout Catholic Germany. Attempts were made to reform the discipline and the liturgy of the Church, aiming to bring the Church into line with the new theology. Many advocated the abolition of popular devotions, and also the abolition of clerical celibacy.

The chief proponent of this Germanic Gallicanism was von Hontheim (1701-1790), auxiliary bishop to the prince-bishop of Trier. Under the assumed name of Febronius he published, in 1762, a book on the power of the Roman Pontiff in the structure and government of the Church. The work was marked by most extreme Gallicanism. It received wide acceptance, and it precipitated a powerful anti-papal movement, which was named Febronianism, after the author.

Febronius denied the divine institution and the universal jurisdiction of the Primacy of the Pope. He degraded the Pope to a merely nominal ruler, holding only a primacy of honor. The primacy of the Pope, he continued, was not a special privilege of the See of Rome, but could be separated from it and transferred to another diocese. Febronius maintained: that the Pope was incapable of making laws or irreformable decrees on faith and morals; that the validity of the papal decrees depended on the consent of all the bishops; that the Pope was subject to General Councils, which alone enjoyed the prerogative of infallibility. He advocated the formation of national churches with independent national heads.

To force the Pope to abandon the Primacy, which Febronius called a corruption and a usurpation, the author called upon the bishops to assemble national synods and a General Council. He urged the bishops also to engage in a mighty campaign of education to turn the priests and the people against the Primacy of the Pope. If these steps failed,

Febronius called upon the bishops to appeal to the princes, lay and clerical, to block intercourse with Rome and to take into their own hands the introduction of the changes. As a last resort he urged refusal of obedience to the Pope.

Since Febronius' book was in complete accord with the absolutist tendencies of the age, it was enthusiastically applauded by civil rulers, court theologians, canonists, and lawyers. They saw in it the realization of the dream of a state church subservient to the civil ruler. But the book was condemned in 1764, by Pope Clement XIII, the heroic defender of the Jesuits. The Holy Father exhorted the German bishops to take vigorous measures against the dangerous theories which it advocated. Many bishops, however, remained indifferent; some even showed themselves favorable to the views of Febronius. But the majority of the German bishops suppressed it in their dioceses.

Still new editions and translations gave the book's ideas wide circulation in Germany, France, Spain, and Portugal. A powerful anti-papal movement appeared; it also was called Febronianism. The movement was especially welcomed in Austria, where Joseph II was forcing its principles into usage there, as also in all his dominions. The prince-bishops of Mainz, Trier, and Cologne, at a joint meeting in 1769, presented a catalogue of complaints against the Roman Curia; many of the items were extracted from, or based upon, the work of Febronius.

In 1778, Hontheim made a retraction; but it was valueless, for his commentary on the retraction showed clearly that he had not receded a step from his original position. However, Hontheim—or as he was more popularly known, Febronius—before his death in 1790, expressed regret for the doctrines he had advocated. He died in full communion with the Church.

The most dangerous application of Febronianism was the series of large-scale attempts of the Emperor Joseph II to control and organize the Church in the extensive territories of the Austrian and the Hungarian Crowns. These attempts have been called Josephinism, to which the next chapter will be devoted.

Josephinism

AS EMPEROR, Joseph II possessed no power, only a nominal title, ancient and prestigious, but nothing more. But as the heir of the Hapsburg princes he was a powerful monarch, wielding direct rule over many states, within and without the Holy Roman Empire of the Germans.

Joseph II was shallow by nature, and his education had been adversely affected by the Gallicanism and liberalism of many of his instructors. In early manhood he began to dream of absolutism. It was the age of the benevolent despots. The young prince chose for his ideal Frederick the Great, the King of Prussia, the outstanding benevolent despot of Europe. And as this mighty monarch posed as a rationalist philosopher, so the Austrian heir began also to dream of being a philosopher king.

Joseph's mother, the wise Empress Maria Theresa, kept him in check, but after her death he inaugurated his plans of reform, influenced greatly by his Chief Minister-of-State, Prince Kaunitz, a philosopher, and by other rationalist advisers. They were *plans* and they were *reforms*, for the new ruler started to mix into almost every phase of the lives of his subjects. No doubt he meant well and he desired the good of his people, but it was the good as he, the benevolent despot, conceived it.

Joseph II, impulsive, stubborn and inexperienced, proceeded with headlong haste to impose the sweeping changes suggested by his own disordered imagination or urged by his rationalist advisers. Disregarding political and historical rights, he undertook to reduce the administration of his different dominions, so varied in race, character, and customs, to a dead level of uniformity. Thus, to avoid taking an oath on the Hungarian Constitution, which he intended to change, he conveyed the crown of Saint Stephen to Vienna. He still further exasperated the national feelings of the Hungarians by making German the official language of the kingdom, abolishing at the same time the local governments and annulling the privileges of the nobles and the free cities.

By a stroke of the pen he destroyed the Constitution of the Austrian Netherlands, which had been in force since the times of Maximilian I (1493-1519); he replaced it with a centralized bureaucracy. His craze for "reforms" reached down even to the simple people, going to such ridiculous lengths as, for example: "To save the forests," coffins were prohibited, and the bodies of the common people were to be buried in large trenches, or sewed into sacks.

During these stormy changes, political and social, a far worse tempest was raging against the Church. It was a mighty attack against the Pope and his primacy, against his faithful followers, bishops, priests, and laymen, and against some of the most essential and venerable dogmas of the Catholic Religion. The supreme leader of this ecclesiastical revolt was Joseph II; indeed the term "Josephinism" was coined as its name. Joseph was thoroughly imbued with anti-papal Febronianism, and he fancied himself a "Philosopher." Actually he was the dupe of several sinister advisers, who induced him to invade fields over which the Church alone had jurisdiction — for example: communication with the Holy See, episcopal functions, theological instruction, religious orders, and the services of divine worship.

How inimical to the life of the Catholic Church were the ecclesiastical "reforms" of Joseph II may be judged from the following instances. In regard to the government of the Church: (1) he insisted that all documents issued by the

Holy See must receive the Royal Placet (certificate of permission for publication); so also must all documents of the bishops to their people; (2) he forbade the bishops of his dominions to hold any direct communication with Rome, or to ask the Pope for a renewal of their faculties, which he undertook to confer by his own authority; (3) he insisted that the nominees for a bishopric take their oath of allegiance to himself before their consecration.

In regard to ecclesiastical education: (1) he introduced a system of state-controlled education; (2) he abolished the episcopal seminaries and established central seminaries at Vienna, Budapest, Louvain, and Pavia for the education of the clergy of his dominions (not infrequently freethinkers and religious scoffers were made the professors of the future priests); (3) he forbade the attendance of Austrian students at the Collegium Germanicum at Rome lest they should be brought under the influence of papal teaching; (4) he ordered priests not to preach on doctrinal truths, but only on moral subjects and national economy; (5) under his imperial authority a new catechism, more in harmony with the so-called spirit of the age, was issued.

In regard to religious orders: (1) Joseph II suppressed all monasteries "that did not serve a practical purpose" (36,000 religious were ejected from their religious houses); (2) he severed the remaining communities from their monastic superiors in Rome; (3) he made the admission of novices as difficult as possible.

In regard to religious services: he presumed to regulate the forms of divine worship, religious processions and pilgrimages, the number of feasts to be observed, even the number of candles to be used at Mass (three for a Low Mass).

For such nonsense Joseph II came to be called, all over Europe, "The Sacristan Emperor." But he went to far more dangerous extremes when he arrogated to the State the inalienable right of the Church to legislate about the sacrament of Matrimony, and when he essayed to abolish ecclesiastical impediments in the marriage contract.

These "Reforms," though they exasperated the greater portion of the clergy, and the mass of the people, were encouraged by some weak and time-serving bishops, free-thinking professors, and priests infected with Febronianism.

Pope Pius VI, in Rome, was thoroughly alarmed by the dangers menacing the Catholic Church in the Hapsburg dominions. By personal letters and by communications through his nuncio, the Holy Father sought most earnestly to induce Joseph II to draw back from his policy of state aggression. The Vicar of Christ even journeyed to Vienna to plead with the emperor.

Pope Pius was obliged to leave Vienna without any definite results. But he returned with one very significant consolation: whatever might come from the Emperor and from the court-bishops, the majority of the people and the clergy of Austria were still unwaveringly loyal to the head of the Catholic Church. Nay more, leading them was the prince-archbishop of Vienna, Christopher Anthony von Migazzi, the keen opponent of the Aufklaerung and of Josephinism, and by his side were several other loyal bishops of the Church in Austria. This was truly a substantial victory.

The following year, when Joseph II paid a return visit to Rome, he was induced by the Spanish Ambassador to desist from his plan of a complete severance of the Hapsburg lands from the Holy See.

Just six years of rule remained to Joseph II, and in that brief half dozen years he had to witness the almost total collapse of his "reforms." Before he died, his dominions lay in the state of utter confusion. Angry opposition to his civil and ecclesiastical programs was mounting everywhere. The opposition in Austria has already been noted; it was increasing. In the Tyrol, and in the Slavic states of Bohemia and Moravia, open resistance was threatening. Hungary was in furious rebellion. It was only pacified when Joseph sent back the Crown of St. Stephen and promised to abandon most of his religious, civil, and linguistic schemes.

The Austrian Netherlands (the present Kingdom of Belgium) broke out into open revolution. All classes struck for their ancient Constitution, and all followed the lead of Cardinal Frankenberg and the bishops against the secularizing of the episcopal seminaries. In an effort to save the Austrian Netherlands, Joseph II found himself obliged to turn to the Pope, whom he had so maltreated and despised, in the hope that he might induce the Belgians to return to their allegiance. He promised to withdraw most of the "reforms" that he had introduced. But his repentance came too late to save the Austrian rule in the Netherlands.

Joseph II died in 1790. In history he presents a sad, even a pathetic, picture. He meant well and he desired the best for his subjects. But he was impulsive, sadly lacking in the knowledge of men, and very badly advised by Febronians and by Rationalistic Philosophers. Joseph II composed his own epitaph for his tomb: "Here lies a prince whose intentions were pure, but who had the misfortune to see all his projects fail."

An anticlimax to Josephinism was the attempt of the Prince-bishops of Mainz, Trier, Cologne, and Salzburg to curtail the Pope's power in Germany. Meeting at Ems, in 1786, to protest the setting up of an apostolic nunciature in Munich, they published a notorious document, "The Punctuation of Ems." It was Febronian in every line. In twenty-three articles it aimed at making the German Prince-bishops practically independent of Rome. It lowered the papal primacy to a merely honorary one; it advocated an independence of the Prince-bishops in regard to the Pope which is entirely incompatible with the unity and catholicity of the Church of Christ.

To the disappointment of the four prelates, not a single German ruler gave them support. Joseph II was sympathetic, but upon the advice of no less a person than Kaunitz, for political reasons he withheld his public approbation. Frederick the Great, King of Prussia, actively opposed the document. The supreme refutation came from Pope Pius VI. His document covered the whole ground of the controversy and offered a most masterly defense of the papal rights and privileges. Pope Pius ended with a paternal admonition to the four prelates to give up their untenable position towards the Holy See.

The Archbishops of Trier, Cologne, and Salzburg complied. But not the Archbishop of Mainz; he clung stubbornly to his views, until the storm of the French Revolution broke over his city and territory and put an end to his rule as a temporal prince.

The French Revolution

IN THE LAST decade of the eighteenth century came the deluge, the French Revolution. Through those ten years hurricanes of infidelity and sacrilege lashed and pounded the Barque of Peter with demoniacal fury. In the darkest hours, Catholicism seemingly was reeling towards obliteration. Nor were the terrible onslaughts confined to France. They raged in every European country, wherever the revolutionary armies penetrated. What is more, the revolutionary ideas were rooted deeply in every Latin-American state; later, sometimes even the confiscations and executions were copied.

Long after the frightful blood-baths had ceased, the French Revolution's implacable hatred of the Catholic Church was continued by the heirs of the Revolution in constant anti-clerical campaigns against the Church. Down until World War I, and even after, the numerous and powerful descendants of Voltaire in every Catholic country bent their most strenuous energies to implement his bitter motto, "Écrasez l'infame. Crush out the infamous thing."

The French Revolution was so extensive and so complex that even a brief summarization of it would require dozens of pages. However a few generalizations may be in place. Certainly there was need of great changes in every facet of civic life — political, social and economic, yes, even in the material aspects of ecclesiastical affairs. Unfortunately, the architects and practitioners of changes were, for the most part, inexperienced theoreticians, or "doctrinaires," as the French call them.

But there were far more dangerous men afoot. These were the fanatical revolutionaries, the terrorists. By sinister intrigues, wild mob riots and ruthless assassinations, they mounted to the supreme power. Then they proceeded to clear the way for their materialistic and godless state. They strove to obliterate every civil and religious institution of the past. Against religion they moved with iconoclastic hatred to destroy the entire fabric of Catholicism.

All opponents, from any group at all, they massacred, drowning their protests in blood. The fury of the "Terror" lasted for more than two years; it ceased only when the leaders of its factions killed themselves off. But this did not happen until after they had slaughtered 1,200,000 men and women of France by the guillotines, the mass-drownings, or the fusillades of the revolutionary armies. It has been estimated that a very large number of those sacrificed to *"Liberty, Equality* and *Fraternity"* were humble, simple people.

It is necessary to turn back to June 23, 1789. On that day the ancient Estates General was changed into a Constituent Assembly pledged to draw up an entirely new constitution for France. The change was effected by merging the three estates: The First (the Clergy), 300 members; the Second (the Nobility), 300 members; and the Third (The Bourgeoisie, *Commoners),* 600 members.

The new assembly suffered every legislative defect. It was too unwieldy, with its 1,200 members. Most of these members sadly lacked experience, and they disintegrated into hopelessly squabbling factions. The sessions, moreover, were constantly intimidated by terrorist mobs who thronged the galleries, shouting down speakers and menacing them with bodily injuries and even murder. The last soon became no idle threat.

The outlook for the Catholic Church was daily worsening. Her most malignant enemies, Voltairians, Gallicans and infidel Revolutionaries dominated the sessions of the

Assembly. Now was their opportunity to bury Catholicism in ruins, and they moved quickly and forcibly to the attack. In November, 1789, all ecclesiastical properties were declared the property of the nation; the secular clergy were placed upon the government pay roll.

On February 13, 1790, the Assembly, a purely secular body without any spiritual authority, branded the monastic vows of religious orders of both men and women antagonistic to liberty, and in consequence this Assembly declared them null and void, suppressed all such orders, and forbade them to accept novices. The religious who would abandon their religious vows and return to the world were guaranteed pensions. Those who wished to remain in community life were to be herded without distinction of rule into certain houses selected by the state. These religious, too, were allowed support from the state, but the pensions were irregularly paid.

Hostile municipal authorities and fanatical mobs made the position of these last religious even more precarious. Out of the 37,000 French nuns, only 600 broke their vows and returned to the world. Among the 13,136 French monks and friars, the defections were far, far more numerous.

The climactic blow was hurled on July 12, 1790, when the Assembly, over most strenuous opposition, passed the Civil Constitution of the Clergy. This code purported to be statutes regulating church affairs in the new France; actually it was a well-planned instrument for enslaving the French Church and refashioning it on a Presbyterian basis. The Assembly, a civil institution, possessed no authority in the purely ecclesiastical sphere; yet it essayed fundamental changes, and these without a single consultation with the Holy See. Little wonder that the Civil Constitution of the Clergy surpassed in its Gallicanism the most pretentious documents of Louis XIV.

The Constitution had four divisions: Ecclesiastical Offices, Appointment to Benefices, Salary of the Ministers of Religion, and Residence and Absence. Only the first three divisions will be considered; but in them are to be found the most potent attacks upon the divine structure of the Church, especially the episcopacy and the Pope's primacy.

Here are some of the provisions of the "Ecclesiastical Offices": There should be only one bishop for each of the departments (the new political and administrative divisions of France). Thus with one stroke, 48 episcopal sees together with their seminaries were suppressed. The title of archbishop was abolished; out of 83 remaining bishoprics, 10 were called metropolitan bishoprics and were given jurisdiction over the neighboring dioceses. No section of French territory was to recognize the authority of a bishop living abroad, or of his delegates, and this, adds the Constitution, "without prejudice to the unity of faith and the communion which shall be maintained with the Head of the Universal Church." There should no longer be sacerdotal posts specially devoted to fulfilling the conditions of Mass foundations. All appeals to Rome were forbidden.

Here are some of the provisions of "Appointment to Benefices": Bishops should be appointed by the Electoral Assemblies of the particular departments. They should be invested and consecrated by the metropolitan, and take an oath of fidelity to the nation, the King, the Law and the Civil Constitution of the Clergy. They should not seek any confirmation from the Pope. A bishop might on his appointment announce his election to the Pope as an evidence of his own communion with the Holy See. But it was the metropolitan or senior bishop of the province who should ratify his appointment.

The Cathedral Chapters were suppressed; and in the place of the canons it was arranged that to each bishop should be assigned a council of vicars whose approval should be necessary for the principal acts of episcopal administration. Pastors of parishes (the French term is *"curé"* — the English word "curate" in French is *"vicaire")* were chosen by the Electoral Assembly of the local districts. Thus all citizens, even non-believers, could vote to name the ecclesiastical officials of the Catholic Church, all its bishops and pastors.

As was noted earlier, the first obligation of these bishops and priests was to take an oath of fidelity to the Civil Constitution, which denied to the Holy See any effective power

ST. ALPHONSUS DE LIGUORI

over the Catholic Church in France. The curé (the parish priest) was given the right of selecting any priest of the diocese as his assistant without reference to the bishop. In all cases of disputes between the bishop and his priests, the ultimate decision rested with the secular authorities.

Only one provision need be cited from "Residence and Absence": Neither bishop nor parish priest could be absent from the diocese or parish for more than two weeks without getting permission, the bishop from the *Departmental Assembly*, the parish priest from the *District Assembly*. The emphasis is eloquent.

The Civil Constitution placed the King in an extremely difficult position. If he refused to sign it, he would only supply a new weapon to the extremists now taking over all of France. Yet Louis XVI, a good and sincere Catholic, was heartsick at the thought of establishing a French schismatic church. He turned to the Pope. Pius VI had followed the development of the Civil Constitution with utmost anxiety. He replied to the King on July 11, condemning the measure. For the time being the condemnation was kept secret in the hope that the remedy would come from the French bishops. All parties were watching for what stand the prelates would take.

Archbishop de Boisgelin of Aix, as their speaker, quickly broke the tension. In their name he published a document in which he pointed out clearly the schismatical nature of the law. His brochure was supported by all the bishops of France except seven. A vast body of the parish priests also joined in the condemnation.

The Assembly countered by ordering all clergy to swear allegiance to the Civil Constitution, under pain of expulsion from their ecclesiastical offices. Of 130 bishops only four took the oath; three of these were sceptics and profligates. Of 70,000 priests, nearly 50,000 refused the oath. Among the one-third who took the oath, some were clerics whose lives and ideas portended such a course. Many others did so from their confusion about the issues at stake. But these, and they were quite numerous, repudiated their action as soon as Pius VI made it clear that the Constitution meant open schism.

Schism now became a fact. The faithful clergy, because they refused to take the Constitutional Oath, were called "non-jurors"; the schismatic clergy, because they took the oath, were called "constitutionalists." The non-jurors were driven out of their offices in favor of the constitutionalists. A number of constitutionalist priests were hastily consecrated to bishoprics held by non-jurors.

The majority of the Catholic laity abandoned religious services in the churches to which constitutionalist pastors were appointed. They followed the faithful pastors to private houses where they officiated. During the "Terror," the Catholic people gathered by night in hidden barns and distant places where their hunted priests offered Mass. They guarded and concealed their priests, and they died with them on the guillotines or in the massacres by the furious mobs.

When it was evident that the Assembly would not relent, Pope Pius VI, on April 13, 1791, published the official document condemning the Civil Constitution of the Clergy. It produced the desired effect: as has been noted, numerous constitutionalist priests gave up their oath and embraced the hard lot of the non-jurors. The eighteen constitutionalist bishops, of course, repudiated the Pope's condemnation. All the non-juror bishops published their full acceptance of it. They even offered to resign if such a step would secure peace, but Pius VI did not want them to do so.

The prospects for these heroic bishops and their loyal clergy were persecution, torture and execution. For these faithful Christian shepherds the Revolutionaries reserved their bitterest hatred, slightly less intense than what they felt for Pope Pius VI himself.

The Reign of Terror

FOR FIVE FULL years, beginning with the fall of the Bastille, anarchy pervaded France. Disorder and confusion kept increasing each year as the Revolution progressed. Mobs, led by fanatics and criminals, ruled everything everywhere. They dominated the national assemblies. They poured lawless and blood-thirsty rioters into the streets of the cities. They devastated the forests and the farming lands, demolishing castles and cabins, monasteries and convents, leaving a trail of merciless brutality and murder behind them. They sacrilegiously desecrated urban churches and rural chapels, and regularly they stole precious chalices and sacred vessels to sell to the highest purchasers.

Everywhere in France war against property, public or private, was raging. The civil order was collapsing. There were mutinies in the army and in the navy, and the handing over of 400,000 guns to the newly organized National Guard merely armed the revolutionary forces. As the danger of assassination grew imminent, many nobles and conservative people fled into exile; they became known as *"Émigrés."*

Anarchy paralyzed the national Legislative Assembly. Its 745 members, every one a radical revolutionary, split into hostile factions, contending fiercely for supreme control. The most ruthless group was the Jacobins, so called from their headquarters in the abandoned convent of St. Jacques. Their goal was an extreme socialistic and atheistic republic. Pursuing every intrigue, pushing aside all opposition, holding back from no outrage, the Jacobins swept themselves into complete control of the Legislative Assembly on August 13, 1792.

One of their first acts was to inaugurate "The Reign of Terror." They aimed to consolidate their power by massacre on a grand scale. "We can rule only by fear," said one of their chief leaders. To carry through this bloody tyranny, the Jacobins devised a vast machinery of merciless committees and tribunals, which worked with hellish efficiency.

At Paris were the three great committees: The Committee of Public Safety, The Committee of General Security and the Commune of Paris (the greatest power in the State). Here also was the Revolutionary Tribunal, consisting of Judges and "jurors" who condemned the victims sent to them by the Committee of Public Safety, in batches of 20, 30, 50 or more. Agents of the Committees, "Deputies in Mission," toured the Departments of France to carry out the orders of the Paris officials.

In the Departments, throughout France, were 21,500 revolutionary committees, all modeled on the great bodies of the capital. The local committees were usually made up of ruffians and criminals; their duties were to carry out the orders from Paris, or to act upon their own plans in imprisoning, despoiling and guillotining fellow Frenchmen without trial.

A model of massacring was soon perpetrated in the "September Murders." When all the leading opponents had been arrested under pretense of securing Paris from the advancing Prussians, a wholesale massacre of prisoners in Paris was arranged. The slaughtering began on September 2, and lasted for six days and five nights without interruption.

During that time one archbishop, two bishops, about four hundred priests and one thousand nobles were cruelly killed by bands of murderers in the prisons of Paris. The word was passed from Paris to the mobs in other cities to do likewise, and at Meaux, Rheims, Versailles, Orleans, Lyons and other cities the same sickening scenes of carnage were enacted.

Nothing in their program did the Jacobins carry out with more cruelty and more persistence than their war against Catholicism. They aimed specifically at the annihilation of the Catholic clergy. A large majority of the priests, refusing to abandon their flocks, had to lead furtive lives in forests, in mountain valleys, or in the crowded sections of the large cities. They moved always in constant peril of arrest. Capture meant for them either execution by the bloody guillotine or, if they survived the loathesome prisons, transportation to the malarial swamps of Cayenne. Hundreds and hundreds, perhaps even thousands, of French priests made the supreme sacrifice of the Martyrs.

The Jacobins did not hesitate to induce priests to betray their sacred vocation by marriage, offering them material profits and human applause. But they gained only a few. It is tragic to note that some of these unworthy clerics became the bitterest persecutors of the Church.

Later on, constitutionalist priests, Protestant ministers and Jewish rabbis were beheaded by the guillotine; the atheistic republic had no place for them either.

The Paris Commune, which ruled the whole of the country, prohibited baptism, confirmation, anointing of the sick, marriage rites and Christian burial. The National Convention broke up the Christian family by suppressing marital and parental authority, and by establishing divorce.

To root out Catholic civilization, the Convention supplanted the Christian Era by substituting in its place the Revolutionary Era (the first day of the Year I began on September 22, 1792), the week of seven days by the week of ten days, the Sunday by the Decade, all ecclesiastical feasts by revolutionary festivals. Christmas Day was dishonored by naming it "the day of the dog."

Day after day, in the last months of 1793, the sessions of the Convention were disgraced by scenes of religious mockery. In one, the Constitutionalist Archbishop of Paris openly rejected Christianity. As a sign of his repudiation, he cast off his crozier and mitre and openly trampled upon these sacred symbols of his episcopacy.

The Convention abolished the worship of God, but proclaimed the worship of the Goddess of Reason. The Cathedral of Notre Dame of Paris was transformed into a temple of Reason, and on its high altar was enthroned a notorious actress as the Goddess of Reason on November 10, 1793. Similar outrages were committed in the Departments, where the Jacobins closed, pillaged and desecrated the churches.

The Terror raged as horribly in the Departments as in Paris. Invading armies on the frontiers, and domestic revolts all over France threatened to crush the Revolutionary Republic. But the invaders were driven back, and the revolts, never more than disunited local affairs, were easily overcome by the "Deputies in Mission." Only the sturdy Catholics of La Vendée and a few other western Departments displayed energy, numbers and unity.

The vast terrorism of the punishment for uprisings, beggars description. Every prison was jammed with victims. Only vague estimations can be made of the tens of thousands put to death by the guillotine, by numerous firing squads, by the grape-shot of the artillery cannons, or, as in Lyons, by the mass-drownings in the Rhone. Everywhere total confiscations, mountainous taxation and wholesale demolition of public buildings instilled terror in the hearts of the survivors of the revolts.

The worst horrors were reserved for La Vendée and the provinces adjoining in the west of France. When the Catholics of these districts saw their king beheaded; their archbishop driven to the mountains; their priests hunted down; their churches plundered, desecrated and handed over to an apostate priesthood; and themselves forced to travel for miles and miles to hear Mass in the recesses of forests and caves, these devoted people rose in arms to defend their Faith. After some initial successes, the fortunes of war turned adversely, and La Vendée became the scene of brutalities, the most horrible committed during the Revolution.

The head of the Revolutionary Tribunal of Nantes put to death 15,000 men, women and children during the last three months of 1793. Prisoners were shot down in general fusillades; between four and five thousand were drowned. they were tied together two by two and driven into the Loire, or placed on large rafts and lighters, and sunk. The rural districts were scoured for the purpose of killing women and children. Jacobin troops sallied forth to pick up Vendeans along the high roads, shooting them in batches of twenty-five.

In 1794, after the disastrous battle and massacre of Le Mans, Turreau, sent by the Commune of Paris at the head of twelve "columns of hell," entered La Vendée from different points. His orders were to exterminate the inhabitants and confiscate their lands. He killed all living things that came in his way, burned crops, mills and villages: 1,500 square miles were devastated, 20 towns and 1,800 villages destroyed. Among the 90,000 slain were 15,000 women and 22,000 children. The remaining population fled to the woods, whence they carried on a desultory but destructive warfare against the republican hordes.

In the autumn of the same year, the smouldering insurrection broke out anew and rapidly spread north of the Loire into Brittany, Maine, Anjou, and Normandy. The insurrectionists north of the Loire were called the Chouans. They fought under independent leaders and received everywhere the support of the peasants, who resented the suppression of their religion and priesthood.

After the fall of Robespierre, the Committee of Public Safety sent General Hoche into the affected Department. Hoche was a wise and able man; he allowed the churches to be reopened, left the clergy unharassed and concluded a number of armed truces with Vendean and Chouan leaders. Hostilities ceased when Hoche agreed to recognize the local authorities, to guarantee freedom, and to admit Vendean and Chouan leaders to command positions in the National Guard.

The Reign of Terror ended in its own sanguinary power-struggles. One day a faction would be wielding supreme rule, a week later its leaders would be waiting their turn at the scaffold of the guillotine.

On March 24, 1794, the leading Hébertists, the atheistic, ultra-revolutionaries, were executed. The turn of the Dantonists, the moderate group, came on April 5. As he awaited his fate, Danton remarked: "On just such a day I organized the

Revolutionary Court. I ask pardon of God and of man." He was a strange man, ruthless, yet with a certain basic goodness.

Mingling in all intrigues moved Maximilian Robespierre, the treacherous, the cold-blooded, the exquisite murderer, the very epitome of the Reign of Terror. His day fell on July 27. He attempted suicide, and failed. Then with head bandaged and in great pain, he was obliged to lie all night on a table, while his enemies filed by, taunting and cursing him. Next morning Robespierre was carted off to the guillotine.

The Reign of Terror was over. The churches were re-opened and the priests were not molested in their ministries. But the anti-Christian laws were not repealed.

To stave off certain defeat in 1797, former terrorists, still numerous and powerful, inaugurated the "Second Terror." Mass transportations replaced the guillotine. Imprisonment in the marshes of Rochefort, on overcrowded ships, and in the deadly climate of Cayenne did the work just as effectively. The vast majority of the victims died either on the ships or in the colony. The laws of 1793 and 1794, aiming at the obliteration of the Catholic Church, were enforced with the old virulence.

But Napoleon's *coup d'état*, November 9, 1799, overthrew the terrorist Directory and brought internal peace to France.

The
Directory
and
Pius VI

THE GOVERNMENT THAT ruled France after the fall of the Terrorists was the Directory, called so from its executive of five directors. This government was thoroughly Revolutionary; many of its officials were former terrorists. Its strength lay in the vast numbers of the followers of Rousseau among the populace and in large sectors of the higher officers of the army. With such support it was able to contain the fierce factions in its own ranks and to crush the moderates and the returning *émigrés*. It did not repeal the most odious anti-Christian laws of the Reign of Terror. Such laws were mitigated only by the personal character of local officials.

The three directors who were left, in 1793, introduced again the anti-Christian proscriptions. They inaugurated a second terror. This time transportation to Cayenne was substituted for the guillotine. It was aimed especially at the Catholic priests and proved more effective than the guillotine. Three-quarters of the priests transported from Belgium died within a few months.

Despite all, it was quite evident that Catholicism in France was steadily coming back.

In internal affairs the Directory was caught in turmoils of factions, which eventually destroyed it. But in external affairs the armies of the Republic, owing to brilliant generals and enthusiastic soldiers, were marching from one victory to another over all enemies: Austria, Prussia, Sardinia, Naples, Spain and Portugal. The victorious armies established a whole group of local republics, all satellite states of the French Directory, along the French frontiers and even further.

One sinister fact must be noted: the armies of the Directory were everywhere missionaries of the French Revolution. Wherever they went, they united with the local sceptics and anti-clericals, all disciples of Voltaire and Rousseau, to set up new areas of the Atheistic Revolution.

Still another sinister fact should be noted: the Directory indemnified German princes for lands incorporated into France by lands confiscated from the German Catholic prince-bishops, an action which was to destroy much of the support for the religious activities of these German bishoprics.

The French Revolutionary Republic nourished a special hatred for Pope Pius VI. He had condemned the Civil Constitution of the Clergy, he had praised the non-juring priests, he had suspended the constitutionalist priests, he had received many refugees, he had celebrated solemn obsequies for Louis XVI, he had protested against the occupation of Avignon. But what they had most against him was that he was the successor of St. Peter.

Within two years the Directory's armies were confronting the Pope. In eight rapid victories their young military genius, Napoleon Bonaparte, conquered most of Lombardy, crossed the Po, marched his troops into the Papal States and imposed an oppressive truce on the Pope. He carried special instructions from the Directory to demand that the Pope should revoke all dogmatical and canonical decrees regarding the Church in France.

Pius refused the slightest deviations in matters of faith or morals. Instead he prepared to die at his post, refusing the asylum offered to him by Naples and England.

Napoleon occupied the northern portions of the Papal States, threatened to march on Rome, and eventually forced Pius VI to conclude the Treaty of Tolentino (1797). By this document Avignon was finally abandoned and a war-indemnity of fifteen million francs was paid into the French Treasury. Napoleon waived the religious questions.

The Directory was not satisfied even with these very severe terms. It wanted the complete destruction not only of the temporal power, but of all Papal authority.

Napoleon was more farsighted than the Directory. Though but a nominal Catholic, he foresaw the inevitable resurrection of Catholicism; already it had made considerable progress all over France. He looked forward to the favor of French Catholics for his present and possibly his future plans. It has been said that Napoleon had sent a secret message to Pius VI, reading: "I am not an Attila, and if I were, remember you are the successor of Leo I."

The Directory, however, spared no pains to destroy the Papacy. After the Peace of Tolentino, it sent to Rome as ambassador of the French Republic, Joseph Bonaparte, elder brother of Napoleon. The ambassador was a thorough revolutionist. He made his house the resort of domestic and foreign revolutionists, who went busily to work stirring up agitations against the papal government. In a purposely inspired street riot, an attaché of the French Embassy was killed. Here was the pretext long desired by the Directory. At once General Berthier marched his troops into the city.

Five days later, against the protests of the people, the General overthrew the pontifical government and proclaimed the Roman Republic, February 15, 1799. The wild excesses of the Paris atheistic mobs were reproduced in the city of the Popes. The symbol of the Roman Republic was the statue of Liberty with the tiara under her feet.

It was hoped to force Pius VI to flee the city. But in this his enemies were confounded. The aged Pontiff, eighty-two and very seriously ill, refused to leave. Fearing lest the presence of the Pope might foster disaffection of the Romans against the French, the Directory decided to seize the Pontiff and by force take him away as a prisoner. Their agents acted with calculated brutality. One wrested the Fisherman's Ring from the sick Pope's finger. He was the same one who harshly answered the old Pope's pleas to be allowed to die in Rome by remarking that one died the same way everywhere.

Pope Pius was pushed into a cheap carriage and hastily driven away, accompanied by a guard of surly troopers. He was first taken to Siena and then to Florence. But the devoted love of the bystanders as his coach drove along the roads frightened the Directory. So with absolute indifference to his condition, the sickly old man was driven over the Alps to Grenoble and finally to Valence.

All through that painful journey one continual occurrence struck deeply both the agents of the Directory and the Roman prelates who accompanied Pius VI: the crowds of simple people, Italian and French, who came all along the way to reverence the dying old Pope and to beg his blessing. All that the weakened Pontiff could do was to smile back his fatherly thanks. He succumbed to his sufferings at Valence, on August 29, 1799.

The Pope was buried by his helpless friends in a common graveyard. The municipal officer of the commune of Valence certified the decease "of the said Giovanni Angelo Broschi, exercising the profession of a Pontiff." Then he sent to Paris his report, which pompously concluded with, "the late Pope has just died. We have seen the last of them and the end of superstition." So exulted the Voltairians and the Rousseaunians everywhere.

But their celebrations were soon to die in abrupt silence. A new Pope was to be elected, and in honor of his persecuted predecessor, to take the name, Pius VII!

When it became known that Pius VI was dead, Cardinal Albani summoned the conclave to meet in Venice. Why Venice? Because Venice was now safe territory. Two years before, the puppet Revolutionary Republic of Venice had disappeared, and the region was once again under Austrian control. Many Italian and some French Cardinals had found refuge in the city of the Adriatic.

The conclave was opened in the Benedictine monastery of San Giorgio Maggiore on November 30, 1799. There arose a considerable conflict between the supporters of the Austrian pretensions and the supporters of a continuation of Pius VI's policies. At length the union of several neutral cardinals with the party supporting Pius VI's plans assured the election of Cardinal Chiaramonti. After the new Pope's unanimous election on March 14, 1800, he chose the name Pius VII, as has been noted.

No more suitable man could have been found to meet the difficulties which menaced the Catholic Church. As Bishop of Imola he had shown his realization that a new era had dawned and that the true interests of the Church demanded meeting the republican ideas which had come to supplant the old theories of royalty. At his coronation he received not only the congratulations of Austria, Spain, Naples, Sardinia and Russia, but the devoted prayers of all loyal Catholics.

Owing to better political conditions, the new Pope was able to return to Rome. On July 3, 1800, Pius VII made his solemn entry into the Eternal City, amid the enthusiastic greetings of the people. All parties were delighted to have a Pope again in their midst, and Pius VII was not the man to stir up bitter memories by a policy of severity.

There remained France to face and its rising leader, the First Consul, Napoleon Bonaparte. There were both bright possibilities and grave difficulties.

Napoleon
and
Pius VII

IN THE AUTUMN of 1799, the specter of anarchy again arose in France. The Directory's days were numbered and civil war was impending. On November 10, the Directory was overthrown by Napoleon and his soldiers in a *coup d'état*. On November 15, a different government, with an entirely new constitution was proclaimed. It was called the Consulate, because the three executives who governed the new state were given the title, Consul. Actually only one, the First Consul, ruled, and he was endowed with practically supreme power. The other two possessed only consultative votes.

Napoleon was designated First Consul, and for a ten-year term. France was now a military monarchy under the guise of a republic. The Consulate actually endured for but three and a half years, and then the First Consul became Emperor of the French, Napoleon I.

The First Consul, Napoleon, devoted much of his great ability to the internal reorganization of France. High among his projects was the restoration of Catholicism. Though personally indifferent in religion, he had become convinced that without the Catholic religion the re-establishment of civil order in France would be an impossibility. Besides, he judged that the restoration of Catholicism might secure for him the support of the vast body of French Catholics. He considered too that this restoration might reconcile the clergy to the new order and break the last bond by which the ancient dynasty was still connected with the country.

Consequently he opened the churches again to public worship, set free the clergy still detained in prison, altered the form of the oath of the Constitution, abolished the *Decade*, and permitted the observance of Sunday as a day of rest. These were all preliminary measures, intended to prepare the way for the act which was to restore official relations with the Holy See, namely the Concordat between France and Pius VII.

While returning from his mighty victory over the Austrians at Marengo, Napoleon began overtures for a settlement with the Papacy. Pius VII in Rome spared no time entering negotiations. He sent two representatives to Paris to examine proposals with two representatives of the First Consul. One of these last was the skillful and unscrupulous ex-bishop Talleyrand. Various schemes and counter-schemes were proposed and rejected. At last Napoleon gave his approval to one of the plans. It was submitted to Rome in February, 1801.

In many ways the plan was unacceptable to the Papacy. A new draft, more in accordance with the wishes of Pius VII, was drawn up at Rome. Napoleon, very much irritated, ordered his minister at Rome to break off negotiations unless his terms were accepted within five days. To prevent the rupture, the Pope, on the suggestion of the minister, sent his most capable representative, Cardinal Consalvi, in haste to the Paris negotiations. Talleyrand at last had met his match.

Consalvi, one of the supreme diplomats of modern times, was quite able to cope with the machinations of Talleyrand and the First Consul. He was unmoved by Napoleon's angry mutterings or by his threats of casting aside the Pope and setting up a national church with the aid of the Constitutional clergy. Consalvi calmly proceeded to argue point after point of the proposed concordat. Several times the negotiations were on the verge of being broken off as Consalvi held steadfastly to his principles in the face of exorbitant demands. Agreement was at last reached, and Napoleon ratified the Concordat. Consalvi set out for Rome to secure Pius VII's ratification. He encountered serious objections at the Papal Court, for only by extensive concessions had Napoleon's ratification been obtained. Eventually the College of Cardinals by a large majority declared that it was lawful for the Pope to ratify this Concordat. Pius VII did so on August 15, 1801.

The Concordat, as its preamble stated, was a solemn treaty between France and the Holy See.

Its first article guaranteed the free and public worship of the Catholic religion, subject, however, to such police regulations "as public safety might demand in the judgment of the government." Consalvi struggled hard against this restriction, suspecting a sinister motive behind these police regulations. But, on being assured that they referred to processions and the like, and fearing lest further resistance might lead to a rupture, he gave his consent. Future events proved that Consalvi's suspicions were only too well founded.

The second article provided for a new division of the French dioceses, reducing the 136 bishoprics to 60. The reduction and the realignment were to be made by the Holy See in concert with the French Government.

The third article arranged that the Holy Father was to ask the bishops who were losing their sees to resign them for the good of the Church. He was to deprive of their sees those who refused.

The fourth article described the plan for the choosing of the new bishops: the First Consul was to nominate them; but the Pope was to give them their canonical institution. This procedure was to be followed for the choosing of all future bishops.

There were seventeen articles in all. Only a brief account of the rest may be given within the limits of this chapter. Bishops were to appoint the parish priests, who had to have the approbation of the government. All cathedrals and churches which had not been alienated could be put to use again. However, the holders of confiscated church properties were to remain in undisturbed possession (Pius VII agreed to this only for the sake of peace). In compensation, the government pledged to make suitable provision for the maintenance of the clergy. It has been conjectured that the compensation was about one-ninth of what had been confiscated.

The Concordat, more often a sorrow than a benefit for the Church, lasted until 1905, when the anticlericals ruling

France unilaterally revoked it. Even in the beginning, it met with considerable opposition. Forty-five of the dispossessed bishops immediately resigned their sees, most of the others followed shortly, and one small schism lasted for a long time. Napoleon forced all the Constitutional bishops to resign. A fierce opposition persisted in republican circles, chiefly in the army.

On Easter Sunday, April 18, 1802, the Concordat was solemnly proclaimed at Paris and at Rome. But the Roman celebrations lapsed quickly into silence when the news arrived from Paris that at the proclamation there was appended to the Concordat a series of restrictive laws, known as the Organic Articles, and published as though they formed part of the Concordat. Neither Pius VII nor Cardinal Consalvi had ever been informed of any restrictive laws. The Organic Articles took away much of the liberty that had been conceded in the Concordat.

The Organic Articles numbered seventy-seven. In summary, they forbade the publication of all papal documents; the decrees of councils, even general councils; the exercise of legislative powers; the convocation of a national, provincial, or even a diocesan synod without the authorization of the government. The Council of State was empowered to hear all charges of abuse of ecclesiastical jurisdiction. The bishops were hampered in the administration of their dioceses, and the curés, in the work of their parishes, by all kinds of petty restrictions. The four Gallican Articles were to be taught in the seminaries, and the use of a common catechism (Gallican in spirit) was enjoined.

The Gallicanism of the Organic Articles was on a par with that of the Civil Constitution of the Clergy, or of the church policies of Louis XIV. Cardinal Consalvi now saw his worst suspicions of the "Police Regulations" more than verified. The Organic Articles are not to be attributed entirely to Napoleon's love of deception. Anti-Christian forces were still so strong in France that he feared the possibility of a rejection of the Concordat. So he resolved by an unfair interpretation of the "Police Regulations" clause to publish a series of regulations which would nullify to a great extent the liberty contained in the Concordat.

POPE PIUS VII. Portrait by Jacques Louis David. *The Louvre, Paris.*

ERCOLE CARDINAL CONSALVI. Secretary of State to
Pope Pius VII. Portrait from an engraving.

Pope Pius VII, through the French Minister in Rome, protested immediately against the publication of the Organic Articles. A few days later, in a public allocution he renewed his protest. He protested at least twice more through Cardinal Consalvi and Cardinal Caprara. Even two years later, in 1804, Pope Pius attended the coronation of Napoleon only in the hope that he might secure the repeal of the Organic Articles.

On May 8, 1804, the national legislature of France conferred on Napoleon Bonaparte the title of Emperor. His elevation was ratified by a plebiscite of over 3,500,000 votes against 2,500. Napoleon invited Pius VII to his coronation. After long, anxious deliberations, Pius VII consented, in the sole hope of promoting religion in France, especially by the repeal of the Organic Articles, as has been noted.

At the ceremonies in Notre Dame, Pius followed the ancient rite for the coronation of emperors. He first anointed Napoleon, then he reached for the crown to place it upon the ruler's head. But Napoleon snatched the diadem from the Pope's hands and placed it himself on his own head. Napoleon then crowned his wife, Josephine. It was a boorish insult, this new emperor's self-crowning, but it was only the climax of several acts of disdain and neglect which he displayed towards the Pope during the pompous celebrations. Pope Pius VII, the common father of Christendom, reduced to the role of a mere spectator, was invited for the sole purpose of enhancing with his prestigious presence the brilliant imperial pageant.

The Pope, however, was there for one purpose only, the repeal of the Organic Articles. The circumstances of the coronation left no hope for their removal. Sore was the disappointment of Pope Pius.

Then it was proposed to Pius VII that he should fix his residence at Paris—and it was hinted that the Emperor had the power to enforce his wish. Calmly the Pope replied: "For such an emergency my resignation is already in the hands of Cardinal Pignatelli. The moment I am deprived of my liberty I will cease to be Pope, and become once more the Benedictine monk, Barnaba Chiaramonti." After that no obstacle was placed in the way of his departure.

The return of Pius VII to Rome could be described just as his journey to Paris has been: "He traversed Italy and France through a people on their knees." The simple common folk strove to express their sympathy, love and loyalty for their Holy Father, so unjustly treated. They intensified their religious fervor by reverently gazing on his saintly person and by witnessing his gentle humility. The strength of Pius VII was in the vigorous faith and warm affection of his spiritual children. Napoleon enviously observed of them, "they will travel thirty leagues to be blessed by the Pope."

Emperor
Napoleon
Against
Pope Pius VII

AFTER THE IMPERIAL coronation, Napoleon's power expanded tremendously. He made France strong, bringing tranquillity to the nation and giving it prosperity. He occupied the northern Italian principalities and annexed them to the French realm. The satellite republics, established by the Revolution on the frontiers, he transformed into kingdoms and principalities; though he kept them still satellites by naming his own brothers or his favorite generals to be their kings or princes. Similarly, after conquering Naples, Spain and Portugal, he turned these nations into satellite kingdoms. Upon the ending of the ancient German Empire, consequent upon his decisive defeats of Austria and Prussia, Napoleon found several southern and western German states eager to possess his favor. He organized them into the Confederation of the Rhine, under his domination, of course. His victories over the Russians gave him Polish allies and a powerful influence in a possible restoration of Poland.

England alone defied Bonaparte. Because of her overwhelming victory in the naval battle of Trafalgar she was still mistress of the seas. The French Emperor decided that the island-kingdom could only be brought low by a mighty land campaign against all her international commerce. So he devised the Continental System, in which all his satellites and all his allies were to join France in a total boycott of every commercial relation with England. The venture turned out to be one of Napoleon's few great failures. It was too vast and too personal; even his own relatives violated it. Nevertheless Napoleon's power continued to mount; it reached its summit during the years 1810-1812, when Napoleon was the master of Europe from Portugal to Poland, and from Sicily to Denmark.

The most obvious aspects of Napoleon's dominance were political and military. But it was also materialistic, ruthless and unscrupulous. Many of the generals and officials were Voltairian sceptics; hence the dominance at times was distinctly anti-religious. The new legal system, the Code Napoleon, allowed civil marriages and divorce, and introduced these into the Italian annexations. Imperial forces invading Spain abolished more than one-third of the monasteries of the Catholic nation. Everywhere the enemies of Catholicism welcomed the arrival of imperial armies enthusiastically.

During the decade between 1804 and 1814, Emperor and Pope were in continual conflict. Where he could, Pius VII yielded for the sake of peace; but where right and principle were concerned he stood inflexible. The common father of Christendom could not join the Continental System, nor could he sanction the spoliation of Naples, nor regard Napoleon's enemies as his own. As the guardian of Christian morality he could not sanction the marriage and divorce laws of the Code Napoleon, nor could he comply with Napoleon's demand that he dissolve the lawful marriage of Jerome Bonaparte, his brother, and Jerome's American wife. (Jerome's marriage with Miss Patterson at Baltimore, in 1802, did not fit in with Napoleon's plan to make his brother King of Westphalia in Germany and to marry him to a German princess.) Pius VII found the first marriage valid. It had been performed by Bishop John Carroll. Jerome, a weakling, discarded his American wife and attempted marriage with the German princess.

To intimidate Pius VII, in 1808, Napoleon ordered General Miollis to occupy Rome. In a dignified reply, the Pontiff declared that during the occupation he would consider himself a prisoner in the Quirinal Palace, and that he would decline all negotiations. During the first years of his captivity, Pius VII had to witness unheard-of violence in his domains. Napoleon, as "successor to Charlemagne," revoked the donations of Pepin and Charlemagne, and annexed four papal duchies to his new puppet kingdom of Italy. The Holy Father saw cardinals and bishops banished, papal officials arrested and papal subjects sentenced to death. Napoleon demanded the suppression of religious orders, the abolition of celibacy and the erection of a French Patriarchate. Nothing was left to the Pontiff but to address an encyclical of protest and remonstrance to the Catholic world.

On May 18, 1809, Napoleon by a formal decree abolished the temporal sovereignty of the Popes. The Papal States were transformed into French departments; Rome was made the second city of the Empire; the Pope was assigned a salary of two million francs and the possession of the papal palaces. The decree was promulgated in Rome on June 10. Amid the booming of the cannons of the Castle of St. Angelo the papal flag was hauled down, and the tri-color was hoisted over the Eternal City. On that very day, Pius VII signed a bull of excommunication against Napoleon and his agents, without mentioning names. The mighty Emperor had only ridicule for the action of the Holy Father. "What does Pius VII expect from denouncing me to Christendom? Does he imagine that the arms will fall from the hands of my soldiers?" Three years later the scornful questioner found *literal* answers in the snowy wastes and freezing colds of the retreat from Moscow.

General Rodet, on orders, seized the Quirinal Palace on July 5. He battered down the doors and, axe in hand, entered the room where Pius VII, with Cardinals Consalvi and Pacca, awaited. When the Holy Father firmly refused his demand to abdicate as a temporal ruler, the General arrested Pius VII and Cardinal Pacca, his secretary. Under military guard both were escorted out of Rome and Italy, across the Alps to Grenoble and back to Savona. Here the Holy Pontiff was detained a prisoner for three years. Pacca was separated from him and confined to the Alpine fortress of Fenestrella. In the meantime the foreign cardinals in Rome were ordered to retire to their respective countries;

twenty-six of the other cardinals were brought to Paris, so that they might be under the power of Napoleon in the event of the death of Pius VII.

The conflict between Emperor and Pope, now prisoner at Savona, continued unabated. One striking episode was the Emperor's divorce and remarriage. In 1796, Napoleon had married a widow, Josephine de Beauharnais, in a civil ceremony. The marriage was most probably valid; in 1796, the presence of a parish priest was morally impossible. Just before the coronation, at the urgent request of Josephine and the order of Pius VII, Cardinal Fesch, uncle of Napoleon, armed with all the necessary faculties, performed a secret ecclesiastical ceremony. The Emperor asserted that he took part only to appease the scruples of his wife. In the eyes of the Church, if the civil marriage had not been valid, the new ecclesiastical ceremony at least externally placed the matter beyond all doubt: they were now validly married.

As Emperor of the French he desired a lineal descendant, and his marriage with Josephine was childless. Now, in 1809, at the pinnacle of his power, he decided to sacrifice Josephine and to seek a marriage with Maria Louisa, daughter of the Hapsburg Emperor of Austria, Francis I. The Senate quickly granted the divorce. But the Court of Vienna demanded an ecclesiastical decision about Napoleon's former marriages. In the marriage problems of royal persons the only competent authority to give decisions is the Pope. Napoleon did not dare to submit the question to his prisoner at Savona. Instead he referred the case to a local church court of Paris. But as the court was incompetent, and its decision of annulment was dictated not by Canon Law but by abject servility to the Emperor, its decision was void of legal value. The decision served, however, to calm the consciences of the Court of Vienna and of its compliant archbishop. But Pope Pius VII, from his imprisonment at Savona, protested the whole procedure.

Napoleon *invited* the bishops and *ordered* the cardinals to return to Paris to adorn by their presence the celebration of his victories and of his marriage with the Hapsburg princess. Consalvi and twelve other cardinals absented themselves from the marriage festivities. Napoleon was furious at their defiance. He ordered the arrest of these heroic cardinals, the confiscation of their properties, and their exile to various French cities. He even forbade them to wear their cardinalatial robes. Hence the thirteen were referred to as "the black cardinals," in contradistinction to the "red cardinals" who supported the Emperor.

Napoleon found in the gentle patience of Pius VII an insurmountable obstacle to his grandiose ambition of becoming the master of the Church as well as of the State. The Holy Father paid little heed to his wild threatenings; he ignored his personal insults. The Emperor, in his anger, cut down the number of bishoprics, suppressed numerous monasteries, seized the properties of the prelates who rejected the Organic Articles, and filled the dungeons of Fenestrella with churchmen. But all to no purpose; the Sovereign Pontiff quietly but definitely refused to yield. The mighty commander of nations stooped to the pettiest meanness in his treatment of the prisoner of Savona.

The Holy Father was quartered in a poorly furnished set of rooms in the bishop's house. His few faithful servants were sent away. No cardinal nor ecclesiastic in whom he trusted was allowed to see him. His ring was taken away from him. His desk was rifled; even his letters were opened and read by an imperial official before being delivered. He was put on prisoner's allowance; his household expenses were reduced to about seventy-five cents a head daily. So the Holy Father was compelled to live almost entirely on alms during his three years' confinement at Savona.

But in spite of all, Pius VII could not be induced to infringe on the laws of the Church. Napoleon next turned to working his will through a National Council — "My Council," as he called it. Though there were some surprising manifestations of loyalty to the Pope, the Council was dragooned into accepting a proposal empowering an archbishop of a province to install newly-appointed bishops, if the Pope would not do so within six months. Pope Pius consented to the decree, providing that the installation be performed in the name of the *Pope only*. Napoleon in high dudgeon declared that he would henceforward initiate bishops without any papal interference. When the fathers again asserted their independence and loyalty to the Pope, the Emperor closed the Council on July 11, 1811, and ordered the arrest of three bishops who had prominently opposed his wishes.

Shortly after the more independent bishops had departed, a group of about eighty of the compliant bishops were assembled. Yielding to threats and promises, they accepted the proposals of the Emperor. A deputation of imperialist cardinals and ecclesiastics went to Savona to persuade Pius to accept the proposals. Pius agreed, but authorized the archbishop to confer the canonical institution only in the name of the Pope. Napoleon was by no means satisfied. He resolved, however, to delay the arrangement of this and several other religious problems until he should have returned from his Russian campaign. So he marched off with his soldiers—to Moscow!

Concordat of Fontainebleau

ON JUNE 16, 1812, six days before the declaration of war against Russia, Napoleon had Pope Pius VII transported to the Palace of Fontainebleau, thirty-five miles south of Paris, to prevent a possible British rescue of the Pontiff from Savona. The prisoner status was unchanged, for the Holy Father was allowed no visitors except "red cardinals" and imperialist ecclesiastics. In December, Napoleon was back in Paris after the overwhelming Russian disasters. He gave thought to a reconciliation with the Pope. It was a useful policy, if not a very necessary one. An exchange of New Year's greetings was made; and on January 18, 1813, Napoleon presented himself at Fontainebleau.

However, only a week of stormy interviews followed, about which very little definite information can ever be known. The Emperor ruthlessly pressed his proposals for dominating all episcopal appointments. He did not hesitate on occasions to try to terrify the Pope with his raging and direful threats.

The Holy Father's situation was truly a sad one. His health, seriously impaired by the rigors of Savona, failed him; and he was now, at seventy-three, a painfully sick old man. Alone, without advisor or assistant, he was pitted against a pitiless antagonist backed by court ecclesiastics, who were ready to support the Emperor's demands with slanted precedents and partisan theology. Why wonder, then, if in these circumstances he was drawn into concessions which if ever ratified, would have been a betrayal of the Church. An agreement, known as the "Concordat of Fontainebleau," was signed on January 25. The most important paragraph dealt with the canonical institution of bishops; it provided that if the Pope did not concede this institution six months after the nomination, it could be bestowed by the archbishop, or senior bishop of the province. This concession, in the final analysis, would have put all the French and Italian bishops and archbishops in the Emperor's power. The entire document was represented to Pius VII as only the preliminaries to a concordat. The words of its preamble stated that it was intended only "to serve as a basis for a definitive arrangement." But on February 13, Napoleon had the "Concordat of Fontainebleau" published (just as it stood) as a law of the State. This act was most unfair to Pius VII; the Emperor had no right thus to convert "preliminary articles" into a definitive act.

A few days previously, on February 9, in accordance with one of the provisions of the "Concordat," the "black cardinals" were recalled from their exile. Consalvi, Pacca and DiPietro hastened to Fontainebleau. When they arrived, they found the condition of Pius VII pitiable in the extreme. He was in deep melancholy, burdened with the bitterest remorse for what he had done in a moment of weakness and refused to be consoled.

The three cardinals immediately began a careful scrutiny of the agreement. Then they declared that the concessions were impossible and should be recalled by the Pope. Needless to say this view found no favor with the imperialist cardinals, but in the end it won out. With the advice of Consalvi, Pius VII prepared a retraction of the "preliminary articles." In his letter of March twenty-fourth to Napoleon, the Pontiff reproached himself for having signed these articles and disavowed the signature which he had given.

Napoleon ordered the Pope's letter to be kept strictly secret. Acting on his own authority, he ordered the "Concordat of Fontainebleau" to be binding on the Church. Then he filled twelve vacant sees. He had Cardinal DiPietro removed from Fontainebleau, and threatened to do the same to Cardinal Pacca. However, the news of the Pope's retraction kept spreading everywhere; and opposition from the clergy and laity against Napoleon's religious usurpation was appearing in Belgium, France and Italy. Pius VII issued a brief in May, 1813, declaring all recently appointed bishops unlawful and schismatical, and their exercise of jurisdiction null and void.

Finally on January 22, 1814, as the Allies were getting ready for their advance on Paris, the order was issued that the Pope was to start immediately for Savona. On his arrival he was treated with all due respect by the officials. On March 17, the prefect of the area informed Pope Pius VII that he was free to leave. Two days later he set out for Rome. The journey was veritably a triumphal progress. People everywhere along the route crowded to catch a glimpse of the venerable pontiff who had so bravely withstood the threats of Napoleon. The enthusiasm of the Roman populace welcoming their own pastor of pastors can only be imagined.

Pius VII's kind heart harbored no enmities. After the fall of his persecutor, Napoleon, he gladly offered a refuge in his capital city to the members of the Bonaparte family: Princess Letitia, the deposed emperor's mother; his brothers Lucien and Louis; and his uncle Cardinal Fesch. So forgiving was Pius, that upon hearing of the severe captivity in which the imperial prisoner was held at St. Helena, he requested Cardinal Consalvi to plead for leniency with the Prince-Regent of England. When he was informed of Napoleon's desire for the ministrations of a Catholic priest, he sent to him the Abbé Vegnali as chaplain. Princess Letitia, in 1818, in a letter to Cardinal Consalvi, acknowledged most gratefully all the kindnesses of Pius VII and of his great minister, remarking that they had been the only protection and support her family possessed in their sorrows.

Nine years remained to Pius VII. Though venerable in age he worked tirelessly, restoring the Roman Congregations, and reopening the national colleges for seminarians at Rome. With his great assistant, Cardinal Consalvi, he obtained from the Congress of Vienna most of the Papal States in Italy, and through the same skillful diplomat he negotiated several concordats, especially with German states. He solved the Veto Controversy in Ireland by allowing the Irish hierarchy to make the final decision, which eliminated the royal veto in the election of Irish bishops. The aging Holy Father erected new bishoprics in various European countries — thirty-two in France alone.

American Catholics must always venerate the memory of Pius VII for his organization of the American hierarchy in 1808. He raised the first see, Baltimore, to metropolitan rank, and elevated Bishop John Carroll to be the first Archbishop. He created suffragan sees at Boston; New York; Philadelphia; and Bardstown, Kentucky. In 1820, he added two more suffragan sees — one at Charleston, South Carolina, and the other at Richmond, and finally a third suffragan see at Cincinnati.

These last years of the Holy Father were not without their sore trials: the secret revolutionists among the Carbonari in Italy, the anti-religious revolutions in Spain and in Portugal, and the almost continual domineering policies of Prussia and other German states.

Undoubtedly the greatest act of the declining years of Pope Pius VII was the restoration of the Society of Jesus. It was the one he most desired to achieve. Circumstances in the early years of his pontificate prevented his reversal of the suppression of 1773. But whenever the opportunity offered itself, Pope Pius did what he could. In 1801, he gave full and formal confirmation of the Society of Jesus in White Russia, where it had never died out. This brave act of the Holy Father enabled ex-Jesuits everywhere, but especially in England and in the United States, to unite with the persisting remnant of the old Society. In 1804, he restored canonically the Jesuit order in the Kingdom of the Two Sicilies. By 1814, sincere Catholics were urgently praying for the complete restoration. No one cherished the hope more than did the Supreme Pontiff. And sharing in his desire were such eminent Cardinals as Consalvi, Litta and Pacca. When Pius VII returned from Fontainebleau, his mind was made up to bring about a universal restoration, in spite of any and all clamors of the old enemies of the Jesuits, or of any of their new foes, the anti-clerical liberals. The Bull of Restoration was soon completed.

On August 7, 1814, the universal restoration of the Society of Jesus became an accomplished fact. On that day, Pope Pius VII proceeded through the streets of the Eternal City, crowded with the jubilant populace, to the Church of the Gesù, where he said Mass at the altar of St. Ignatius. Then in the Sodality Chapel, in the presence of a notable assemblage of eighteen Cardinals, many high dignitaries and 150 survivors of the old Society, the Pontiff had the solemn Bull of Restoration read. Few could restrain their tears, especially when Pope Pius VII received the aged veteran priests who had lived through forty years of sorrow and loneliness to this day of the complete fulfillment of all their hopes and prayers.

In the Bull of Restoration, Pius VII says explicitly: "We would reckon it a grave fault in the sight of God were we in such a need to spurn such richly blessed help which the special rule of Divine Providence offers us, and were we in the barque of Peter, so tossed here and there by the storm, not to accept the skillful and seasoned rowers who offer themselves to break the billows of the sea threatening us every moment with disastrous shipwreck." In conclusion Pius VII declared the Brief of Suppression to be completely revoked. The Society of Jesus was therefore free again to serve the Pope throughout the whole world at whatever tasks he should wish to assign to its members.

Bourgeois Liberalism

THE HUNDRED YEARS between the fall of Napoleon, 1814, and the eruption of World War I, 1914, proved a dolorous century for Catholicism. Time and again, the Church was persecuted in almost every country of Europe, North America, South America, Africa and Asia. The attackers aimed at subverting the Church to hostile governments, or at excluding her from public society, and in certain cases, even at annihilating the Catholic religion. Frequently the onslaughts resulted in wholesale destruction of ecclesiastical edifices and institutions, in total confiscations of Church properties, in bloody outrages on clerics and devoted lay people, and in numerous banishments of bishops, priests, religious brothers and religious sisters. The nineteenth was a century of persecutions, indeed.

To appreciate the wide extension of forces hostile to the Church, her enemies must be grouped according to their specific programs. The most numerous, most powerful, and most persistent were the Liberals, the heirs of the *Enlightenment*, the *Aufklaerung*, and the French revolution. ("Liberal" is used solely as a party term.) The conflict of Liberalism with Christianity will be given fuller treatment later. The Regalists came next; they took part in the Conservative Reaction (Austria, Prussia, Russia and France), which aimed at restoring the old monarchies. The dangers which the Regalist Reaction constituted for the Church were: first, the revival of Gallicanism, Febronianism and Josephinism; secondly, the embarrassment of the Papacy due to Austrian extensions of power in the Italian peninsula.

The advances of strong Protestant states must then be considered. One of these states was the vigorous Kingdom of Prussia. Prussia persecuted the Catholic Poles, and planned to Protestantize the Catholic ecclesiastical states in Westphalia and in the Rhineland, which it had obtained at the close of the Napoleonic wars. The supreme Protestant state, however, was England, exalted by her tremendous victory over Napoleon, hailed as the Mistress of the High Seas, and acknowledged as holder of the industrial and financial leadership of the world. Protestants everywhere looked up to Britain as their patron and, if the need called, their champion. England welcomed the role. Though bloody implementation of her prejudices had long gone, the large majority of England's classes, high and low, were still strongly anti-Catholic in spirit.

Lastly, there was the mighty Russian Empire, which had assumed leadership and protection of all Eastern Orthodox Christians against the Popes of Rome. Russia had little toleration for either the Latin Catholics or the Oriental Catholics who accepted the spiritual leadership of the Roman Pontiff. Her ruthless persecutions of the Catholic Popes, the Catholic Lithuanians and the Catholic Ruthenians, evidenced her enmity for the Popes and for their loyal, heroic adherents.

Liberalism, as the most inimical of the anti-Catholic forces, has need of further explanation. The term "Liberal" has been given so many variant meanings, from broadmindedness and humane social reform to explicitly irreligious legislation. It has been used of persons, ideas, political parties, philosophical speculations and theological teachings. Since the days of the *Enlightenment* in the late eighteenth century, Liberalism has been applied more and more to certain tendencies in the intellectual, religious, political and economic life which implied a partial or total emancipation of man from the supernatural, moral and divine order.

Usually the principles of 1789 (the French Revolution) were considered the *Magna Carta* of this form of Liberalism, called by some "Integral Liberalism." The fundamental ideas of this nineteenth-century Liberalism proposed an absolute and unrestrained freedom of thought, religion, conscience, creed, speech and politics. The necessary consequences of these proposed ideas were: not only the abolition of the Divine Right of Kings, but of every kind of authority derived from God; the relegation of religion from the public life into the private domain of one's individual conscience; the absolute ignoring of Christianity and the Church as public, legal and social institutions. Finally, Integral Liberalism denied that for man the supreme source of authority is God. Disregarding the moral law and repudiating divine Revelation were only to be expected of the heirs of Voltaire and Rousseau.

The Liberalism of the *Enlightenment* was first developed by doctrinaire intellectuals. Their theories were activated and spread over Europe by the armies of the Revolution — so much so that at the Restoration of the Bourbon monarchies there existed in every European nation a strong Liberal party vigorously opposed to the "Holy Alliance" of Austria, Prussia, Russia and France. These parties and their programs were classified as "Bourgeois Liberalism." Their membership was drawn from the middle classes: the manufacturers, bankers — heirs not only of the Rationalist Revolution, but also of the Industrial Revolution. With them were lawyers, litterateurs and politicians, all disciples of Voltaire or Rousseau. As sons of the Revolution they were closely bound together, locally and extranationally, by anti-Christian Masonry.

The natural development of doctrinaire Liberalism adapted itself to the interests of the propertied and moneyed classes. Since the clergy and the nobility had been dispossessed of their political power, the bourgeois groups were the only classes which could make use of their new institutions. The ordinary people were not sufficiently instructed and organized to do so. The rich industrial classes, therefore, were from the beginning and in all countries the mainstay of Liberalism; and Liberalism for its part was forced to further the interests of the manufacturers and financiers. Bourgeois Liberalism enjoyed its highest favor in France during the reign of the citizen-king, Louis Philippe, 1830-1840. But it also flourished in Germany and in Austria — in fact, in practically every Continental nation.

The characteristic traits of Bourgeois Liberalism were: materialistic and sordid ideals, which cared only for unrestrained enjoyment of life; and egoism in exploiting the economically weak. True to its revolutionary antecedents, it engaged in systematic persecutions of Christianity and especially of the Catholic Church and her institutions. It displayed a frivolous disregard of—even a mocking contempt for—the divine moral order. It manifested a cynical indifference in the choice and the use of slander, corruption and fraud in fighting its opponents and in acquiring absolute mastery and control of everything.

It took Bourgeois Liberalism fifty years to push up to the high plateau from which it dominated the European scene for the succeeding fifty years. In passing, one cannot help but note the fact that it was in this stretch of domination that Bourgeois Liberalism unwittingly generated the forces which were to destroy it: Nationalism, Socialism and Communism. Only a summarization of the several conflicts of the first fifty years can be given here.

In the upward push, three periods can be discerned: the first (1815-1830) was the struggle of the Liberals to overthrow the restoration of the old monarchies; the second (1830-1848) was the victorious establishment of Liberalism in most European states, with the greatest success in France; the third (1848-1877) was the definite control of the governments of France and Italy, the maintenance of vigorous Liberal parties in Switzerland, Portugal, Spain, Germany, Austria, Hungary, Belgium and England.

For the ordinary people this period was "confusion worse confounded." Often the partisans of Liberalism infiltrated the most legitimate causes: liberty, political freedom, social reform, economic justice and patriotism. In many cases they took over the leadership. It was hard for Catholics to defend themselves and drive out the intruders. Often they were split between old loyalties and new aspirations. It was next to impossible to repulse the bold assertiveness of unscrupulous leaders, especially when they were backed by mobs. There was little that could be done to block the intrigues, skillfully planned in the lodges of secret societies.

The Catholic Church suffered grievously, immensely and continually. Not only were churches and monasteries destroyed, but the vital economic resources were confiscated on a wholesale scale. Anti-clerical mobs did not always stop at tearing down churches and convents; sometimes they plunged on to bloodshed and sacrilege. One constant objective was the abolition of Catholic education. Not only were the Catholic common schools closed down and private schooling in secondary education under religious auspices prohibited, but the centuries-old Catholic universities were turned into state institutions to become hotbeds of scepticism and atheism. Religious orders were abolished; monks, priests and nuns were forbidden to lead their religious lives, or were forced into banishment. Some liberal states made it a distinctive goal to turn themselves and their people into a secularized society. Hence even nursing nuns were driven from their hospitals, and chaplains were forbidden entrance into them. The thought was nourished that in such a secularized world Catholicism would cease to exist.

There is no need for surprise at such plans and actions. Bourgeois Liberalism was merely an extension into the nineteenth century of the Enlightenment and the Revolution. But one need only remember: Peter's barque was still sailing the seas in the nineteenth century.

The Catholic Revival of the Nineteenth Century

STRANGE AS IT may seem, the direful century of Liberalism's endless warring upon Catholicism was also the glorious century of Catholicism's modern revival. Most significant among the features of the revival was the veneration of the Popes which developed during this century of tribulations. There had existed nothing parallel to it in all the previous history of the Church. And long before this century had ended, devoted respect and filial affection for the Holy Father had become well nigh universal among Catholics. And so, this veneration has remained to our own day—the warmest tie, and one of the strongest, binding the Catholic people of every race and of every color to the Vicar of Christ, the Sovereign Pontiff of the Catholic Church.

The revival of Catholicism in the nineteenth century had many other inspiring elements. There were the supreme shepherds of the flock themselves, the seven Popes, all of worthy life, four of extraordinary accomplishment; there were the dedicated clerical leaders, from cardinals and bishops to diocesan priests and religious-order priests. There were the national revivals, in which lay and clerical scholars, theologians, philosophers, litterateurs, journalists and orators met the challenges of the sceptical rationalists, defended the Faith, promoted Christian culture and enkindled religious devotion and Catholic piety. Then there was the glorious flowering of sanctity: several canonized saints, and large numbers of men and women of extraordinary holiness of life; the revivifying of the older religious orders, and the founding of several hundred congregations of religious priests, brothers and nuns. One must not be unmindful—this was the century of the appearances of our Blessed Mother at Lourdes, La Salette, Rue du Bac and Knock.

Finally there was the widespread manifestation of the apostolic spirit, evidenced by the tens of thousands of missionaries, priests, nuns and brothers, who carried the Gospel to the remotest areas of the five continents. And this apostolic spirit was evidenced, too, by the countless European Catholics, of all classes and ranks of society, who banded together in missionary societies to send money and supplies to the active missionaries toiling in the "fields afar." But above all, the revival of the nineteenth century was crowned by the dogmatic decrees, the scriptural directives and the vital social encyclicals of Leo XIII and St. Pius X.

And yet at the end of the Napoleonic era, the Church's prospects for recovery were truly disheartening. As the preceding chapter revealed, her enemies—whether rationalist liberals, or Protestant monarchs, or Russian autocrats—held complete ascendency. Everywhere in the Catholic world the Church was faced with the gigantic task of rebuilding the thousands of ruined churches and monasteries, demolished by revolutionary mobs or in the clashings of battling armies. And there were scarcely any financial means, even to begin the reconstruction. The confiscation of Church resources by the anti-clerical revolutions had been total. Similarly, vast losses followed the secularization of Church properties when the German ecclesiastical states were handed over to lay princes.

The outlook for the clergy was equally depressing. The wide depletions in their ranks, due to the holocausts of the guillotines and of the Cayenne swamps, or to the enormous youth-levies in the great national wars, were not refilled.

Nor could they be; for after all the destruction there remained pitifully few seminaries, and the few surviving seminaries had been robbed of their essential financial resources. There was hope, but only in the virtues and faithfulness of the surviving clergy, from cardinals to humble curates.

These post-revolutionary priests were heroes. They stood staunchly loyal to their priesthood in spite of the abuse continually hurled at them by the anti-Catholic world, the scornful gibes of bourgeois politicians, the nasty innuendoes of foul scribblers and the obscene curses of street-ruffians.

The most overwhelming deficiency in the Church's life at the time was the destruction of the great religious orders. These for centuries were stalwart supporters of the Church and the papacy, and potent agents of the ecclesiastical life and worship. Father Hughes, the renowned English historian, believes that one would have to go back 1,200 years to St. Gregory the Great's time to find fewer Benedictine monasteries. As for the great order of preachers and theologians, the Dominicans, it took them more than half a century to become again the strong support of the Faith. An earlier chapter has detailed the losses suffered by Catholic education and by the Catholic missions in the suppression of the Jesuits.

The ousting of the Church from her pre-eminence in education was a most serious disaster. This expropriation took away her universities and turned them into state institutions, given exclusively to the pursuit of secular knowledge. Their professional staffs were made up largely of Voltairians; and these with the student bodies, who were largely influenced by them, became cynical proponents of infidelity and immorality. Generally the new secular universities abolished the faculty of theology, which had been the focal point of the Medieval Catholic university. If some retained this faculty, they often did so grudgingly. Associations of Catholic professors and students were occasionally tolerated, but seldom were they accorded academic recognition. Frequent and bitter conflicts also raged between laic states and the Catholic Church over the management of secondary and primary schools. The Church more often emerged as the defeated party.

Truly in the mid-nineteenth century there was much that was disheartening in the prospects of Catholicism. The "intelligentsia" of her opponents dismissed the Church and the Papacy (in their minds, both were identical) as only imposing ruins, tottering relics of bygone times. Von Ranke wrote in 1837, "The day of the papal power is gone forever." But wait, forty years later, in surprise he had to write, "The Papacy has entered upon a new epoch." The "intelligentsia," concentrating on the sinking material power of the Popes, were quite unaware of their steadily rising religious prestige.

The opening paragraphs of this chapter have emphasized the significance of the growing prestige of the Pope, and also listed some outstanding features of the Catholic Revival. Here some pertinent considerations are in order. The Church's survival of the Revolution and her subsequent vigorous life aroused admiration all over Europe. People everywhere were stirred by the heroism of the Popes, the clergy and the Catholic common people, by the long vistas of the Church's history, and by her saving and all-satisfying dogmatic and moral teachings. More and more inquiring souls became convinced of her divine guidance and protection.

At length in the second quarter of the nineteenth century, the great spiritual revival came into existence. It kept expanding through the rest of the century and into the next also, bringing into the Church hundreds of thousands of converts, among them many notable intellectuals. One salutary development of the revival was a more independent attitude on the part of both clergy and laity towards the state, especially towards any state that was threatening encroachments upon the spiritual domain. Catholics everywhere were now prepared to stand up staunchly for the rights of the Church.

One of the most significant acts of Pius VII — and he made it on the eve of the Catholic Revival — was the restoration of the Society of Jesus. On August 7, 1814, at Rome, in the splendid old church of the Jesuits, the Sovereign Pontiff published the Bull of Restoration in the presence of eighteen cardinals, many high dignitaries, and 150 survivors of the original Society.

In the Bull, the Pope noted that he had received an almost universal request from all parts of the Christian world for a complete restoration of the Society of Jesus. Pope Pius affirmed that the rebuilding of holiness after the most deplorable disasters of recent times had occupied all his thoughts, and that it was a duty which he must perform.

Pius VII was looking to the future; he was planning particularly for the Jesuits to be effective auxiliaries of the Popes in the oncoming Catholic Revival. For the moment he was well aware that the Restoration meant little more than permission for a few old priests and a couple of hundred recruits to live in community and to call themselves "The Society of Jesus." None of them entertained any illusions about occupying the old position of the Jesuits in the Catholic world. They had not the men. Most of the old Society were long dead. Youthful aspirants were few, and their training would take years. Nor had the handful of Jesuits any resources. Their old colleges, churches and properties were permanently in the hands of others; the prospects for new foundations were practically nil.

In the initial decades the growth of the Society was insignificant and greatly hindered by anti-clerical forces; then followed a steady development despite numerous and most vicious attacks. In the first sixty years of the Catholic Revival the numerical increase in the Society of Jesus (from 500 in 1814, to 9,260 in 1874) was, to say the least, providential. And during that period the Jesuit order had become a vigorous force in the Revival, thus realizing Pius VII's hopes and plans that the Jesuits would provide loyal and powerful assistance to the Popes.

A few instances of the Jesuits' labors for the Church may be cited. The great parish missions, preached year after year in Europe and in America, brought back countless people to the sacraments and strengthened all Catholics in the Faith. The widespread promotion of devotion to the Sacred Heart and to the Blessed Mother enkindled loving worship in the hearts of all believers. The Jesuit colleges, with their groundwork of faith, sent out generations of youths solid in belief and loyal in devotion to the Popes. The works of Jesuit theologians were of great value in the development of the teachings on the Immaculate Conception and on the infallibility of the Popes. The Jesuit writers untiringly defended the Papacy and the Faith from all attacks; they made their learned journals, the *Civiltà Cattolica*, the *Stimmen aus Maria Laach*, *L'Études* and the *Month*, literary arsenals for the papal cause. The theologians of the Society had important parts in the First Vatican Council, especially in regard to the prerogatives of the Pope. During the revival, Jesuits took up again the work of the missions in Asia, Africa, North and South America.

Since 1814, the services rendered by the Society of Jesus to the Pope have frequently been stamped with Christ's cross. The attacks upon the Jesuits were but parts of the attacks upon the Church and the Popes. The assailants were the same: Liberals from the European Masonic lodges, Hegelian politicians of absolute nationalist states, and Atheistic Communists. The calumnies of the literary assaults upon the Society were ultimately aimed at the Papacy. Except in Spain, Mexico, China and the Commune of Paris, the attacks were not unto blood—although from 1814 to the present, 177 Jesuits have been murdered by anti-Catholic forces. The persecutions aimed at the Jesuits of this period have been continual rounds of banishments and of total confiscations of colleges and institutions. Twenty times during the period were the Jesuits so dispersed. The enmity for them has been more persistent and more fundamental than any of the opposition of the earlier days. In such irreconcilable conflicts the Jesuits must suffer because of wholehearted loyalty to the Holy Father. But that is just the loyalty which St. Ignatius Loyola wished for the soldiers of his Company of Jesus.

Revival in France and Germany

NEVER DID a movement seem more hopeless than the Catholic Revival in France in the early decades of the nineteenth century. The majority of the intellectual class was infected with Voltairianism, and so also was an even larger majority of the bourgeoisie (the governing class). As for the proletariate, the dwellers of the slums and the remote rural areas, they were crassly ignorant of the Faith; there had been few priests left to instruct them after the Revolution.

The revival began with the writings of Chateaubriand, De Maistre, and other Catholic authors, who fearlessly proclaimed the Catholic religion and the Holy See as the only secure foundations on which to restore civil society. The most famous of the new books was Chateaubriand's *The Genius of Christianity;* it is one of the treasures of literature. Now the proponents of "The Enlightenment" had sought to destroy Christian dogmas by holding them up to ridicule, and so had deluded many cultivated minds. Chateaubriand proved that this derided religion was the most beautiful of all, and likewise the most favorable to literature and art.

De Maistre's book was more solid; it was entitled *On the Pope.* In it the author exalted the dignity and the sovereignty of the Pope in the Church, and he strongly maintained the infallibility of the Pope. De Maistre's book dealt Gallicanism a decisive and final blow.

The revival was not long in operation when it began to produce magnificent works of Christian charity. In 1833, a professor of the University of Paris, as pious as he was learned, Frederic Ozanam, founded the Society of St. Vincent de Paul. Ozanam's idea was to oppose the reigning Voltairianism by the service of God in the service of the poor, and to create a means of reconciliation in the struggle between the classes and the masses. His appeals found a most remarkable response among the educated classes. Before long, 17,000 members were personally visiting and aiding 20,000 poor unfortunates in the slums of Paris. Before 1848, five hundred conferences were working in France, and the Society was firmly established in England, Ireland, Belgium, Spain, North America, and still other countries. Earlier, in 1822, Pauline Marie Jaricot had founded at Lyons the Society for the Propagation of the Faith. By 1841, because its membership was open to all grades of people, its rolls counted 700,000, and it was spreading through the world. No country, in the nineteenth century, sent so many missionaries and martyrs into the mission lands as France.

During the revival, the number of French religious more than doubled what it had been before the Revolution. Pulpit oratory flourished again as Dominicans, Jesuits, and other preachers filled the cathedrals and churches of France with their sermons. The firmness of the bishops, following the example of Cardinal de Bonald, Archbishop of Lyons, successfully defeated the repeated attempts to revive Gallicanism in the seminaries. One should remember that these holy achievements were carried on while anti-Catholic liberalism, securely in the saddle, was waging war upon the Church.

In the 1830's fairly young men led the revival. They were: Lamennais, a priest; Lacordaire, a priest; and Montalembert, a layman. Learned and eloquent, they attacked relentlessly both radical liberals and conservative Gallicans. Lamennais

PAULINE JARICOT. Foundress
of the Society for the
Propagation of the Faith.
A contemporary portrait.

FREDERIC OZANAM. Founder
of the Society of St. Vincent
de Paul.

came to be looked upon as the most eminent personality among the French clergy. In ability the two colleagues were his equal. Yet it was from these devoted men that very serious trouble arose. They urged that the Church abandon her past connections and take the lead in the contemporary democratic movement. Its proposals for liberty had a special attraction for them; and they advocated that the Church work for accepting some of them, or make some adjustments with these new ideas of liberty. On October 16, 1830, Lamennais founded a paper called *L'Avenir* (The Future), to propagate his program; Lacordaire and Montalembert joined him as associates in the venture.

The intentions of these young enthusiasts were good, but their policies were imprudent, their demands exaggerated, and their language immoderate. The violent language of *L'Avenir* in its attacks upon the bishops and the seminaries, as well as upon the government, stirred up a whirlwind of protests. The editors suspended the paper and appealed to Rome. They received an adverse decision. Pope Gregory XVI condemned many of the principles and methods of *L'Avenir*. The Pope, out of personal regard for the three editors, did not mention their names. All three accepted the decision. But shortly Lamennais returned to his old ideas. Lacordaire and Montalembert would not follow him. Ever constant in the Faith, they both later became glorious pillars of French Catholicism. Lamennais' end was tragic. He gradually renounced his ecclesiastical functions, and within a few years abandoned all outward profession of Christianity. After his apostasy, he moved further into heresy. He died rejecting all religious ministrations, yet he had once been the most eminent priest in France.

Lacordaire became the greatest of modern pulpit orators. His conferences at Notre Dame, expounding Catholic philosophy and theology, filled the vast cathedral each Lent for 21 years, with throngs from all walks of life, and from all conditions of belief and unbelief. Lacordaire entered the Dominicans and restored the venerable Order of Preachers to its former high position in France.

Montalembert, as a legislator, became the leading French champion of Catholic education in all its divisions. He gained the favor of the French bishops, and aroused them, as they had never been before, for the godly education of youth. Montalembert, as a writer, became outstanding; his *Monks of the West* revived the consciousness of the debt civilization owes to monasticism. His pen was always at the service of the Church and of the cause of liberty. Montalembert is recognized as one of the greatest Catholic laymen of modern times.

The Catholic Revival in Germany was truly amazing. Cardinal Pacca had declared: "The Church in Germany can be preserved only by a miracle." In Napoleon's time Catholicism lay prostrate in most of the German states. By the Great Secularization of 1803, the Church had been deprived of her freedom of action, her properties, her monasteries and her schools; she had been betrayed by some of her prelates and priests; and she was paralyzed by the indifference of large sections of the masses. All that was left to this anemic Church was the patient prayerfulness and the silent resistance of those of her priests and simple lay people who did not falter in their loyalty to the Faith. They proved to be much more numerous than they had appeared to be.

Bearing down upon the stricken Church were powerful enemies: Protestant Prussia, bent upon protestantizing its new Catholic territories in Westphalia and the Rhineland; the ubiquitous doctrinaires of the *Aufklaerung*, who dominated the intellectual circles; the numerous followers of the Revolution; and finally the heirs of the last two groups, wielding far more power than either, the anti-Catholic liberals. These last controlled most of the governing bureaucracies in the German principalities. The liberal bureaucrats were all state-absolutists, and they bitterly opposed Catholicism. Significantly, all their relations with the Holy See were modeled on Napoleon's Concordat and his Organic Articles.

In some Catholic circles, notably among frightened and cowardly prelates, there still lingered memories of the old heretical Febronianism and Josephinism. Prussia's preeminence enhanced the importance of the rationalistic and materialistic universities at the expense of the Catholic universities. Unfortunately in these last, owing to state influence, scepticism and infidelity had made some entrances.

The German Revival was an extraordinary affair. It came from the very heart of the people. Despite the indifferences of the masses, there existed a vital element of priests and humble lay people. Early in this century had occurred the fruitful Viennese apostolate of St. Clement Mary Hofbauer, C.SS.R.; and a few decades later came the tremendous parish-missions of the restored Jesuits, preached in all parts of Catholic Germany. The vital element withstood oppression and prayed for better days. It was not long when their ranks began to receive numbers of distinguished scholars; some were ecclesiastics, but more were laymen, and several of these were converts.

The new recruits were soon the leaders of the revival, inspiring their co-religionists with their own forthright courage. They were militant Catholics, too, and they insisted on being heard in every sphere of learning, culture, and political affairs. Above all, they emphasized the apostolate of the pen for the knowledge and the defense of Catholicism. The unmeasured attacks upon the Church and her new converts, made during the Tercentenary of the Reformation (1817), roused the born Catholics from their torpor to produce energetic refutations in books, pamphlets and periodicals.

Two centers prepared the way for the literary revival. The first was the Munster Circle, under the direction of the Princess Amalie Gallitzin. Two famous authors participating were Count von Stolborg and Frederick Schlegel. One of the chief supporters was the future Archbishop of Cologne, Droste von Vischering. The second center was the Munich Circle, founded by Bishop Johann Sailer and led by Joseph Goerres, the strongest and most gifted champion of Catholic Germany in the field of religious and political matters. Goerres later founded the Munich School, in which he and his coterie of Catholic professors gave German Catholicism the highest intellectual prestige. Catholic leaders from Italy, France, and England visited Munich to meet and take part in discussions with Goerres.

The Cologne Affair was decisive for German Catholics; it welded into close unity all elements of the Revival. Prussia, in 1825, extended to the 1,500,000 Catholics of the Rhine provinces and Westphalia the regulation that the children of mixed marriages must be educated in their father's religion. Already hosts of young, unmarried Prussian executives had been sent into these almost entirely Catholic states; and they were expected to marry young Catholic girls of the area. It would then be only a question of time before the ruling class would be Protestant. The Catholic clergy refused to comply with the order. At the government's request, the bishops asked for instructions from the Holy See. Pius VIII gave the decision; it was that children of mixed marriages were to be educated only in the Catholic religion. His successor, Gregory XVI, confirmed his decision. Thereupon Archbishop von Spiegel of Cologne and three of his suffragan bishops, without any knowledge on the part of the Holy See, entered into a secret conspiracy practically to ignore the papal brief. The Bishop of Trier, one of the signers, repented on his deathbed and informed the Pope of the plot. Bunsen, the official Prussian representative, falsely denied the fact.

Archbishop von Spiegel was eventually succeeded by Clement Droste von Vischering, a prelate of unimpeachable loyalty to the Church. On discovering the secret pact, he sent a declaration to Berlin, announcing that he would carry out the brief of Pius VIII. The government's answer was, on November 30, 1837, to arrest the fearless Archbishop with a great display of military force and imprison him in the fortress of Minden. The following year the Archbishop of Gnesen in Silesia was arrested by the Prussians for the same reason; he was confined in the fortress of Colberg.

The intense excitement caused in Germany and in the entire Catholic world by the arrests of the Archbishops indicated how much public Catholic loyalty had grown in the Catholic Revival. In December, 1837, Gregory XVI gave an allocution on the affair. His words were received enthusiastically by Catholics in Europe and America. The remaining two bishops who had signed the pact withdrew their signatures. The Prussian government tried to justify its measures, but the Holy See published documents which dissolved all contradictions.

The National Council of the American Bishops at Baltimore sent words of admiration and encouragement to the "new Athanasius." Joseph Goerres wrote for the dispute one of his greatest books, giving it the title *Athanasius* to compare the Archbishop of Cologne with the heroic Father of the Church, St. Athanasius of Alexandria. Goerres completely refuted the arguments of the government and of the anti-Catholic press. The Prussian scheme was defeated all along the line, and the old Catholic practice was everywhere restored. The German Catholics would continue to grow from strength to strength to become the admiration of their fellow Catholics throughout the world.

Northern Spring

AT THE OPENING of the nineteenth century, the Catholics of Ireland and Great Britain were emerging from a long night of two hundred and fifty years of persecution. The laws denied them practically every human right. After 1750, a change slowly set in, and by the century's close the worst of the laws had been revoked. Still some very oppressive ones remained, especially those excluding Catholics from membership in Parliament and from high governmental offices. The persecutions of Irish and English Catholics, owing to different local circumstances, varied so much that the sufferings of each group must be treated separately.

In 1800, the Catholics of Ireland numbered slightly more than 3,000,000. They constituted about two-thirds of the whole population. Though not legally slaves, the three million were so, for all practical purposes. They could own neither lands nor cabins. They could rent no more than ten acres, from which they could be evicted on notice. In abject poverty they eked out the barest existence. There were a few exceptions: a handful of Catholic nobles maintaining a tenuous possession of landed estates, and small groups of professional men and merchants in the towns who had achieved a modest competence. But all Catholics were barred from the Irish Parliament and from all civil offices. The sole reason was their Catholic Religion.

The landlords, holders of most of the estates and of the monopoly of political power, were descendants of the anti-Catholic Elizabethan and Cromwellian conquerors. They formed what was called the "Protestant Ascendency"; with some noble exceptions, they were intensely anti-Catholic. Even the best among them, with still rarer exceptions, were adamant for "A Protestant king, a Protestant aristocracy and a Protestant government."

The amelioration of Catholic grievances was prompted by the fear of French invasions, during the American Revolution and especially during the French Revolution. The ameliorations were also due to the contemporary spirit of rationalism, which blunted the religious feelings of Protestants and of Catholics. It was at this time that some of the Catholic nobility and professional men apostatized to retain properties, or to achieve worldly success.

And yet, as this half-century of Catholic relief laws was coming to an end, bloody attacks were being made upon Catholic peasants to drive them from their farms so that they might be replaced by Protestant peasants. Organizations such as the Orange Society (founded in 1795) in the North, and the North Cork Yeomanry in the South, waged a reign of terror against rural Catholics. An insurrection of the outraged Catholics was deliberately provoked by governmental agents and then extinguished in blood.

Hopes for Catholic emancipation were held out to the beaten Irish people to win their support for the union with England. The union came in 1800. Then the hopes and promises were dropped completely.

In the last quarter of the eighteenth century, while England's population totaled 13,000,000, Catholics in England counted only 60,000. They were grouped into four districts, each governed by a vicar-apostolic, a missionary bishop without local title. Many of the Catholics belonged to the nobility and the wealthy class; there was, however, a considerable percentage of servants and laborers in the North and in London. Crushed by centuries of persecution, the English Catholics sought only to be left alone. Newman in his *Second Spring* touchingly describes their furtive lives.

In 1778 and 1791, the British Parliament passed Catholic Relief bills. They were contemporaneous with the Catholic Relief bills passed by the Irish Parliament at the instigation of the British Privy Council. Both series revoked numerous and similar anti-Catholic laws, and both retained similar oppressive laws, notably those excluding Catholics from Parliament and from high offices. Strong opposition greeted the English bill of 1778. A proposal to extend it to Scotland was rejected by the powerful opposition of the Presbyterian clergy and prevented by violent city riots that destroyed Catholic churches and the properties of Catholic merchants. The English opposition was very strong, culminating in the Lord Gordon Riots of 1780.

Lord George Gordon, an eccentric fanatic, organized a demonstration to the House of Commons against the Catholic Relief Bill. His 60,000 followers degenerated into a wild mob that terrorized London for five days. The chapels of the Catholic foreign ambassadors, and other Catholic churches, were torn down; and their altars, sacred vestments and furniture were piled up in the streets and given to the flames. Prominent Catholics and their Protestant friends — especially members of Parliament—were brutally assaulted in the streets; their residences were burned down or looted. Order was restored only when the troops were commanded by King George III to attack the mobs. The riots ceased in a day. The Lord Gordon Riots were the last violent attack upon English Catholics.

During the next three decades, the small body of English Catholics were plagued by internal dissensions. New relief laws were expected; even emancipation was hoped for. In 1782, a small group of laymen, mostly nobles, founded the Catholic Committee to look after Catholic interests in England. From the beginning, the Catholic Committee was distrusted by some of the vicars-apostolic and by large numbers of the clergy and the laity. The reason for the distrust was that the members of the Committee represented the liberal, anti-papal party then prominent in continental countries. Some of their priestly advisers were radicals, and this fact confirmed the suspicions of the majority of the English Catholics. The members of the Committee, though well-meaning, lacked the theological knowledge needed for solving the intricacies of church-state affairs. Further, they tended to usurp the place of the bishops and of the Pope. They arrogated to themselves the conducting of Church affairs independently of the bishops; they also advocated the choosing of bishops by the flocks. Their views on the powers of the Pope and on his infallibility seemed very much like Protestant views.

A bitter conflict broke out on the occasion of a new Catholic Relief bill. The Committee negotiated with the government without the knowledge of the bishops. The crux of the trouble was a new oath for Catholics. Some of the Committee's proposals on the oath were actually heretical. The bishops condemned the oath. The Committee's influence was strong; but it was checkmated by the pamphlets and interviews of Doctor Milner, a priest who was later to be the Vicar-Apostolic of the Midland district. For his heroic services to the Church, Dr. Milner was called "The Athanasius of England."

The orthodox Irish oath of 1778 was acceptable to the bishops, and they succeeded in having it substituted for the offensive and degrading oath that had been first proposed. The Catholic Relief bill was passed in 1791. Though many evil laws were removed, many very distressing statutes were retained, notably the exclusion of Catholics from Parliament and high civil offices. The Catholic Committee was dissolved in 1792. Conflicting views remained and were to break out into much more essential battles in a few years.

After the union of England and Ireland in 1800, Emancipation became a very vital interest for the Catholics of both countries, now that the common Parliament at Westminster alone could abolish penal laws. Most of the struggle would be in Ireland because of its three million Catholics and its thirty bishops. But there would also be intense activity among the sixty thousand English Catholics and their four bishops. Realizing that emancipation could not be much longer delayed, the British government moved for some control over the Catholic Church in Ireland and in England. It sought the power of veto on nominations to bishoprics and also on papal documents entering both realms. The English Catholics were rather willing to concede the veto, so anxious were they for emancipation. But there was one outstanding opponent, Bishop Milner; and he fought the veto unflinchingly in his writings and by his interviews.

The Irish hierarchy chose this intrepid bishop to be their English agent against the veto. His strenuous opposition displeased many of his own countrymen. In 1813, Bishop Milner was expelled from the Catholic Board and was repudiated by his three episcopal colleagues. On the other hand the entire Irish hierarchy publicly thanked Bishop Milner and defended him strongly before the authorities in Rome. A great assembly of the Irish Catholic laity voted their public thanks to the undaunted bishop.

The Irish bishops unanimously and adamantly refused to accept the veto. And they refused just as strongly the government's offer of salaries for the priests. The entire body of the Catholic laity of Ireland, with a few rare exceptions, enthusiastically supported their bishops. The opposition of the Irish bishops, backed by their three million lay people, weighed heavily in the struggle, not only for Irish, but also for English Catholic emancipation. This was evidenced in the Quarantotti incident.

Msgr. Quarantotti was Secretary to the Congregation of the Propaganda and had charge of routine affairs during the imprisonment of Pius VII and the dispersal of the cardinals. He exceeded his authority when, in 1814, he sent a rescript to Dr. Poymter, the Vicar of the London district, advising him and the bishops of both countries to accept the veto. The British bishops, always excepting Dr. Milner, were ready to comply. But in Ireland a perfect storm of opposition arose; every bishop, all the priests, and the vast majority of the laity totally rejected the suggestion. When Pius VII was released, he issued an instruction substantially nullifying Quarantotti's rescript. The veto proposal eventually faded out. The independence of the Catholic Church in Ireland and in England was assured.

Emancipation was finally won by Daniel O'Connell, a devout Catholic and an astute leader. His strong religious convictions gave him the perseverance to overcome the hostility of the Protestant ascendency and the apathy of the downtrodden Catholics. When the government declared his organizations illegal, he founded new ones that surmounted the objections. He kept his enthusiastic followers

JOHN HENRY CARDINAL NEWMAN. Photograph in his later years.

JAMES CARDINAL GIBBONS, Archbishop of Baltimore. For
forty-four years Cardinal Gibbons was the beloved and
revered leader of the American Catholics. He was the sturdy
champion of the workingman.

always law-abiding. To raise funds he established "The Catholic Rent," to which every Catholic was asked to contribute at least a penny a month. This was in the range of the hundreds of thousands of poor peasants, and made them participants in the cause. He also enlisted the cooperation of parish priests, who were the natural leaders of the humble peasants.

The climax came in 1828, when O'Connell sought election for Parliament from County Clare. He openly declared that he would not take the oath against Transubstantiation, which all members of Parliament were required to take. Ignoring all pressures, the Catholic peasants defied eviction and voted for their champion. O'Connell was elected by an overwhelming majority. The government, faced by the alternatives of emancipation or the threat of civil war, passed, in 1829, the Act of Catholic Emancipation. O'Connell was admitted to the House of Commons. The emancipation opened Parliament and most high offices to Catholics. It removed many grievances, but not all. The impoverished Irish peasants, most of the nation, had to pay tithes for the support of the Episcopal Church until its disestablishment in 1871.

In the mid-nineteenth century, two events of great importance occurred for English Catholics. One was the stream of converts flowing from the Oxford Movement; the other was the re-establishment of the hierarchy. When John Henry Newman and his devout Oxford scholars sought to revivify the moribund Established Church, they found their ideal church in the Catholic Church of Rome. They bravely sacrificed their careers and made their submission to that Church (1845). Some 800 ministers and lay persons followed them. In a few years the stream of converts increased to many thousands. It continues to this day. The converts brought high culture and new vigor to the furtive, though ever faithful, older Catholics. Let one example be cited: the great literary figure and loving spirit of Cardinal John Henry Newman.

In 1850, Pius IX elevated Bishop Wiseman, Vicar of the London district, to be Cardinal Archbishop of Westminster; he also appointed eight suffragan bishops. The Holy Father thus re-established the English Catholic hierarchy. He was careful to pick out new titles for the appointees, none of which were in use in the Established Church. But wild protests were raised. Some 7,000 noisy demonstrations, at which effigies of the Pope and the Cardinal were burnt, were held before the year was out. Cardinal Wiseman issued an appeal to the English people. His calm, powerful reasoning allayed the storm and brought home to the English Protestant people that the Pope's action was a purely domestic affair for Catholics and had not a single design against the Established Church. The turmoil quickly died down. A period of remarkable growth ensued for the English Catholics.

Italian Unification and the Roman Question

THE IDEA of Italian unification arose towards the end of the eighteenth century, possibly in resistance to Napoleon's invading armies. Before long the intense nationalism of the French troops had so far impressed the defenders that they began to aspire to an Italian nationalism. This last could only be realized by a union of the age-old sovereignties that ruled the Italian peninsula. These were: in the north, the Kingdom of Sardinia-Piedmont, the Duchies of Milan, Tuscany, Parma and Modena, and the Republic of Venice; in the center, the Papal States; in the south, the Kingdom of the Two Sicilies (Naples and the island of Sicily).

Unification would be extremely difficult. Its problems were complicated further by the boundary adjustments of the Congress of Vienna (1814-1815), which gave to the Hapsburg Emperor of Austria the Duchy of Milan (Lombardy) and the territories of Venezia. The adjustments also installed Hapsburg archdukes, the Emperor's kindred, as dukes of Tuscany, Parma and Modena. The Congress of Vienna thus made Austria the most powerful force in the Italian peninsula, and Austria was inimical to unification.

Unwittingly the Congress gave the proponents of unification a strong rallying point: they could now claim to be the champions of Italian independence against foreign domination. And Austria, with deep internal problems and powerful rivals, was by no means as mighty a power as she appeared to be.

Regionalism was the outstanding feature of the Italian scene. The seven sovereignties that had ruled for centuries in the peninsula varied markedly in traditions, customs and temperament. Even though the splendid Italian literature was the common treasure of all, the language of the people differed from place to place because of the dialects which prevailed. As regards the economy, a new variation appeared in the second quarter of the nineteenth century: a manufacturing economy in the industrialized Sardinia-Piedmont, and the old agricultural economy in the rest of the peninsula.

How was unification to be achieved? Should Italy be a federal union, or a single centralized state? Should Italy be a monarchy, or a republic? More perplexing were the questions: How would the Papal States fit into the unification? What would become of the Pope?

Of all the Italian governments, that of the Papal States was the oldest; founded in 750, it had been in existence for eleven hundred years. Its fundamental purpose was unique, the maintaining of the religious independence of the Pope. Some of the medieval emperors had tried to stretch their protectorate into a domination of the Holy See. Each had failed. In more recent times Napoleon had abolished the ancient state. When he changed his Italian conquests into departments of France, he had included the Papal States. He had named Rome "The Second City of the Empire," to rank after Paris. However, his Italian plans had evaporated after Waterloo.

In the mid-nineteenth century, some distinguished Italians proposed a federal union under the presidency of the Pope. The plan was hardly realistic. The Pope could not be the civil head of a great national state. He was, first and last, the religious ruler of the universal Church, which embraced millions of communicants, drawn from every nationality. His complete independence must be evident to all. Hence the fundamental purpose of the papal lands was the guaranteeing of that independence. The extent of the papal territories would depend upon the circumstances of particular times.

Trying to reconcile independent papal lands with a centralized United Italy produced an agonizing dilemma for countless Italians, loyally patriotic and devotedly Catholic. And so the perplexing Roman Question arose. It would last for a century until its solution by the Lateran Treaty (1929). The splendid Roman avenue, constructed to commemorate the Lateran Treaty, the Via della Conciliazione, leading up to the Piazza San Pietro, testifies to the excellence and the general acceptance of the Lateran solution — the Vatican City State, hardly bigger than a large city park, an independent token-state that clearly emphasizes the necessary neutrality of the Pope. Excellent solutions, especially in Church and State affairs, often imply the gravest problems and the strongest conflicts; but they also imply the most profound faith and the most constant prayer.

The grave problems have been stated, the strong conflicts must now be considered. Later the profound faith and the constant praying of the Italian Catholics will be described. In Italy, as in every European country of the nineteenth century, anti-clericalism held a powerful attraction for certain intellectuals, or pseudo-intellectuals. Some became Voltairian opponents, and others Rousseaunian revolutionists. The armies of the French Directory, wherever they marched, spread French revolutionary ideas. This was especially true in the satellite republics they set up in Italy. These armies were preceded, or followed, by the anti-religious French Masonic lodges in whose secret meetings were planned the wars on Catholicism. Napoleon, despite his opportunist gestures towards the Faith, and his imperial patronage of religion, was an anti-papalist.

The masses of the people remained loyal to the Holy Father, as is evidenced by their opposition to the Directory's Roman Republic, and by their enthusiastic welcome of

Pius VII, as he returned from Fontainebleau. Austria's preponderance in the Italian peninsula after the Congress of Vienna, as was noted, aroused many recruits for the unification. Austria's protection of the Papal States during revolutionary outbreaks unfortunately gave the false impression of an alliance of the Pope with a foreign foe of unification. The anti-clericals exploited this impression to obtain a leading position in the unifying movement.

Only a brief summarization of the events of the unification can be given here. The first attempt, that of the Carbonari in 1820, ended in failure. The second attempt, that of the Young Italy movement, led by Mazzini in 1848 and 1849, ended in the short-lived Republic of Rome and in the flight of Pius IX to Gaeta in Naples.

The third movement was the successful one. It was led by the King of Sardinia, Victor Emmanuel II. Actually, it was the work of his able Prime Minister, Count Cavour, a bourgeois liberal. In 1859, the armies of Sardinia and her ally, Emperor Louis Napoleon III of France, drove the Austrians out of Lombardy and almost all of Venezia. Within two years the Sardinians had taken over the whole of the peninsula, including the Kingdom of the Two Sicilies, and all the Papal States except Rome and a small area around the city. In 1861, the Kingdom of Italy, with Victor Emmanuel II as its king, was proclaimed. Florence was made the capital. Pius IX held on to Rome and its environs, but only because of the French army which the Catholics of France had forced Louis Napoleon to send for the Pope's protection. In 1870, the Franco-Prussian War forced the withdrawal of this French army. The Italian troops marched on Rome. On September 20, they captured the city and ended the temporal sovereignty of the Popes. Rome was proclaimed the capital of United Italy.

Moral protest was the only course left to Pope Pius IX. He had condemned the excesses of the revolutionaries in the unification movement, and he had excommunicated (without naming names) the destroyers of the Papal States. Now, upon the fall of Rome, he issued a solemn protest against the deprivation of his means of protecting his spiritual independence in directing the universal Church. Further, he published the decree *Non expedit,* forbidding Catholics to vote or to take part in the new government. Then he voluntarily made himself the "Prisoner of the Vatican."

The Italian parliament in 1871 passed the Law of Guarantees, which provided: (1) the Pope was accorded the prerogatives of sovereignty, and his person was declared inviolable; (2) three palaces were given to the Pope, and an annual pension of $650,000.

Pius IX rejected the Law of Guarantees as a unilateral settlement, merely a parliamentary act which was revocable by another parliamentary act and hence no permanent guarantee at all. He refused the pension. The Pope's distrust was confirmed by the subsequent numerous anti-clerical and anti-Catholic laws. These were the reasons why his successor, Pope Leo XIII, the most conciliatory of modern Popes, maintained the policies of Pius IX: constant protests, seclusion in the Vatican, and retention of the *Non expedit* decree. True, the prohibition for Catholics against being elected or electors left a free field to liberal, radical and, later, socialist persecutors, but it also developed a disciplined Catholic body. Time, as always, was with the Church.

It would be painful and useless to enumerate the persecutory laws enacted against Italian Catholics, especially when the radical leftists were in power. Similar programs were being implemented by their revolutionary brethren in other Catholic countries. All were descendants of Voltaire and Rousseau, of secularist liberals and Marxian socialists.

The programs suppressed religious orders and confiscated their properties; laicized education at all levels, but especially in the primary schools; demanded the faculty for the state to confirm the appointment of bishops; harassed the public worship of the Church; forced priests and seminarians into military service; and destroyed Catholic charitable and social societies. These nefarious laws were accompanied by vile attacks from the anti-Catholic press, and by premeditated insulting demonstrations.

Perhaps the worst was the attack upon the casket of Pius IX. On the night of July 12-13, 1881, while the remains of Pope Pius IX were being quietly transferred from the

Vatican to their final resting place in the church of St. Lawrence-outside-the-walls, a mob of ruffians, abetted by the police, attacked the cortege with the avowed intention of throwing the casket of Pope Pius into the Tiber. The outrage was foiled by courageous young Catholic men of Rome, who fought a desperate street battle with the ruffians and saved the corpse of the saintly Pontiff from the disgraceful insult.

In the solution of the Roman Question, of vital importance was the profound faith of the Italian Catholic people. This is a fact which has not been sufficiently recognized. It was obscured by the noisy machinations of anti-clerical revolutionaries, actually and always a clamorous minority. The quiet, prayerful lives of the majority manifested their intense loyalty to Catholicism.

Holiness is one of the first tests of genuine religion. From 1815 to 1915, there dwelt in Italy forty-four persons who have been raised to the altars of the Church. Twenty-three have been canonized and twenty-one, beatified. Eight of these were martyrs in China. Here only a few can be cited: St. John Bosco, friend of street urchins, social reformer, teacher, founder of the Salesians; St. Frances Xavier Cabrini, missionary of the continents; St. Pius X, apostle of the Eucharist, defender of the Faith; and Bl. Anna Maria Taigi, devoted wife, mother of seven children, mystic and constant helper of the sick poor.

Another testimony to the deep faith of the majority was the extraordinary growth of religious congregations in Italy during the period, 1815 to 1915, when three hundred new congregations for women were founded, and almost as many for men. Most notable were the Salesians, founded by St. John Bosco, and the Salesian Sisters, founded by St. John Bosco and St. Maria Mazzarello. Today both congregations are worldwide and together total 40,000 members.

The foreign mission apostolate had a special appeal to the loyal Italian Catholics of this period. Their missionary priests and nuns, many driven from their country, served zealously on numerous frontiers of Catholicism, and on none more than in China, Argentina, California and the Rocky Mountain areas of the United States.

In their own homeland of Italy, loyal Catholics advanced solid projects of social reform—all based on Christian principles—that still attract the attention of moderns. Their theologians held leading parts in the revival and adaptation of St. Thomas' theological views. Their apologists courageously and untiringly defended the Church in their journals, such as the *Civiltà Cattolica,* from all the bitter attacks of her enemies. In the long struggle they would not be defeated, for they sailed in the timeless barque of Peter. Their strength grew until it helped mightily in bringing on the solution of the Lateran Treaty, the Vatican City State.

Pius IX: Helmsman in the Storm

IN A RECENT chapter, it was stated that the hundred years from the fall of Napoleon to the outbreak of World War I constituted a very sad century for the Catholic Church. The Liberals, heirs of the Enlightenment and sons of the French Revolution, continually and throughout Europe raised tumultuous storms against the Barque of Peter. The might of Protestant Prussia and the power of autocratic Russia moved ominously toward its obliteration. The remnants of Germanic Febronianism still strove to enchain it. Even the course of certain Catholic Liberals was but a dragging of it towards destruction on the shoals and reefs of compromise and confusion.

Liberalism and Revolution eventually faded as spent forces. But into the maelstrom swept fiercer storms, Nationalism and Communism.

Nationalism was a gross caricature of a beautiful virtue, the patriotic love for one's country. The extreme nationalistic state first crushed the rights of its own citizens, and then embarked upon a selfish aggrandizement of power and wealth at the cost of whatever nations lay in its path, all the time fostering hatred and detestation against the peoples of such nations. It waged wars of spoliation which in the final analysis could only lead to universal anarchy.

Such Nationalism developed into a quasi-religion, having for its supreme good the earthly exaltation of the nation. Such Nationalism could only be the complete contradiction of Christianity and its divine Founder, Jesus, who died for all men.

Modern Communism, "Scientific Socialism," as its countless followers call it, was introduced by three events: the issuance by Karl Marx, in 1848, of the *Communist Manifesto;* the organization by him, in 1854, of the *First International Association of Workingmen;* and his publication, in 1867, of the first volume of his famous book, *Das Kapital.* Here is not the place to discuss the economic theories and the social proposals of Marxian Communism. What is of the utmost importance is the recognition of its fundamental philosophy. And that philosophy is a complete materialism, which absolutely rejects God, the human soul and all spirituality. Marx started from a purely materialistic conception of history, according to which all politics, religious and moral phenomena are but states of a process of evolution. His theories of economic determinism and of necessary class-struggle are totally opposed to Christian morals and charity. Marx was a complete atheist, and so were all the outstanding leaders of "Scientific Socialism." He and they were dedicated enemies of Catholicism.

Almost from the beginning, Marxian Communism spread widely among the working classes. Strange as it may seem, the Bourgeois Liberals were the chief reason for this spread. They had garnered most of the wealth of the new industrialism, at the expense of the workingmen, who were reduced in the process to the state of a poverty-haunted proletariat. Moreover, by their attacks on religion and their destruction of religious education, the Bourgeois Liberals had dehumanized and de-Christianized whole areas among the proletariat. Dr. MacCaffrey cogently points out these facts in his *History of the Catholic Church in the Nineteenth Century,* Volume II, p. 500ff.:

"The prevalence of irreligious views and of antagonism to all forms of positive religion among the ruling classes, and in the universities and seats of learning, was bound to have its effect on the masses of the people.... Materialism and atheism were undoubtedly the basis for the system sketched by Marx, and go far to explain the success which Socialist agitation achieved during the nineteenth century.... In many respects Socialism is but the logical consequence of Liberalism, however much Liberals may protest against such a close connection. It was Liberalism which rendered most of the universities of the world centers for the propagation of atheism and infidelity. It was Liberalism which sought, and seeks, to drive religion from the schools and colleges, and to introduce in its place some vague species of moral instruction separated from all dogmatic beliefs, and unavailing as a deterrent of crime because deprived of divine sanction...."

While all the external storms were raging, the Church's defense was hampered by proposals of certain extremists among the Catholic Liberals, which would reject or curtail the authority of the Holy See. These proposals aimed at certain changes in ecclesiastical doctrine and discipline in accordance with the anti-ecclesiastical liberal Protestant theory and atheistic "science and enlightenment" prevailing at the time.

One group objected to revival of scholastic philosophy, and advocated the freedom of philosophical and historical investigation from the control of theology or of ecclesiastical authority. Such views were opposed by loyal Catholic scholars who urged the importance of returning to the system of philosophy which had been identified so long with Catholic teaching; they also urged the necessity of controlling the conclusions of philosophical and historical studies by the supreme authority in the Church.

Through the tempestuous seas, under the darkening skies, against the relentless attacks, the Barque of Peter was kept on a steady course by its helmsman, Pope Pius IX. The sovereign Pontiff aimed at a reaffirming of the *Magisterium* of the Catholic Church, and at a rallying of all the sons and daughters of the Church to enthusiastic support of the *Magisterium*.[1] Let it be recalled that Christ Himself established the

---

1. The *Magisterium,* technically, is the office of teaching and safeguarding the truths of the Faith, bestowed on the Pope and the bishops by Christ.

POPE PIUS IX

Felici

POPE LEO XIII

Felici

VATICAN COUNCIL I. A nineteenth-century print.

Magisterium when He commanded His apostles to teach all nations whatsoever He had taught them — promising that He would remain with them even to the consummation of the world — and when He declared that the Holy Spirit would teach them all truth and abide with them forever.

The reaffirming of the *Magisterium* was achieved first by a striking exercise of its teaching power, then by a public listing of the contemporary heresies opposed to the Catholic Church, and finally by a clear and exact definition of the foremost component of the *Magisterium*, the infallibility of the Pope.

The exercise of the *Magisterium's* teaching power was the definition of the Immaculate Conception of the Blessed Virgin Mary. In 1849, Pope Pius IX issued a letter to the bishops of the Church requesting them to explain their views and the opinions of their flocks on the subject of the Immaculate Conception. The replies of most of the bishops were favorable to the definition. The Pope then appointed a commission of learned theologians to examine the replies and the tradition of the Church. After the theological commission had submitted its report, a number of bishops were invited to be present in Rome for the definition.

On December 8, 1854, Pius IX solemnly promulgated the Bull, *Ineffabilis Deus*, by which it was defined as of Catholic faith that the Blessed Virgin Mary in the first moment of her conception was preserved from all taint of original sin.

The Pope's definition *implied* Papal infallibility, since he acted not with cooperation of a general council, but by his own independent and sovereign authority in laying down a doctrine which must be accepted by the whole Catholic Church. The definition of the Immaculate Conception was received with enthusiasm. Hardly a dissentient voice was raised either against the doctrine itself, or against the action of the Pope. The apparition at Lourdes, and the century of miracles and of enormous pilgrimages at the Grotto, certainly manifested divine approval.

The listing of contemporary errors appeared on December 8, 1864, in a document entitled: "A Syllabus containing the most important errors of our time, which have been condemned by our Holy Father, Pius IX, in allocutions, at consistories, in encyclicals, and other apostolic letters." The listing contains eighty erroneous propositions, selected from condemnations found in thirty-two papal documents.

The reception of the Syllabus among Catholics was assured by the love and obedience which they bore towards the Vicar of Christ. No sooner had it made its appearance than it was solemnly accepted in national and provincial councils by the episcopate of the whole Church. But by the enemies of the Church, the Syllabus was received far differently. No papal utterance had stirred up such a commotion for years. Many professed to see in the Syllabus a formal rejection of modern culture and a declaration of war by the Pope on the modern state.

Anthony J. Haag, S.J., sums up the significance of the great document in the old *Catholic Encyclopedia* (1912), Vol. XIV, p. 369: "The importance of the Syllabus lies in its opposition to the high tide of that intellectual movement of the nineteenth century which strove to sweep away the foundations of all human and divine order. The Syllabus is not only the defense of the inalienable rights of God, of the Church, and of truth against the abuse of the words *freedom* and *culture* on the part of unbridled Liberalism, but it is also a protest, earnest and energetic, against the attempt to eliminate the influence of the Catholic Church on the life of nations and of individuals, on the family and the school. In its nature, it is true, the Syllabus is negative and condemnatory; but it received its complement in the decisions of the Vatican Council I and in the encyclicals of Leo XIII. It is precisely its fearless character that perhaps accounts for its influence on the life of the Church toward the end of the nineteenth century; for it threw a sharp, clear light upon reef and rock in the intellectual currents of the time."

Reaffirmation of the *magisterium* was completed by the First Vatican Council's dogmatic decrees, especially the one defining papal infallibility. In 1867, Pius IX indicated his intention of summoning a general council. His intention was met with most vociferous opposition from Catholic "Liberals" who had protested against the Syllabus. They dreaded the possibility of the Council's defining papal infallibility, though the Council was not being summoned for that purpose. The denial of papal infallibility was one of the chief doctrinal errors of the times; it struck at the validity of the pontifical acts of the last three hundred years, it weakened the effects of contemporary papal decisions, and it endangered the very root of faith.

At once opposition within the Church was organized to counteract the Pope; its activities were loudly applauded by the entire anti-Catholic press. Some of the opposition even sought the intervention of secular powers to prevent the Council's existence. But in the face of all clamor, on December 8, 1869, Pius IX solemnly opened the Vatican Council. One of the first acts of the council fathers was their definite profession of the faith that the Council of Trent had proclaimed. A second act was their definition of the supernatural order, with a condemnation of the opposing errors.

The plans of the opposition received a mighty check when some five hundred bishops petitioned the Holy See to permit a proposal for the definition of papal infallibility. The council fathers were practically unanimous as to the doctrine itself. A minority, about a sixth of the Council, held that the definition was inopportune. The opposition outside the Council now raised a furious journalistic attack. But their bitterness failed completely.

After a full and fair deliberation, the Dogma of Papal Infallibility was defined on July 18, 1870. The vote of the Council was 533 to 1. Fifty-five bishops of the opposition were permitted by Pope Pius to leave Rome before the vote. Every one of these bishops shortly afterwards gave a public acceptance of the definition as an article of Faith. Two hundred bishops, who had been unable to take part in the Council, immediately sent in their adhesion.

Everywhere, in all continents, local councils and synods unanimously and immediately accepted the decree. The Catholic laity matched the enthusiastic loyalty of the clergy. Only a pitiful handful of stubborn intellectuals, priests and laymen, left the Catholic Church. Their minimal church quickly faded into obscurity. The first Vatican Council had rallied the whole body of Catholics to a loyalty unprecedented in the history of the Church.

The
Kulturkampfs

REVIVING CATHOLICISM was severely tested during the half-century following Vatican Council I, by ferocious attacks aimed at its enslavement, even at its obliteration. The German adversaries named their campaign *Der Kulturkampf* (the Struggle for Civilization). When the label is used in the singular form, it designates the German conflict only. But it can be used in a plural and less distinctive sense of all the other anti-Catholic campaigns, for their objectives and their methods were the same as those of the Germanic onslaught.

"Civilization" had the same meaning for all the attackers: the laic and secular culture, the materialistic and rationalistic world of Bourgeois Liberalism, with its exaggerated scientism, its state absolutism that overruled the sanctuary, and its greedy ever-extending nationalism. The German Kulturkampf will be treated first; it was the most powerful of all.

Prince von Bismarck was the author of the German Kulturkampf. In 1871, he suppressed the Catholic section in the ministry of worship of the Kingdom of Prussia, the largest state in the Empire, larger than all the others put together. Bismarck was Prime Minister of Prussia as well as Chancellor of the new German Empire. Prince Bismarck claimed that the unity of the Empire demanded the nationalization of the Catholic Church and her subjection to the State. He entertained the hope of winning the German hierarchy to his plans. But he was completely disappointed; the German bishops, instead, with singular loyalty, accepted all the decrees of the recently completed Vatican Council.

The Iron Chancellor then determined to dominate the Catholic hierarchy by force. Besides suppressing the Catholic section of the Prussian ministry of worship, he put all pulpit utterances under surveillance. Shortly afterwards he expelled the Jesuits, and with them the so-called affiliated congregations (Redemptorists, Christian Brothers, Vincentians and Religious of the Sacred Heart). All Catholic seminaries were closed; and the students were required to attend courses of philosophy, literature and history in the state universities and to pass state examinations. On the other hand, apostate and excommunicated priests were given government protection, and a number of Catholic churches were turned over to the recently formed sect of "The Old Catholics."

The government's animus was manifested in Bismarck's announcement: "Whatever we shall do, be assured of this, that we shall never go to Canossa." His reference was to the celebrated self-imposed penance of the medieval German Emperor, Henry IV, before Pope St. Gregory VII at Canossa in Tuscany. The resistance of the Catholics was characterized by the reply of their leader, Ludwig Windthorst:

"We hear that it is to be a question of war to the knife against us; we on our part are desirous of peace, but if you insist upon war, why, then you shall have it." And the German Catholics—bishops, clergy and people—rose as one man for their faith. Every measure of religious tyranny was met by the protests of the clergy, jointly or individually, and by the passive but effective condemnations of the laity.

In the Reichstag, the imperial parliament, the battles for the Church were heroically fought by the Catholic Center Party under the direction of Windthorst and Mallinckrodt. Small in the beginning, the Center Party was overwhelmed in every roll call of votes. Yet in the midst of all defeats, they never ceased to enunciate boldly the principles of law and truth, and they never let their strong cohesion weaken in the least.

After some years, increases in their numbers gave them the balance of power in the Reichstag. In every question that concerned religion, the Center Party stood undauntedly and unyieldingly the champion of the Church in Germany. In this mighty struggle of the bishops, priests and laymen of Catholic Germany, Pius IX never ceased in his encouragement of these brave children of St. Boniface.

For his chief aide in the Kulturkampf, Bismarck appointed an ultra-liberal, Dr. Falk, to be his minister of worship. Dr. Falk was directly responsible for the whole anti-Catholic legislation. These iniquitous laws, passed for several years in the month of May (hence their name, the May Laws), suppressed every free exercise of papal jurisdiction in Germany, prevented the authorities of the Church from punishing disobedient members, deprived the bishops of free appointment to benefices and forced them to submit to the government the names of candidates.

Any bishop or priest who, in exercising the functions of his sacred office or in administering the sacraments to his people, transgressed the restrictions of the May Laws, was first fined for every single case, then deprived of his income, and finally imprisoned or exiled either from a specified district or from the Empire.

Pius IX, in his encyclical of February 5, 1875, declared the May Laws null and void, because they were directed against the divine Constitution of the Church. Falk retorted by restricting all state support and exemption from military service to the sect of the Old Catholics and to such clergymen alone as should subscribe to the May Laws, offering thus a reward for apostasy.

Under the operation of the May Laws, all the bishops and 1,770 priests were imprisoned, exiled, or died without being replaced; 9,000 religious, 7,763 of them women, were driven from their peaceful homes into misery and destitution, *after* the expulsion of the Jesuits and affiliated orders; 601 parishes, comprising 664,697 souls, were entirely destitute of spiritual care, while 584 other parishes with over 1,500,000 souls were inadequately served.

And yet before the passing of a single decade, the mighty Kulturkampf had ground to an ineffectual stop. The loyalty of the German Catholics to the Church and to the Holy Father remained unshaken. Not one theological student had enrolled in the course of studies prepared by the government. Not one state-appointed priest obtained episcopal recognition. The handful of priests who submitted to the May Laws

WILHELM
EMMANUEL, BARON
VON KETTELER,
Bishop of Mainz.
Pioneer in social
reform and
champion of the
working classes.

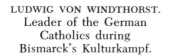

LUDWIG VON WINDTHORST.
Leader of the German
Catholics during
Bismarck's Kulturkampf.

was truly insignificant. In the whole Kingdom of Prussia, such clerics numbered scarcely twenty; and they were shunned by the Catholic people as traitors.

In the dioceses deprived of their pastors, the episcopal powers were extended by the exiled bishops to delegates unknown to the public but promptly obeyed by the Catholics. The Bishop of Paderborn personally administered his diocese from Belgium.

Archbishop Ledochowski of Gnesen-Posen, in the part of Poland then held by Prussia, heroically defied all the persecutions, especially the order that all religious instruction in the schools must be given in German and not in Polish. He was fined several times and then ordered by the state to resign his bishopric. He was arrested and confined in the dungeon of Ostrowo. Pius IX's reply was to raise the heroic prelate, though still in prison, to the Cardinalate. The Prussian government declared him deposed from his bishopric and in a short time exiled him from the kingdom. Cardinal Ledochowski found refuge in Rome. From the Eternal City, the banished prelate continued to rule his archdiocese. An association of his young priests secretly discharged their pastoral duties in the vacant parishes. Espionage and priest-hunts proved of little avail and soon fell into universal contempt.

By 1878, the defeat of the Kulturkampf was evident. Bismarck himself realized that he was completely checked by the unflinching loyalty to their faith of the German Catholics. The government was not unwilling to come to terms, if only some face-saving opportunity were offered. The opportunity came with the election of Pope Leo XIII. On the very day of his election, the new Pontiff addressed a letter to the Emperor in which he expressed his sorrow at the strained relations existing between the German Empire and the Catholic Church. Bismarck seized the chance to open negotiations. He was on his way to *Canossa.*

As has been noted, there were in the last half of the nineteenth century several other kulturkampfs, although the term was never applied to them. They occurred in France, Italy, Spain, Portugal, Austria, Hungary and the Latin-American republics. They varied in duration and intensity, but all were aimed at the destruction of Catholicism, and all were directed by the Grand Orients, or similar governing bodies of European anti-clerical Freemasonry.

The French attack became the exemplar for all the rest. It was the longest, lasting from 1879 to 1914; it was the bitterest; and it inflicted the worst damages upon the Catholic Church. One of the chief reasons for its successes was the hopeless political fragmentation of the French Catholics on the question of the old Monarchy and the Third Republic. In vain did Pope Leo XIII beg them as a matter of vital practicality to accept the Republic, so that Catholics could work with better-minded Liberals for the obtaining of justice for Catholicism. The divisions were too deeply rooted. Needless to say, the ruling clique of anti-clericals and their allies, the growing Socialists, would give no hearing to Pope Leo's efforts for reconciliation.

Relentlessly the enemies of Jesus Christ and His religion moved toward their goals: a laic educational system, a laic society and a laic world. Step by step, they banished all religious education from all schools, colleges and universities. They suppressed all religious orders and congregations; the Jesuits were the first to be abolished. They even expelled the nursing sisters from the hospitals. They persecuted the secular priests, drafting the seminarians and the priests into the armed forces and compelling them to serve the full periods as combat soldiers. They confiscated the properties and resources of all the religious: priests, brothers and nuns.

By the laws of 1901, 1902 and 1904—especially by the Law of Associations—they completed their work. There was not a religious house left in France. Nor was a single religious—priest, brother or nun—permitted to live and practice his or her vocation in France.

What happened to these religious men and women, who now without resources were so heartlessly thrust out upon the world? With sorrowing hearts they set out upon the lonely road of exile. But God blessed their sacrifices. In a very short time they were accomplishing wonders spreading His kingdom in Canada, the United States, the

British Isles, and almost everywhere in the fields afar of the Catholic missions.

It only remained for the anti-clericals to break off official relations with the Holy See, and to abolish the concordat, and their work of decatholicizing France would be completed. By a series of petty maneuvers, the government broke off diplomatic relations with the Vatican in 1904. In the following year, it abrogated the concordat and passed the law accomplishing the separation of Church and State.

Who now owned the cathedrals, the churches, the episcopal residences, the rectories, the seminaries, the schools and the properties, movable and immovable, of these institutions? The anti-clerical government answered that it was not the Church, since the Church no longer existed in the eyes of the law, but it was the State. To hold such properties and to manage them, the government proposed setting up Associations of Worship. These associations were to be responsible only to the State, and they were to be entirely independent of the bishops. They were given complete control; they might obstruct the bishops, and they might produce schisms.

Pope St. Pius X solemnly condemned the Associations of Worship as opposed to the Constitution of the Church. The bishops of France unanimously accepted his decision. As scarcely any Associations were formed, the government dropped the project. However, the government ordered the clergy to seek the permission of the civil authorities for the holding of religious services. Pius X forbade any compliance with such an order. The entire clergy of France faithfully accepted his directive.

The separation of Church and State was the darkest hour in the decatholicizing of France. But shortly, brightness began to appear, and it grew steadily and surely. A new courageous spirit was animating the clergy and the faithful laity; it was a spirit nurtured in the wisdom of Leo XIII's encyclicals and intensified in the heroic firmness of St. Pius X. French Catholicism, robbed of its material resources, grew in moral power and spiritual vitality. Liberated from the domination of civil politicians, it became most loyal to the Holy See.

Voluntary associations, established in most of the French dioceses, raised funds for the maintenance of public worship, and for the support of the clergy. Similarly efforts were made, and with considerable success, to raise funds to re-establish several of the free primary schools closed by the suppression of the religious congregations.

Anti-Christian legislation was widely ignored in France. Fanatical anti-clericalism began to fade; it had brought only division and shame to the nation. It ceased to be a powerful force during World War I. On the other hand, the rejuvenated Catholics continued advancing, bringing most dedicated and most valuable services not only to the Church in France but to the Church Universal and to the Holy Father.

Modernism

ORDINARILY, MODERNISM MEANS an acceptance of what is deemed modern; it generally involves a distaste for what is considered out-of-date. In the first decade of the twentieth century, Modernism became the technical title for a contemporary Rationalistic movement. In general, one might say that this Modernism aimed at the radical transformation of human thought in relation to God, man, the world, and life—here and hereafter—which had been prepared by Humanism and the eighteenth-century Enlightenment, and was solemnly promulgated at the French Revolution. Through the following century the movement was effected by further rejections of dogma by Liberal sceptics.

Modernism, though possessing neither a definitive creed nor an organization, fostered agnosticism, rationalism, higher criticism of the Bible, and the theory of the evolution of religion.

Doctor MacCaffrey summarizes Modernism thus: "The system of Modernism...was clearly a reaction against authority and in favor of individualism. In the place of the motives of credibility usually put forward as a groundwork for Christian revelation, and of the external teaching authority of the Church, it endeavored to set up the inner consciousness and experience of the individual as the basis and criterion of faith; and instead of regarding the Catholic dogmas as absolute and objective, it looked upon them merely as relative and varying formulas by which the individual endeavors to express the inner manifestation of the divinity. By confining human knowledge to the knowable or phenomenal world, and faith to the unknowable world, all possibility of a conflict between faith and reason, it was contended, was finally removed." So one could hold that Jesus, in the world of reality, was only a man; but in the world of faith one could pray to Jesus as God.

St. Pius X in his decree *Lamentabili* lists for condemnation sixty-five modernist propositions. The greater number concern the Holy Scriptures, their inspiration, and the doctrine of Jesus and of the apostles, while others relate to dogma, the sacraments, and the primacy of the Bishop of Rome. The last erroneous proposition, the sixty-fifth, is especially significant: "Modern Catholicism can be reconciled with true science only if it is transformed into a non-dogmatic Christianity; that is to say, into a broad and liberal Protestantism." [1]

A remodelling, a renewal according to the ideas of the twentieth century—such was the purpose of the modernists. Loisy, their foremost leader, declared that avowed modernists aimed "to adapt Catholicism to the intellectual, moral and social needs of today." The spirit of this plan of reform may be summarized under the following heads:

(1) a spirit of complete emancipation, tending to weaken ecclesiastical authority; the emancipation of science, which must traverse every field of investigation without fear of conflict with the Church; the emancipation of the State, which should never be hampered by religious authority; the emancipation of the private conscience, whose inspiration must not be overridden by papal definitions and anathemas (excommunications); the emancipation of the universal conscience, with which the Church should be ever in agreement;

(2) a spirit of movement and change, with an inclination to a sweeping form of evolution such as abhors anything fixed and stationary;

(3) a spirit of reconciliation among all men through the *feelings* of the heart, a process in which logical reasoning played no part.

Many of the modernists favored an understanding between the different Christian religions on a basis of agreement that must be superior to "mere doctrinal differences."

1. *Encyclical Letter of Pope Pius X, On the Doctrines of the Modernists (Pascendi Dominici Gregis)* and *Syllabus, Condemning the Errors of the Modernists (Lamentabili Sane)* Available from the Daughters of St. Paul, 50 St. Paul's Ave., Jamaica Plain, Boston, Ma. 02130.

Concluding this necessarily brief summary of the essential principles of Modernism, one could say that this system, if accepted, would erase all Catholic teachings in the vital areas of philosophy, theology, Sacred Scriptures, and the history of religions. So St. Pius X, in his encyclical *Pascendi*, "On the Doctrines of the Modernists," wrote: "And now with our eyes fixed upon the whole system, no one will be surprised that we should define it to be the synthesis of all heresies." [2]

The storm raised up against the Church by Modernism was one of the most severe that she has ever had to sustain. It persisted through two decades, the last of the nineteenth century and the first of the twentieth. The most vital teachings were attacked: the validity of the Bible, the Godhead of Jesus, the actuality of the Church, its sacraments and its infallibility. The prospects were indeed alarming; rationalistic biblical criticism, sceptical church history, false philosophies and false theologies were infecting the young priests and the seminaries. If through them the infection were to pass to the people, the loss of faith would be appalling.

The proponents of Modernism were particularly active in France and in Italy, though a few also worked in other countries. Modernism was never an organized sect with a definite creed and an official leadership. Rather it was a movement, a collection of small groups, or cliques, of various rationalistic views. They wielded considerable influence among sections of the clergy and the Catholic intelligentsia. Foremost among the leaders were Abbè Loisy in France; Father Tyrrell, an English ex-Jesuit, in France and England; and Don Buonaiutti in Italy.

The movement was opposed most vigorously by orthodox Catholics, who were numerous and vocal. For some years a furious literary war raged; books, pamphlets, articles (in old reviews and in new reviews) flooded Europe. Even great secular journals entered into the conflict.

But when the debates echoed in the seminaries and in the pulpits, the time for decisive action had come. The hierarchies of Italy and of France began issuing pastorals of warning against incipient heresies that would raise havoc

2. *Encyclical Letter of Pope Pius X, Pascendi Dominici Gregis*, above printing, p. 48.

POPE ST. PIUS X

with the faith of the Catholic people, especially with the faith of the simplest.

In his very first encyclical, Pope Pius X affirmed that he would take the utmost care to guard the clergy from being ensnared by certain new proposals in scriptural studies, theology and history which were but preparing the way for rationalism. Giuseppe Sarto was one of the kindest of men, and one of the meekest too, but he could be the sternest and the most adamant when the faith of his Catholic flock was in serious jeopardy.

Of all the pontifical documents directed by Pius X against Modernism, three are of supreme importance: the Decree *Lamentabili Sane,* which the Pope had the Holy Office publish, July 3-4, 1907, to condemn 65 distinct modernistic propositions (it is called also the Syllabus of Pius X); the Encyclical *Pascendi Dominici Gregis,* which the Holy Father himself published on September 8, 1907, and in which he expounded and condemned the system of Modernism; the Motu Proprio *Sacrorum Antistitum,* issued on September 1, 1910, by the Sovereign Pontiff, in which he produced the oath against Modernism, and the obligation incumbent on all priests to swear to it. The Decree *Lamentabili* has already been treated in this chapter.

The Encyclical *Pascendi Dominici Gregis* is a masterly treatment of the entire question of Modernism. In the introduction, St. Pius X laid down the gravity of the danger, pointed out the necessity of firm and decisive action, and approved the use of the term "Modernism" for the new errors. In the beginning, Pope Pius gave a very methodical exposition of Modernism. Next he followed its general condemnation with a word as to the corollaries (consequences) that might be drawn from the heresy. The Holy Father then went on to examine the causes and the effects of Modernism, and to indicate the necessary remedies. The application of these remedies he described in thirteen paragraphs. They were indeed energetic remedies.

Pius X was not satisfied with merely diagnosing the evil. He would make certain the obedience of all the Catholic clergy. In the Motu Proprio *Sacrorum Antistitum,* after calling attention to the injunctions of the encyclical *Pascendi* and also to the provisions that previously had been established under Leo XIII for preaching, Pope Pius prescribed that all candidates for the priesthood, all who exercised the holy ministry of the priesthood or who taught in seminaries and similar ecclesiastical institutions, superiors of the orders of regular clergy, officials of the Roman Congregations—all must take an oath, binding themselves to reject the errors that had been denounced in the encyclical *Pascendi* and the decree *Lamentabili.* Such was the Oath against Modernism.

Pope Pius continued his enforcement of the stern remedies which he had prescribed in the encyclical *Pascendi,* either personally or through the Roman officials. He ordered all bishops to purge their clergy of modernistic infections. In consequence of papal and episcopal actions, heretical books were banned, unorthodox journals were condemned, and several of them disappeared in a short time. Recalcitrant teachers were dismissed, as were negligent seminary officials. The last is well illustrated by the dismissal of the superior of the seminary of Perugia for having permitted his seminarians the reading of Loisy. In grievous cases, heretically-minded priests were excommunicated.

The condemnation and the stern measures of its implementation fell like a thunderbolt upon the Modernistic movement. Most of the people affected submitted unreservedly to the authority of the Church. There were, unfortunately, some notorious exceptions: Loisy in France, Tyrrell in England, Buonaiutti and Murri in Italy (Murri was reconciled a year before his death). However, the number of priests who left the Church were few, only some thirty in all. In contrast, the vast majority of Catholics wholeheartedly welcomed St. Pius X's course in nullifying the evil threats of Modernism.

St. Pius X was above all a positive shepherd of the flock of Christ. One of the chief goals of all his labors was the deepening of the sanctity and piety of the clergy. A holy priesthood would ever breed valiant champions of the Faith. Hence he spared no pains to make the Catholic priesthood a learned body of servants of God and of God's people.

Nothing preoccupied him more than improving, intellectually and spiritually, the priestly seminaries. Thus he insisted on solid Thomistic philosophical studies for the seminarians. Thus, too, he worked so hard to establish at Rome the Biblical Institute. He would have it be a center for biblical studies which would give assurance of unquestioned orthodoxy and scientific worth.

St. Pius had crushed the evil thrust of Modernism; he planned to prepare the Church to meet any future recrudescence of that Modernism which he himself had called the synthesis of all heresies.

Holiness in the Modern Age

THE CHURCH'S CONSTANT survival has ever puzzled her adversaries. They do not realize that the primary reason is God Himself, guiding and protecting His Church. They have not listened to the Divine Savior's declarations: "Upon this rock I will build my church, and the gates of hell shall not prevail against it." "Do you think that I cannot ask my Father, and he will give me presently more than twelve legions of angels?" "The Paraclete, the Holy Spirit, whom the Father will send in my name, he will teach you all things." "And behold I am with you all days, even to the consummation of the world." Nor have they scrutinized the four essential marks which Christ impressed upon His Church: oneness, holiness, catholicity and apostolicity.

The proclaiming of belief in the four marks of the Church has always been one of the most cherished practices of faith for Catholics. In every Sunday Mass and in the Masses on the great feast days, when priests and people are concluding the Nicene Creed, how emphatically do they pronounce their belief in the one, holy, catholic and apostolic Church.

Since previous chapters have more conspicuously treated the first, third and fourth marks, this chapter will be concerned only with the second mark, the extraordinary holiness of the Church. Actually it will illustrate and illuminate even more the other three marks, by revealing the spirit, the energy and the numbers of the Church's defenders and propagators.

The Church of Christ must be holy, for Jesus founded His Church to guide mankind to holiness through her. The doctrine of the Church must be holy. Never has she approved the smallest sin, never has she tolerated the slightest error. In the face of the bloodiest persecutions, the most sacrilegious despoliations and the most wholesale desertions, the Church has never compromised with the world, the flesh, and the devil. Ever and always she has exhorted her children to strive for the highest ideals of every virtue. She has had but a single goal for her followers, their most generous and great-souled love of God. *Our Savior is the ideal of the Church.* To Him she channels all the thoughts, aspirations and actions of her children.

The Church must be able to supply the means which will help men to live according to her holy doctrine. Christ has given to His Church a superabundance of means. First He sent the Holy Spirit to her, to teach all things and to remain with her until the end of time. The Holy Spirit is not only the supreme teacher and guide of the Church; He also is the re-vivifier of her supernatural life, He is the inspirer of all the good desires and works of the members of the Church.

In the sacraments the Church has particularly efficacious means of increasing holiness in her sons and daughters. These are the visible signs which were instituted by Christ to produce and increase sanctifying grace in our souls. Each sacrament also imparts special graces in accordance with its nature, for the more effectual overcoming of evil, or the more facile practice of virtue. Think for a moment of the marvelous reconciliations, strengthenings, dedication and union with God that have resulted from the frequent use of the sacraments of Penance and the Holy Eucharist.

Finally, the prayers in the manifold sacramentals and devotions of the Church are always linked with graces which make easy the accomplishment of sanctity.

If the Church is holy, if she possesses so many means to holiness, she must actually produce saints in every age. What is a saint? In answering, one must distinguish between

THE TWENTY-TWO MARTYRS OF UGANDA. A contemporary
African portrayal, depicting each of the saints with the
symbol of his martyrdom.

ST. FRANCES
XAVIER CABRINI.
First American
citizen to be
canonized.

BLESSED MAXIMILIAN
KOLBE, O.F.M.
Martyr of the prison
camp of Auschwitz.
Put to death August 14, 1941.
Beatified, October 17,
1971 by Pope Paul VI.

essential holiness, extraordinary holiness, and canonized holiness. Essential holiness consists in the possession of sanctifying grace. Those who depart this life adorned with it will enter heaven, and will be saints eternally. They will belong to the heavenly host, which St. John describes in the *Book of Revelation:* "I saw a great multitude, which no man could number, of all nations and tribes, and peoples, and tongues, standing before the throne, and in the sight of the Lamb."

Now as members of the Church Triumphant, the saints are continually interceding for the members of the Church Militant, here below, that they may be strong, brave and victorious in the battles with infidelity and immorality. How can their intercessions fail, these cherished servants of the almighty and eternal God?

Extraordinary holiness refers to men and women of conspicuous goodness in the Church on earth. And they have never been lacking. They are often referred to in popular admiration as living saints. Strictly, of course, they cannot be called saints until the Church, after their deaths and after the most careful investigations, declares them saints.

Some are outstanding as heroic leaders in ardent championship and in staunch defense of Catholic doctrines and Catholic morality. Others are conspicuous leaders in the spiritual and devotional life, people of prayer and mortification, living the spiritual law of God to the best of their ability, and ever joyfully accepting any interior or exterior sacrifice which the crucified Savior places upon them.

All these Christian heroes, with profound humility, by word and by personal action, exemplify the highest ideals of Christianity. Their holiness is truly the living answer to the jibes and slurs of the sceptical and immoral. These holy men and women of God come from every class and occupation. Many of them seal their testimony with their life-blood. Assuredly they vindicate the mark of "holy" for the Church on earth.

Canonized holiness comes from the Church's official declaration of sainthood. It consists of two parts: beatification and canonization. If the decree contains a precept, and is universal, in that it binds the whole Church, it is a decree of canonization. If it only permits veneration, or if it binds under precept but not with regard to the whole Church, it is a decree of beatification. Canonization does not necessarily follow beatification; many of the Blessed are not canonized. The processes in both cases usually last for several years.

The investigations are conducted with scrupulous accuracy and precautions; all testimony must be given under oath. What must be established is that the holy person under consideration practiced the theological virtues to an heroic degree. In the case of the martyr, it must be established that he, or she, was put to death particularly and really out of hatred for the Faith. For the Blessed, two real miracles are required; they must have occurred after his death and through his intercession. For the Canonized, two new miracles are required; and they must have occurred after his beatification, and through his intercession. The most competent physicians are called in to examine the impossibility of a natural cure in each case.

Only the strictest rules of evidence are permitted in the local episcopal court, or in the Congregation of Rites in Rome. The Pope makes the final decision, which he publishes in a solemn decree. This solemn decree is an exercise of his infallibility. Canonization is the way the Church chooses her heroes for the inspiration of her people.

It is possible at this point that an objection may be urged: "In the primitive Church and in the Middle Ages there were saints, of course; but where are they in our days?" The answer is that *the Church of our times is quite as prolific of saints as she was in the ages that are past.* Let the nineteenth century be cited as an example.

This was the century in which many made use of the power of politics, of art and science, of the acquisitions of modern culture, as weapons against the Church. This was the century which brought about depravity in morals and spread abroad gross infidelity; yet this century is nevertheless not inferior to any preceding age in the number and greatness of its saints.

A recent compilation of the holy men and holy women who *lived* in the nineteenth century and who were raised to the altars of the Church revealed 61 saints, of whom 23 were martyrs; and 265 Blessed, of whom more than half were martyrs. The martyred saints included 22 Negro youths from Uganda. The martyred Blessed included over 140 Asiatics, Chinese, Japanese and Indo-Chinese. The Oriental martyrs had a good percentage of lay men and women, and even children.

In the saints and the Blessed of the nineteenth century is the same joyful, enthusiastic martyrdom as in the days of Nero, the same burning zeal for souls, the most intimate spirit of prayer, heroic love of neighbor, faith firm as a rock, angelic chastity, royal magnanimity, cheerful love of the cross, childlike humility and simplicity, seraphic love of God. There is the same power of working miracles. And there are the same supernatural gifts of grace just as in the most glorious ages of faith.

With the saints and the Blessed are the holy Catholic men and women whom their brethren esteemed as "living saints," the faithful priests and religious sisters, and the uncountable ordinary Catholic people, the adorers of the Blessed Sacrament, the worshipers of the Sacred Heart, the clients of Mary's Rosary—all these formed the spiritual forces against which the Gates of Hell stormed in vain.

Heroes
of God

A MEANINGFUL appreciation of Catholic holiness in modern times calls for more than an enumeration of sixty-one canonized saints and two hundred sixty-five beatified, and more than a prudent reckoning of the numerous persons of holy life, the "living saints" of popular esteem. It calls too for more than a listing, or an assessment, of heroic achievements in the worship of God and in the service of His Church. Indeed the reflective cataloguing of saintly people and their holy deeds, even if restricted to a single century, would prove an interminable task. It would have to include people of every social station from the papal throne to the humblest hearths of prayerful peasantry.

Their holy lives vindicated the validity of Catholic truth and morality. Their saintly examples inspired the members of Christ's Mystical Body. Their prayers and sufferings, manifesting the almighty power of God's grace, prevailed over the hosts of infidelity and moral turpitude.

A summary treatment such as this can only present a few brief samplings. These will generate some appreciation of Catholic holiness in the modern age.

Best known among the holy ones of modern times is St. Thérèse of Lisieux, the "Little Flower of Jesus," as she has been lovingly called by the millions of her clients.

H. Daniel-Rops, probably the most widely informed of modern Church historians, has called her the greatest saint of modern times and has affirmed her supreme importance for a knowledge of our modern Church.

There are three important considerations in the life of St. Thérèse: the swift and worldwide growth of her veneration; her autobiography, *The Story of a Soul,* written at the command of her superiors; and the beautiful devotion which she developed and advocated, "The Little Way of Sanctity."

The life-story of this humble little saint can be briefly told. She was born at Alençon in 1873. At the age of fourteen she entered the convent of the Carmelites at Lisieux, where she followed quietly and faithfully the life of prayer, silence and penitence of the daughters of St. Teresa of Avila for a little more than nine years. She died in 1897, at the age of twenty-four, after six months of excruciating sufferings from tuberculosis and from interior spiritual agonies. Only a handful of relatives and friends attended the funeral of this obscure young Carmelite. Few, even among her convent sisters, surmised her sanctity.

The superiors in the next year published her autobiography. At first only a few thousand copies were printed. But as *The Story of a Soul* began to be read, a great demand for it arose; in a few years hundreds of thousands of copies were being read all over Europe and in the New World too. It truly was a classic of spiritual literature, and it merited translation into thirty-five languages, including one into Hebrew.

Reports of favors, spiritual and temporal, even of miracles, attributed to Sister Thérèse's intercession began to flow in from all parts of the Catholic world. The little Carmelite's memory was especially treasured by soldiers in the trenches of World War I; they carried her picture, or wore her medal on a chain about their necks. Had she not suffered from the cold, as they were? Had she not died after frightful physical pain and a terrible feeling of abandonment, as they might have to do? And now, did she not carry for them the hopes of peace and final happiness?

So great had the devotion to Sister Thérèse become that the Holy See dispensed with the customary fifty years' waiting period and ordered the official opening of her cause. In 1923, Pius XI beatified Sister Thérèse; and in 1925, only twenty-eight years after her death, he canonized her and ordered her feast to be celebrated by the entire Latin Church.

Pius XI was a very learned scholar and a most solid-minded person; he was the last man to be swept away by any emotional storm. Pius XI continued to manifest his strong devotion to this youthful Carmelite saint. In 1927, he proclaimed her the Patroness of the Foreign Missions, thus associating St. Thérèse with St. Francis Xavier, the Patron of the Missions; and he also made her the Patroness of all works concerning Russia.

The veneration of the humble nun of Lisieux continued to grow. Articles and books about her were issued in the hundreds. Numerous churches and chapels under her invocation were arising throughout the entire Catholic world. In 1937, the then Cardinal Pacelli, as special delegate of Pius XI, consecrated in Lisieux the Basilica of St. Thérèse of the Child Jesus. It would now be hard to find a Catholic home without a picture of the Little Flower of Jesus.

Most important in the astonishing growth of devotion to St. Thérèse was her autobiography. At her death she had left three writings on the facts of her life. These she had authorized her sister, Mother Agnes of Jesus, also a nun of the convent of Lisieux, and its prioress for three years, to organize for publication. Mother Agnes combined the three manuscripts into one text, changed a bit the order and the style of the original documents, and published the autobiography as *The Story of a Soul*.

As has been noted, it gained immediate acceptance. Eventually the number of copies in the original French and in all the translations passed well over the million mark. Its uniqueness, personal appeal, self-revelation and deep spiritual wisdom made *The Story of a Soul* one of the great modern books of holiness. But more than all else, it became the vehicle for transmitting to the world St. Thérèse's "Little Way of Sanctity."

What was this "Little Way" of St. Thérèse? It consisted in an awareness of God's fatherhood and in a childlike

ST. THÉRÈSE OF LISIEUX. An actual photograph of the saint taken by her sister Celine in March, 1896, one year before Thérèse's death.

dependence on Him. It came to the little Carmelite, pondering over what would be her special service for God, when she read in the prophet Isaiah, "Whosoever is a *little one*, let him come to me." Benedict XV, the initiator of the cause of Sister Thérèse, remarked that this approach to God "contained the secret of sanctity for the entire world."

The "Little Way" was not new; it was only a fresh repeating of fundamental Catholic truths. Pius XI defined it: "It consists in feeling and acting under the discipline of virtue as a child feels and acts by nature." It was an attitude of a soul in relationship with God. Benedict XV declared: "There is a call to the faithful of every nation, no matter what be their age, sex, or state of life, to enter wholeheartedly upon this way which led Sister Thérèse of the Child Jesus to the summit of heroic virtue."

Saint Thérèse supernaturalized the whole of daily life. Her simplicity and perfection in sanctifying small things and in consecrating daily duties became patterns to numerous "ordinary people." She declared: "My little way is the way of spiritual childhood, the way of trust and absolute self-surrender." Here is a striking and a charming piece from her writings:

"Being a child means not attributing to yourself the virtues you practice or believing yourself capable of anything at all; it means recognizing that the good God places the treasure of virtue in the hands of His child to be used when there is need of it—but it is still God's treasure. Finally it means never being discouraged by your faults, because children fall frequently but are too small to hurt themselves much."

Pius XI proclaimed in the Bull of Canonization that St. Thérèse had fulfilled her vocation and achieved sanctity without going beyond the common order of things.

The Little Flower also taught ordinary people how to supernaturalize human sufferings. This was especially true after she became a victim of tuberculosis; then her life became one long trial of bodily and spiritual sufferings. Yet it was just at this time that St. Thérèse gave the most remembered of her utterances: "I have never given the good Lord anything but love, and it is with love that He will

repay me. After my death I will let fall a shower of roses."
"I will spend my heaven in doing good upon earth."

During the last six months, often exhausted and racked with pain, she had the fearful experience of bitter temptations against faith, especially the feeling of abandonment by God. Once in her dereliction she was heard to cry, "I did not think that it was possible to suffer so much." But in all this bodily and spiritual suffering, she recognized the cross of Christ, and with love she embraced it. St. Thérèse died on September 30, 1897; her last words were, "My God, I love You."

H. Daniel-Rops declared that the message of St. Thérèse of Lisieux is the most complete and relevant retort to modern atheistic humanism. Nietzsche coined the phrase, "God is dead." Karl Marx left no consideration for God in his materialistic paradise. But St. Thérèse opposed them and all their followers with an irrefutable answer: her "Little Way" of trust and absolute self-surrender to God.

Consider her humble origins and her hidden life, the amazing rapidity and world-wide growth of her veneration, the universality and vitality of her "Little Way," the stark heroism of her last dark hours, the universal acclaim at her elevation to the altars of the Church, and her heavenly responses to her earthly clients. Only the living God could produce St. Thérèse of Lisieux.

Clerical
Holiness

IN HOLINESS the clergy of the modern age compare favorably with the clergy of any other period. One of the Popes, Pius X, has been canonized, and three or four others have been talked about as worthy of the honor of the altar. It would be impossible to count the bishops, priests and brothers who have been canonized, or beatified, or (in the popular esteem) have lived like saints. A few names will be cited as examples of the rest.

St. Clement Mary Hofbauer, C.SS.R., 1751-1820, "The Apostle of Vienna," spent the last twelve years of his life reviving faith and morals in the glorious capital of the Hapsburg domains, the leading city of the Germanic world. The "Enlightenment" and Josephinism had wrought havoc in Vienna. But as a preacher, confessor and director of souls, St. Clement gained an extraordinary influence on all classes, from the Emperor Francis down to the poorest inhabitants. The holy Redemptorist never spared himself. He constantly preached his simple sermons on faith and morals in the churches of the capital and its environs.

Daily he spent hours in his confessional, to which flocked not only the heartsick poor, but ministers of state and university professors. He devoted special care to the spiritual development of the youth. By his understanding and sympathy, he gained numerous converts. So great was his love for the sick that he is said to have been present at 2,000 death beds.

The Apostle of Vienna did more than any other single individual for the extinction of Josephinism. The attempt, at the Congress of Vienna, to establish a National German Catholic Church independent of the Popes, was defeated by the influence of St. Clement Mary Hofbauer and his devoted friends.

The saint died on March 15, 1820. Pius VII spoke thus of his dedicated champion: "Religion in Austria has lost its chief support."

St. John Baptist Vianney, the Curé of Ars, was born near Lyons in 1786. The Napoleonic wars considerably delayed his seminary studies, and these, because of his extremely limited education, proved very difficult for him. He was ordained in 1815. Three years later, he was designated curé (pastor) of the parish of Ars, an obscure hamlet some miles from Lyons. With only average intelligence and a very meager sacerdotal education, the new curé seemed poorly fitted for the priesthood. But if John Baptist Vianney could scarcely serve the Church by his learning, he could serve her well by his holiness. Even before ordination, he was far advanced in spirituality and in the practice of virtue.

The chief labor of the Curé was to be the direction of souls. He was not long at Ars when people from other parishes began coming to him; then penitents came from all parts of France, and finally from many countries of Europe. For the next forty years, this out-of-the-way hamlet was the center of a great spiritual revival. In the last ten years of his life, St. John Vianney spent from sixteen to eighteen hours a day in the confessional. Bishops, priests, religious, young men and women in doubt as to their vocation, sinners, persons in all sorts of difficulties sought his counsel. The sick were even carried to him.

In 1855, the number of pilgrims reached twenty thousand a year. Very distinguished persons journeyed to observe the holy Curé and to listen to his daily sermons. His direction was characterized by common sense, remarkable insight and supernatural knowledge. His brief sermons were simple in language and filled with the imagery of daily life and country scenes. Yet they breathed faith, and that love of God which was his own life-principle and which he infused into his audience.

The Curé's message was carried to his hearers as much by his manners and appearance as by his words. He was blessed with the gift of miracles, notably of supernatural knowledge and of the healing of the sick, especially of little children.

But the greatest miracle of St. John Baptist Vianney was his own life. From his early years he practiced mortification; and for forty years his food and sleep were insufficient, humanly speaking, to sustain life. All this time he labored unceasingly, with unfailing humility, with patience and cheerfulness. Death came on August 4, 1859.

St. Pius X proposed St. John Baptist Vianney as a model to the parish clergy. It was most fitting that he should do so, for like St. John, the holy priests of the parishes rally the laity to the side of the Vicar of Christ.

A pioneer bishop in the United States is the third exemplar of clerical holiness in the nineteenth century. He is Bl. John Nepomucene Neumann, the fourth bishop of Philadelphia. Bl. John was born in Bohemia in 1811. He came forth from priestly studies a profound theologian. He had also become a master linguist, fluently speaking six modern languages. Later, as bishop of Philadelphia, he learned to speak Gaelic, that he might help the many Irish immigrants of his flock.

John Neumann possessed an apostolic soul. Inspired by the letters of a missionary in America, Father Baraga, later bishop of Marquette, he immigrated to New York on the completion of his seminary studies. Bishop Dubois straightway ordained him and sent him to exercise his priesthood in the environs of Buffalo. After four dedicated years, he entered the Redemptorist order and spent three more zealous years at Pittsburgh.

Archbishop Kenrick of Baltimore, who esteemed him highly, recommended him for the see of Philadelphia. At the suggestion of the archbishop, Pius IX gave Father Neumann a command of obedience to accept the bishopric of Philadelphia, a diocese that had suffered much from lay-trustees and from anti-Catholic outrages. Archbishop Kenrick consecrated him bishop, on March 28, 1852.

The diocese of Philadelphia comprehended a large territory: the eastern half of Pennsylvania, the southern half of New Jersey, and the whole of the state of Delaware. Its Catholic population was not at all numerous, and consisted mostly of poor immigrants. Churches were few and, except for the see-city, were widely dispersed. In his solicitude for his flock, Bishop Neumann visited the larger congregations once every year and the smaller ones every two years. In the country places he would remain several days, preaching, hearing confessions, confirming, visiting and anointing the sick. Once he walked twenty-five miles and back to confirm one boy. In five years he erected fifty churches.

Bishop Neumann was indefatigable in the cause of Catholic education. He devoted special care to improving the standards of seminary training. A constant topic of his exhortations was the necessity of parish schools. At his consecration there were but two parochial schools in the Philadelphia diocese; when he died, eight years later, there were nearly one hundred. In those few years the pupils had increased twenty-fold. To staff his schools he brought in the Christian Brothers and six congregations of Sisters. It might be noted that he proved himself the staunch friend of the Colored Oblate Sisters of Baltimore.

Bishop Neumann played a conspicuous part in the First Plenary Council of Baltimore. At the invitation of Pius IX, he was one of the bishops who went to Rome to be present for the Definition of the Immaculate Conception. Bishop John was always a dedicated advocate of the rosary of Mary, the Virgin Mother. He was most zealous in his promotion of the devotion to the Blessed Sacrament; he was the first American bishop to introduce the Forty Hours devotion into his diocese.

Bishop John Nepomucene Neumann was a small, humble man. Even while he lived he was revered for his holiness. After his death, which came on January 5, 1860, stories of his virtues started to spread, and reports of favors attributed to his invocation began to circulate. He received the title "Venerable" on December 15, 1896. He was beatified by Paul VI, on October 13, 1963. Bl. John is the first American bishop to be raised to the altars of the Church.

The fourth example of modern clerical holiness we shall treat is St. John Bosco. He has been called the best representative of the Church in the nineteenth century. Pius XI said of him: "In his life the supernatural almost became the natural and the extraordinary, ordinary." He was born near Turin, in northwest Italy, in 1815; and he died in Turin in 1888. He was canonized in 1934, by Pius XI.

According to the Italian custom, being a secular priest, he was called "Don." It was not long before his countrymen were affectionately speaking the words, "Don Bosco." When the knowledge of his good deeds and wise thought became world-wide, the affectionate title was heard everywhere.

Don Bosco, almost from the day of his ordination in 1841, made himself the devoted friend of the abandoned street-gamins of Turin. For these poor, friendless waifs he very soon began planning spiritual training, technical education and even dwelling places. For them he became a far-seeing educator, a wise social reformer, and an eloquent preacher. For them, and others like them, he founded two religious congregations, the Salesian Fathers and Brothers, and the Salesian Sisters.

These two congregations were to help him in caring for and educating poor and oppressed youths of both sexes, and they were to continue his works when he was no more. At his death the two congregations were carrying out his ideas in 600 houses. Today, still loyal to the purposes of their founder, the Salesian Fathers maintain 1,393 houses, and the Salesian Sisters, 1,351. Here certainly is a cumulative answer to those who accuse the Church of not befriending the poor.

From his earliest contact with poor boys, Don Bosco never failed to see under the dirt, the rags and the uncouthness, the spark which a little kindness and encouragement would fan into flames. Gentleness and good humor were his unfailing attitudes. His pleasant outings with his urchins

BLESSED JOHN N. NEUMANN. Vatican workers unveil tapestry prior to beatification ceremony on October 13, 1963. After ten years as a Redemptorist Father, Bl. John Neumann was consecrated the fourth bishop of Philadelphia. He was the first American bishop to be beatified.

ST. JOHN BOSCO. Actual photograph from the later
nineteenth century.

ST. ELIZABETH ANN SETON. An early portrait.

ST. BERNADETTE SOUBIROUS. Actual photograph of the saint taken one year after the apparitions of Lourdes (1858). Bernadette at this time was fifteen or sixteen.

to favorite spots in the environs of Turin set the pattern for all his later activities.

Since these excursions took place on Sundays, Don Bosco would say Mass in the village church and give a short instruction on the Gospel. Breakfast would then be eaten, followed by games. In the afternoon, Vespers would be chanted, a lesson in the catechism given, and the rosary recited. It was a familiar sight to see him surrounded by kneeling boys preparing for confession. Religion was emphasized, but it was done amid wholesome surroundings and joyous companions. From these outings developed his technical schools, and later his cultural schools.

In Don Bosco's educational work, religion had the first place; so he wrote: "Frequent confession, frequent Communion, daily Mass — these are the pillars which should sustain the whole edifice of education." For him education's chief object should be to form the will and to cultivate the character. Once Don Bosco said: "Instruction is but an accessory, like a game; knowledge never makes a man because it does not directly touch the heart. It gives more power in the exercise of good or evil, but alone it is an indifferent weapon, lacking guidance."

In this spirit Don Bosco operated his manual schools, shops and night classes. From his schools went forth innumerable boys and men whose main business was the saving of their souls. And they remained faithful through life to the Church and to their particular countries. In his higher schools the same results were evidenced.

To cite but one instance: before Don Bosco's death in 1888, such schools had prepared for their clerical studies over 6,000 priests, 1,200 of whom remained in the Salesian congregation. To all his students, lay or clerical, St. John Bosco, great-hearted and kindly, had but one lasting message: "Serve the Lord with gladness."

In modern times the Church and the Holy See have been faithfully served by none more than by the holy women of the religious orders and congregations. Today there are more than a million Catholic sisters in the cloisters, schools and hospitals. It would be safe to say that far more than half belong to institutes which were founded in the last two centuries.

The number of enclosed contemplatives is relatively small, for theirs is a unique vocation. Let St. Thérèse of Lisieux be their representative. Better known are the religious women who teach the children of the flock, or who nurse the sick and dying at home or in the foreign missions. It would be impossible to list either the names of all the congregations or the scenes of their labors, or their outstanding members. Here only the names of a few can be cited as examples of innumerable heroines of the domestic scenes, or of the foreign missions.

Americans: St. Elizabeth Seton, Mother Katherine Drexel; Italians: St. Mary Mazzarello, St. Frances Xavier Cabrini; French: St. Julie Billiart, St. Madeleine Sophie Barat; Germans: Mother Pauline Mallinckrodt; Mother Franziska Schervier; Irish: Mother Catherine McCauley, Mother Mary Aikenhead.

Among the sisters rescuing the fallen women may be cited: St. Marie Euphrasia, St. Marie Michaela Desmaisieres. Of the nursing sisters, mention can be made of St. Catherine Labouré and the almost anonymous Little Sisters of the Poor. In the new apostolate of the mass media, there is Mother Thecla Merlo. Among the modern martyrs in the Orient are several women who have been beatified; and certainly, St. Maria Goretti, the modern St. Agnes, must be remembered. Nor can our Blessed Mother's own messenger, St. Bernadette Soubirous of Lourdes, be forgotten.

Finally there must be noted Bl. Anna Maria Taigi, a devout member of the Third Order of the Trinitarians. She was a loyal wife, the mother of seven children, and the nurse of her aged parents. In 1937, Pius XI beatified this holy wife and mother.

Yesterday
and
Today

THE STORMS from the gates of hell upon the Rock of Peter and against Peter's Barque will persist until the end of time. Christ's prophetic words, "shall not prevail against it," imply obstinate persistence. So does His divine promise: "Behold, I am with you all days even to the consummation of the world." And so also do His warnings against the seductions of numerous false prophets. St. Peter, the first Pope, in his first epistle, writes with similar prophetic warning: "Be sober and watch; because your adversary the devil, as a roaring lion, goes about seeking whom he may devour."

Peter's cautioning prediction has been cherished by the Church through all the ages, and most strikingly in our century by Pope Leo XIII's prayer to St. Michael, so beloved by many Catholics: "Holy Michael, the Archangel, defend us in the day of battle; be our safeguard against the wickedness and snares of the devil. May God rebuke him, we humbly pray; and you, Prince of the heavenly host, by the power of God, thrust down into hell Satan and all the other evil spirits who roam through the world, seeking the ruin of souls."

The assaults launched against the Church and the Papacy during our own twentieth century, now ending its third quarter, have been among the worst in the entire history of Catholicism. Fearsome in power and numbers, enormously extended in activities, ruthless in execution, they posed the threat of complete destruction. Certainly their period is comparable with the periods of the early persecutions, the fall of the Roman Empire, the dark ages, the religious revolts of the sixteenth century and the French Revolution.

More than once, the modern antagonists of Christ celebrated their moments of wholesale triumph. It was in such moments that good men feared that the forces of evil would be in control for the next thousand years. So remarked Kurt von Schuschnigg, the former Chancellor of Austria, whom the Nazis deposed and imprisoned for four years until his liberation by American soldiers.

The Catholic Church has tenaciously resisted every attack made upon her during the twentieth century. Grievously has she suffered. But she has survived all the terrible onslaughts. Her continuing existence strikingly evidences the promised eternal presence of her divine Sustainer.

For one thing, during these perilous decades, the Barque of Peter has been blessed by saintly and capable pilots. In the history of the Church, it would be hard to find a succession of such worthy and vigorous Popes as St. Pius X, Benedict XV, Pius XI, Pius XII, John XXIII and Paul VI. From these pontiffs has come the heroic and steadfast leadership that has unfailingly inspired the whole Catholic people, the codification of canon law, the widest development of the foreign missions, the most unyielding defense of Catholic dogma and Catholic morality, the continual insistence on social justice and the liberties of workingmen, the fostering of Christian spirituality and devotional life—especially in regard to the Holy Eucharist and the convoking of the Second Vatican Ecumenical Council.

In their turn the twentieth-century Popes have been blessed with the tremendous loyalty of their Catholic people, lay and clerical. Intense devotion has been given them by countless millions of the laity, a devotion that has been pro-

POPE PIUS XI

Felici

POPE BENEDICT XV

Felici

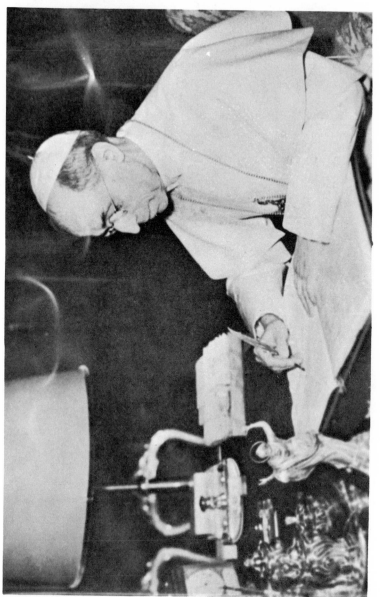

POPE PIUS XII

Felici

moted and participated in by their bishops and priests. The affectionate loyalty for the person of the Pope, which had developed after the disasters of 1870, assumed enormous proportions in the twentieth century.

Crowds of Catholic pilgrims from every race on the globe have constantly converged on Rome to kneel before the Sovereign Pontiff, to receive his blessing for themselves and for their families and friends at home. More vividly than ever before has the Pope become the "Holy Father" to over 566,775,000 Catholics.

During this present century, Rome became the headquarters of great international societies: the Society for the Propagation of the Faith, the Society of St. Vincent de Paul, the Apostleship of Prayer and the League of the Sacred Heart, and the Sodality of the Blessed Virgin.

To strengthen their acceptance of the Faith, modern Catholic men and women have formed themselves into societies based upon their individual labor or professional occupations. In consequence, thousands of organizations representing all classes have appeared: farmers and factory-workers, students and professional men, artists and journalists. Varied and numerous as these organizations are, all of them emphasize their fundamental loyalty to the Church and the Papacy.

Still other lay groups have sought active participation in the apostolate of the Catholic Church. One example of these last groups is the Legion of Mary, noted for its social labors all over the world, and especially its heroic services in Communist China for the preservation of the "hidden" Church. Another example is the Serra Clubs, groups of laymen whose single purpose is the fostering of priestly and religious vocations.

Especially powerful have been the services rendered to the Church by the Knights of Columbus in the ninety years of their existence. For several decades they have been the largest lay society among Catholics; today they number 1,184,545 members. They have participated in many apostolic projects for Catholic apologetics and Catholic higher education. Indicative of their enthusiastic labors is their monthly magazine *Columbia.* Having the largest circulation of any

Catholic monthly (1,200,000), *Columbia* is wholeheartedly dedicated to the Faith and to the Holy Father.

The International Eucharistic Congresses, held in veneration of the Holy Eucharist, have become a mighty source of loyalty to the Catholic Church. Since the first congress, in 1881, forty such gatherings have been held in important cities on the five continents. Each one was presided over by a papal legate, except Bombay and Bogotà, both of which were presided over by Pope Paul VI in person. Each congress has drawn enthusiastic crowds of clergy and laity from distant parts of the world. In the twentieth century the attendance has become enormous; as early as 1932, in Dublin, the attendance was 2,000,000. Modern communications, radio and television, bring uncounted participants to the International Eucharistic Congresses.

Another prolific source of loyalty are the hundreds of devotional shrines. Only a few of the greater ones can be instanced here. But of all, great or small, this can be said: their exercises continue the year round, and their dedication to the Faith and to the Holy Father is characterized by strong personal devotion.

Among the great shrines may be mentioned Lourdes, with its uncountable pilgrims from every nation kneeling to pray to Our Lady of the Immaculate Conception, and with its soul-stirring processions for the blessing of the sick; Fatima, where Pope Paul VI adorned Our Lady of Fatima with a great-sized rosary before a pilgrim throng; Guadalupe, where Indian clients kept the shrine of "Nuestra Señora" open during the bloodiest persecutions; and Our Lady of Czestochowa, the base of Catholic Poland's resistance to atheistic tyrants, and the shrine which preserves the Polish people as one of the strongest Catholic nations to this day.

But the greatest pilgrimage center of all is Rome. From the earliest centuries, Catholic pilgrims have streamed to Rome to kneel at the tombs of St. Peter and St. Paul, to pray at the burial places of the early martyrs, and to venerate the homes of the medieval saints. The pilgrims have never ceased their journeyings to Rome. Indeed today they are coming, in even larger numbers than ever before.

All the resources described above, the Church has had to employ in withstanding the mighty attacks of her twentieth-century antagonists. Only the chief oppositions can be discussed here. These were/are external foes: Secularism, Communism, Nazism and Fascism; and internal foes: Recrudescent Modernism and Anti-Papalism.

Secularism is the supreme enemy of Catholicism. It is the wellspring of all contemporary intellectual opposition, and it is the basis of all physical offensives. Secularism can be defined as the exclusion of God and religion from life. The secularist immerses himself in material possessions, pleasures, comforts and powers. Secularism has become the life-philosophy of countless numbers in every social class.

As the product of French Illuminism, German Aufklaerung and nineteenth-century Positivism, it has gained wide acceptance in university circles, especially when some agnostic scientists promulgated a crudely atheistic theory of evolution. Rationalist litterateurs and philosophers popularized this particular theory, rendering immense damage to faith and morals. Given the agnostic character of much of common education, worldliness and earthy morality were soon spreading among large areas of the ordinary people. It is not surprising that Marxian Communism and state absolutism were so readily accepted among laboring classes.

In this secularism, which rejects God's unchangeable moral laws for glib pronouncements on "contemporary mores" (contemporary moralistic customs) are to be found the roots of the present-day utter collapse of morality. This terrible catastrophe has dragged large sections of modern society down into the viciousness of ancient paganism. All the Popes of the twentieth century have relentlessly struggled against secularism and its materialistic and animalistic evils. They have battled to save their own people from contamination, but they have also fought for the protection of all people of good heart.

Communism, on the basis of military and political power, is the most fearful enemy of Catholicism. Its ultimate professed aim is to establish a worldwide dictatorship of the working class, but a dictatorship founded exclusively on materialism and atheism. Karl Marx, originator of the proposal, was himself a complete atheist; he cursed religion as "the opiate of the people." All leaders of the two mightiest Communist empires, Russia and China, have been militant atheists or total materialists. Today Communism wields iron dominion over one-third of the world's population and, through Communist sympathizers, exercises potent influence in large sectors of the rest.

Opposing Forces

THE RUSSIAN COMMUNISTS were the first to wage all-out war against God and religion. All the rest, including the Chinese, only followed the Russian grand-plan. In the beginning the Russians made it an absolute rule that every party member must be an atheist. Then they moved to liquidate Christianity. They ruthlessly slaughtered priests and bishops; they imprisoned many more, or banished them to Siberia. They confiscated all ecclesiastical properties, demolished many churches, and converted many others to secular uses.

From the beginning, too, the Russian communists strove to make all children hate God. The accomplishment of that horrible evil was one of the chief goals of their new system of common education. They prohibited all public religious instruction; they even forbade parents to teach religion to their children until they were eighteen years of age. For the older youth, they devised an educational program which they labeled "Scientific Atheism." To bolster their atheistic plans, they established anti-God museums and anti-God lectures. Such is the atheistic war Russian communism waged against God and religion. It was literally copied by other communist bodies: witness the frightful persecutions in Mexico, Spain, Poland, Hungary and China.

Nazism has now been dead for almost thirty years. In its day (1933-1945), it may have been the most powerful enemy of Catholicism; certainly it was the most skillfully organized. It dragooned Germany into a totalitarian system of government, based upon an absurd theory of racial supremacy. The Nazis drew some of their leaders from that large section of the intellectuals who were secularists and materialists, and the bulk of their followers from the working-class socialists and materialists. As a one-party government, they controlled all politics, but they aimed further—to dominate society, business and education.

War with Catholicism was inevitable. First the Nazis moved to force all Christian sects into a single national church. Failing in this, they strove for complete domination of German Catholicism. Priests were punished for preaching against the Nazis' program of eugenics, particularly against sterilization. The Catholic press was abolished when it published a letter of Pius XI, criticizing the Nazi administration. Then Doctor von Pastor's monumental *History of the Popes* and Herder's *Kirchenlexicon* (a great Catholic encyclopedia) were suppressed under the pretext that they were "out of harmony with the official conception of German history."

Hundreds of Catholic religious were charged with gross immorality and were condemned without fair trials. Twenty thousand Catholic schools, with a total of three million pupils, were closed. Religious instruction in public education was forbidden. Despite stories of wide defections, the bulk of the German Catholics stood faithful. They heeded Pius XI's encyclical, *Mit Brennender Sorge* (With Burning Solicitude). The Holy Father wrote the document in German. It was one of the most powerful encyclicals ever written by a successor of St. Peter.

The German bishops, led by the dauntless Cardinal Faulhaber, faced unflinchingly the overwhelming Nazi forces. In 1942, when the Nazis were at their zenith of power, the German hierarchy, headed by three heroes—Cardinal Faulhaber, Bishop von Galen and Bishop Ehrenfried—dispatched a letter of protest to the Nazi Government, written in such bold terms that it won the commendation of the world.

Fascism, a form of totalitarianism, should be discussed here. In a Fascist state, a single political party holds iron rule over a nation and over every activity of its citizens.

Usually it is deeply rooted in secularism and materialism; one of its chief principles is the absolutism of the state. Fascism, under Mussolini, took over in Italy in 1922; and it held power for twenty-one years until 1943, when it was ousted with the help of the allied forces of almost all Italian parties.

Conscious of the tremendous power of the Papacy and of the instinctive loyalty of the Italian people to Catholicism, the Fascists in the beginning had passed several laws favorable to the Church. In 1929, they concluded with the Holy See the Lateran Treaty, which provided the ending of the Roman Question by the establishment of the independent Vatican City State, the acknowledgement of Catholicism as the official religion of Italy, the setting up of religious teaching in the state schools, and the acceptance of the validity of canon law in the Italian courts.

But a permanent harmony could hardly be expected between absolutism and Christian freedom. The Fascist officials and the Catholic officials mutually mistrusted one another.

A dangerous crisis arose in 1931, when the General Secretary of the Fascist Party and the newspaper *Lavoro Fascista* proclaimed in public that there was no room in Italy for *Catholic Action* (associations of lay people for religious action under the direction of the bishops). Pius XI had founded *Catholic Action*, and he treasured it very much. So he publicly replied to the Fascists' assertion. Fuel was added to the fire when Mussolini in a radio broadcast rudely commented on the Pope's words. The strong-minded Pius XI quickly answered with one of his greatest encyclicals, *Non abbiamo bisogno* (We have no need).

Pius wrote this document in Italian so that he might reach not only the Fascists but all the Italian people. He wrote also for the whole world, for he sent the encyclical out of Italy secretly, to be published without hindrance from the Fascist censors. In this encyclical, Pius XI denounced the Fascist ideology as a "real pagan worship of the state," irreconcilable with Catholic doctrine and man's natural rights. The Fascists attempted no reply.

During the second half of the present century, Catholicism has had to endure several internal storms. False teachings have challenged the most fundamental doctrines and institutions of the Church. Notorious clerical defections have further darkened the scene. In consequence of these modern denials and revolts, bewildering confusions are burdening the loyal hearts of the faithful clergy and laity, still the overwhelming majority of the Catholic body. Internal storms, however, have been common enough in the two thousand years of the Church's history; and the same history shows the Church surviving and overcoming each one of them.

Space permits only a brief listing of the principal false teachings of our day. First is the reappearance of Modernism; St. Pius X's statement, in 1907, that Modernism is the synthesis (assemblage) of all heresies is just as valid today. Then there are the attacks on Catholic doctrines, especially: denial of the Pope's powers and primacy; rejection of the magisterium of the Church (its infallible teaching office); and the advocacy of a false type of ecumenism, which would sacrifice essential doctrines for the sake of attaining the dubious benefits of a vague union with other religious bodies.

Contemporaneous are the assaults on Catholic moral teachings. Some assailants deny that there ever was, or ever can be, an unchangeable moral code; and they include the Ten Commandments. Some further reject definite norms of morality, and they make each man a law unto himself. The result has been world-wide moral chaos.

Now this moral chaos has been greatly augmented by a materialistic interpretation of the theory of evolution, which rules out God, original and actual sin, Jesus the God-man's redemptive sacrifice on Calvary and in the Mass, and which also rules out Baptism, confession and the Holy Eucharist as meaningless.

Weakening of Catholic ideals has brought sad results to the Church. A case in point is the over-emphasis which some writers on social Christianity have placed upon secularistic humanitarianism. Uncritical preoccupation with secularistic methods and solutions has lessened the conviction of some Catholics regarding the supreme importance of God-centered Christian charity.

But the saddest losses are in Catholic education. There have been most discouraging decreases in the ranks of religious teachers and in vocations to the teaching congregations which serve primary and secondary education. Many religious seem to have lost the perception that there is no holier or nobler vocation than the training of boys to be future priests or future staunch laymen, or the training of girls to be future Catholic virgins or future Catholic mothers.

In higher education there is the danger of Catholic institutions becoming secular colleges and eclectic universities. Unfortunately there is here also a fading out of Catholic convictions. This is especially true of the conviction that the primary purposes of Catholic higher education are the service of God and the communicating of Catholic culture and of Catholic thought to the world.

Finally, there is the current emergence of Gnosticism, a hoary old heresy that has sought to destroy Christianity in every century. "Gnosis," a Greek word, means a secret knowledge which is shared only with adepts and which purports to guarantee their salvation. Actually Gnosticism leads to Pantheism. Gnostic adepts are ever a disruptive force. A re-emerging of these strange sectaries is always a harbinger of evil.

Such are the storms menacing the Church in the last quarter of the twentieth century. But the sovereign Pontiffs will overcome them, as their predecessors dispersed the tempests of the past, and as their successors will silence the tumults of the future. The Popes wield a single weapon. It is the sword of God's truth, the eternal doctrines of His religion and the unchangeable prescripts of His moral law. Employing modern communication media, the Popes issue continually encyclicals, regulations and instructions that meet every exigency.

Felici

POPE JOHN XXIII

POPE PAUL VI

VATICAN COUNCIL II. Ceremonies for one of the opening
sessions.

"I am
with you
all days..."

THE MOST STRIKING effort of the Church in the twentieth century was the holding of the Ecumenical Council of Vatican II. The Council was initiated by Pope John XXIII and brought to completion by Pope Paul VI.

To quote Pope John, Vatican II was to be a pastoral council: "This sacred Council has several aims in view: it desires to impart an ever increasing vigor to the Christian life of the faithful; to adapt more suitably to the needs of our times those institutions which are subject to change; to foster whatever can promote union among all who believe in Christ; to strengthen whatever can help to call the whole of mankind into the household of the Church."

The Council issued sixteen documents directive of every phase of the Church's life. While Vatican II was not primarily a doctrine-defining council, it safely guarded the fundamental teachings and the essential organization of the Church. Pope Paul in his address concluding the council speaks very clearly:

"The teaching authority of the Church, even though not wishing to issue extraordinary dogmatic pronouncements, has made thoroughly known its authoritative teachings on a number of questions which today weigh upon man's conscience and activity, descending, so to speak, into a dialogue with him, but ever preserving its own authority and force; it has spoken with the accomodating friendly voice of pastoral charity; its desire has been to be heard and understood by everyone."

And so the two Popes achieved many updatings of the practices of the Church without changing a jot or tittle of Christian Faith or Christian Morality.

Storms, external or internal, never cease to blow against the Barque of Peter. Some appear more menacing now than ever in the past. The Popes, however, will stand firm in the various crises, and the vast majority of their Catholic people will faithfully support them.

The personal loyalty of modern Catholics for their Holy Father has been noted in previous chapters. Here one might well consider the innumerable prayers "For the Holy Father and for his intentions" which uncounted Catholics of all ranks of the clergy and of the laity, not only every day, but frequently in each day, send to the throne of God. And one should ponder deeply on the numerous Catholic martyrs of the twentieth century; they certainly must be intercessors for the Barque of Peter and its helmsmen, the Popes.

Among these heroic souls should be remembered: Bl. Maximilian Kolbe, O.F.M., who died in a Nazi prison camp; Father Miguel Pro, S.J., who fell before a firing squad in the Mexican persecutions; the twelve bishops, the fifteen thousand priests and nuns who were slaughtered in the Spanish Civil War; the frightful holocausts for Christ under the Nazis, the Russian Communists and the Chinese Communists. Mention might be made here of the twenty-two African martyrs of Uganda. They were put to death in 1885 and in 1887; but they were canonized in 1964, by Pope Paul VI. Tertullian's words are still true: "The blood of the martyrs is the seed of the Church."

The Popes, and with them their faithful Catholic flocks, continuously persevere through the dark hours and the fierce tempests, because of their confidence in the words of the Godman, Jesus Christ:

"And I will ask the Father, and he will give you another Paraclete, that he may abide with you forever" (Jn. 14:16).

"The Paraclete, the Holy Spirit, whom the Father will send in my name, he will teach you all things, and bring all things to your mind, whatsoever I have said to you" (Jn. 14:26).

"And behold I am with you all days, even to the consummation of the world" (Mt. 28:20).

INDEX

A

B

M

Machiavelli, *The Prince* 220
Maistre, Joseph de 501
Malachy O'More, St. 144
Manicheism 180-181
Manila (16th-18th centuries) 400-402
Marcionism 50
Marcus Aurelius 39
Margaret Clitherow, St., martyr 322
Marozia, Princess 116
Marsiglio of Padua 202
Martin de Porres, St. 416, 418
Martin, Pope St., martyr 99
Martin of Tours, St. 54
Martyrs
  modern Catholic 590
  North American 419
  of the Religious Revolution 320-324
Marx, Karl 527
Massacre of St. Bartholomew's Eve 334, 335
Materialistic, secularistic culture and education 527
Matilda, Countess of Tuscany 124, 126
Maximilian, Duke of Bavaria 357
Mazzini, Giuseppi 522
Medieval
  Church and learning 190-195 ;
  Church's struggle for freedom 154-174
  hymns 191, 192
Middle Ages
  moral deterioration in 216-220
  weakening of the authority of the Church in 196-199
Milner, Dr. John 513, 514
Mission(s)
  apostolate to aborigines (1500-1750) 377-384
  difficulties for, in India 382-387, 390
  heroism in medieval missions 185-186
  in the Philippine Islands (16th-18th centuries) 401-402
  in Spanish America 404-408
  medieval achievements 186-189
  of New France 419, 420
Modern Church's resistance and survival of contemporary attacks 574

Modern Saints of the Church 550-556
Modernism
  definition and essential teachings 542, 543
  history of conflict 544-546
  recrudesence of, theological, intellectual, disciplinary 583-585
  St. Pius X's condemnation of and his strong measures against it 546, 547
Mohammedanism (Islam) 92-96
Monasteries, Irish, English, Frankish, destroyed by Norse 110
Monasticism 81-91
  prayer and labor 82-86
  reform in the Dark Ages 120, 121
Monophysite Heresy 61
Montalembert, Count Charles de 502, 505, 506
Montanism 50, 51

N

Nantes, Edict of 335
  revocation 373, 374
Napoleon
  conflicts with Pope Pius VII 480
  divorce and remarriage 482, 483
  excommunication by Pius 481
  imprisonment of Pope at Savona 481-484
Napoleonic Era
  discouraging prospects for Church at end of 496-498
Nationalism, ultra 526-527
Nazism 581-582
Nero 35
Nestorianism 59, 60
Neuman, Bl. John Nepomucene 564-565
Newman, John Henry Cardinal 517
Nicholas the Great, Pope St. 119, 131
Nicholas of Cusa, Cardinal 295, 296
Nineteenth Century
  Catholic Revival 495, 496, 498
  enemies of Catholicism 490, 491
  French Catholic Revival 501-506

Nobile, Robert de, S.J., missionary
   among the Brahmins 388-390
Norbert, St. 142
Normandy 111
Normans of Sicily 124, 126

O

O'Connell, Daniel, 514, 517
"Old Catholics," sect 535, 536
Olier, Jean Jacques 331
Oratory of Divine Love 280
Ostrogoths 71
Otto I 109, 112, 156
Oxford Movement 517
Ozanam, Frederic 502

P

Pagan Humanism
   evil effects on some in the
      clerical ranks 220
   faction in the Renaissance 217
Papacy
   immediately before the Council
      of Trent 276-279
   infallibility of, definition of
      532, 533
   modern veneration of 495
   of the twentieth century, saintly
      and capable 574
   recurrent attacks on, in the Late
      Middle Ages 227, 229
   two unworthy pontiffs in the
      Dark Ages, one at least in the
      late Middle Ages 115, 220, 221
Paris, University of 190
Patrimony of St. Peter, The 98
Paul, St. 24, 44
Paul III, Pope 278, 279
Paulinus of Nola, St. 82
Peace of God, The 118, 119, 120
Pelagianism 61
   semi-Pelagianism 62
Pepin the Short, donation of the
   Lombard conquests to the
   Pope of Rome 101
Peter Claver, S.J., St., missionary
   to the negro slaves 413, 414
Peter Damian, St. 124
Peter Paxmany, Cardinal 304
Peter's Primacy, St. 19, 55
   power of the keys 24, 27, 44

Philip II, King of Spain 338, 340
Philip IV, King of France 158, 171
Philip IV, the Sacrilege of Anagni,
   against Boniface VIII 173
Philip IV, (Secularist and Galli-
   can) 174
Philip Neri, St. 306-307, 309
"Philosophism," infidel and ra-
   tionalist 421
   origins 426
"Philosophisme" (French) 428, 429
Photian Schism 129, 131, 132
Pignatelli, S.J., St. Joseph 441
Pilgrimage shrines, hundreds
   through the Catholic world 578
Pirkheimer, Caritas, Abbess of
   Poor Clares of Nuremberg 224
Pius V, Pope St. 291, 292, 306
Pius VI
   condemnation of the Civil Con-
      stitution of the Clergy 459, 467
   conflicts with the French
      Directory 467-469
Pius VII
   harassed by Napoleon at Fon-
      tainebleau 485
   held prisoner by Napoleon at
      Fontainebleau 485-487
   last nine years: restorations,
      sorrow at anticlerical uprisings
      487-488
   repudiation of concessions
      forced at Fontainebleau 487
   return to Rome 487
Pius IX 522, 523, 527, 531, 532,
   533, 536
   and the Magisterium of the
      Church 527, 528
Pius X, St. 540, 543, 544, 546, 547,
   548
   efforts for the holiness and the
      learning of the clergy 547, 548
Pius XI 582, 583
Plunkett, Bl. Oliver, martyr 321,
   323, 324
Poland 109
   loyalty to the Catholic Faith
      372, 578
Popish Plot (Titus Oates) 374, 375
Portuguese Friars' early missions
   in India 382